AF544855

THE JOURNEY OF
JOHN W. MOSLEY

CHARLES L. BLOCKSON, CURATOR
AFRO-AMERICAN COLLECTION
TEMPLE UNIVERSITY

• • • • • • • • • • • • • •

QUANTUM LEAP PUBLISHER, INC.
Philadelphia, Pennsylvania

Published by Quantum Leap Publisher, Inc.
229 West Upsal Street, Suite 704
Philadelphia, Pennsylvania 19119
800-843-1066
Library of Congress Cataloging-in-Publication Data is available: 92-029011
Manufactured in Mexico by R. R. Donnelley & Sons Company
Published: October 1992
ISBN 0-9627161-7-0

Dedication

To
The John W. Mosley Family,

TERESA STILL MOSLEY,
his wife,
AND JOHN MOSLEY, JR.
AND CHARLES MOSLEY,
his sons

PREFACE

The Journey of John W. Mosley is too long overdue. His images not only document African Americans in Philadelphia and their relationships with prominent national figures but also the common place. His photographs provide strong visual records of the day-to-day work ethics, social activities and culture of African Americans which are regular occurrences within any large city. He also captured the activities of Black children in their homes, in their schools and at play. The collection supports the concerns of historians, sociologists, artists and scholars who are beginning to redress the past and who use photographs to cite examples of their theories. John W. Mosley's photographs were very carefully composed, and when shooting in the studio, lighting was a fundamental concern. Throughout his career, he was very much concerned with composition, the placement of his subjects and props. Mosley created atmospheres, whether in the studio or on location, quiet, lively and intimate. The events and the experiences are remembered not only because Mosley was there to document them but because of the way he captured their emotional impact on film. The events are timeless and symbolic of a communal respect for subject and photograph. His posed portraits are formal and impressive, denoting a conscious act between the photographer and his subject. With the photography equipment that he had to work with, his photographs are exceptional and show a great technical skill. The following pages contain a unique and highly skilled photographer's interpretation of the city that he knew best Philadelphia. As you turn the pages and experience John W. Mosley's journey, you will witness a man committed to telling a visual story about particular events, communities and individuals with great care. The book chronicles a thirty-year span of the photographer's professional career, from the late 1930s through the 1960s. This period witnessed an unusual chain of events in history. The photographs are not meant to be read as an illustration of an event or activity. Historically, a photographic image was seen as a static object; but in today's society, the photograph has become interactive. From the initial glance at John W. Mosley's photographs, the viewer begins a visual interrogation. Each photograph is layered with subtleties that should not be glossed over. Race and representation of race pride in his photography can be used as a catalyst for critical discussions in classrooms and homes as well as in photographic galleries. As you take the visual experience with Mr. Mosley, consider the period in which the image was produced, ask questions about the photographer's vantage point. Did John W. Mosley have a political agenda in creating fundamentally different statements about the Black community in Philadelphia? I believe that it is accurate to respond to this question in the positive.

Deborah Willis
Smithsonian Institution

FOREWORD

"One mind for
the white man
to see,
Another that I know is me."

An old African-American folk expression

"**M**osley was our most magnificent and our most beloved photographer - he was everywhere, always on time and never late, mind you," said one admirer and client. "Although he did not drive, he was always on the move." John W. Mosley was born in Lumberton, North Carolina, in 1907, a town about one hundred miles from Raleigh. He was instilled with religion at a very early age. His father was a Baptist minister. He also worked in the profession of barber. He worked in this profession so that his wife could stay at home with their children. John's older sister, Carolyn, was a teacher and a role model for her younger brother. She taught at a private boarding high school and placed John and one of his brothers there. She had a great influence on her brother's life. Through her initiative, John acquired a strong academic foundation. In high school, John played football. He later attended Johnson C. Smith College. Mrs. Irene B. Mosley, John's sister-in-law, states, "John was very industrious! He was a fine person and lived a good clean life." Mosley was described by those who knew him as "a slender, medium height, soft-spoken man whose eyes were on the positive." One of his favorite dishes was ice cream. He was very athletic and participated not only in football but in tennis and ping-pong as well. He enjoyed going to other athletic events such as track and field, basketball, boxing and baseball. He also enjoyed playing chess and checkers.

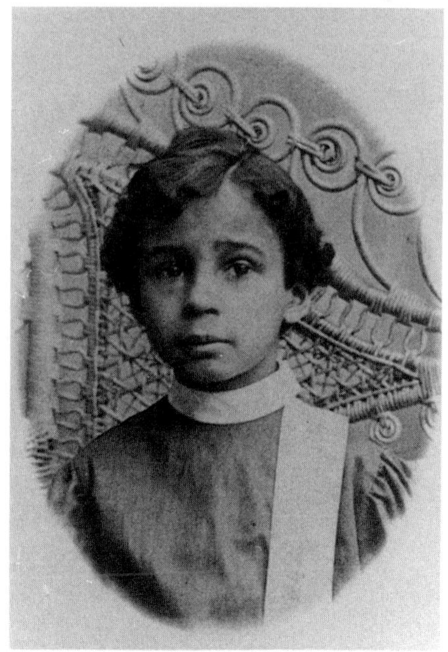

John W. Mosley as a child.

John W. Mosley's love for photography started in the 1920s, when he became fascinated with the art from a simple box camera. He was thrilled by his ability to set forth living action into a permanent visual record. He recognized in that instance that photography, from the moment of its invention, was one of the most moving and powerful instruments of communication to be devised. Mr. Mosley was still a young man when he left North Carolina and migrated to Philadelphia in 1934. He acquired employment at the Barksdale Photography Studio located at 8th and Market Streets where he learned the rudiments and techniques of his chosen profession.

His photographs began to appear in every major African-American newspaper along the eastern seaboard. Mosley's enthusiasm and commitment to his craft enabled him to capture nearly four decades of change. During these decades, he witnessed changes in culture, politics and fashions. His photographs offer telling images of personalities and events in Philadelphia and other areas of the nation. He photographed five United States presidents; Franklin D. Roosevelt, Harry S. Truman, Dwight D. Eisenhower, John F. Kennedy and Richard M. Nixon, during their visits to the city; as well as Senator Robert Kennedy, Constance Motley, Mrs. Daisy Bates, Clarence Muse, Dick Gregory, Loraine Hansberry, Pearl Bailey, Harry T. Burleigh, James DePreist, Nat King Cole, Judith Jamison, Nina Simone and scores of prominent actors and actresses. His close friend Robert Queen, retired editor of the *Philadelphia Independent*, wrote that Mosley once estimated that his scenes of the Atlantic City beach alone might run into "nearly a batch of 25,000 and contained nearly a million faces." Mosley's work was not limited to Philadelphia and Atlantic

City. On various occasions, he traveled to New York City, Baltimore and Washington, D.C., with his cameras, taking photographs for *The Philadelphia Tribune, The Pittsburgh Courier* and other newspapers. Amazingly, he still managed to cover up to four events a day, often working seven days a week. Because of his love for photography, he had indefatigable resolve when it came to his profession. On his way to and from various events, he also photographed buildings, landscapes, streetscapes, children and ordinary people. Teresa, Mosley's wife, recalled that her husband carried his cameras with him whenever he went outdoors. Subjects of interest to him included street scenes, funerals, weddings, family portraits, the famous and lesser-known people who lived in or frequented the Philadelphia area. Elaine Vance Ellis, a native Philadelphian, remembers Mosley, who took photographs of her as a teenager in portrait and group shots. However, she was unaware that he took photographs at her wedding. Years later, upon discovery of the photographs recently in the Blockson Afro-American Collection, she states, "It's amazing! He was everywhere!" Teresa Mosley explains how her husband was able to do this. She states, "When he went to take pictures at functions, he went in and left when he had achieved his goal in order to get to the next affair. He did not drink, argue, curse or smoke so he was able to move freely at affairs, going unnoticed by most participants." African Americans in Philadelphia were constantly writing Mosley to request his services. Being the dedicated and humble man that he was, Mosley would always be there. On some days his itinerary was impossible, but he would do his best. He would tell his wife, "My ox is in the ditch," whenever he did not complete a newspaper assignment on time. But, these were rare occasions. He usually managed to get the job done. Herschell Gordon, a friend, states that "He [John W. Mosley] knew everyone." Particularly, he was acquainted with all of "the movers and shakers" of Philadelphia. When the prestigious Pyramid Club was organized in 1937, Mosley was appointed the club's photographer and art director. As such, he took photographs of Pyramid members, who were prominent leaders in Philadelphia, and celebrities who visited the club. Many of the photographs were published in the club's annual pictorial album.

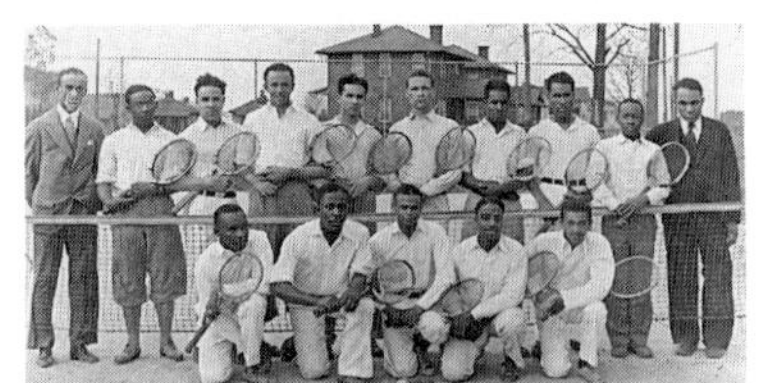

John W. Mosley in Philadelphia late 1930s

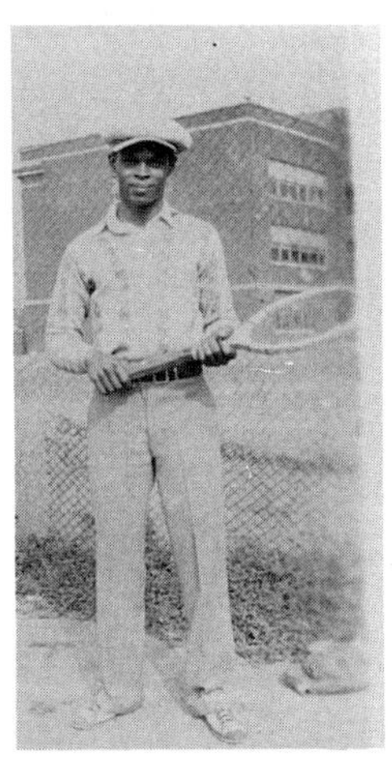

John W. Mosley late 1930s

According to Mrs. Teresa Mosley and others, John Mosley's headquarters was at the Christian Street YMCA for more than twenty years. Prior to his marriage, he lived in the YMCA, where he maintained his darkroom. The Christian Street Y was a perfect location for him because it was "the meeting place" for many African-American organizations and social groups from the mid-1930s on. The Christian Street Y had a special function for South Philadelphia residents. It was a place where they gathered for recreational activities and socializing. On many occasions, John Mosley "took on all comers and defeated most in checkers and ping-pong" between processing his film. When time permitted him to relax, his wife, Teresa said, that, "John enjoyed music, especially big band music, jazz, and opera." Among the thousands of photographs in his collection at the Blockson Collection are his personal autographed promotional photographs of many leading musicians. He also took many photographs of leading jazz personalities who came to Philadelphia, such as Eubie Blake, Jimmy Lunceford, Blanche Calloway, Cab Calloway, Lester Young, and Erskine Hawkins, dating back to 1934.

John W. Mosley was very proud of his African-American heritage. He also believed in helping his people. Mrs. Mosley states that, "He loved his race and his two sons, John Mosley, Jr. and Charles. However, photography was his life. He was independent enough to do his own editing: it was a full-time job." Another acquaintance of Mr. Mosley recalls that "He had a kind of smile - an oriental smile. He used it and disarmed his subjects with that smile of his. He had a philosophy all of his own in that he tried to bring this enlightenment and refinement into African American activities. He had a way of saying what he had to say and then he would laugh. He knew how to quietly come through places and get what he wanted and move on." Perry Triplett, on numerous occasions, transported Mr. Mosley to his photographic assignments. He took him to many different points of destination and watched him cover events such as Lincoln and Cheyney Universities' graduations, the Philadelphia 76ers basketball games, the Philadelphia Cotillion Society Balls, baptisms and a host of other activities. Mr. Triplett stated that he never minded the busy schedule because Mr. Mosley was very knowledgeable and worldly in his view. Thus, the time that Mr. Triplett spent with him was always a learning experience. Mr. Triplett states "Mosley had an enormous mental capacity for photographic memory. He was a genius!" Mrs. Mosley remembers that he went everywhere he could in the Delaware Valley to chronicle African-American life. She states that,"He would not miss the Penn Relays for anything." Mosley was not only everywhere, chronicling African-American life in the Delaware Valley, but he also took pride in investing his money in the best equipment he was able to afford. During his career, he was known to have had at least twenty different cameras. Mr. Mosley took pride in his craft and had great technical skills. When a Mosley photograph was completed, it was his photograph from beginning to end. Mrs. Mosley states, "John would use our bathtub after making sure the water had the right temperature. He would wash the photographs and place them in the dryer while processing them." Mr. Mosley always produced quality products for his clients. The Reverend Inez Thompson states that, "Everybody, it seems, could not wait until John Mosley developed his photographs. You know, having your photograph taken by him was considered an honor. " Mrs. Mosley recalls that she met her husband at the South Broad Street U.S.O. when he was taking photographs during World War II. She states, "John loved photographing beautiful women in bathing suits, fashion models and semi-nudes. How he got them to pose for him, she did not know. The Reverend Thompson states that families sent their daughters to finishing and modeling schools, so many were trained. She states, "This was an era of beautiful women. They were viewed in a positive manner." Some of the photographs of women who modeled were termed "Sitting Pretty." In today's terms, some of the photographs might be viewed as slightly risque for that period of time. However, many women of that period state, "We did not want our boys looking at photographs of other races, when we have beautiful women in our own race." This was particularly true during World War II. John W. Mosley not only captured African-American life but also was conscious of his work as art. As an artist, he conducted studies in light and shadow and was able to capture human emotion through the lens of his camera. He was able to get his subjects to relax. They confided in him. He was able to develop a type of intimacy between his subjects and his camera. They would show him their private side. Although he took many photographs of other people, it was rare that he posed for others. He did not like to get his photograph taken. Perhaps his humility and shyness played a role in his refusal to be part of the public record or perhaps he was just moving too quickly taking photographs of others. Most of the photographs of John W. Mosley taken during his adult life were self-portraits. He would set a camera time and pose. When John W. Mosley died in 1969 at the age of 62, he resided with his wife in West Philadelphia. At the time of his death, the journey of John W. Mosley had taken him through many intricate paths in Philadelphia's African-American communities and included a legacy of over thirty years, documenting the people he loved, in the career that he loved-photography.

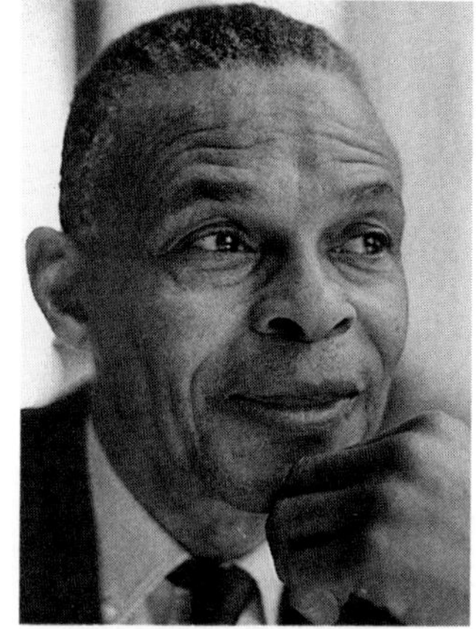

John W. Mosley at age 62.

INTRODUCTION

I have observed this in my experience of slavery,
that whenever my condition was improved,
instead of its increasing my contentment,
it only increased my desire to be free and set me to thinking
of plans to gain my freedom.

Frederick Douglass

This book reflects the journey that John W. Mosley undertook to preserve the proud heritage of African-Americans through the lens of his cameras. The contribution of Mosley's work is that he vividly captured the modern life experiences of African-Americans in an urban landscape from the 1930s through the 1960s. The thirty-year period that he covered was an important time when a number of significant historical events occurred in American history. This period represents a stage that some refer to as "The Middle" in African-American history when a number of changes took place in Philadelphia's African-American communities. Yet, it also represents a period of strength and stability in Black families when many traditions continued. During John W. Mosley's journey, he witnessed not only change but also the continuity of culture and tradition. In order to understand what it meant to be an African-American in Philadelphia and what that community represented and how it evolved from the late 1930s through the 1960s, it is necessary to go back in time and attempt to reconstruct those decades. Through this process, we can begin to give an accurate interpretation of Philadelphia's African-American communities during this period. We can then begin to raise other questions to define and study this group. Did they have institutions and organizations? Did these institutions and organizations reflect their values? If so, what were their values? Was the community diverse? What were some of the things that were important to Black people during these decades? What set previous generations apart from the generations that we have today in the city? Is there any continuity in facets of Black life in Philadelphia from this period to the present?

Philadelphia has a rich and interesting history related to African Americans whose origins began with the first settlers. Some were enslaved Africans. On the unspeakable horrors of the institution of American slavery, there is no need to dwell. The African-American presence in early Philadelphia, though never large, was not insignificant, either. From the research, two prominent facts emerge. First, that there was "great diversity in the people and the role they played in the city's history and, secondly, that the exploitation of black people by the dominant society was so sustained that a major theme of black life has been the struggle for freedom from oppression." Despite such drawbacks, Philadelphia was regarded as a city

1. Charles L. Blockson, *Pennsylvania's Black History*, Portfolio Associates, Inc., 1975, p. 1

of opportunity, for it had the largest free African-American community in America. The African-American leaders of this community were very conscious that their greatest strength was through institutions that would allow them to challenge slavery and racism collectively. Out of their awareness, they established the first mutual-aid organization, the Free African Society of Philadelphia, in 1787. They proceeded to establish schools, literary societies, and businesses, including an insurance company, the African Insurance Company. Two of the earliest churches formed by Blacks also emerged in antebellum Philadelphia: the Bethel African Methodist Episcopal Church, founded by the Reverend Richard Allen and the African Episcopal Church of St. Thomas, founded by the Reverend Absalom Jones. Throughout the antebellum period, in Philadelphia and elsewhere, the two most volatile issues were the abolition of slavery and African-American civil rights. Conventions, meetings and written memorials, to state and federal governments, abounded regarding these issues. During this period, hundreds of runaways fled from captivity in the South through the assistance of Underground Railroad agents. A large number of African refugees remained in Philadelphia, while others travelled on to Canada. African-American participation in the defense of the United States goes as far back as the War of Independence, more than 11,000 Black soldiers were trained for service during the Civil War at Camp William Penn, where Broad Street joins Montgomery County. Philadelphia's African-American men and women offered their services in other wars through enlistments and the draft, often confined to segregated units. Today, African Americans continue to play vital roles in an integrated military, where they have greater opportunities for advancement to the highest ranks and for equal treatment in all ranks. The Great Migration of African Americans to Philadelphia and other northern cities began with the outbreak of World War I. They migrated because of oppressive conditions in the South in the forms of violence and segregation. They also came to Philadelphia because of the promise of better jobs, vacated by white workers who were called into the military. A small group of migrants from the Caribbean joined their brothers and sisters, who migrated predominantly from the rural South. Marcus Garvey, arrived in New York City, established the Universal Negro Improvement Association (UNIA) and worked to mobilize Black people. His doctrines of Black nationalism, race pride and Black self-determination were embraced by the masses of Black people in cities, nationally and abroad. A chapter of the UNIA was established by African Americans in Philadelphia. The chapter drew hundreds of followers and continues to meet in the city today. Father Devine, a charismatic religious leader, came forward with one of the best survival programs during the Great Depression of the 1930s. He was a brilliant organizer and businessman with a multi-ethnic following. His conviction and his motto, "Father will provide," resulted in his being termed one of the most outstanding sociological influences of his time. The Depression hit America hard, with Black people experiencing some of its worst impact. Because African Americans were still struggling for "first-class citizenship," they were "the last hired and the first fired." The Civilian Conservation Corps (CCC), established in 1933, provided for conservation work, whereby men between eighteen and twenty-five might have six months' employment in state forests. Others found employment with the Works Progress Administration (WPA). However, the issue of race resulted in projects which reflected segregation and unequal access to employment opportunities. Philadelphia African Americans created their own institutions and organizations and instilled values which cushioned them from the harsh realities of limited access because of racism. By the mid-1930s, Philadelphia's Black citizens had established and maintained organizations such as the Pyramid Club, which was the epitome of African-American cultural, social and civic life. The Club's motto "Dum Vivimus Vivamus" - "While We Live Let Us Live," was the sentiment of Black people throughout the United States from the 1930s through the 1960s. Another of many organizations was the

Quaker City Lodge, which assisted poor Black families with food, fuel and clothing in South Philadelphia. The families were referred to this Elks lodge by the Police Districts at 20th and Fitzwater Streets and 20th and Federal Streets. The years from that period until 1967 in Philadelphia's African-American communities are recalled through the photographs taken by John W. Mosley. His photographs take us through a journey when the name of his people evolved from "colored" and "Negroes" to the present usage of "Blacks" and "African Americans." The photographs represent an era when upward mobility could only come through education. The lack of it caused African Americans to seek ways for self-improvement within the scope of their means, which meant aspiring to achieve excellence in any field or profession that they had access to. They believed in the dignity of work no matter what their occupation or profession. The photographs in this pictorial are from the John W. Mosley Photographic Collection of the Charles L. Blockson Afro-American Collection at Temple University which contains an estimated 300,000 or more negatives, prints and proofs. The images provide a rich visual history of notable personalities and the cultural, social, and political life of Philadelphia's African-American community and beyond. The photographs for this particular publication were carefully selected from the collection. They represent a range of topics and themes. Some contain images and events which have been identified. Others contain unidentified images and events. It is my intent that both the identified and unidentified photographs will stimulate individuals in the community to come forth and assist in the cataloguing process of this valuable collection, works by John W. Mosley have been exhibited at Temple University, the Tyler School of Art, the Charles L. Blockson Afro-American Collection, the Mellon Jazz Festival, the Please Touch Museum in Philadelphia, the Eisenhower Library in Kansas and in Brazil, among other places. This book is the pictorial journey of a proud race of people. On one level, it is an African-American family album. On another level, it is a tribute to a great Philadelphia African-American photograper. Each section of the pictorial is entitled from themes thoughtfully selected and compiled from contemporary and traditional African-American sayings popularized by those inside of the community itself. The sayings or terms actually chosen for this pictorial were those, through consensus, that best represent the images in the photographs. For example, "Tell It Like It Is" represents the oratorical tradition in the African-American community which has been essential in providing accurate information. "The Learning Tree" represents the great regard for education that African Americans have passed from generation to generation, from Colonial times to the present, even during periods when they were being denied equal access to this basic right. It also shows how important values were taught inside of the community itself. "For My People" represents the institutions, organizations and businesses that African Americans established for their own communities, and their commitment to strive individually for the betterment of the group as a whole. Some institutions and businesses were established in response to the realities of racial discrimination and segregation in the City of Philadelphia. Also, this section shows a period when there were a number of thriving Black-owned businesses, which have now disappeared. "A Sense of Purpose" represents African Americans' commitment and dedication to their communities and also their consciousnesses of their responsibilities as American citizens. "God Bless the Children" represents the importance that African Americans have placed on their children, who represent the future. This value is as old as ancient Africa. "The Living Is Easy" represents leisure and recreational activities. It shows the importance of being able to take time out to be thankful and to celebrate life. This sense of optimism enabled African Americans to make positive and uniquely American contributions in oftentimes hostile environments. "The Cotillion" represents the Philadelphia Cotillion Society, founded by Dr. Eugene Raymond Jones. Mrs. Marian Cuyjet, a former member of the Philadelphia Cotillion Society, states that, "Dr. Jones invited

Black Philadelphians from all walks of life to his extravagant events. A committee was set up in the Society, which raised funds for guests that he invited, who were unable to afford to buy the formal attire required for the Cotillions." The Reverend Inez Thompson states that, "The Cotillion mobilized for public view the private lives of Philadelphia's African-American bourgeoisie. It was a showcase. It helped to reinforce Philadelphia as having a rich dance and cultural heritage. It revitalized dance." The Cotillion focused on "family." It helped to reinforce family life in the community. The father had to present his daughter on the night of the Cotillion Ball. The Reverend Inez Thompson continues, "Young ladies who did not have fathers had to get a substitute." It also strengthened the importance of fathers. She states that, "The upper class learned also to appreciate many working class individuals, who did most of the leg work for the Ball such as making the costumes, etc." "The Crusaders" represents a range of strong men and women in the Black community. For example, the Sleeping Car Porters were very important to the African-American communities. Many were very well educated, with college degrees. They kept their dignity during a period when racial discrimination and segregation limited their opportunities. They fed servicemen, and men, women and children who were denied the same services on the trains that whites received. They also provided the community with information. Many of them would take newspapers, magazines, and journals given to them by wealthy whites home for their families and friends to read. "Sitting Pretty" represents an era when many families sent their girls to schools to become refined and to learn proper etiquette. Photographs of African-American women posing were viewed positively. They would give the photographs to husbands or boyfriends. Others were used as "morale boosters" for servicemen during World War II. The Mosley photographs reflect the continuity of culture and introduce the viewer to important values that have withstood the test of time. The captions with unidentified images in them were carefully researched so that they reflect terms and phrases used during the period in which they were photographed. Especially useful were the *Pictorial Album of the Pyramid Club.* The following pages contain a vivid depiction of a people and their communities. It not only represents Philadelphia but the experiences and relationships of African Americans in cities throughout the United States. It is a testimony to the existence of an African-American humanity that warms the heart and soul as it stimulates the eye.

• • • • • • • • • •

ACKNOWLEDGEMENTS

It is difficult to adequately express the sense of gratitude that I feel towards the people connected with the publication of ***The Journey of John W. Mosley***. Their belief and enthusiasm regarding the value of the Mosley photographic collection and their devotion and commitment to the preservation of his photographs has few parallels. I wish to express appreciation and thanks to John W. Mosley's wife, Teresa Still Mosley, a retired Philadelphia school teacher, and her brother, Clarence Still, for donating this important and magnificent collection to the Afro-American Collection at Temple University. Their generosity was a result of nearly 150 years of relations between the Still and Blockson families, a connection which began during the era of the Underground Railroad. In 1858, William Still, the most energetic and adventurous conductor of the Philadelphia Underground Railroad, recorded in his classic book *The Underground Railroad* the name of my great grandfather James, who had escaped from Delaware. This year the Still family celebrated its 123rd family reunion. Largely due to this historical connection, the Still family decided to give John W. Mosley's photographs to the Charles L. Blockson Afro-American Collection at Temple University in 1985. Grateful acknowledgement is extended to Charles A. Powell, the president of Quantum Leap Publisher, Inc., for his kind forbearance during the preparational stages of this project. I would also like to thank the members of his staff: Barbara Jean Hope, John Cooper and Toni Kersey for her magnificent layout and design. A sincere thanks to Deborah Willis for her contribution to the preface of this book. A special thank-you to Dr. William Tash, Zohrah Kazanjian, Lynette Muse, Dr. Richard Beards and other members of the Temple University family. A sincere thank-you to Diane D. Turner for selecting and handling fragile original negatives with understanding care, for performing the tedious task of researching and writing the captions, and for editing and indexing. I would also like to thank the other members of my staff for their support with this project. I am also deeply indebted to the members of Philadelphia's African American community, who graciously assisted us in identifying individuals represented in the John W. Mosley photographs by taking time from their busy schedules to come to the Afro-American Collection. Finally, a special acknowledgement to John W. Mosley, whose love for his community, wisdom, foresight, knowledge and photgraphic excellence, made this book possible.

Charles L. Blockson

MY FAMILY

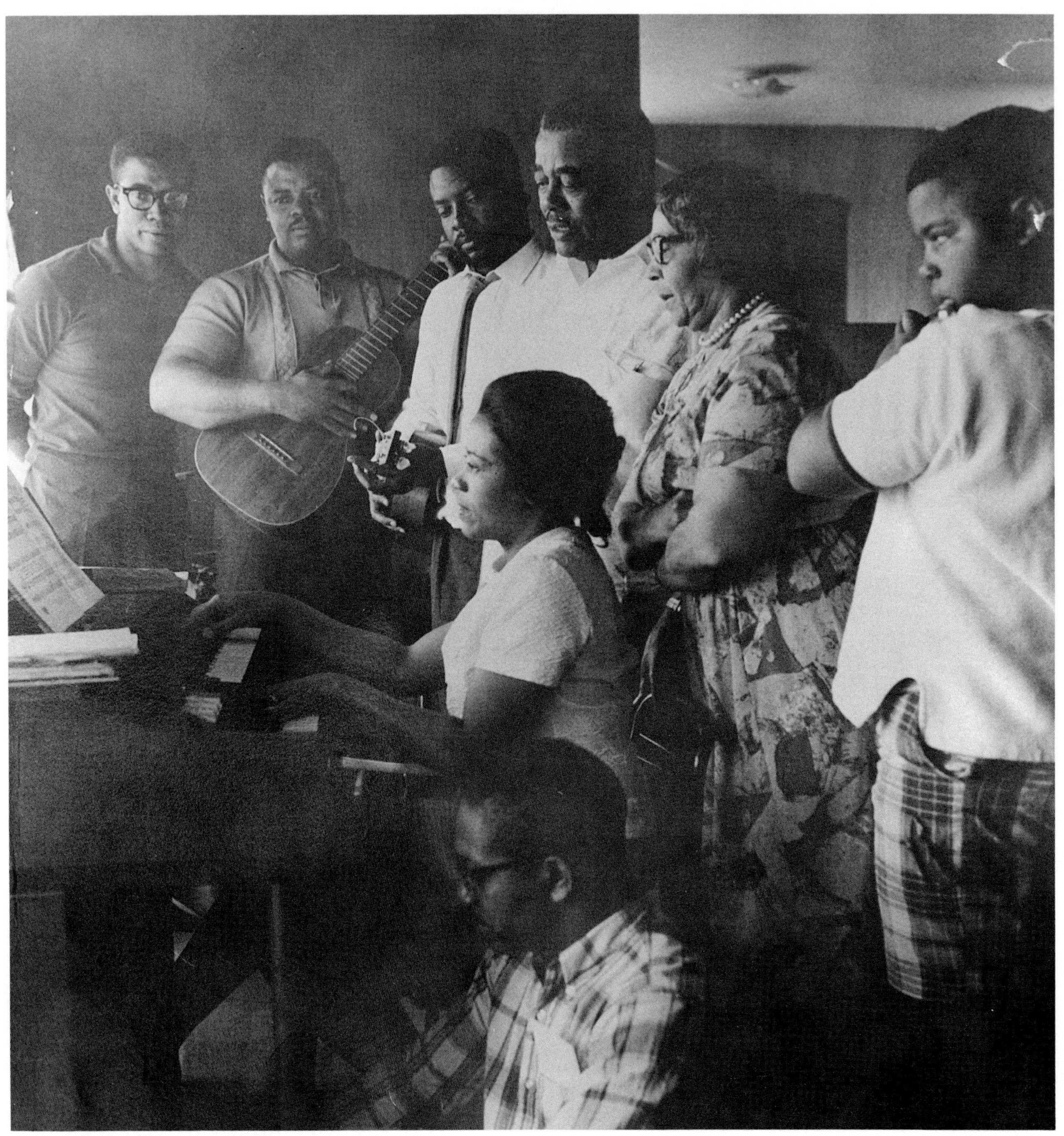

1) Teresa Still Mosley (sitting) plays the piano, accompanied by members of her family (standing from left to right) Cecil Still, Clarence N. Still, Jr., Manny Dongola [from Africa], Clarence N. Still, Sr. [father], Marian Still, Clarence N. Still, 4th, and Charles Wheeler Still (bottom center), early 1940s.

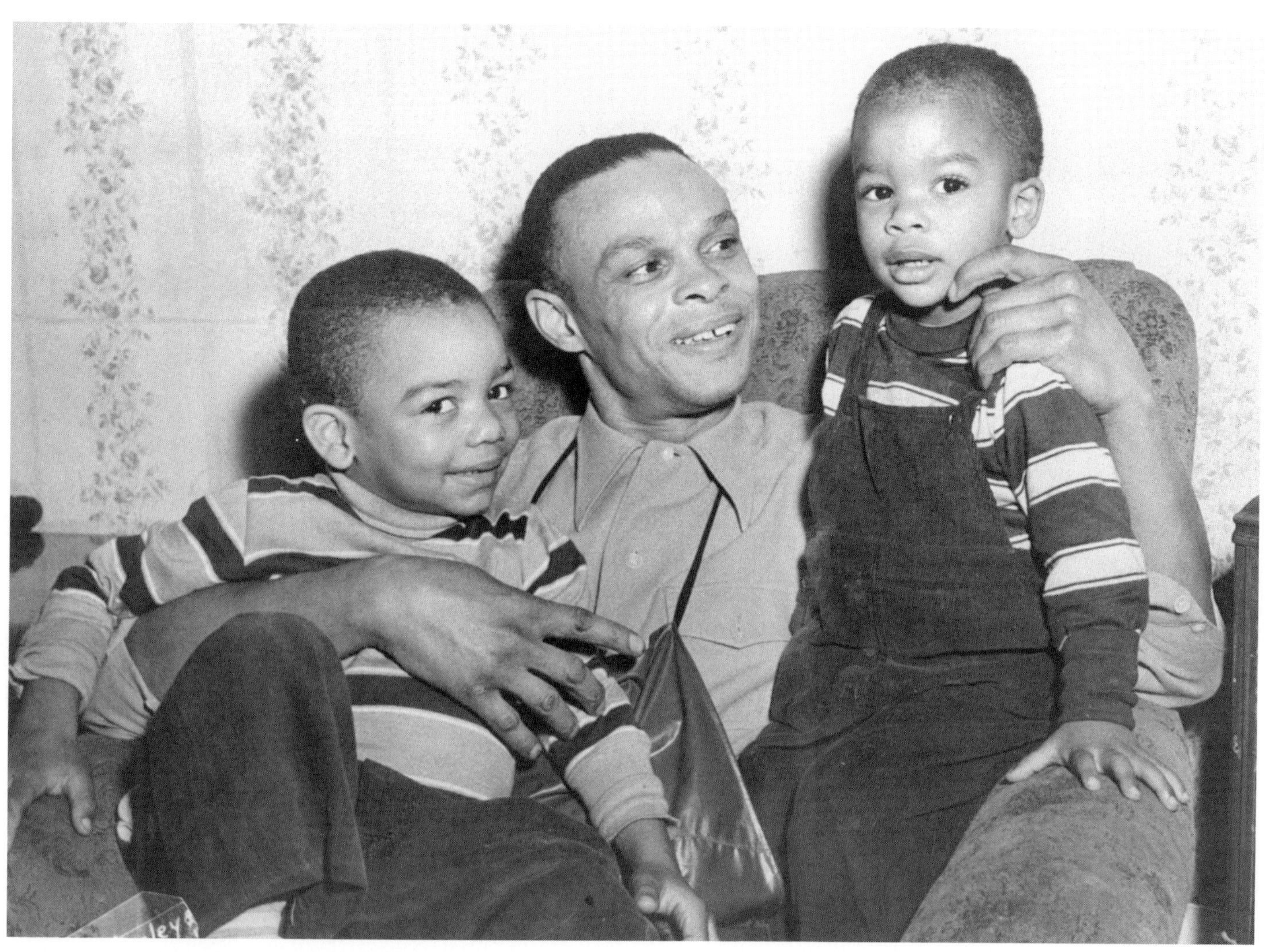

2) John W. Mosley (center) enjoys taking a self-portrait with his two sons John W. Mosley, Jr. and Charles Mosley, 1950s.

TELL IT LIKE IT IS

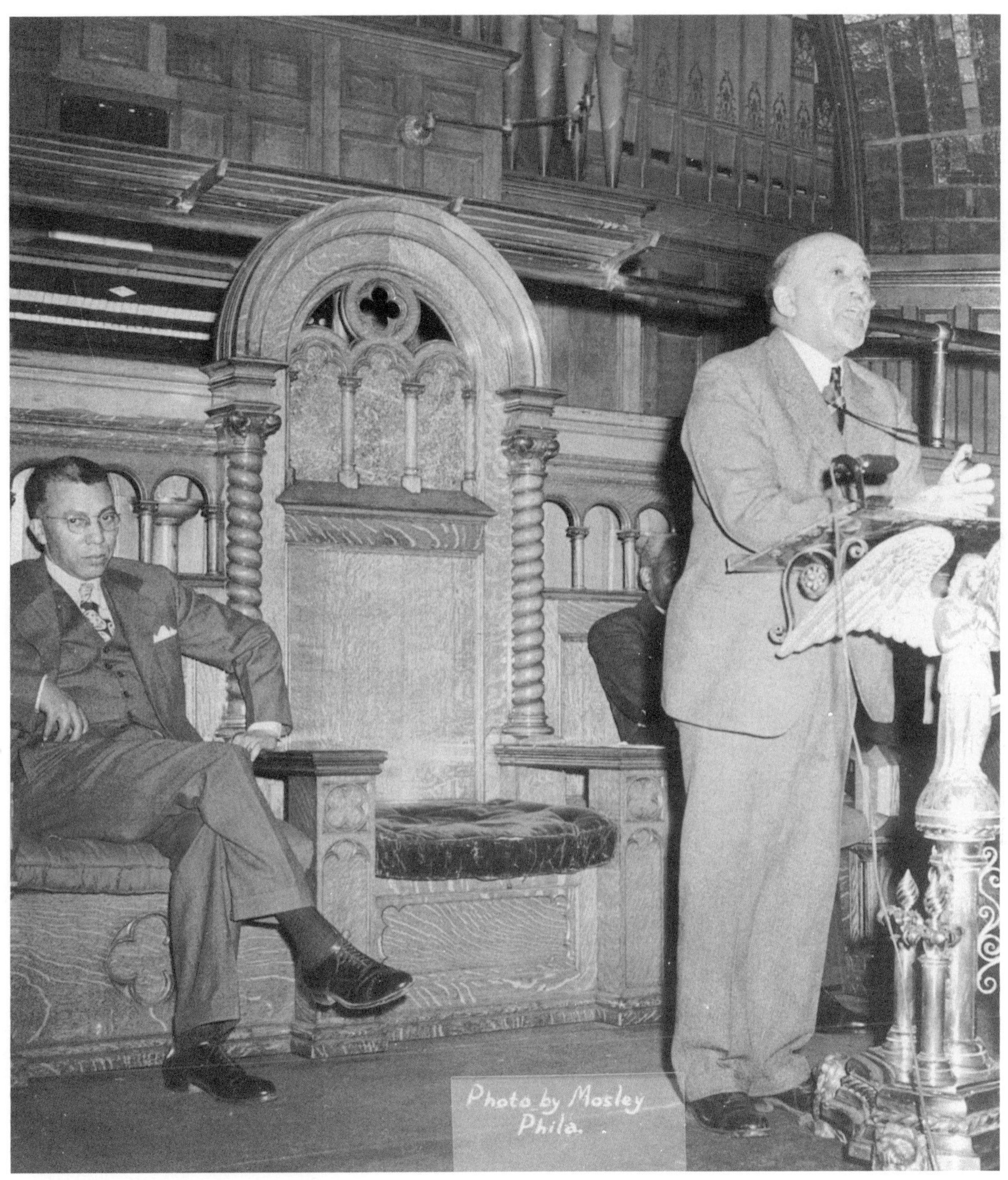

3) W.E.B. Dubois (1868-1963) author, historian, sociologist and educator, speaks at the McDowell Presbyterian Church as E. Washington Rhodes, publisher-editor of *The Philadelphia Tribune*, looks on, February 4, 1945.

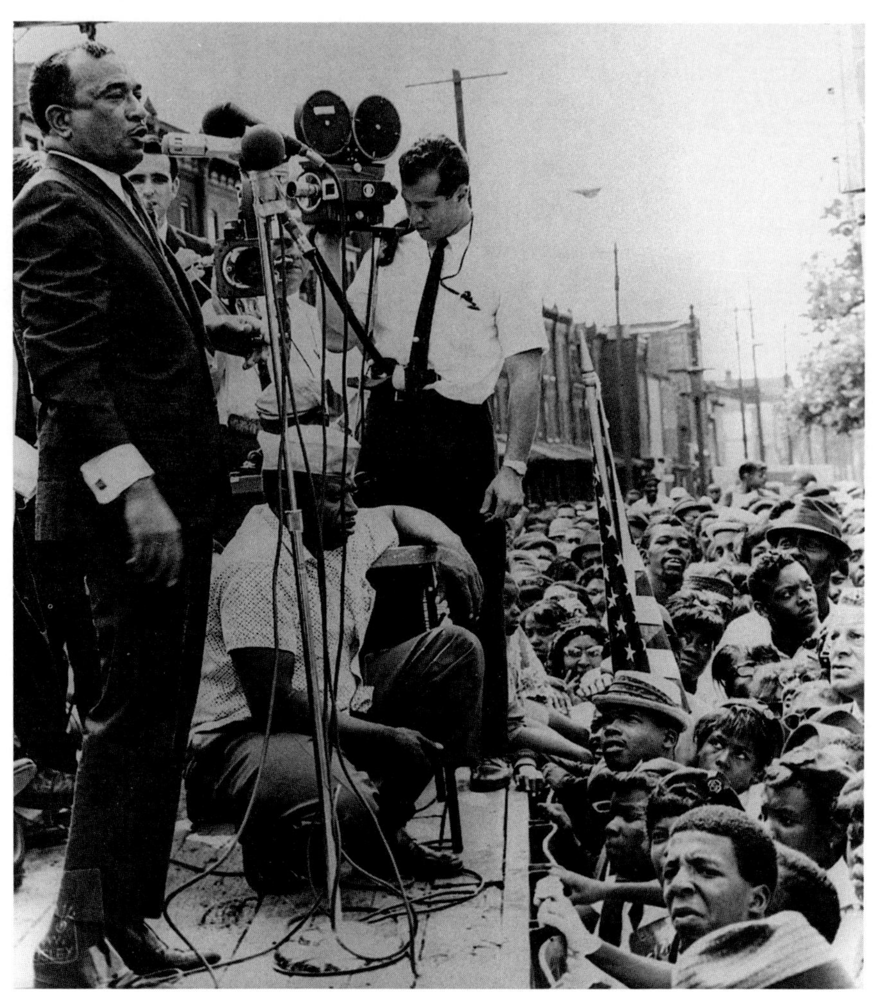

4) Attorney Cecil B. Moore (1915-1976), civil rights activist and former president of North Philadelphia NAACP, addresses a group of civil rights protestors during the campaign to integrate Girard College, 1965.

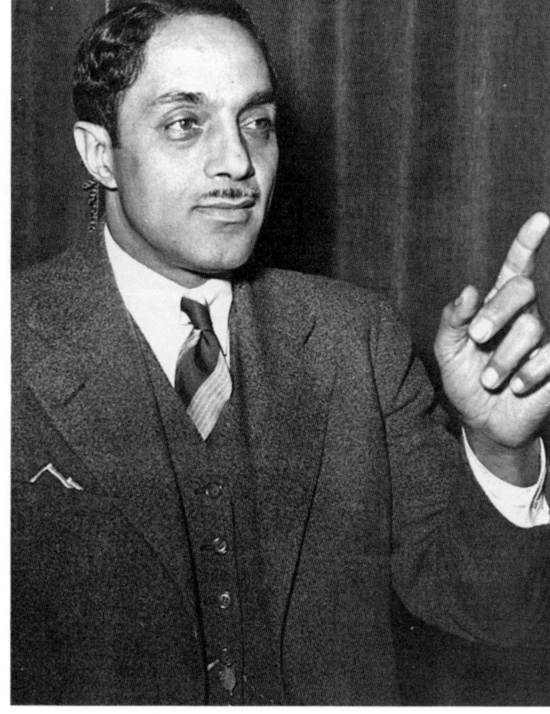

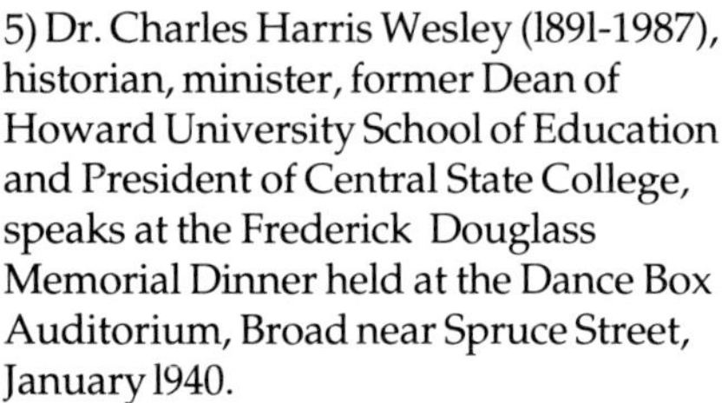

5) Dr. Charles Harris Wesley (1891-1987), historian, minister, former Dean of Howard University School of Education and President of Central State College, speaks at the Frederick Douglass Memorial Dinner held at the Dance Box Auditorium, Broad near Spruce Street, January 1940.

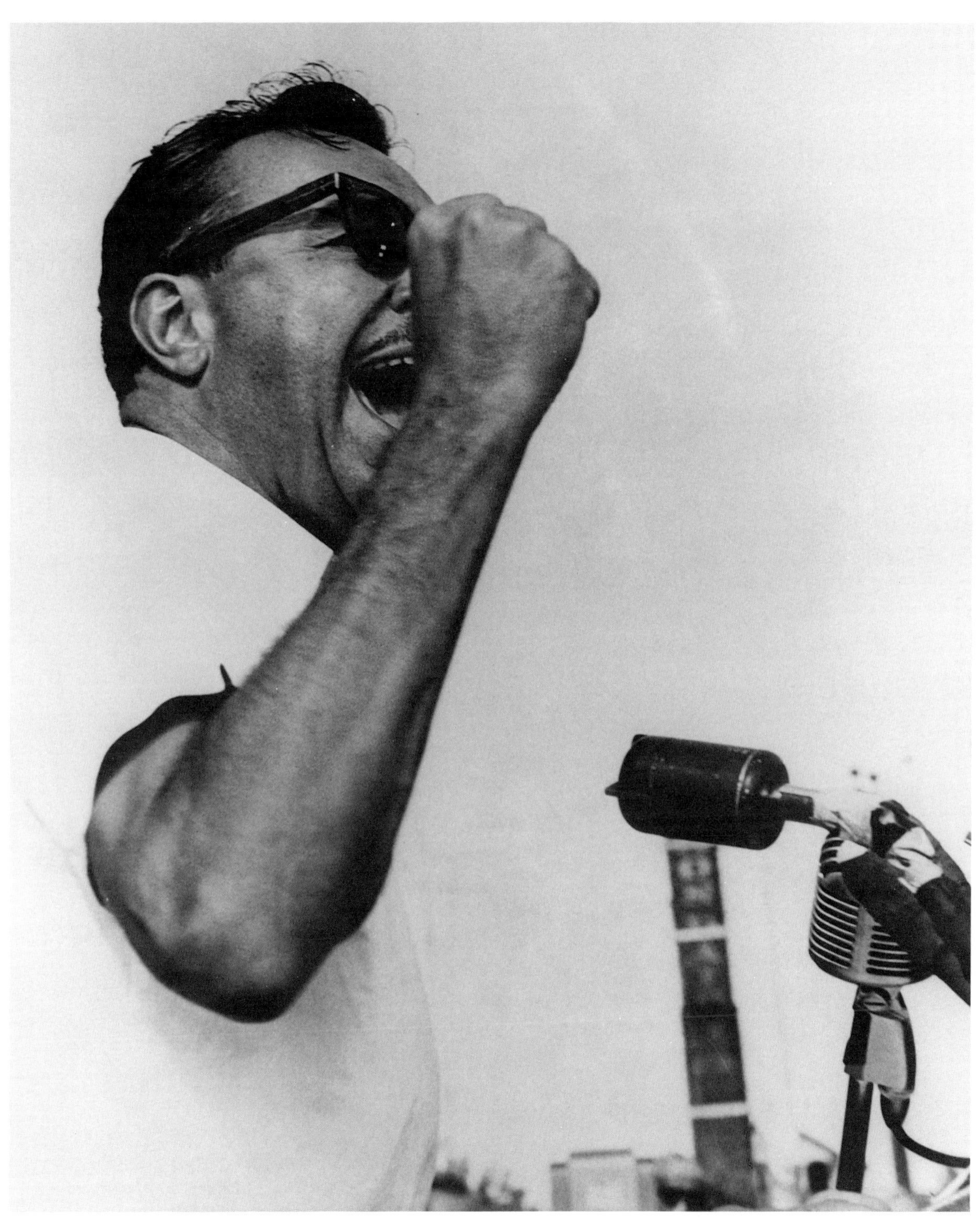

6) The Reverend Congressman Adam Clayton Powell, Jr. (1908-1972), organizer of the 1966 National Black Power Conference, speaks at civil rights rally in Atlantic City, New Jersey, sponsored by the NAACP, August 23, 1964.

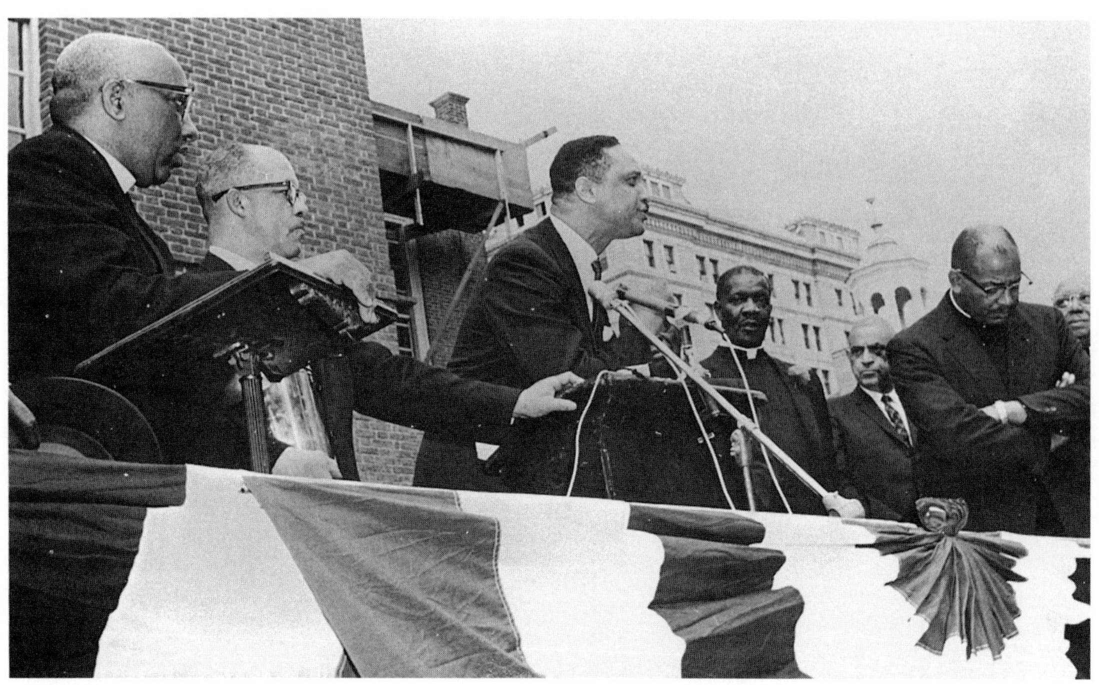

7A) The Reverend Leon Howard Sullivan, creator of Opportunities Industrialization Center (OIC) and first Black member of General Motors Corporation's Board of Directors, speaks at ceremony, mid-1960s.

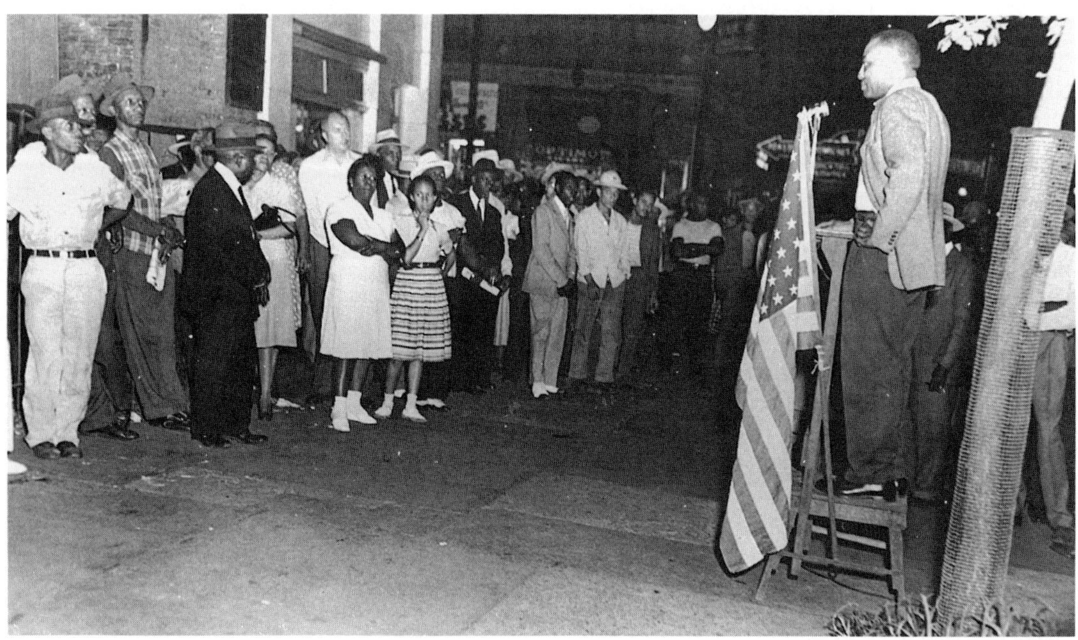

7B) A street corner orator talks as crowd looks on, 1940s.

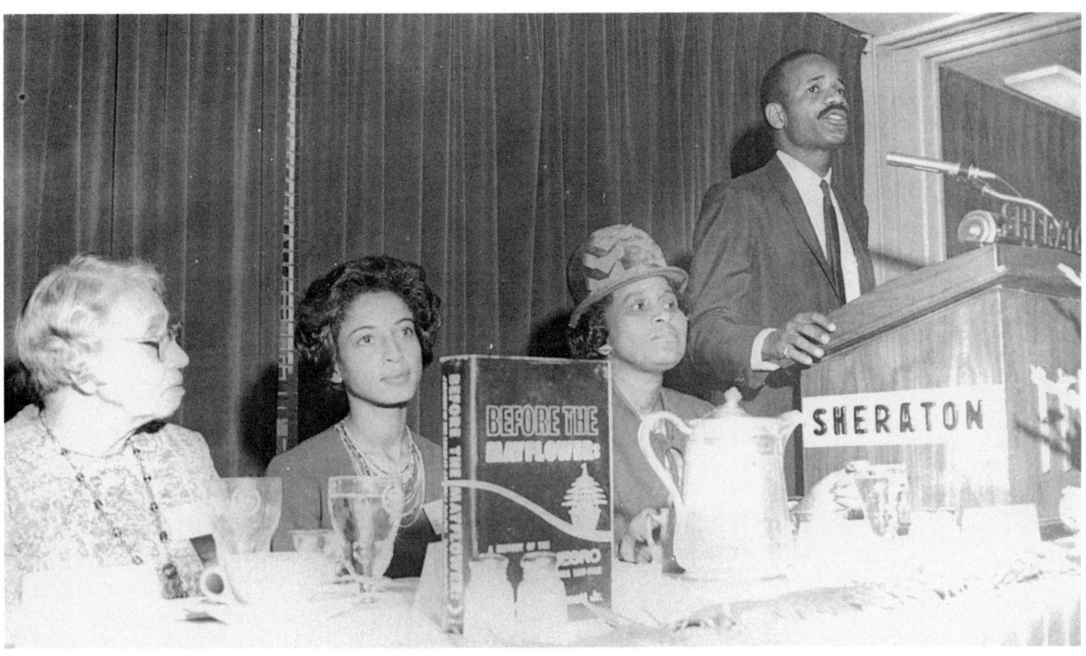

8A) Lerone Bennett historian, writer, journalist, and Executive Director of Ebony, discusses his book entitled *Before the Mayflower* at the Sheraton Hotel,

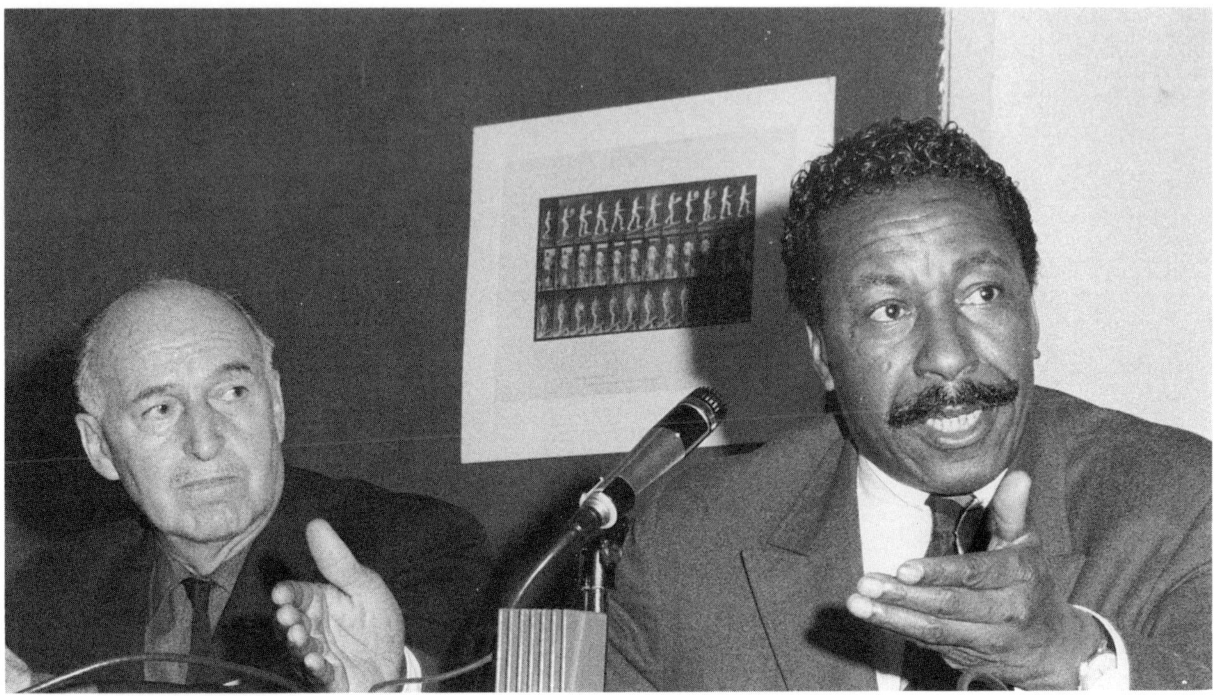

8B) Gordon Parks, photographer, journalist, composer, writer and movie director, speaks, 1960s.

CHILDREN, HOW SHALL I SEND THEE

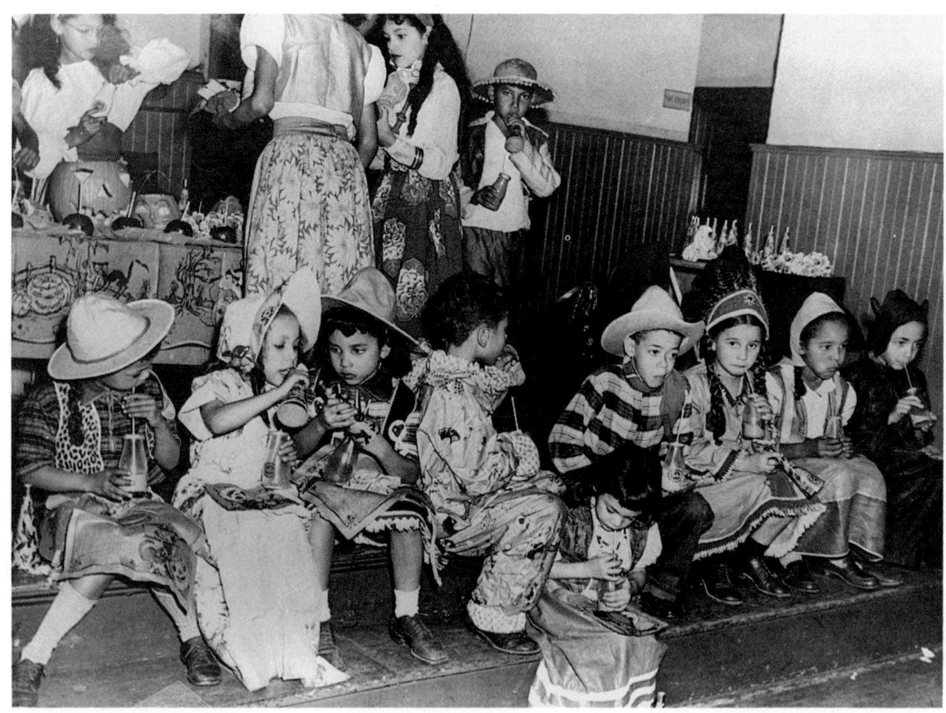

9A) Boys and girls of the Jack and Jill Association enjoy a masquerade party, November 3, 1946. The club was founded in 1938 by a group of Black mothers in Philadelphia, who were interested in expanding social play and activities for their children during a period of segregation in the city.

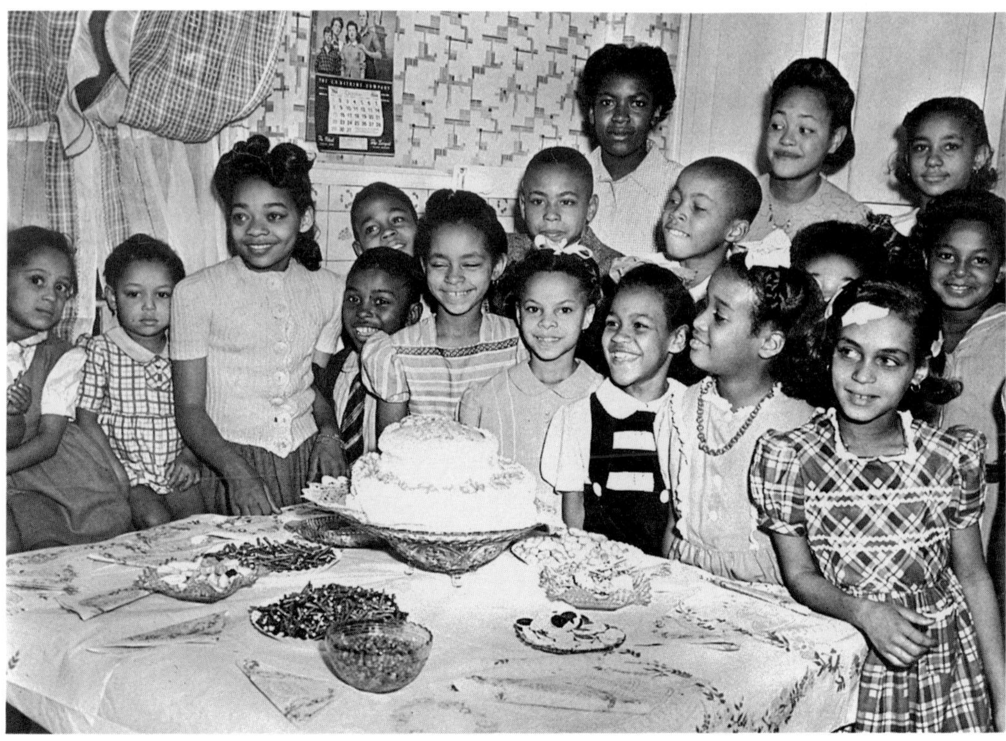

9B) Hamilton girl celebrates her birthday during a party with her two sisters and some friends, 1944.

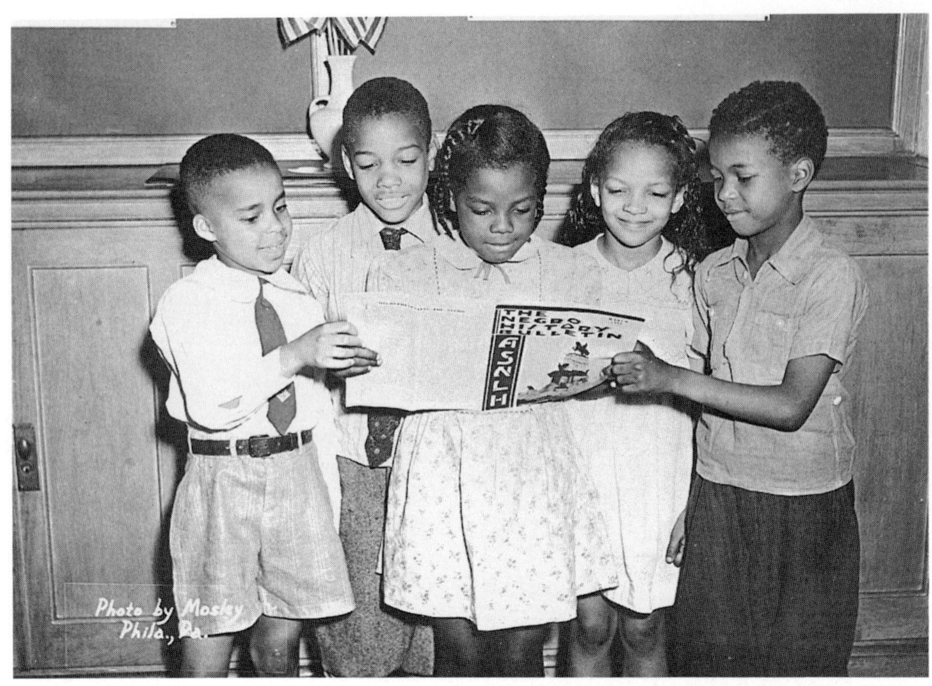

10A) Children learn about their rich heritage at Douglass School May Day, 1944.

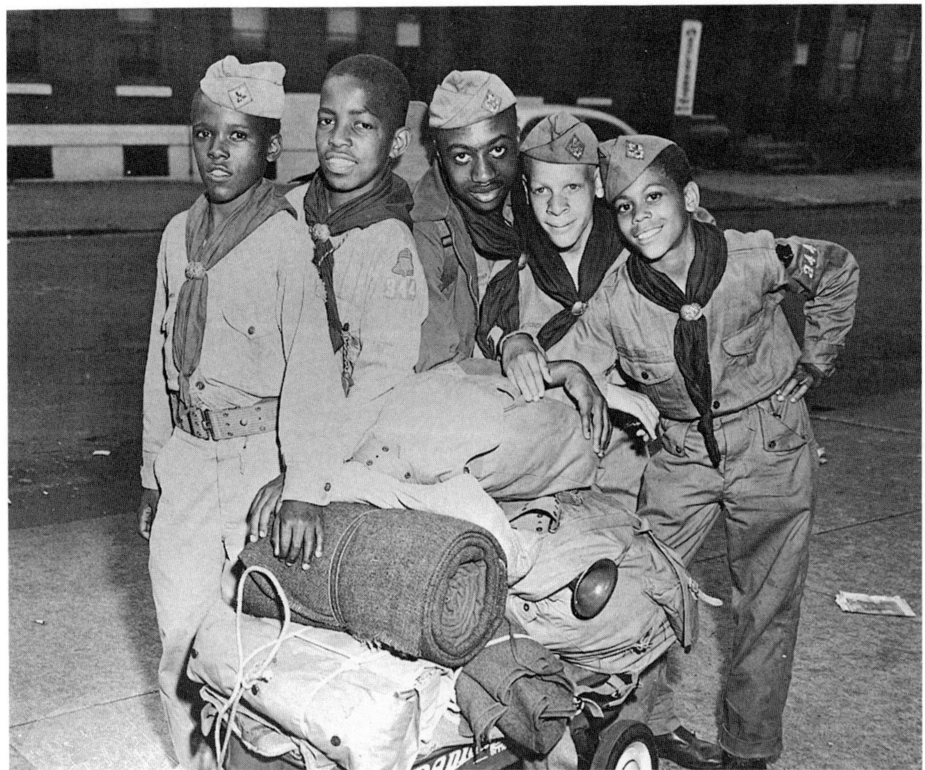

10B) Boy scouts on their way to camping, stop and pose for the camera, June 5, 1949.

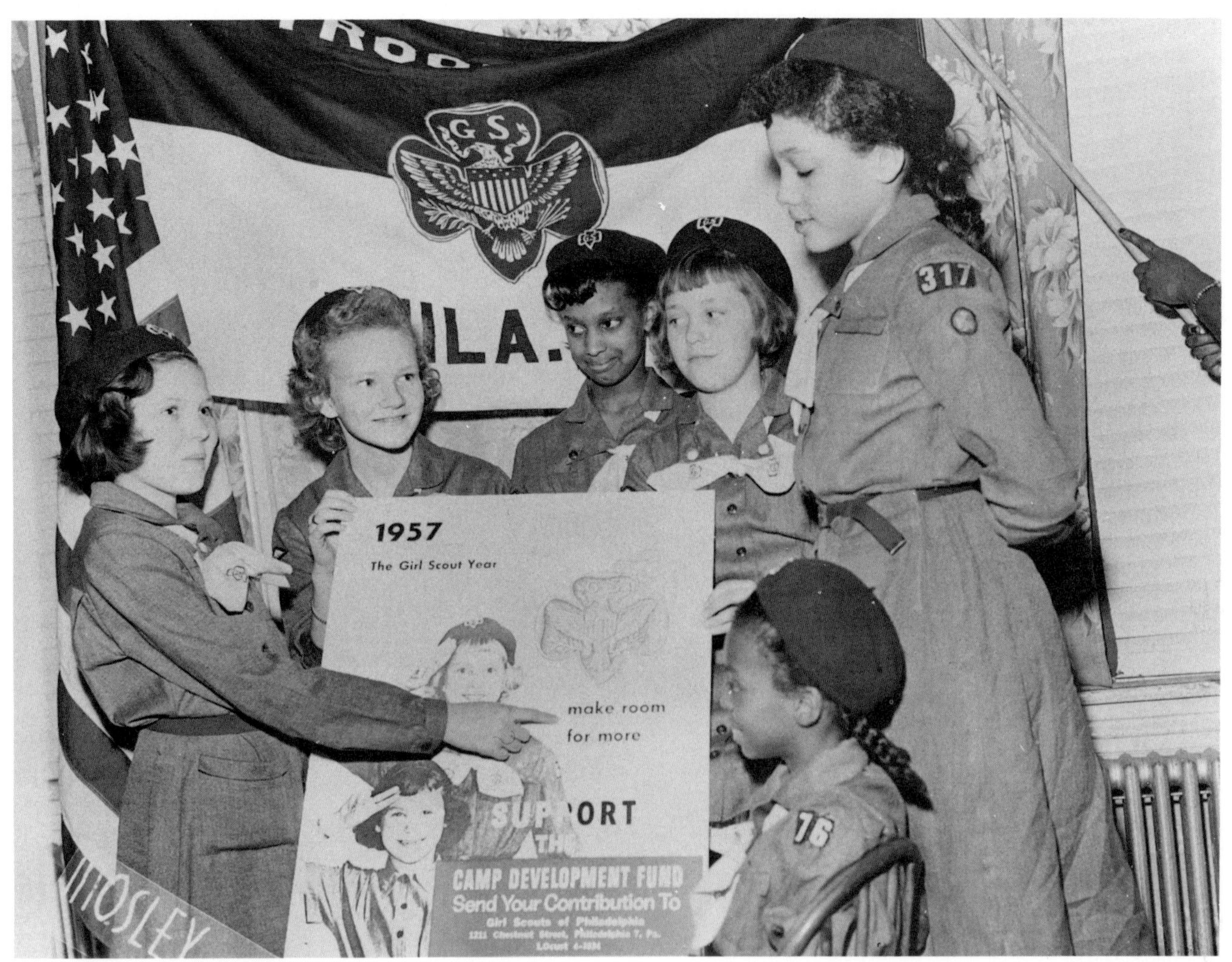

11) Girl scouts solicit for contributions during their Camp Development Fund Drive, March 2, 1957.

STURDY BLACK BRIDGES

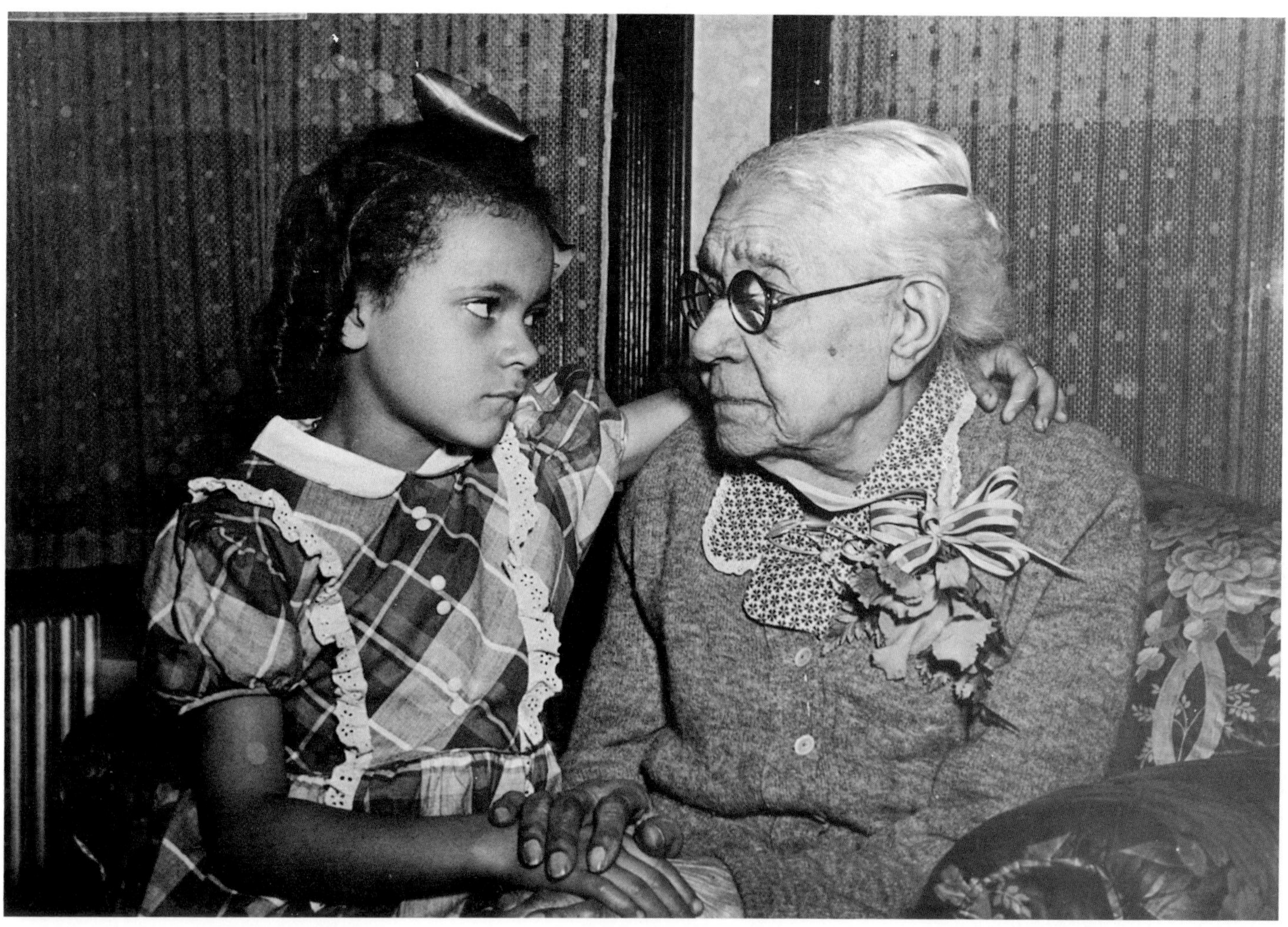

12A)"Love and Understanding," 1945.

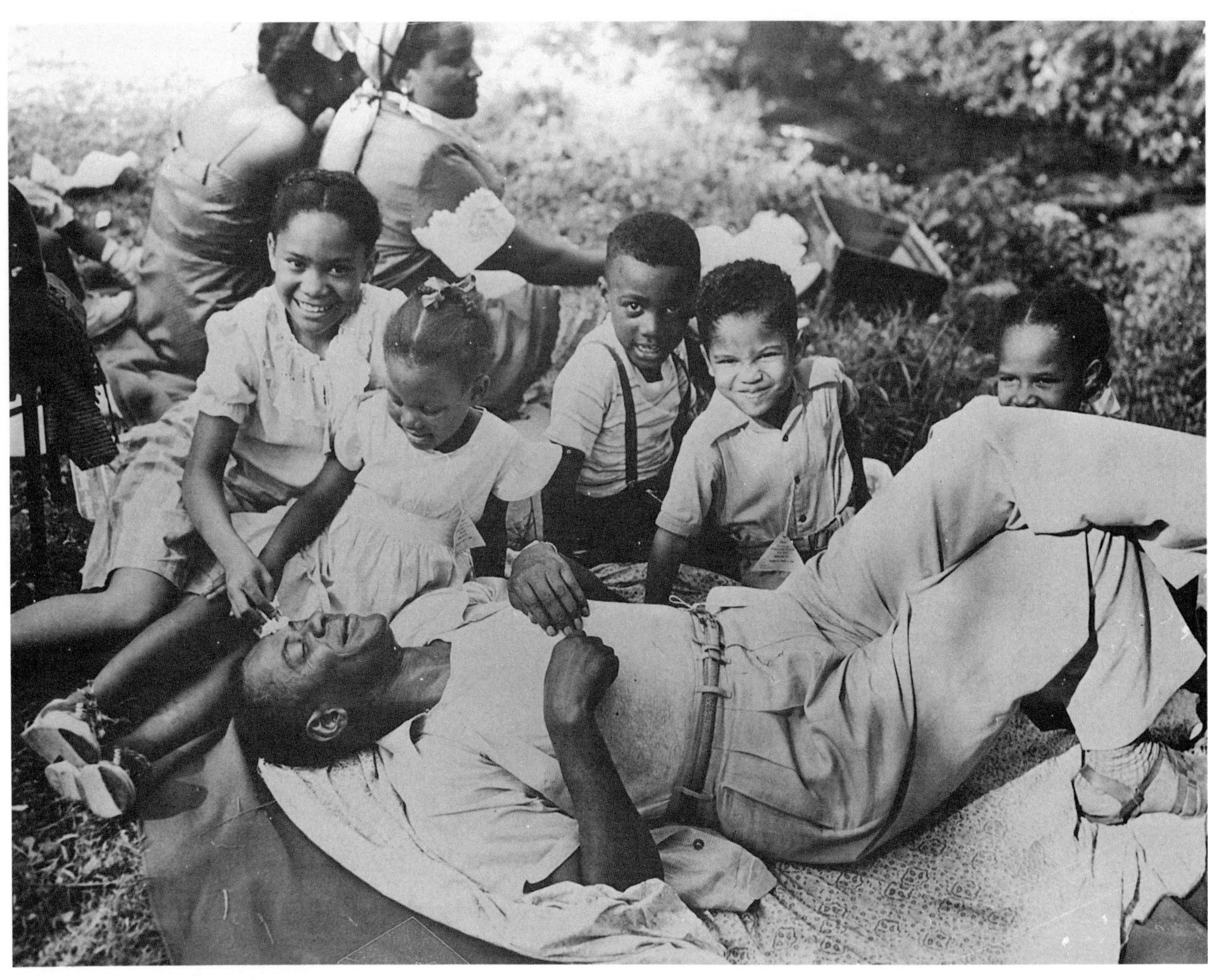

12B)Father plays possum with children on a blanket in the park, mid-1940s.

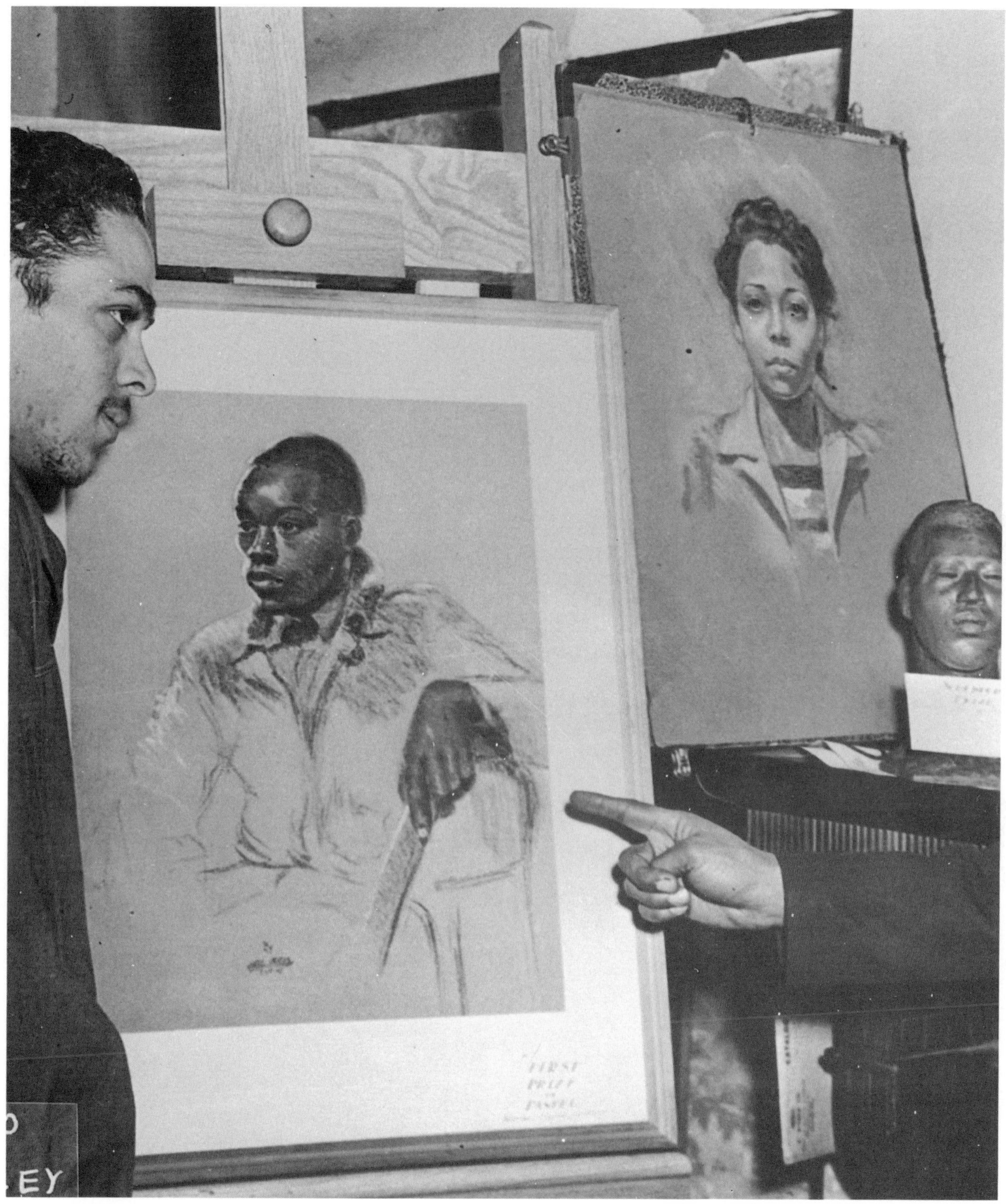

13) Harry Jackson, first-prize winner in an art contest, stands beside his award-winning pastel drawing as John T. Harris, well-known artist and instructor, commends him, 1940.

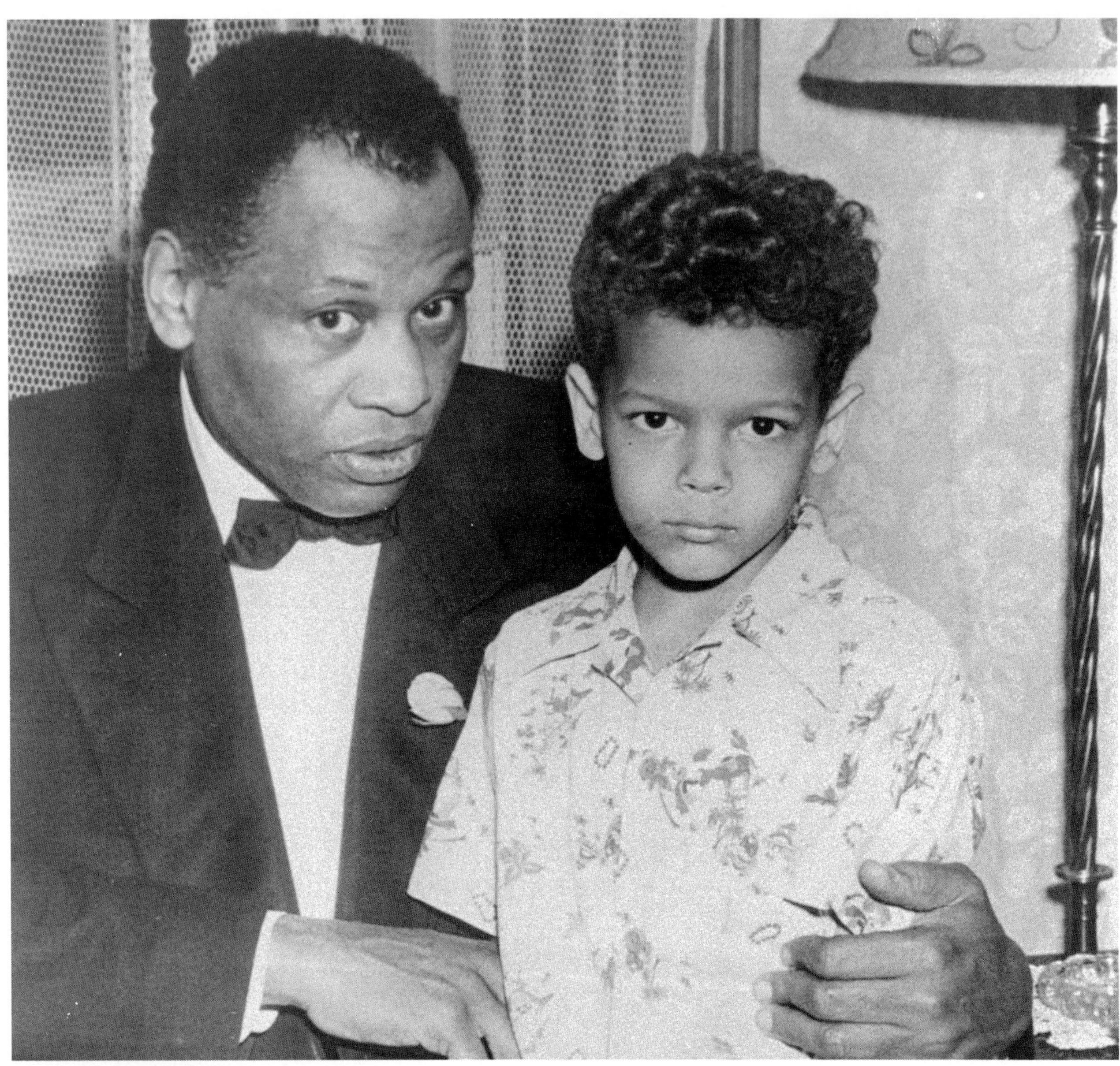

14) Paul Leroy Robeson (1898-1976), actor, athlete, scholar, singer, lawyer, and founder of the Council on African Affairs, passes on words of wisdom to Julian Bond, civil rights activist, son of Dr. Horace Mann Bond (1904-1972) and Mrs. Julia Bond, late-1940s.

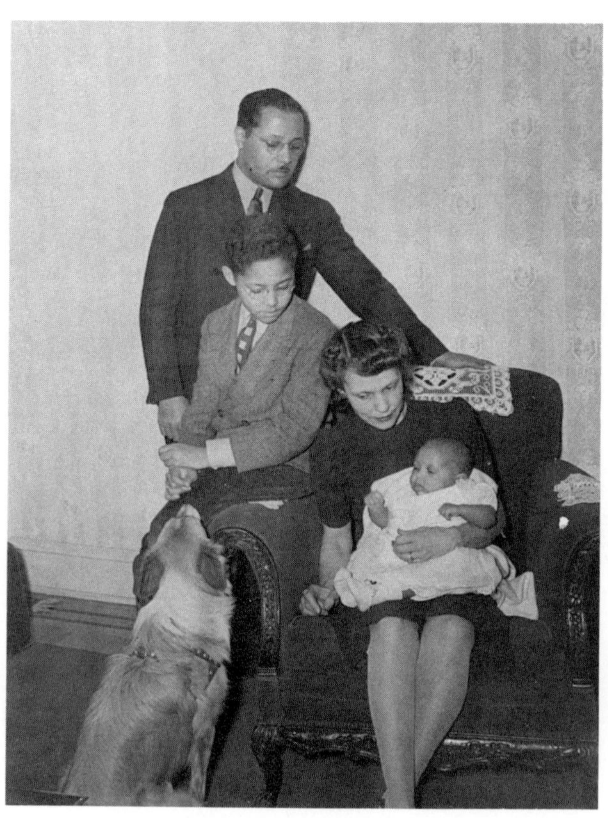

15A) Dr. Russell F. Minton and family, 1940s.

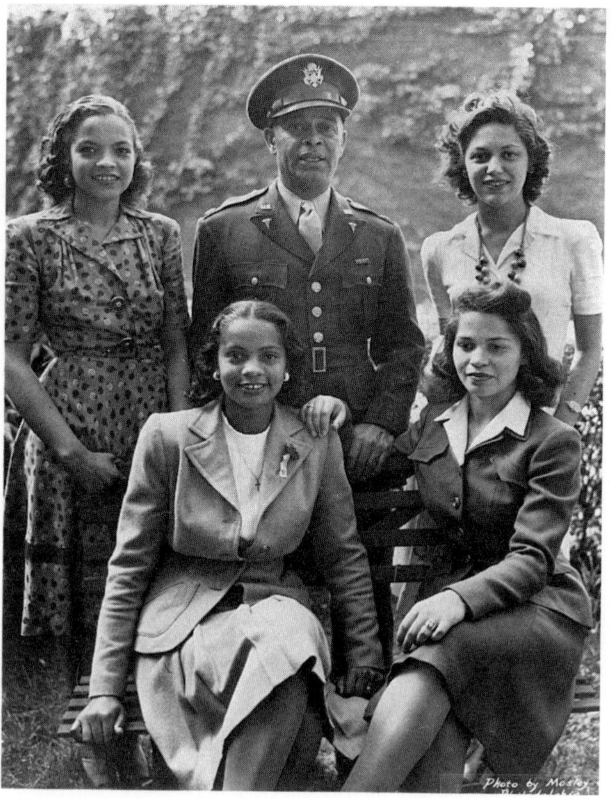

15B) Major DeHaven Hinkson, M.D. (1891-1975), civil rights activitist who served in first and Second World War, with four daughters during the Second World War, 1943.

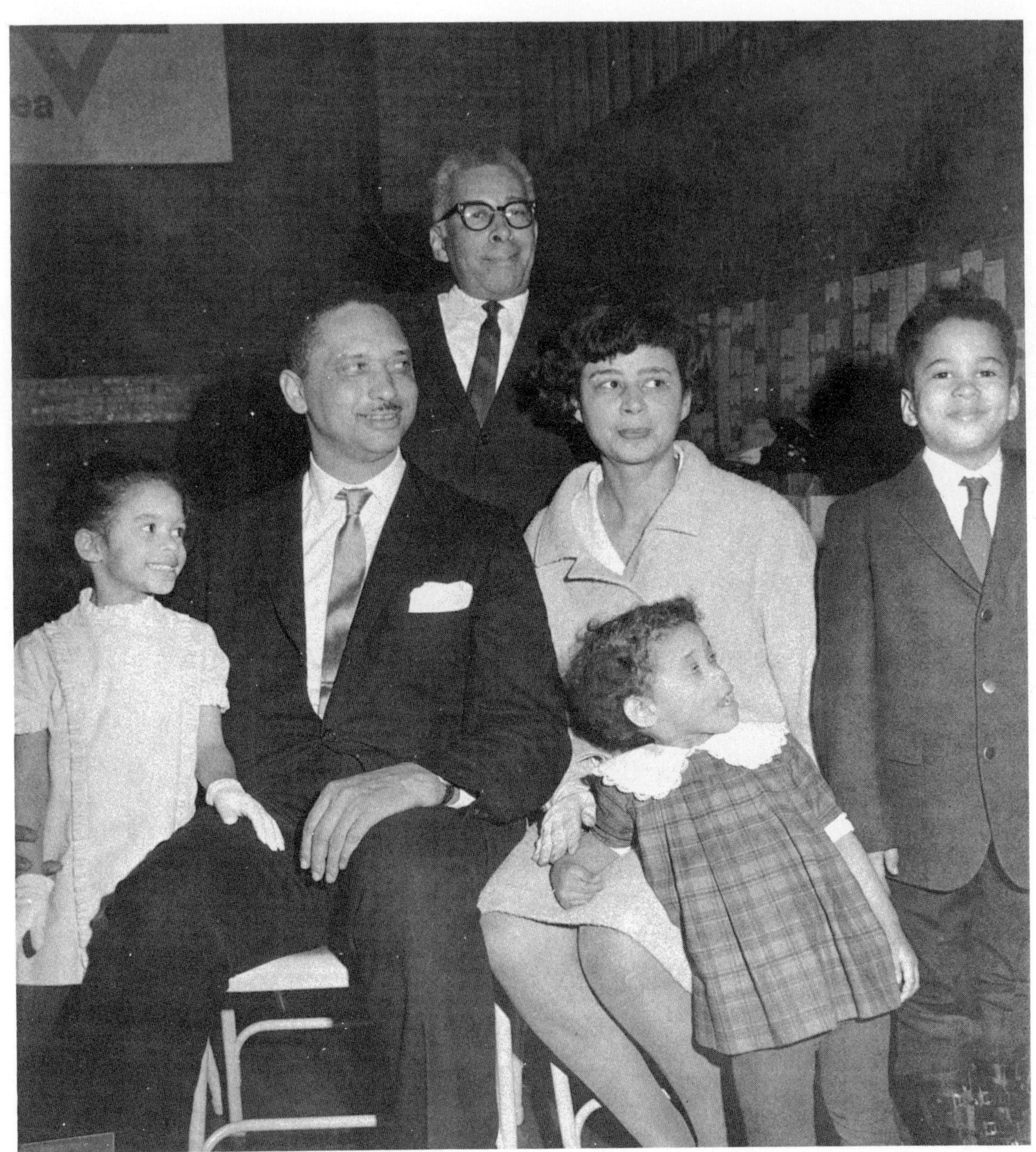

16)The Reverend Leon H. Sullivan with his wife, Grace and their children at the YMCA, 1950s.

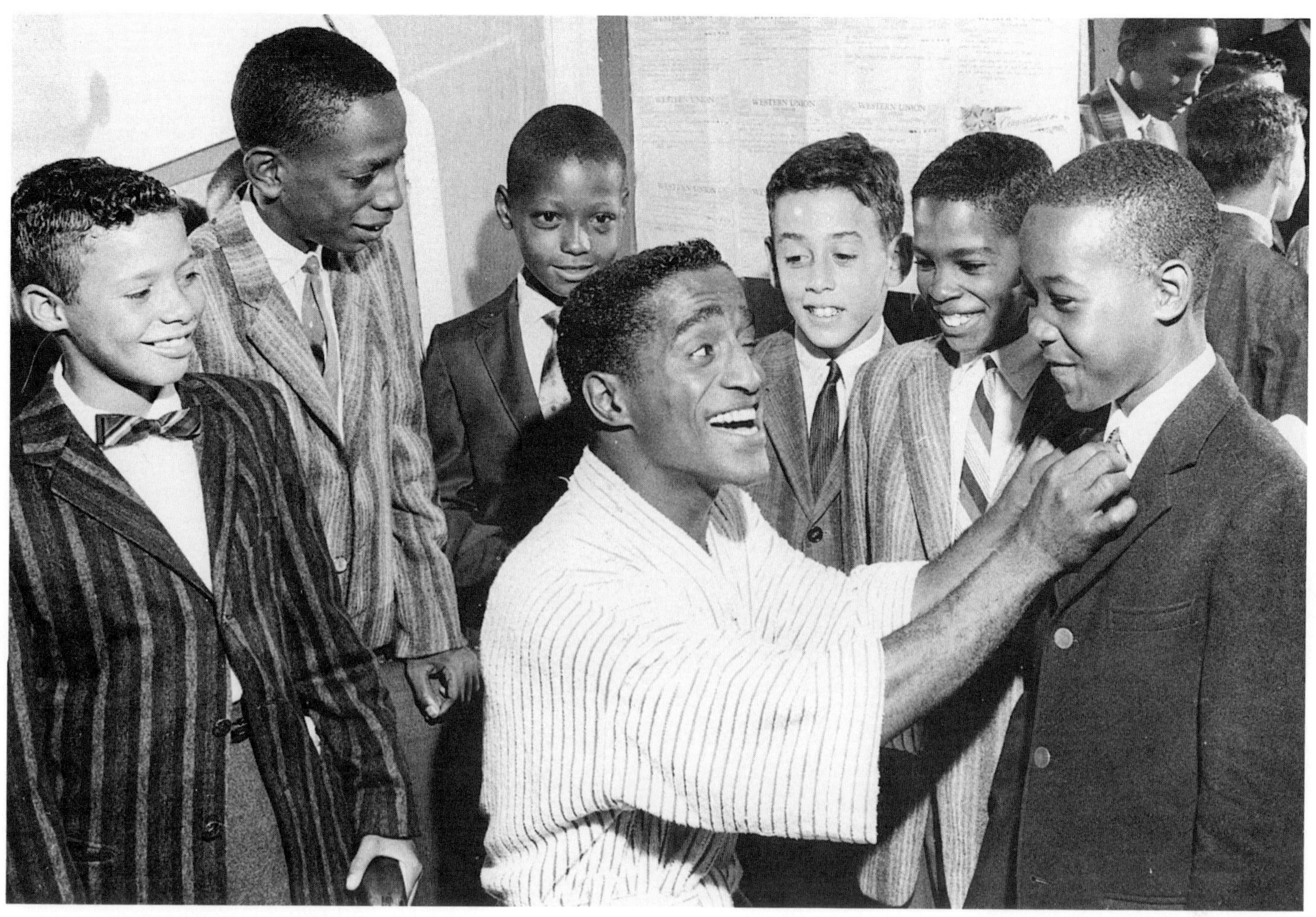

17) Sammy Davis, Jr. (1925-1990) (center), internationally renowned actor, dancer, singer, and civil rights activist, spends time with young men, 1950s.

THE LEARNING TREE

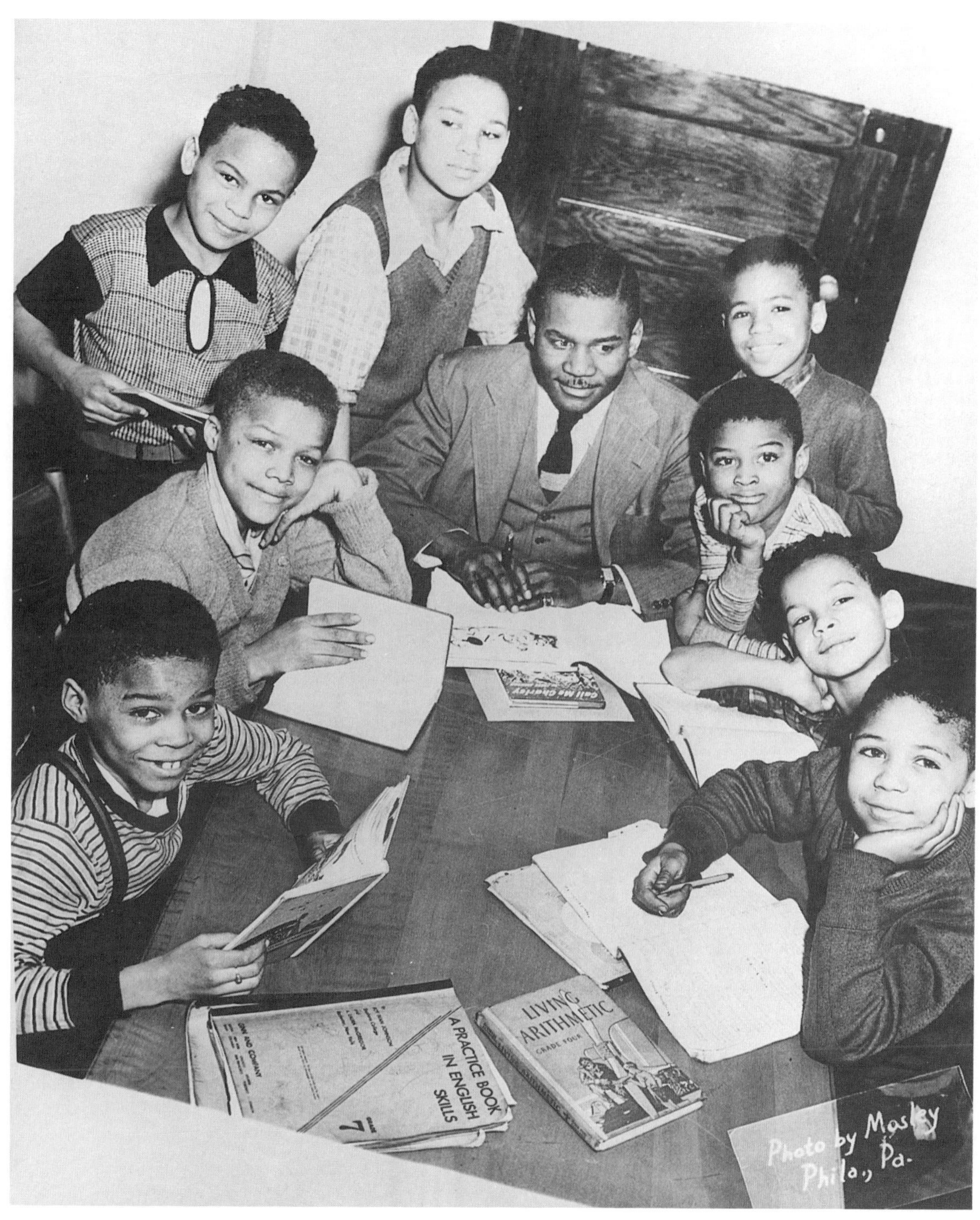

18) Teacher instructs a group of school boys in the basic skills of reading, writing and arithmetic, March 27, 1946.

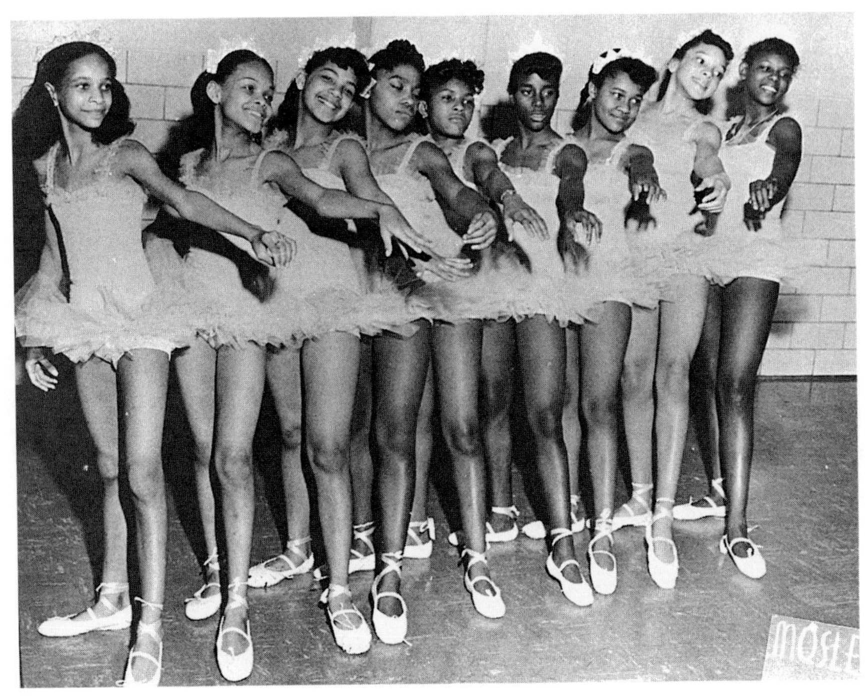

19A) A group of ballerinas pose, 1940s.

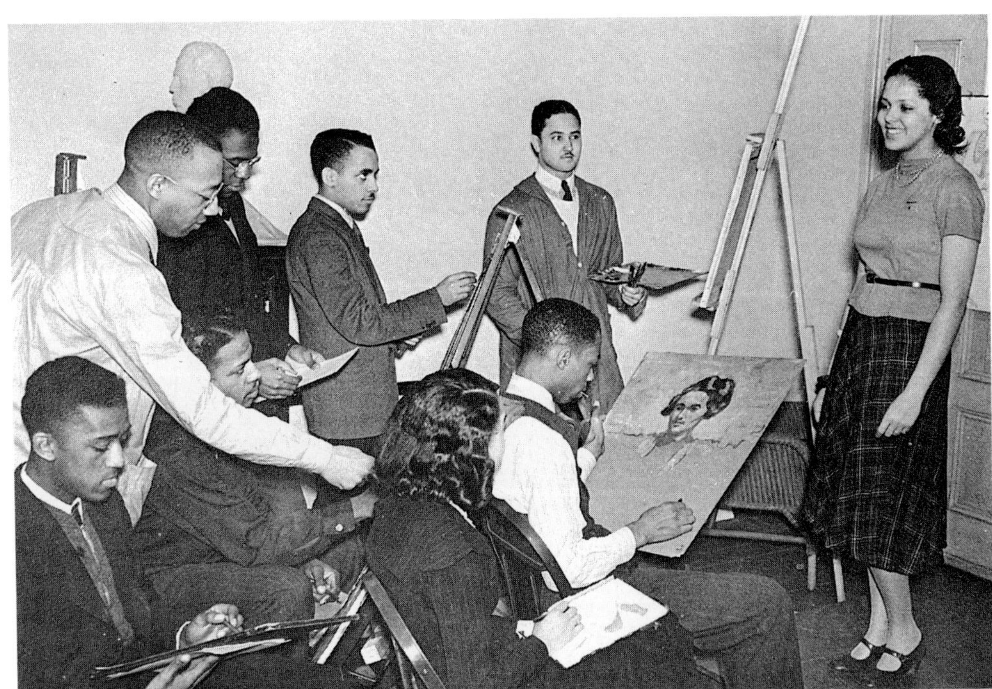

19B) Artist and instructor, John T. Harris, assists his students during a drawing exercise, 1940.

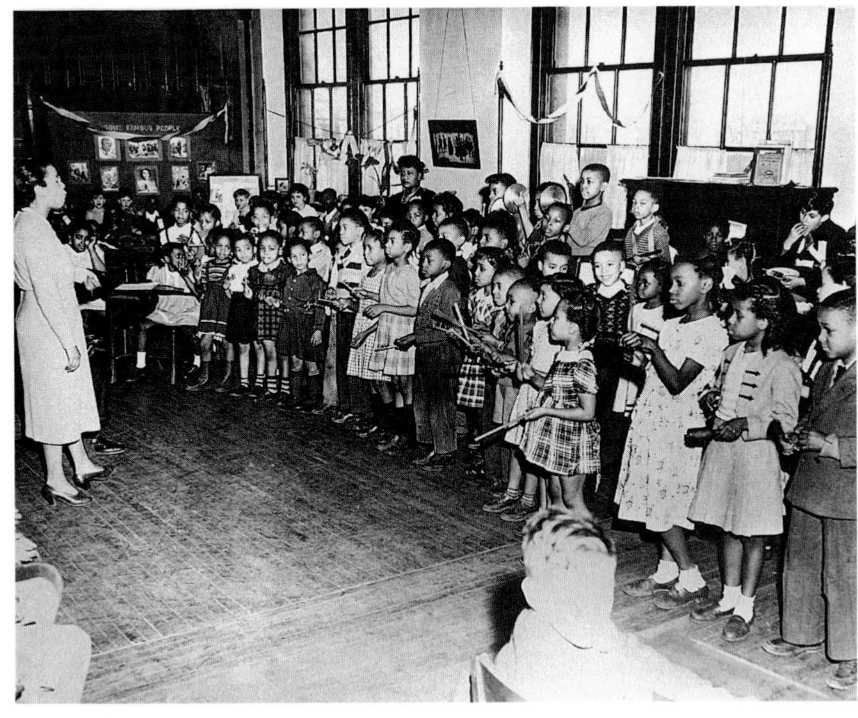

20A) Teacher Sara Gould and students from the Walton School, 29th and Huntington, attend the Arnold School Party, 1940s.

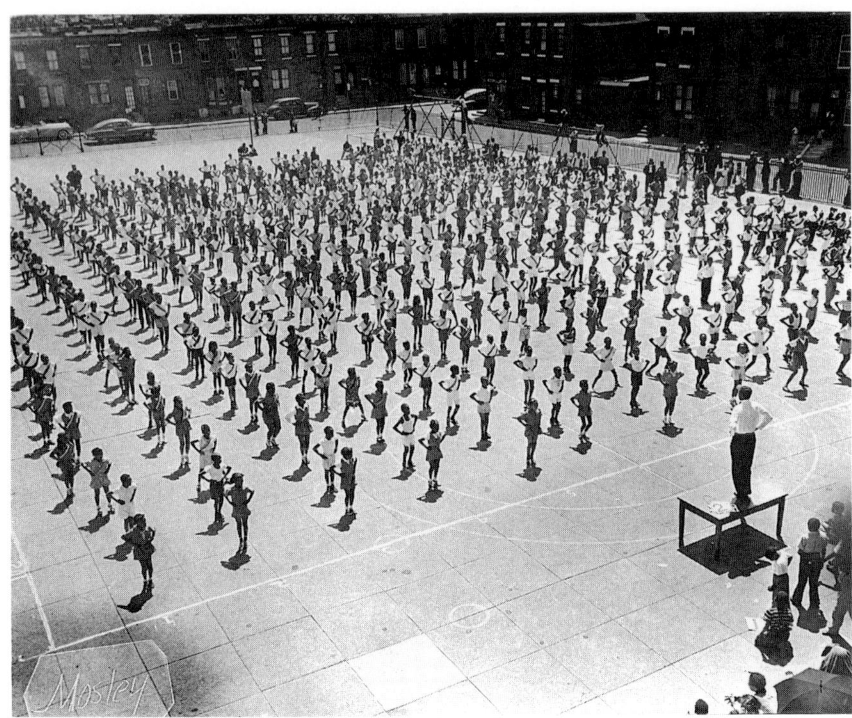

20B) A male instructor leads a group of boys and girls in calisthenics, 1940s.

FOR MY PEOPLE

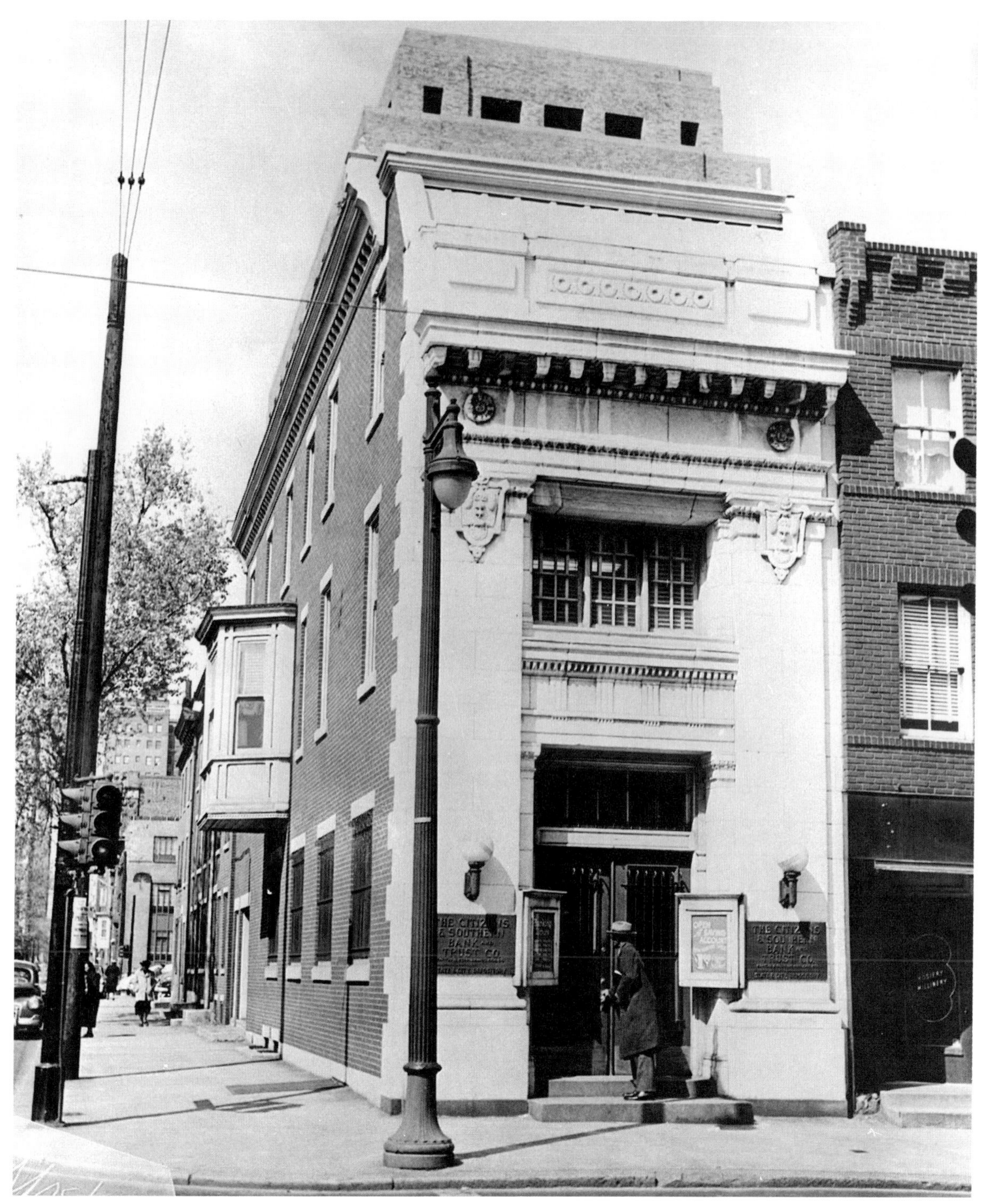

21) Major Richard Robert Wright, Sr. (1855-1947), founder and president of the Citizen and Southern Bank and Trust Company, enters the branch at the N.E. corner of 19th and South Streets in South Philadelphia, 1940s. It was founded in 1921 and was the third and most successful Black bank organized in Philadelphia.

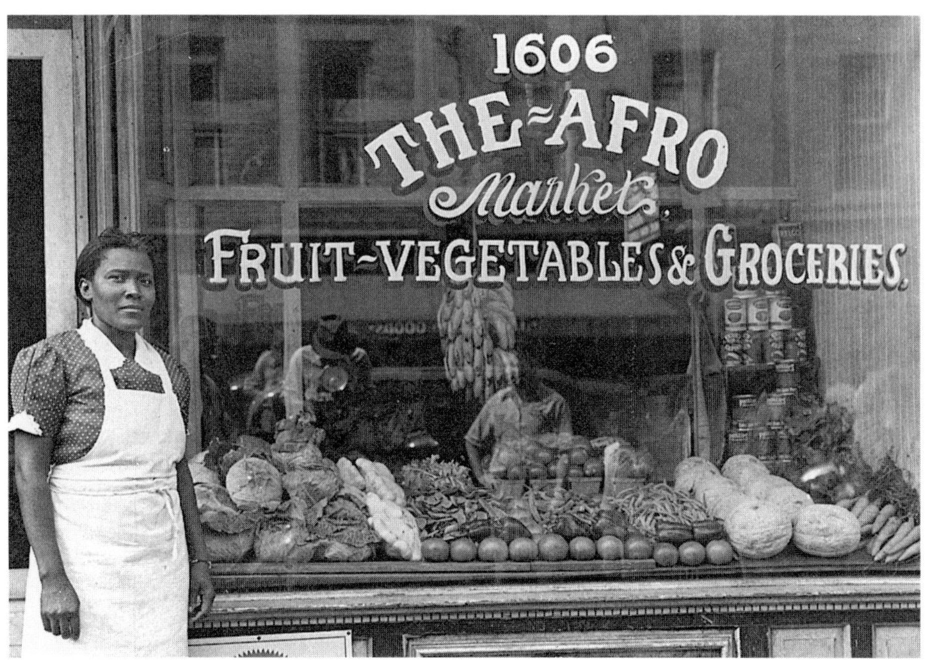

22A) Female grocer stands in front of The Afro Market, 1940s.

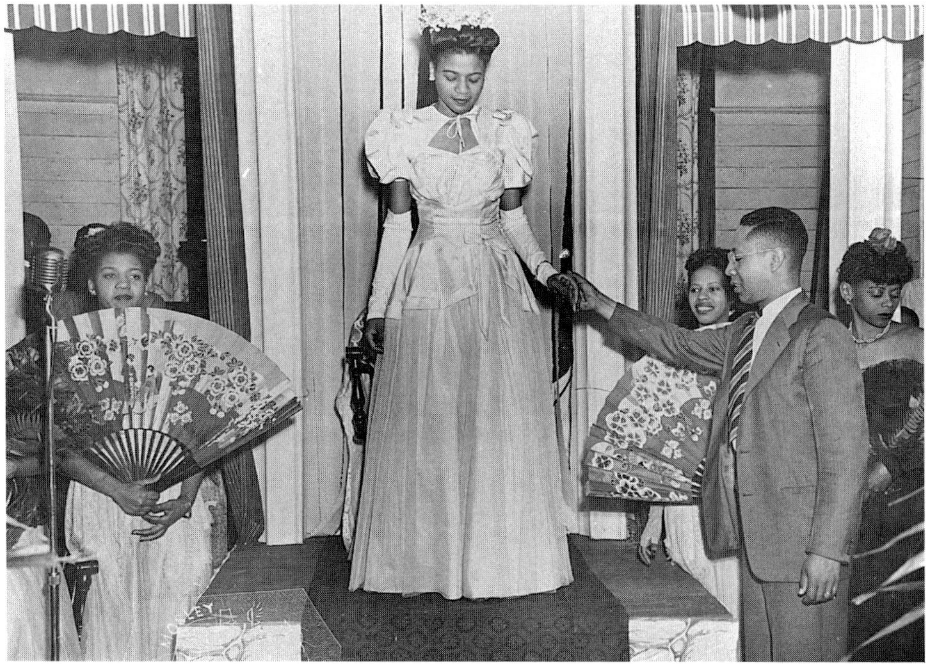

22B) Director of South Broad Street USO, Charles C. Beckett, escorts new queen, Dorothy Chambliss, from platform, Wednesday, May 22, 1946. During the Second World War, Director Beckett was instrumental in providing entertainment and services to Black soldiers during a period of segregation.

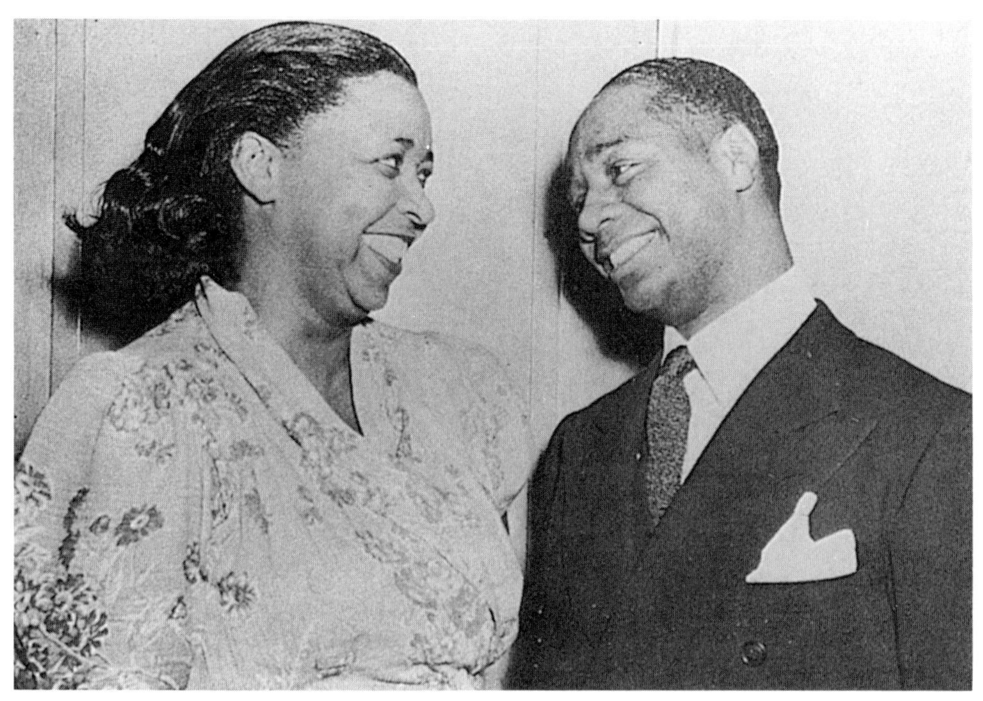

23A) Ethel Waters (1900-1972) (left), entertainer, dancer, singer, night club, movie and stage performer, shares moment with Canada Lee (1907-1951) (right), former welter weight contender, jockey, band leader and actor, 1944.

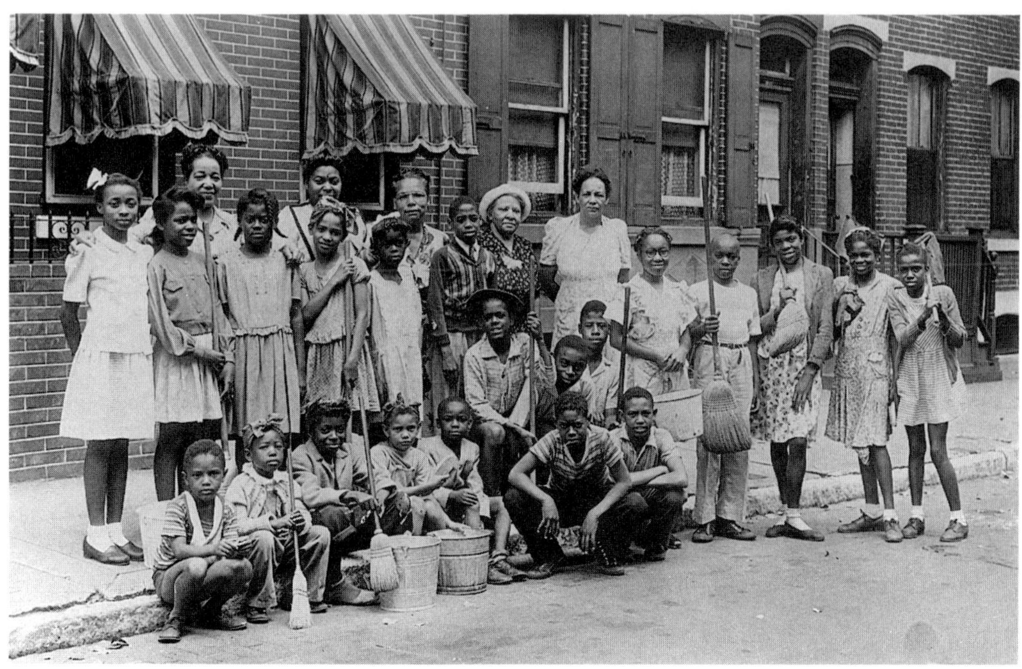

23B) On Montrose Street, adults supervise a group of children who take pride in keeping their block clean, July 8, 1947.

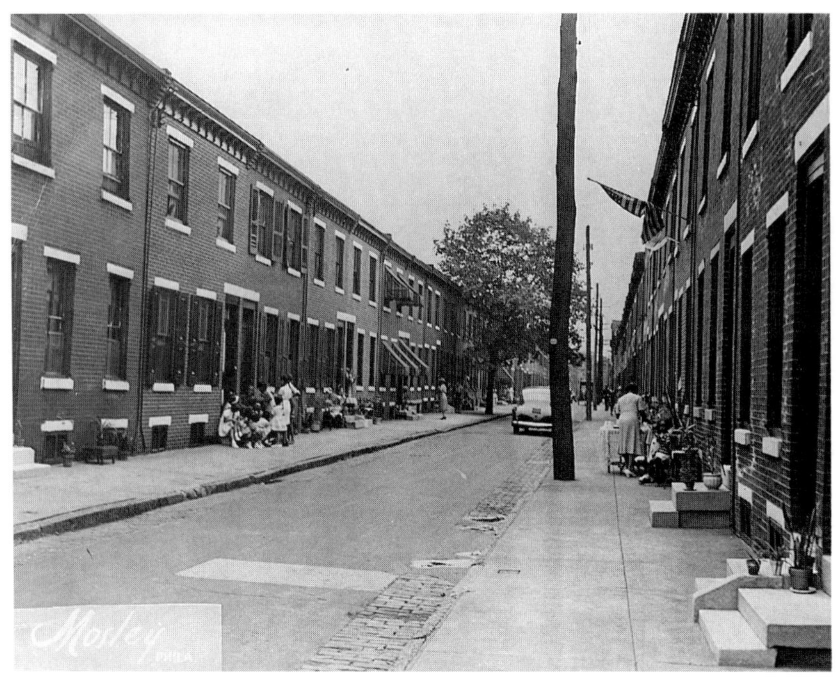

24A) Scene of a North Philadelphia neighborhood adjacent to Girard College, 1945.

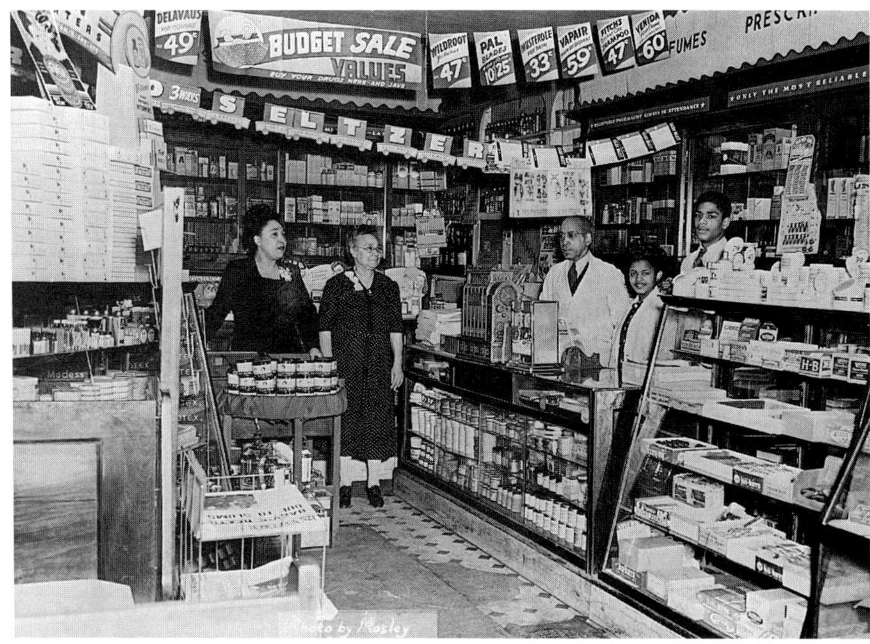

24B) Pharmacist and staff, 1940s.

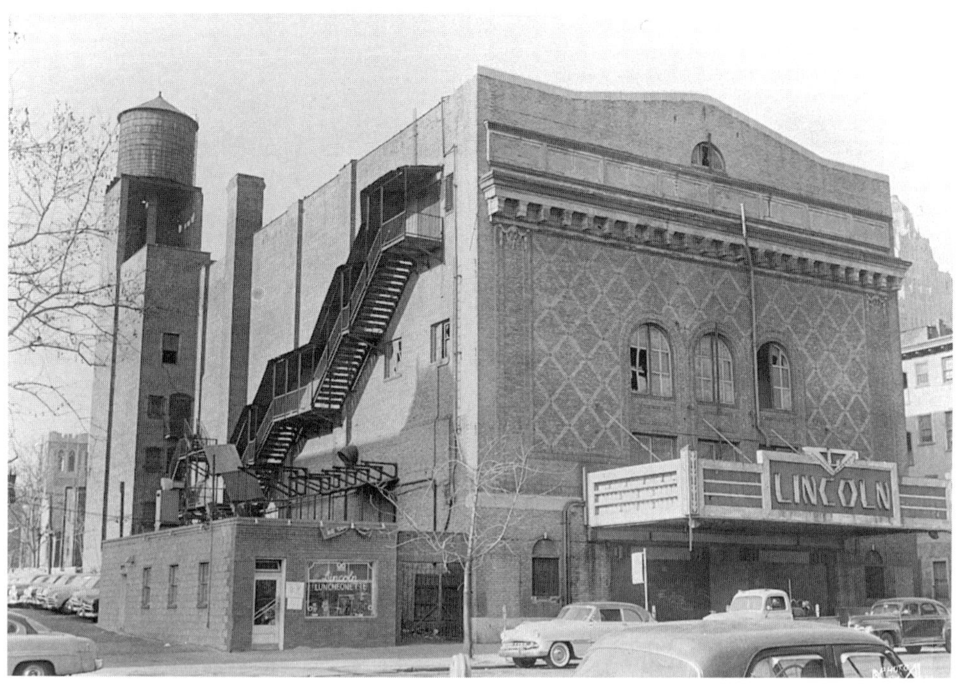

25A) The Lincoln Theater, Broad and Lombard Streets, a popular establishment during the 1930s and 1940s, where renowned Black entertainers and local musicians performed before Black audiences in Philadelphia, December 18, 1954.

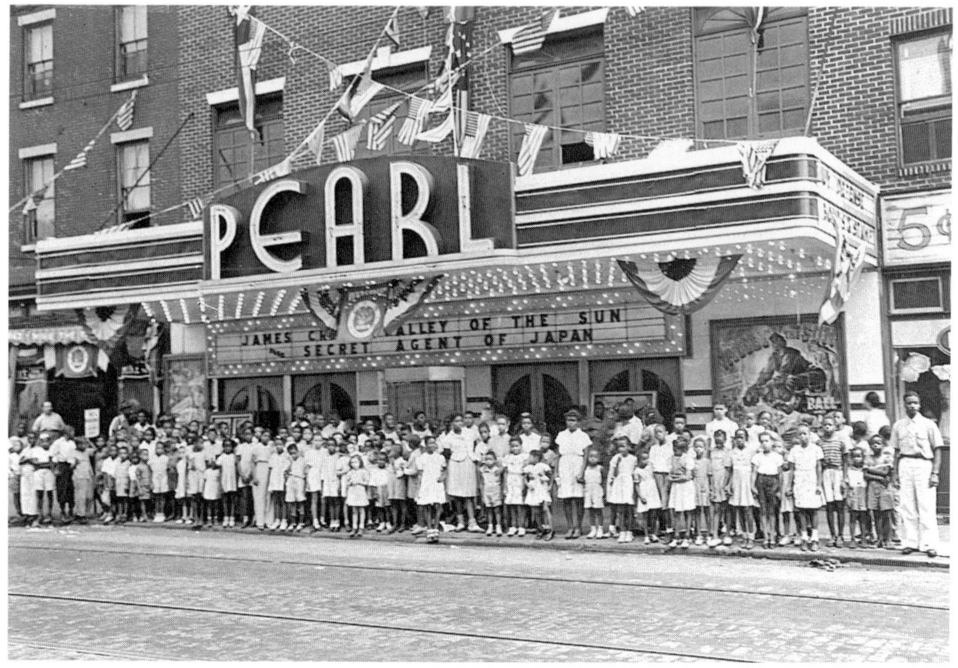

25B) Children in front of the Pearl Theater called the "premiere colored theater" located at Ridge Avenue and N. 21st Street, late 1940s.

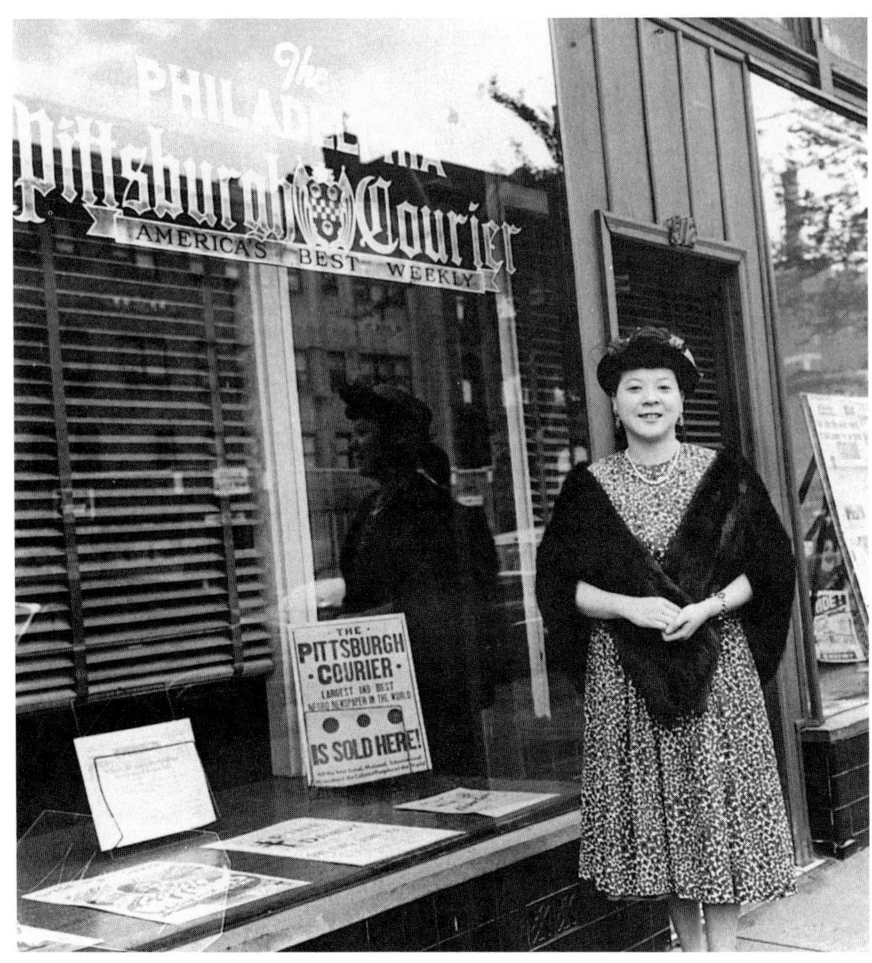

26A) The Philadelphia Pittsburgh Courier office which was located at 2041 W. Columbia Avenue, 1940s.

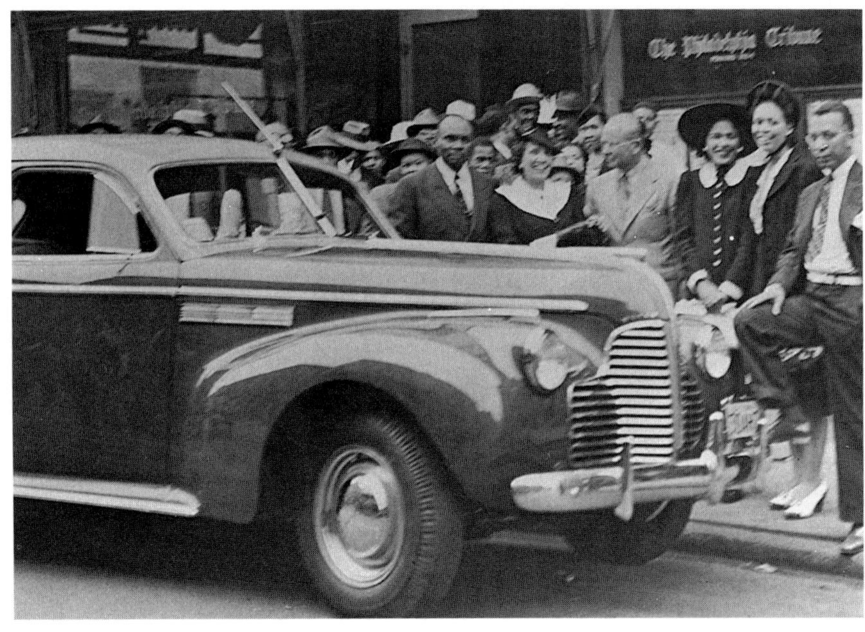

26B) The Philadelphia Tribune office in South Philadelphia, 1940s.

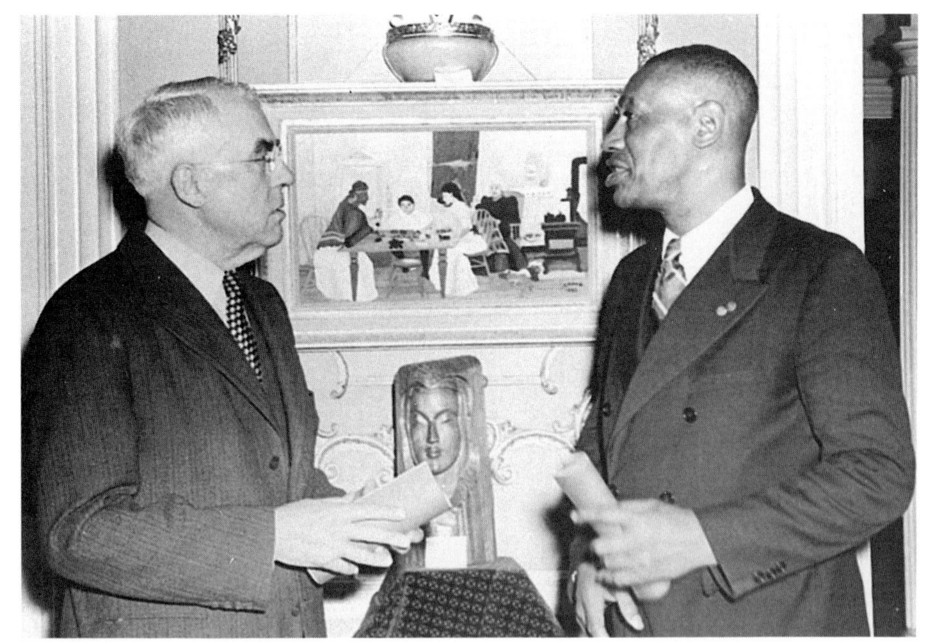

27A) Renowned artist, Horace Pippin (1888-1946), discusses art with Dr. Albert C. Barnes (1872-1951), founder of the Barnes Collection, 1944. In the background, a prize-winning Pippin painting is exhibited.

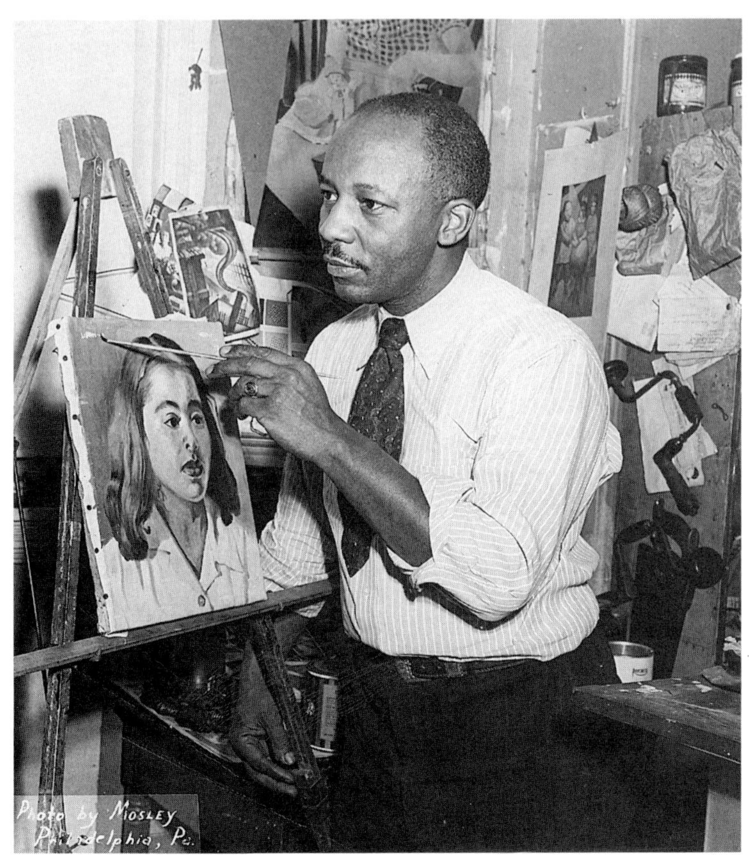

27B) Artist Sam Brown with painting, 1940s.

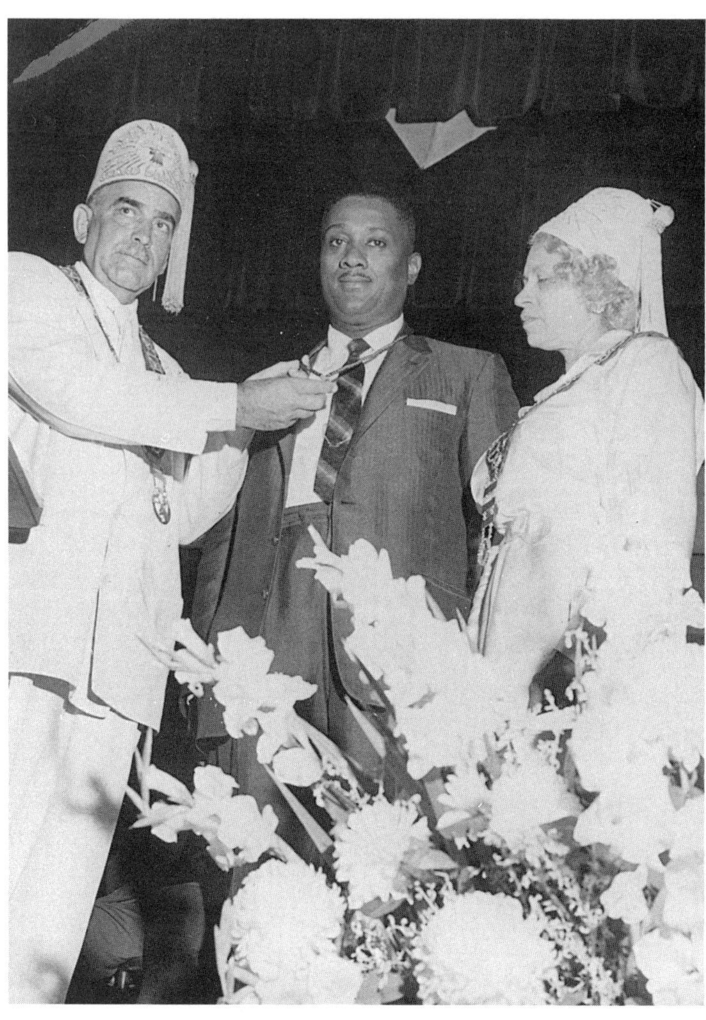

28A) John H. Johnson, editor and publisher of *Ebony*, *Jet*, *Negro Digest*, *Black Stars* and *Black World* receives an award from Exalted Ruler Hobson R. Reynolds at Civil Liberties Meeting as Grand Directoress Alice L. Nichols looks on, 1950s.

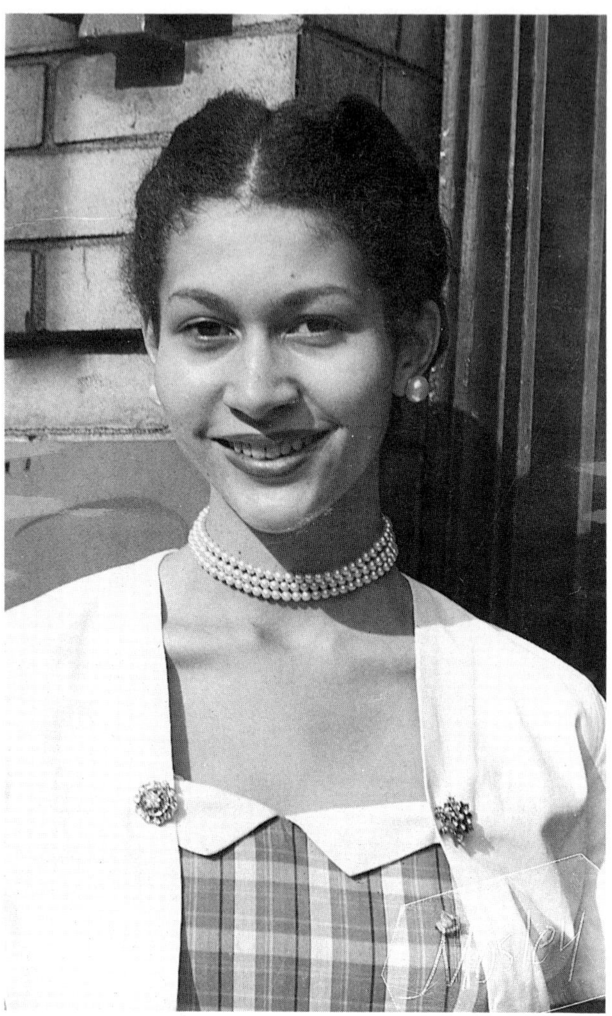

28B) Kristin Hunter, novelist, lecturer, English professor, smiles for the camera, 1950's.

THEY LED THE WAY

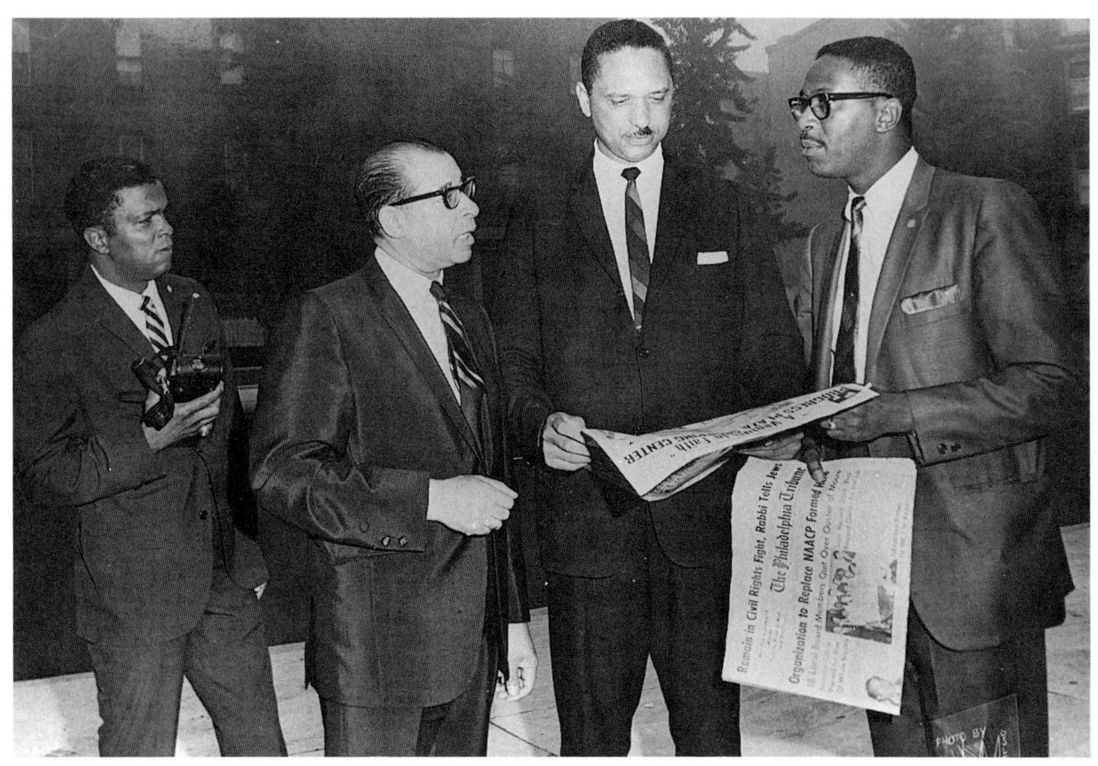

29A) Judge Herbert Cain (second from left) and Reverend Leon H. Sullivan (third from left) converse with two news reporters regarding the Cecil B. Moore and NAACP controversy, 1967.

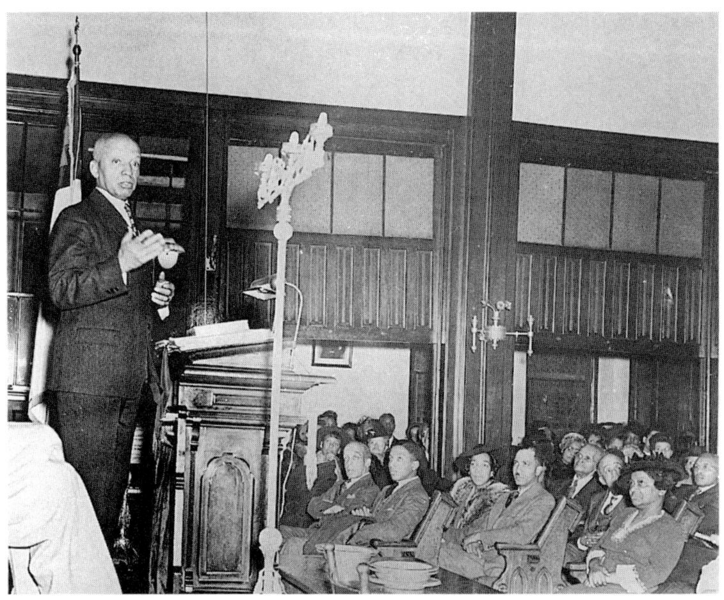

29B) Dr. Carter Godson Woodson (1875-1950), historian known as the "Father of Modern Black History, speaks to a group of Philadelphians as they attentively listen, early 1940s.

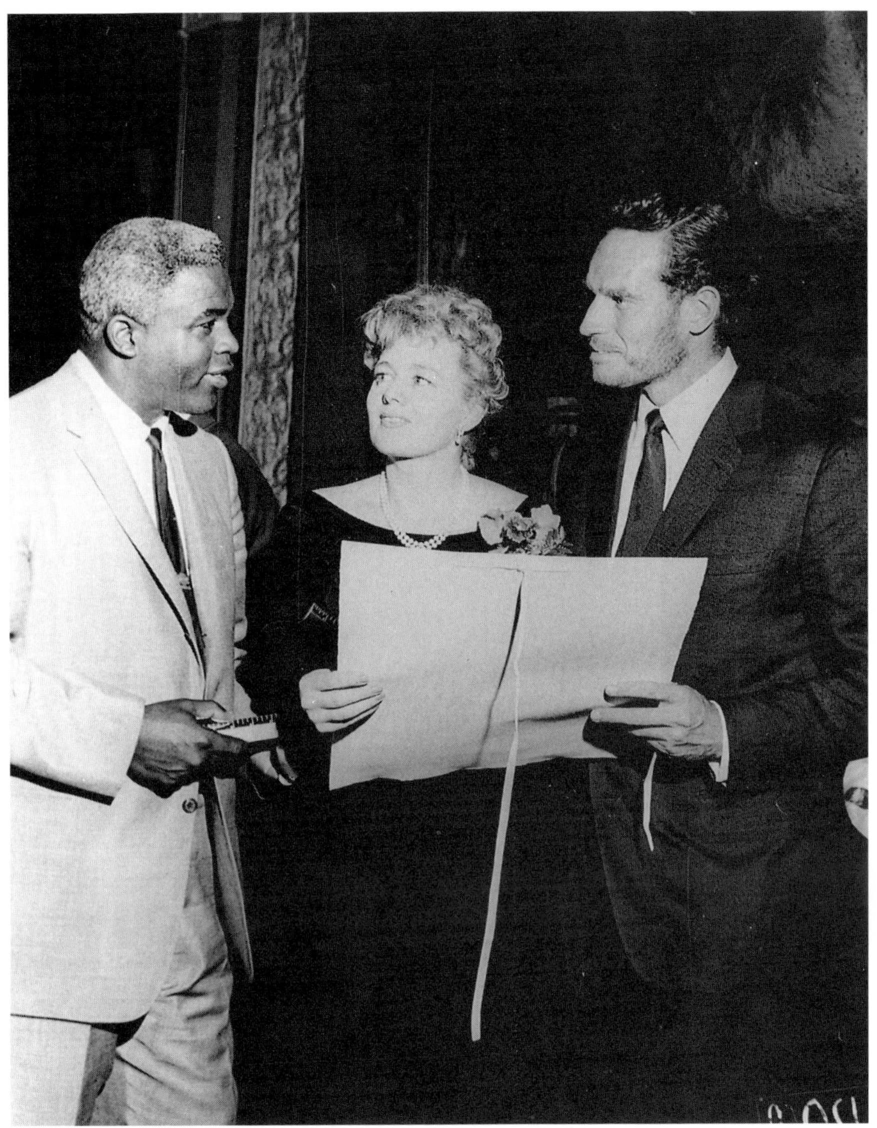

30) John Roosevelt "Jackie" Robinson (1919-1972), first Black major league baseball player, Shelley Winters, actress, and Charlton Heston, actor, converse during a ceremony in Philadelphia, April 18, 1959.

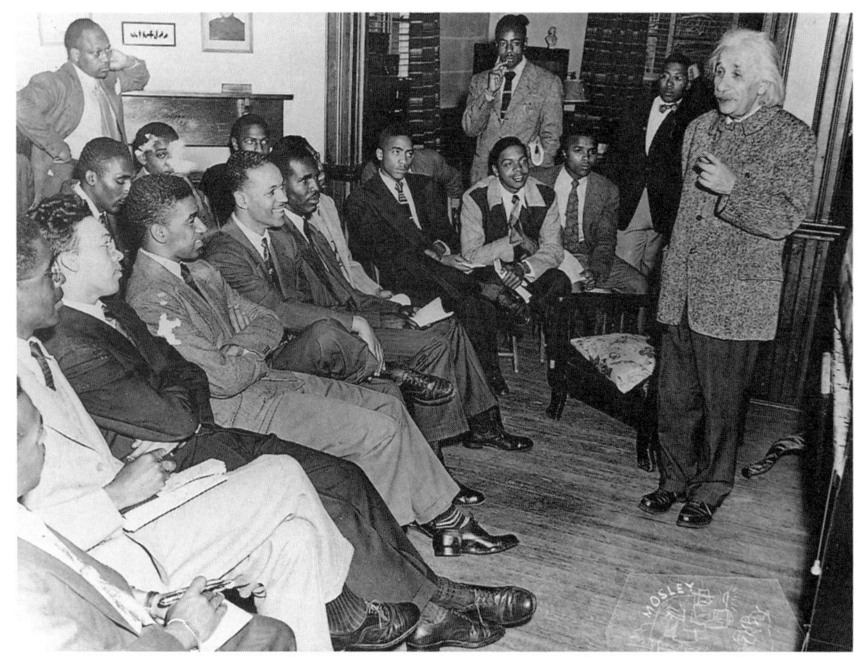

31A) Albert Einstein (1879-1955), physicist, talks to a group of male students at Lincoln University, prior to receiving an honorary doctorate which Dr. H.M. Bond persuaded him to accept, 1946.

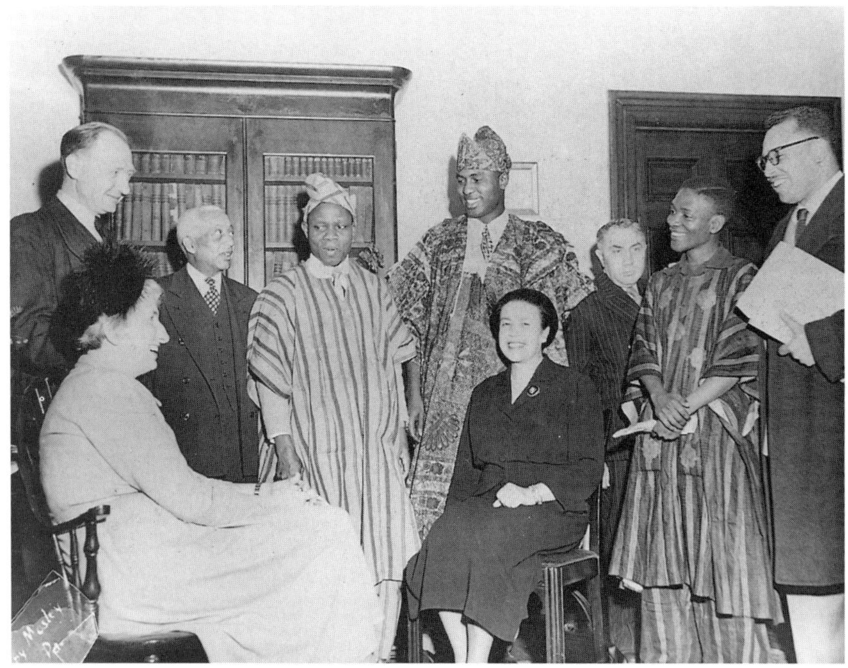

31B) Dr. Alain Leroy Locke (1886-1954) (second from left, standing) of Howard University, first Black Rhodes scholar, author and art historian, and Mrs. Crystal Dreda Bird Fauset (1894-1965) (second from left, sitting), first Black woman in the United States elected to a state legislature, with a group of Africans and others, 1940s.

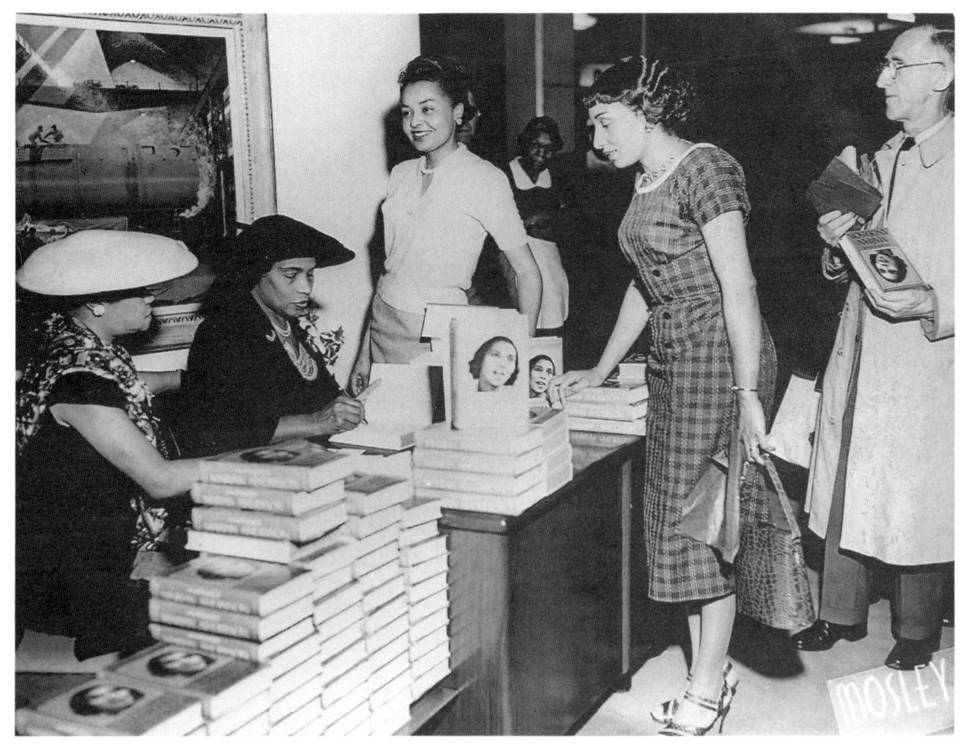

32A) Marian Anderson, renowned concert, operatic contralto singer and delegate to the UN from South Philadelphia, autographs copies of her autobiography My Lord, What A Morning for her fans at Wanamaker's Department Store, 13th and Market Streets, 1956.

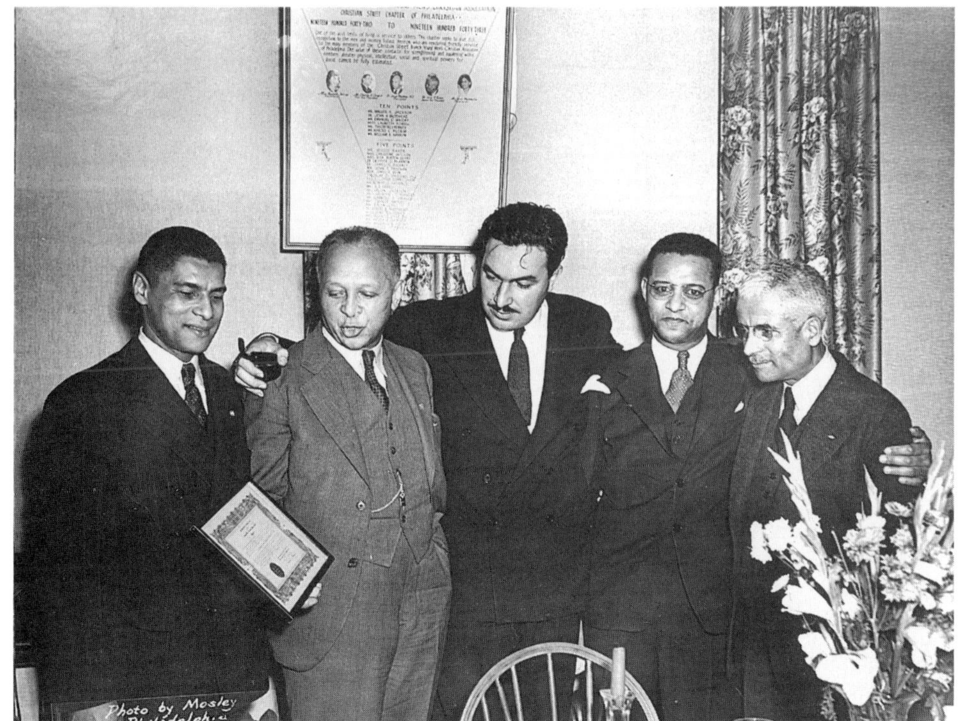

32B) The Reverend Congressman Adam Clayton Powell, Jr. (center) with Dr. James Duckrey (far left), Dr. Leslie Pinckney Hill(1880-1960), President of Cheyney College (second from left) and Dr. James P. Turner (far right) at the Christian Street YMCA, 1944.

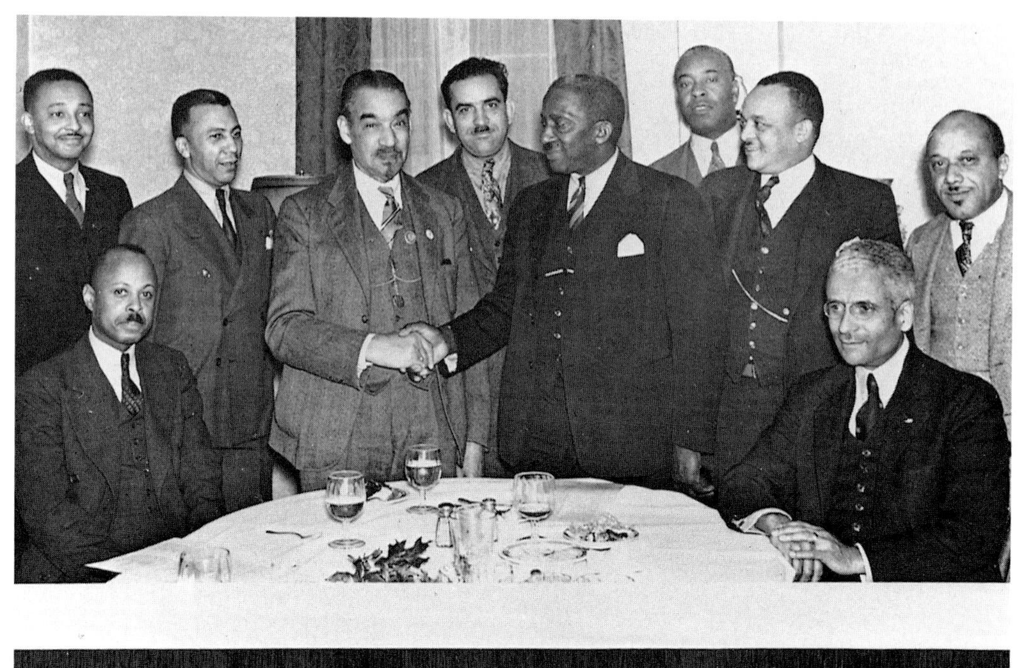

33A) Representative James H. Irvin (third from left) shakes hands with another leader as E. Washington Rhodes (second from left, standing), Hobson Reynolds (fourth from left, standing), Emmanuel C. Wright (far left, sitting), Dr. James P. Turner (far right, sitting) and others look on, early 1940s.

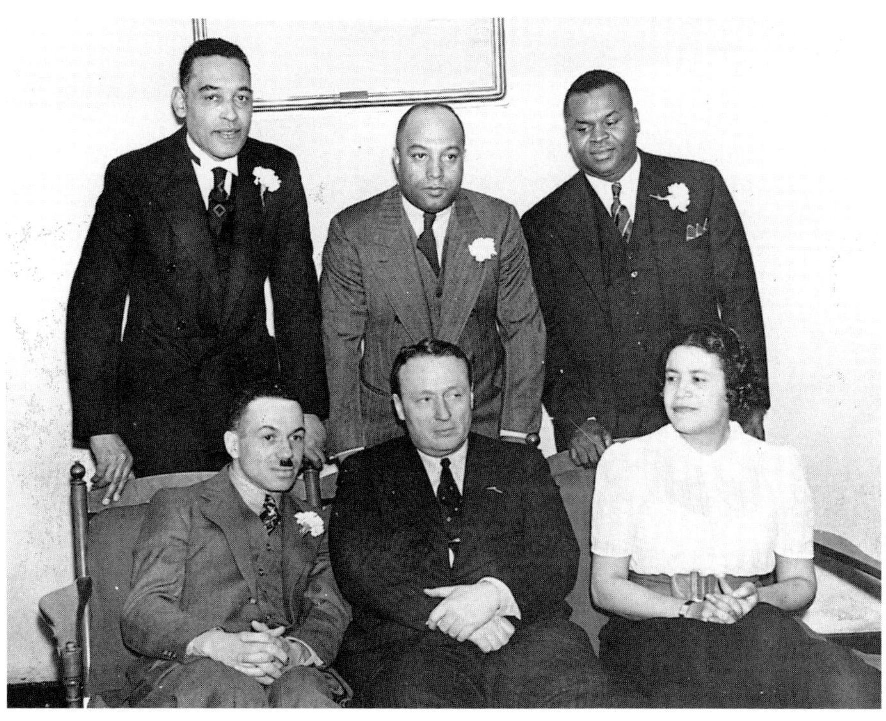

33B)Magistrate Joseph Rainey (left, sitting), Mrs. Crystal Bird Fauset (right, sitting), James Austin Norris (1893-1976) (middle, standing), the Reverend Marshall Shephard (right, standing) with two other men, 1940s.

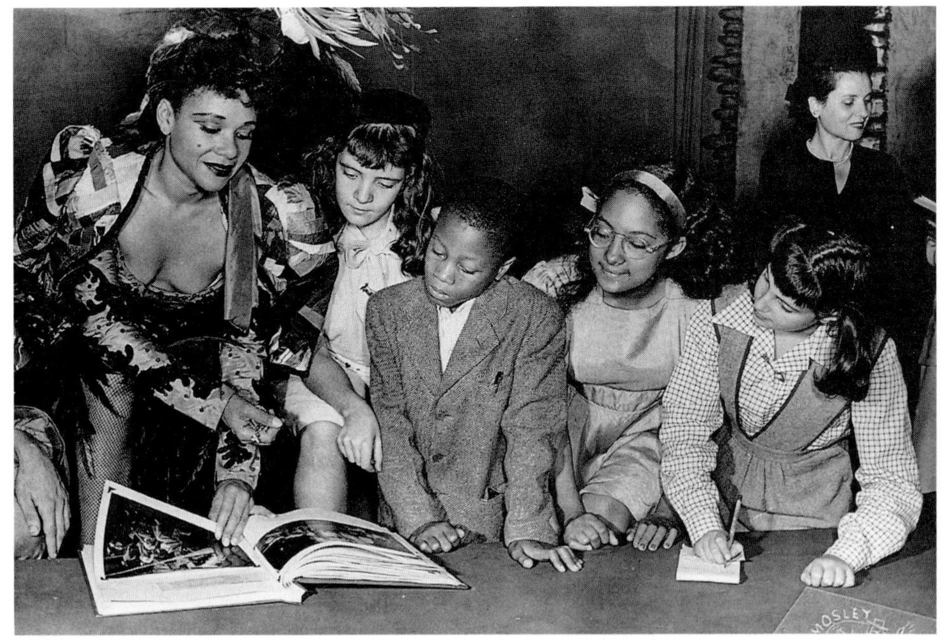

34A) Katherine Dunham, dancer, choreographer, anthropologist and writer, views scrapbook with a group of young people, 1945.

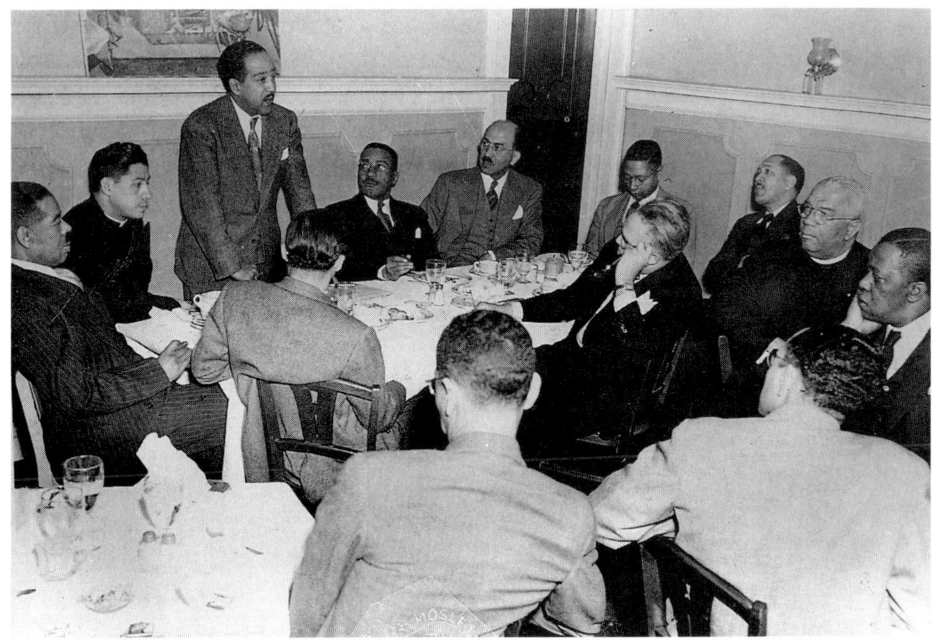

34B) James Mercer Langston Hughes (1902-1967) (standing), poet, novelist, playwright, philosopher and translator, speaks at the Pyramid Club, Girard Avenue as Wayne L. Hopkins (far left), the Reverend Thomas Logan (second left), the Reverend Irvin W. Underhill, Jr. (1896-1982) (fifth from left), Charles C. Beckett (sixth from left) and others look on, 1943.

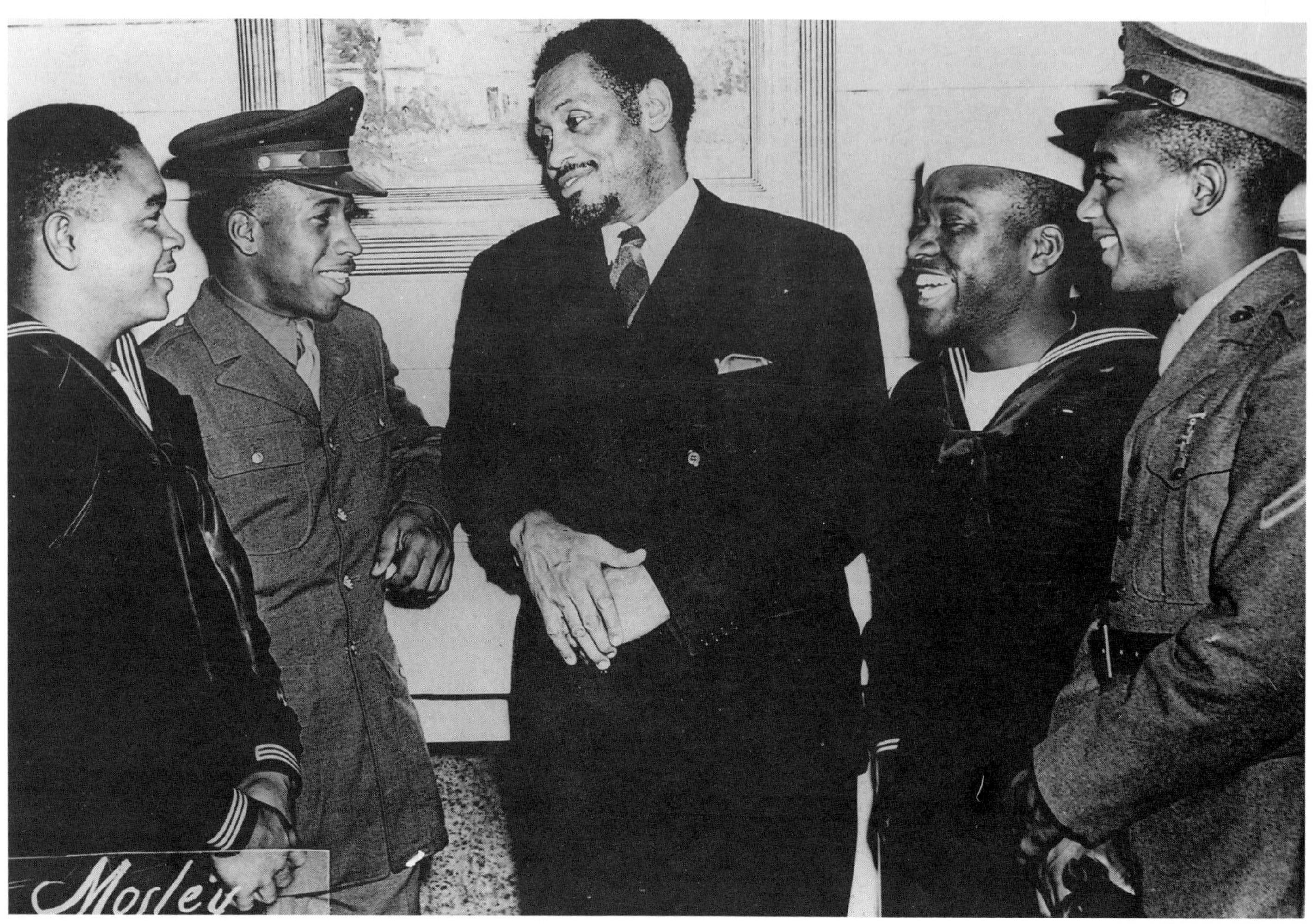

35) Paul L. Robeson chats with a group of World War II servicemen in the South Broad Street USO, 1943.

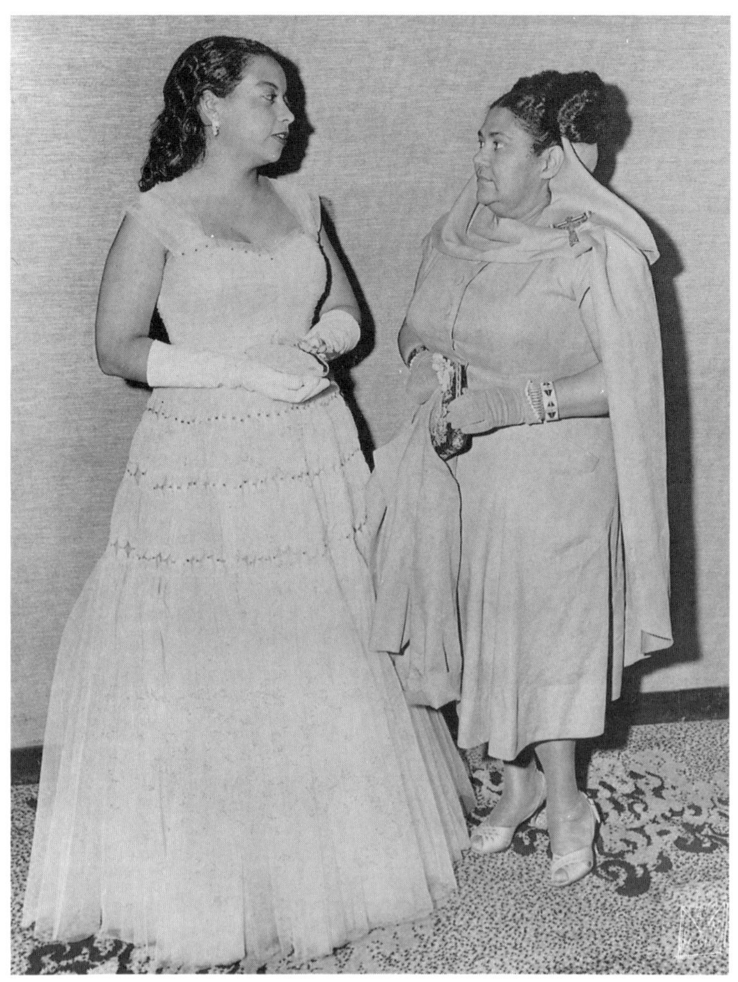

36A) Natalie Hinderas (1927-1987) (left), internationally acclaimed concert pianist and former member of Temple University's music faculty, chats with Dorothy Maynor, opera singer, choral director and founder of the Harlem School for the Arts, 1950s.

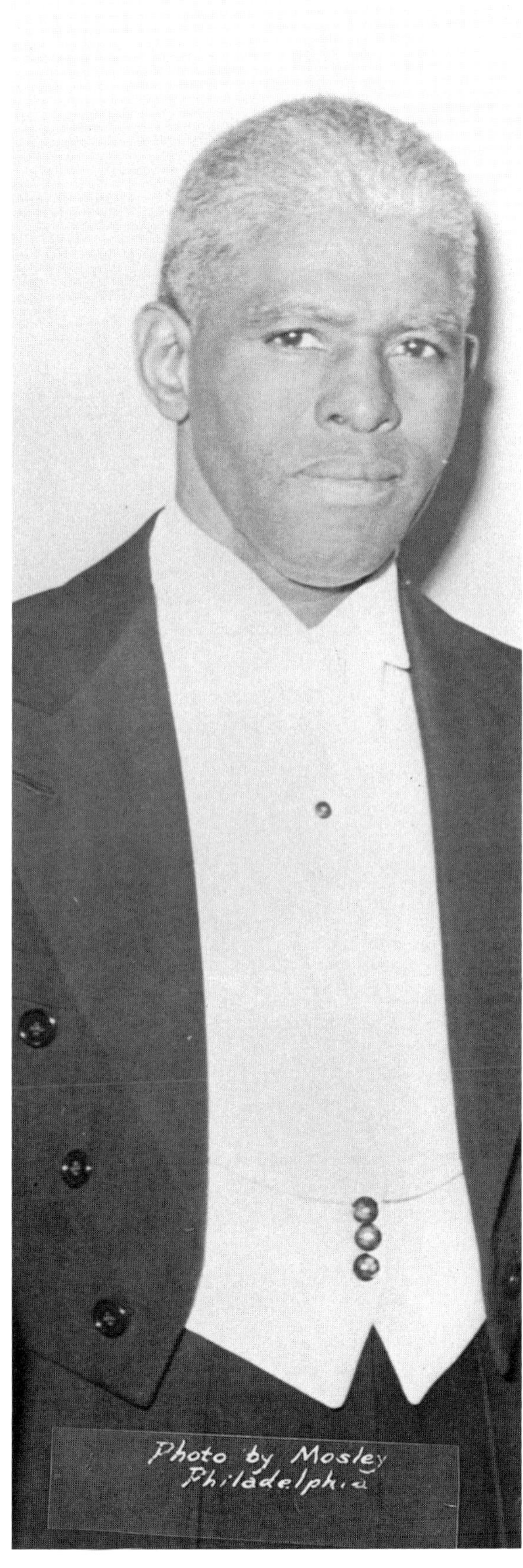

36)Roland T. Hayes (1887-1976), concert tenor singer, in Philadelphia, 1943.

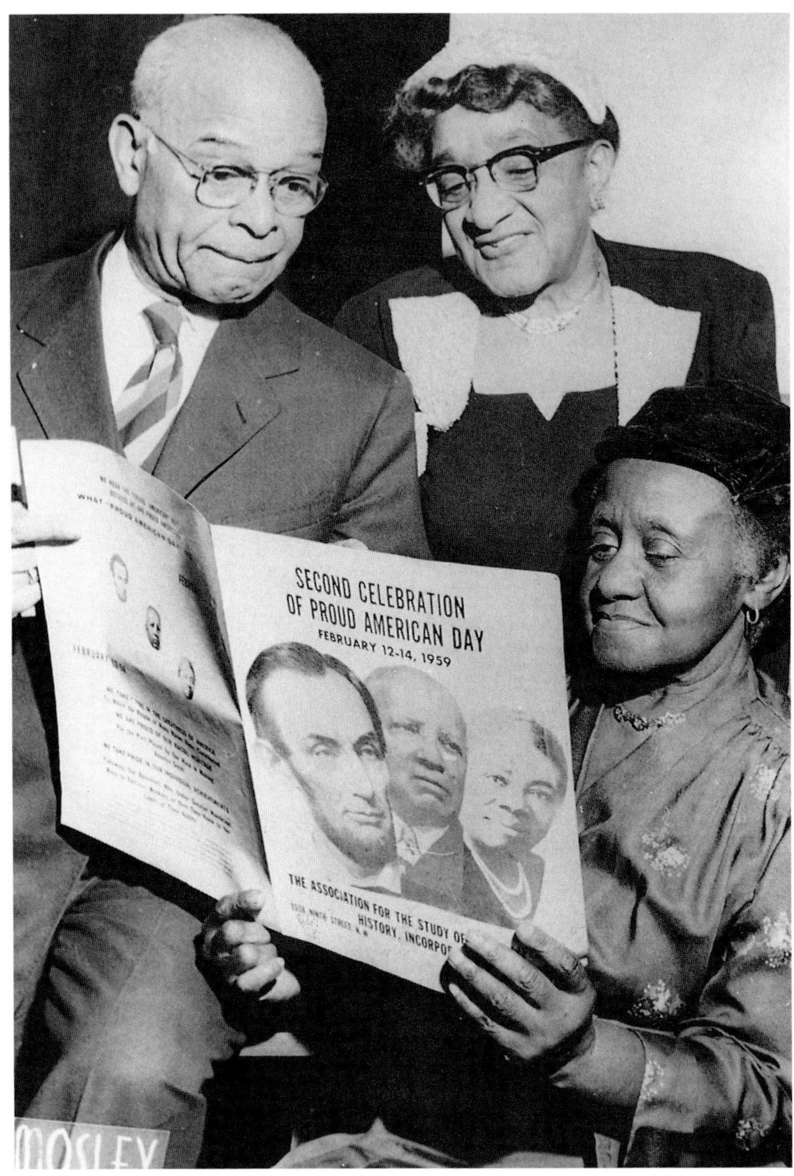

37) Dr. DeHaven Hinkson and two women celebrate Proud American Day, sponsored by the Association for the Study of Negro Life and History, February, 1959.

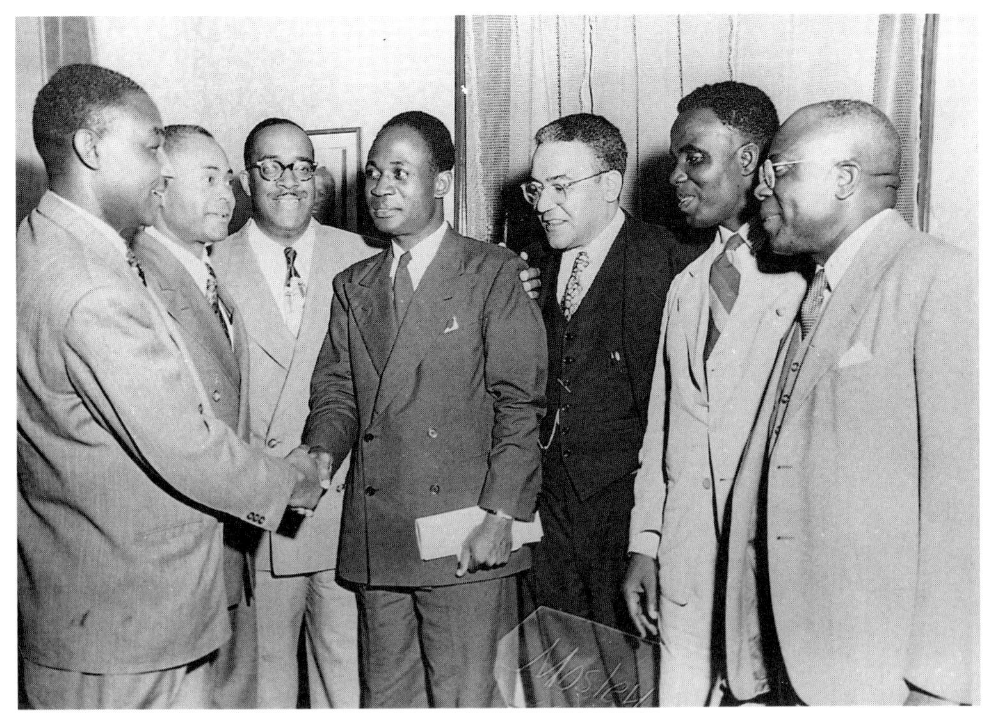

38A) Kwame Nkrumah (1909-1972), the first Prime Minister of Ghana, editor, organizer and educator, shakes hands with Pyramidian the Reverend Leonard G. Carr as the Reverend E. Luther Cunningham (1909-1964) (third from left), founder of the Philadelphia Fellowship Commission, Dr. Horace Mann Bond (fourth from left), Dr. Walter F. Jerrick (far right) and others look on, 1951.

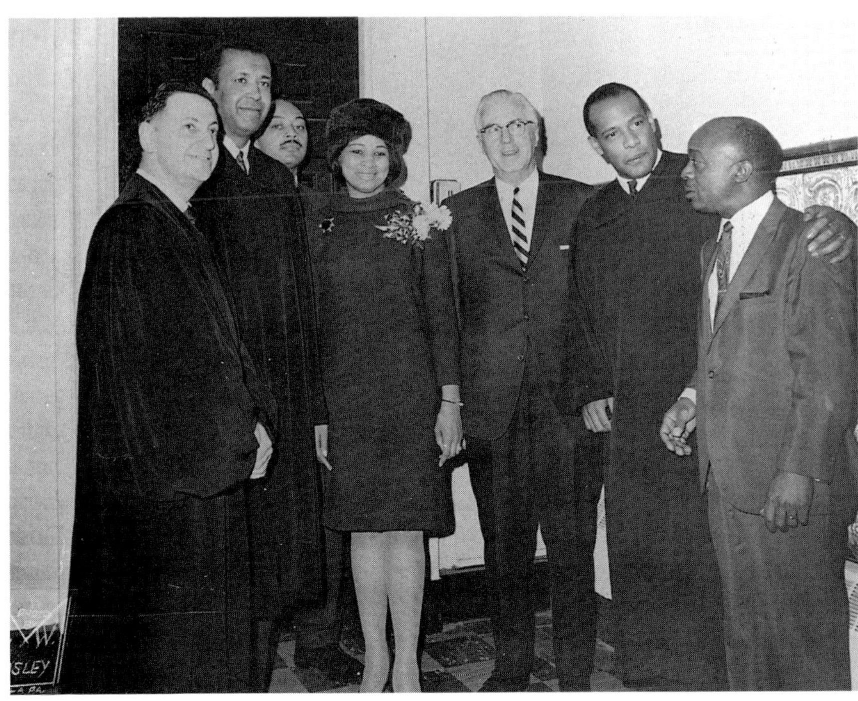

38B) Judges Arlen Specter (far left) and A. Leon Higginbotham (second from left), C. Delores Tucker (fourth from left), Judge Robert N.C. Nix, Jr. (sixth from left) and Nate Middleton (far right), The Pittsburgh Courier news correspondent and others, 1960s.

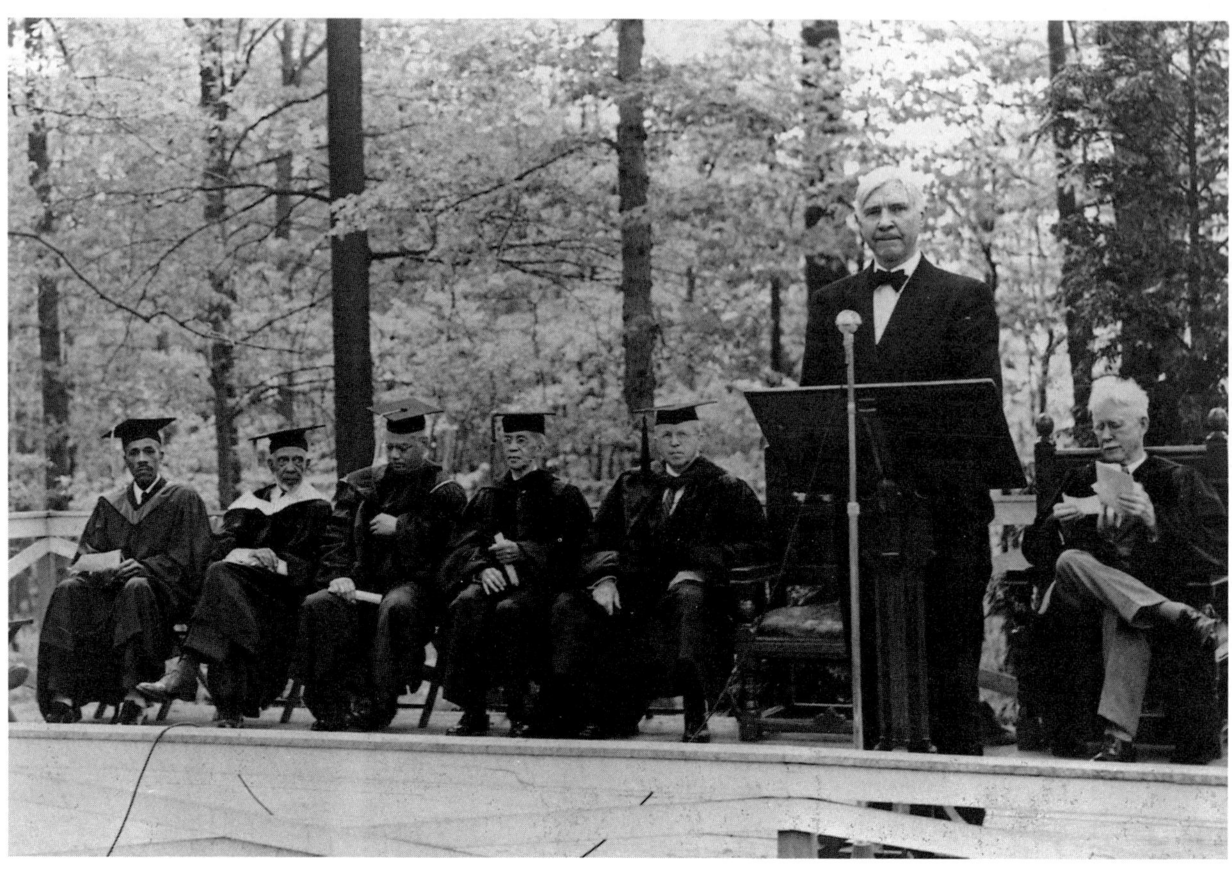

39) Carl Sandburg (1878-1967), author and poet, main speaker at Lincoln University when Langston Hughes recieved an honorary doctorate, Commencement 1943.

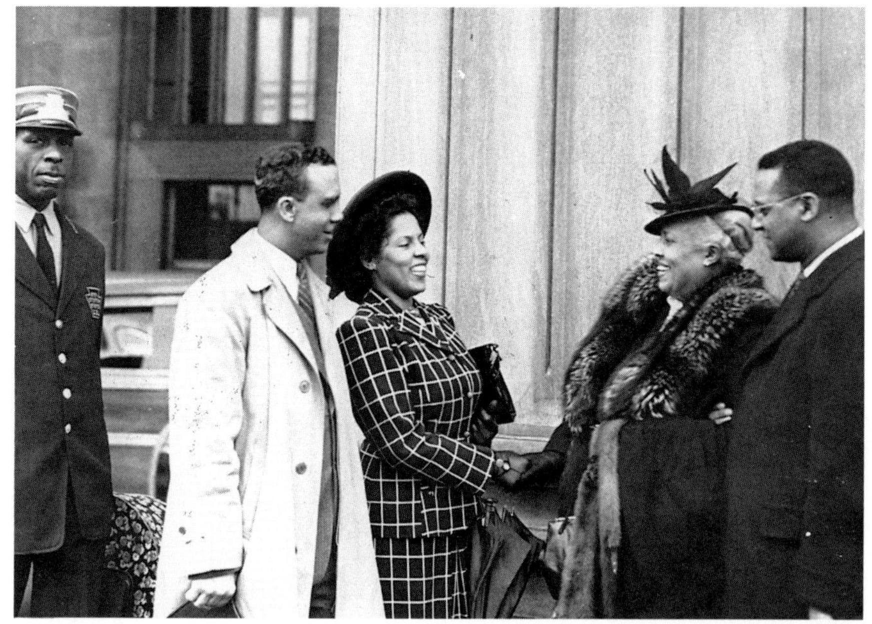

40A) Daisy Elizabeth Lampkin (1882-1965) (fourth from left), political activist, NAACP Field Secretary, suffragist, civil rights reformer and former Vice-President of Pittsburgh, is greeted by Theodore Spaulding (second from left) and others, 1940. She was instrumental in getting Justice Thurgood Marshall to join the NAACP Legal Defense Committee. She was also a mentor to many leaders, including Mr. K. Leroy Irvis, first Black speaker of the Pennsylvania House of Representatives.

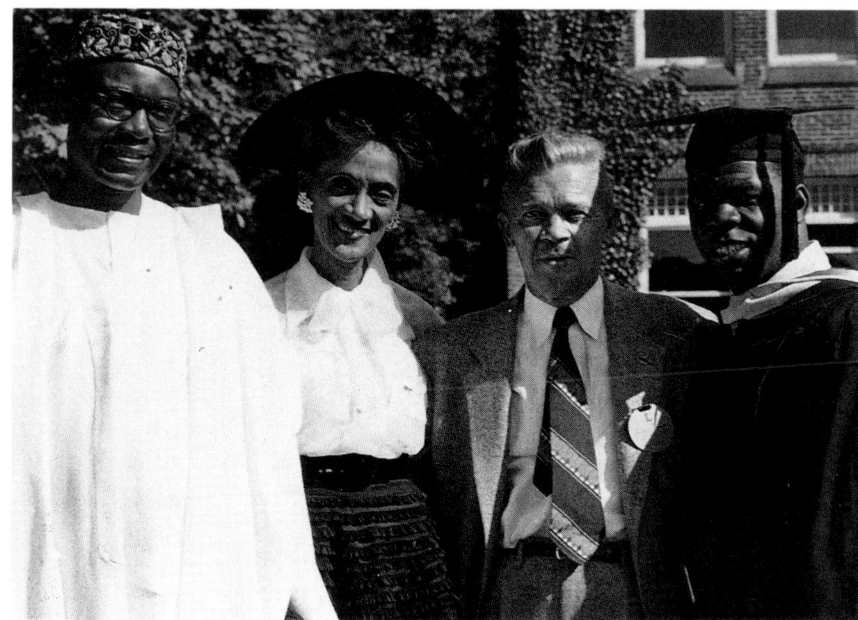

40B) Dr. Nnamdi "Zik" Azikiwe, newspaper editor, author, and first president of the Federal Republic of Nigeria in 1963, at his alma mater, Lincoln University the "Father of Modern Nigerian Nationalism".

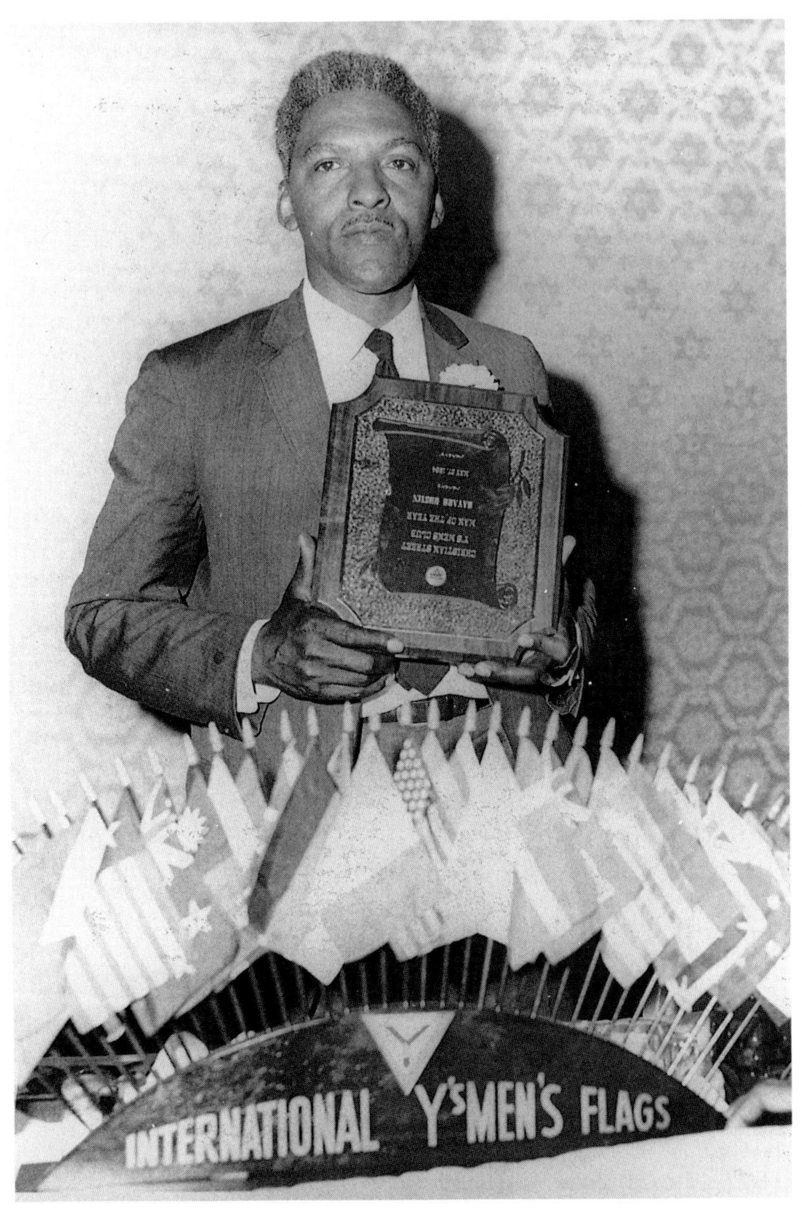

41) Bayard Rustin (1910-1987), civil rights activist, chief organizer of 1963 March on Washington, first field secretary of CORE, former executive director of A. Philip Randolph Institute, receives "Man of the Year" award at Christian Street YMCA, May 27, 1954.

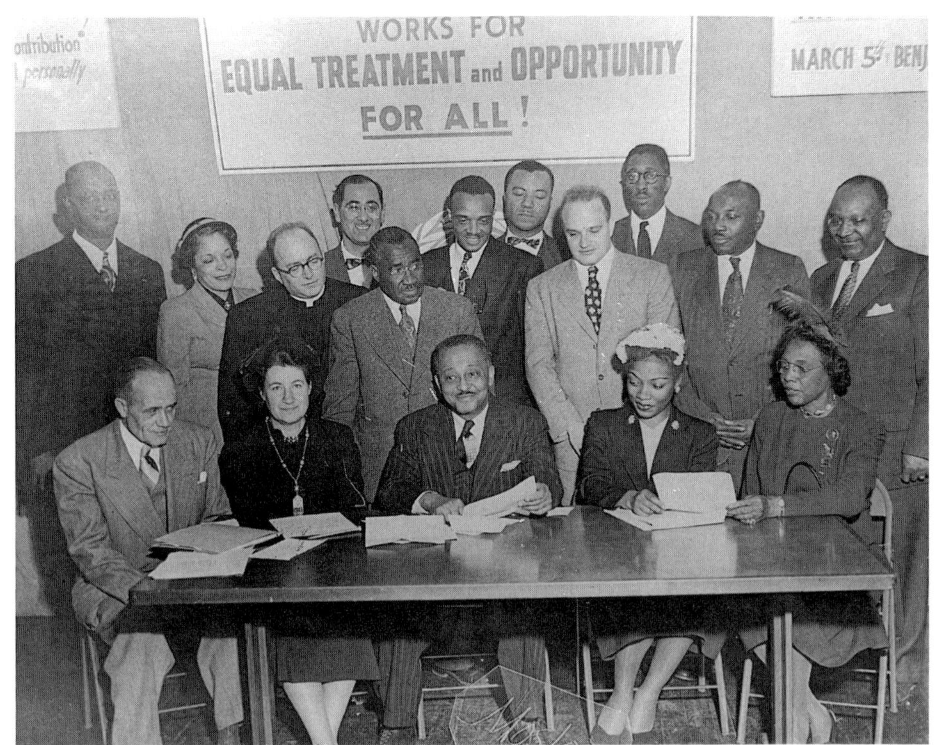

41A) Dr. O. Wilson Winters (second row, second from left), dentist and director of activities of the Pyramid Club, assembles with fellow members of the Philadelphia Fellowship Commission, 1940s.

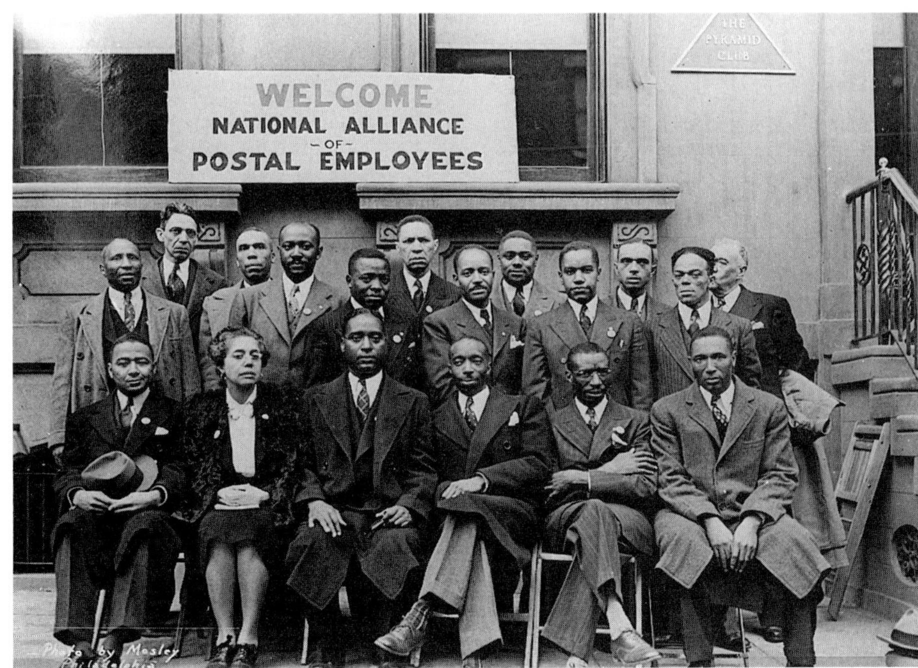

41B) The National Alliance of Postal Employees assemble in front of the Pyramid Club, Girard Avenue, during meeting in Philadelphia, 1940s.

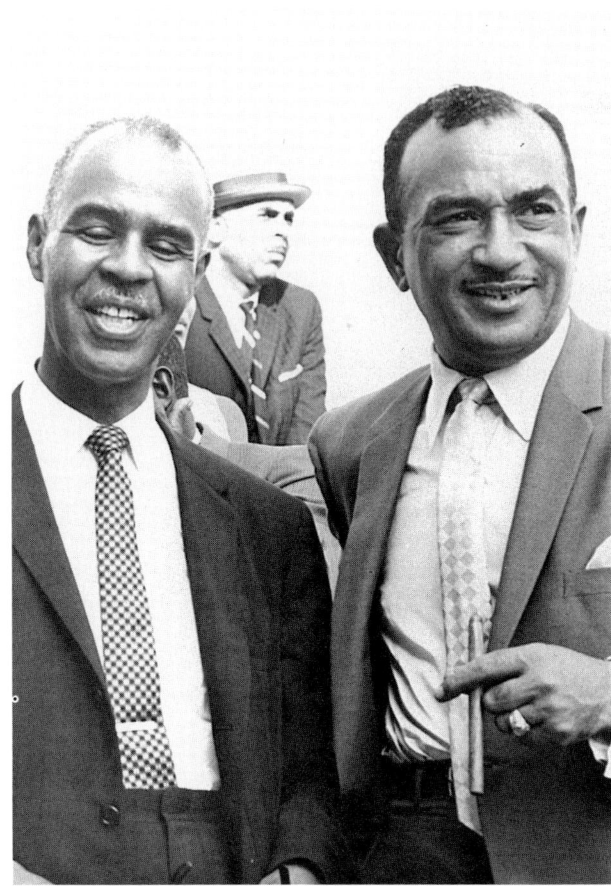

42A) Roy Wilkins, former Executive Secretary of NAACP, columnist, journalist and former dining car waiter, and Attorney Cecil B. Moore, 1960s.

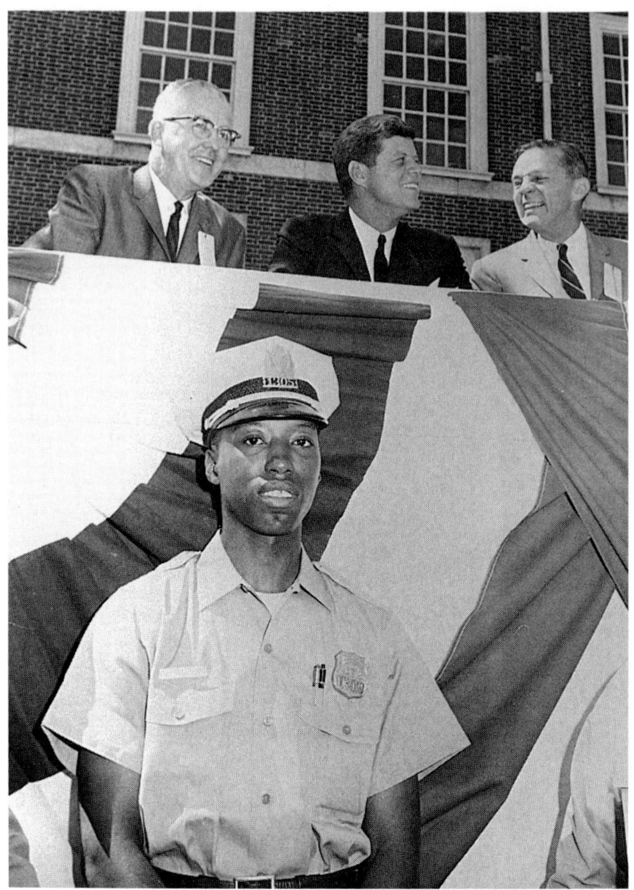

42B) John Fitzgerald Kennedy (1917-1963) (center), former president of the United States, with former Mayor Tate (left) and Senator Joseph Clark (right) at Independence Hall, 1961.

A SENSE OF PURPOSE

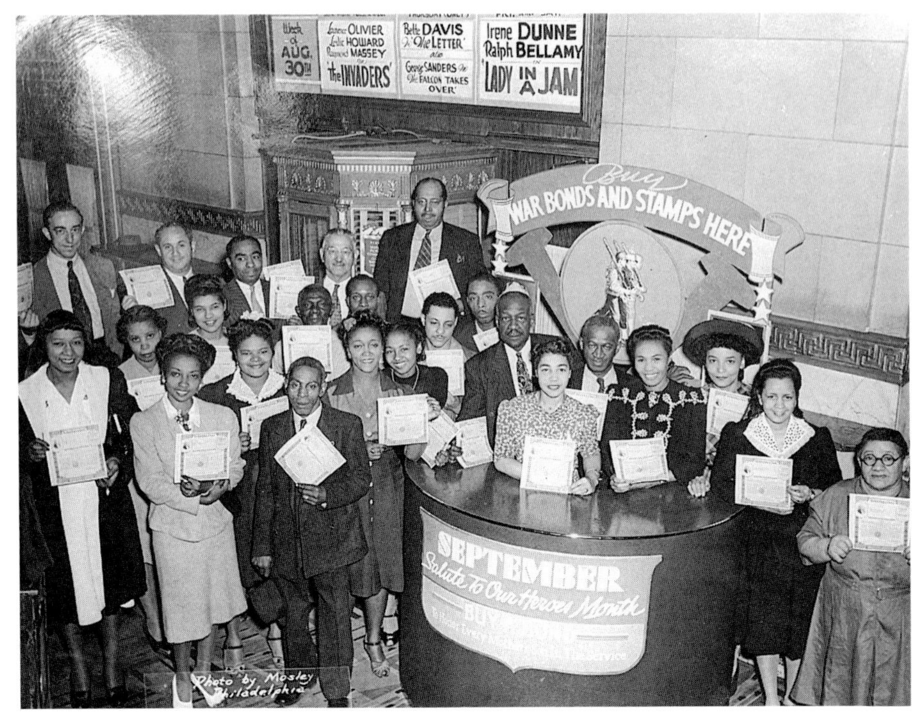

42C) Philadelphia African American citizens demonstrate their loyalty and commitment during World War II by organizing campaign to buy war bonds and stamps to honor servicemen, 1943.

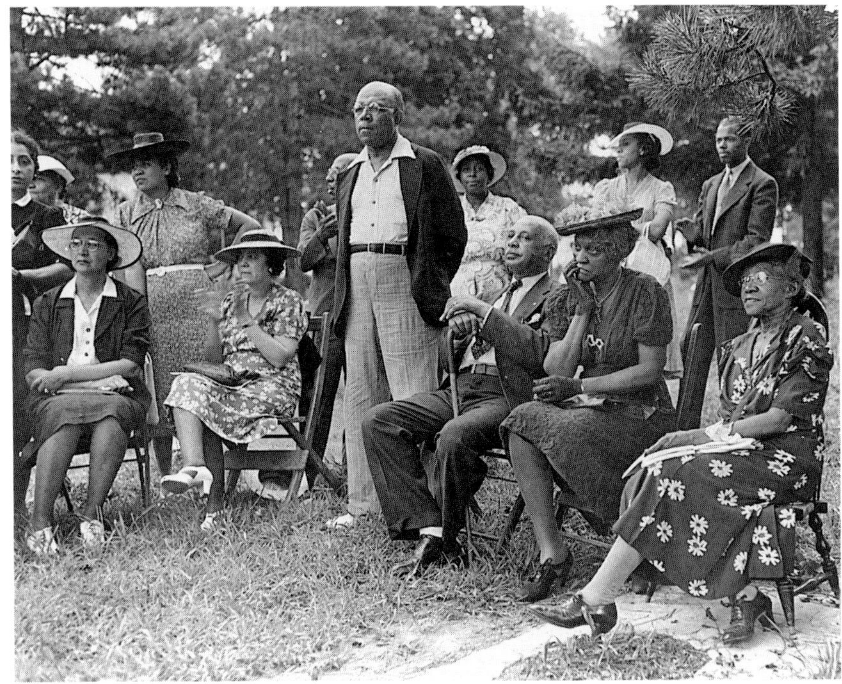

42D) William Christopher "W.C." Handy (1873-1958) (sitting, third from left), band leader, trumpeter, and composer, assembles with a large delegation at the grave of James Allen Bland (1854-1911), entertainer, song writer and composer, who composed the Mummer's Parade theme song "Oh, Dem Golden Slippers" and, at the age of 24, "Carry Me Back to Old Virginny" which was adopted as Virginia's official state song in 1940, August 12, 1939. Mr. Handy, who met Mr. Bland around 1897, stated that he was an inspiration to him. early 1940s.

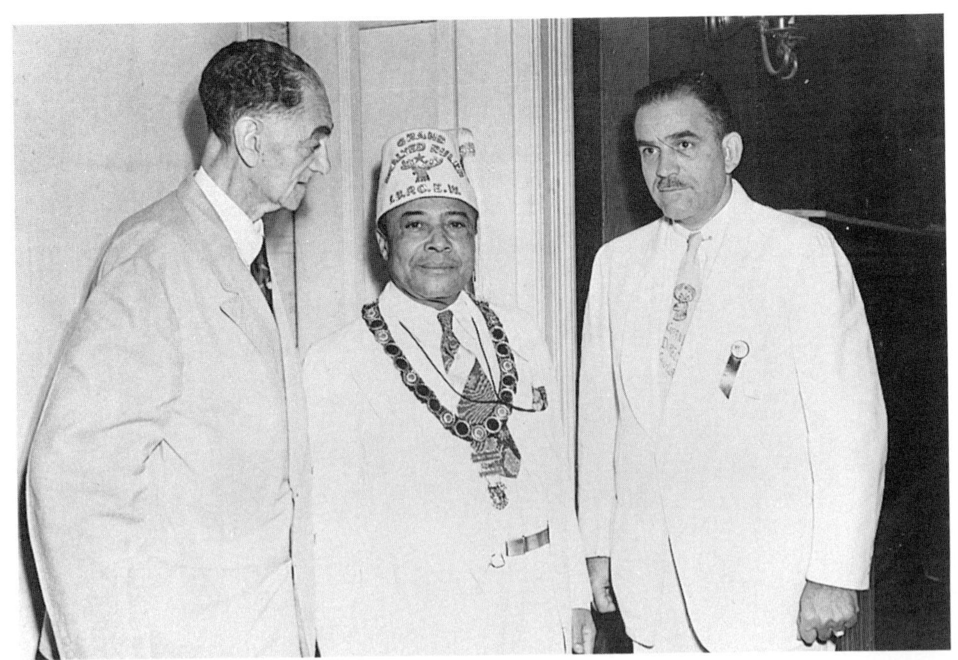

43A) Elks leaders Judge Edward W. Henry (far left), second Black Magistrate, J. Finley Wilson (center), Grand Ruler, and Hobson Reynolds (right) converse, 1945.

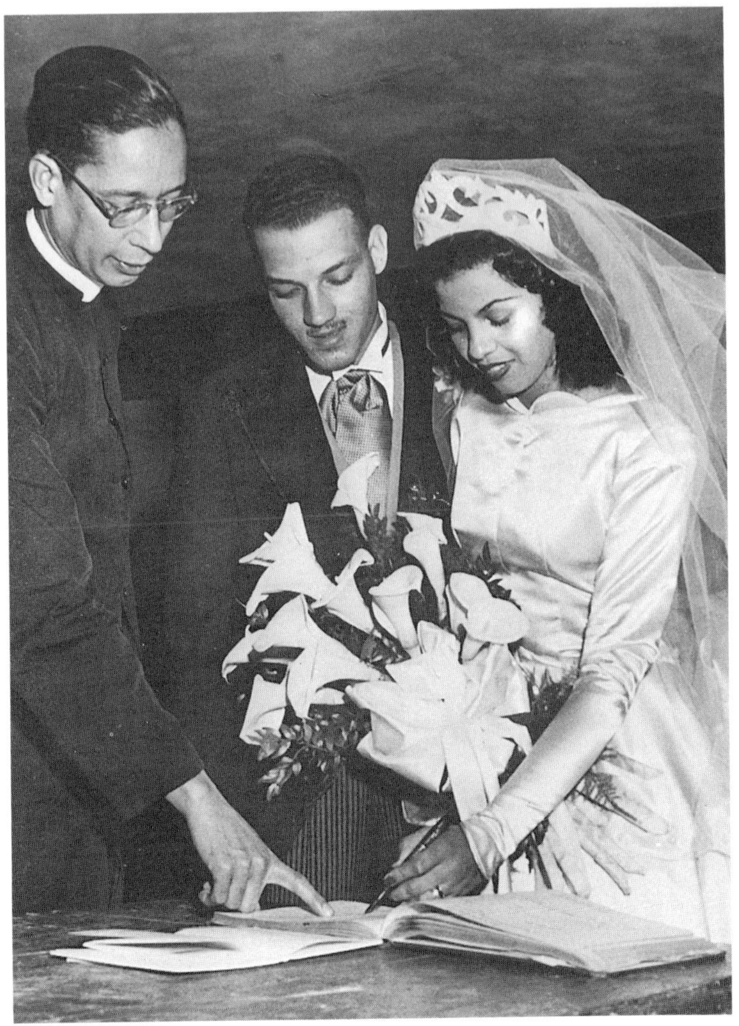

43B) The Reverend Jesse F. Anderson, pastor of St. Thomas P. E. Church, 52nd and Parrish left), instructs Mr. Chew and Ms. Johnson, before marriage ceremony, 1950s.

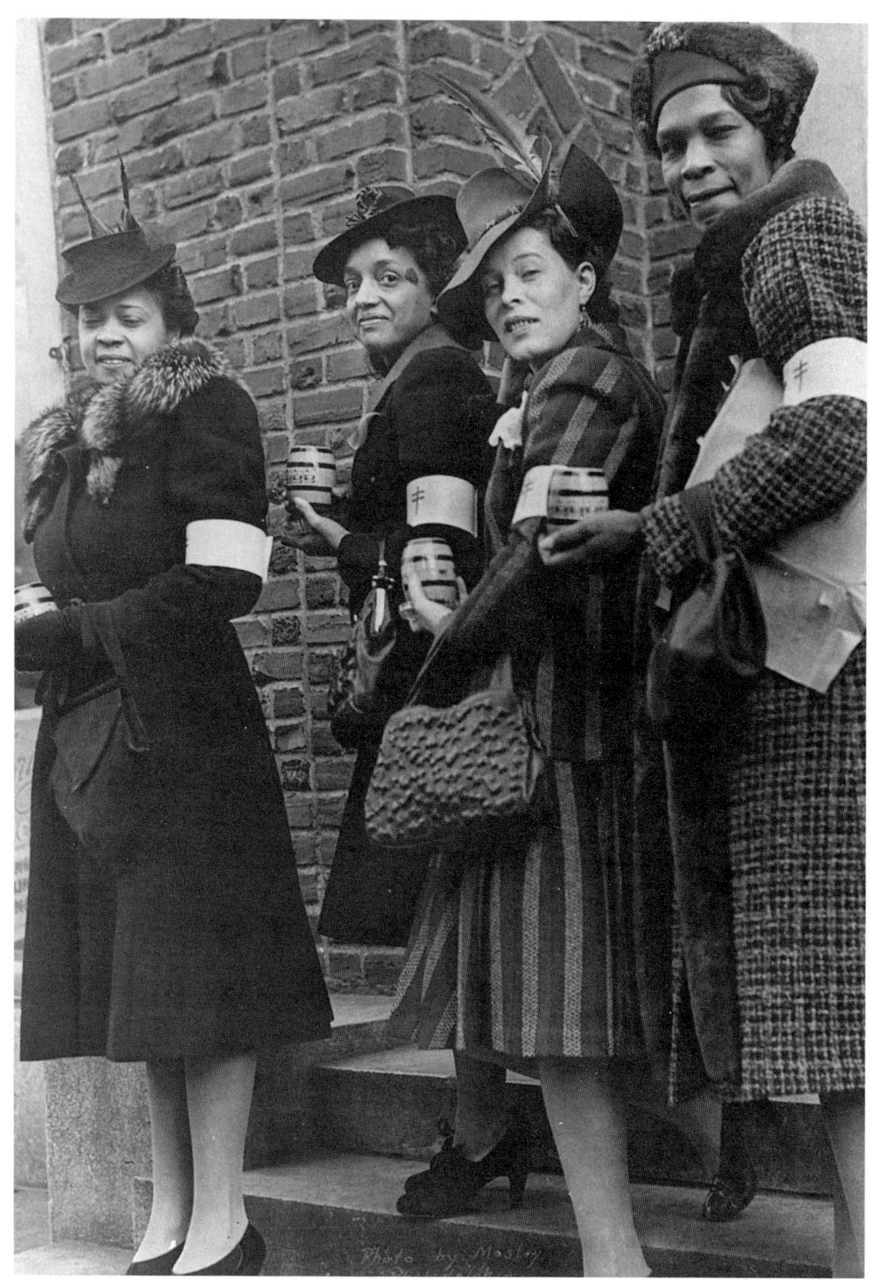

44) Verna Phillips (third from left) and other women collect donations for Easter Seals anti-tuberculois campaign, late 1940s.

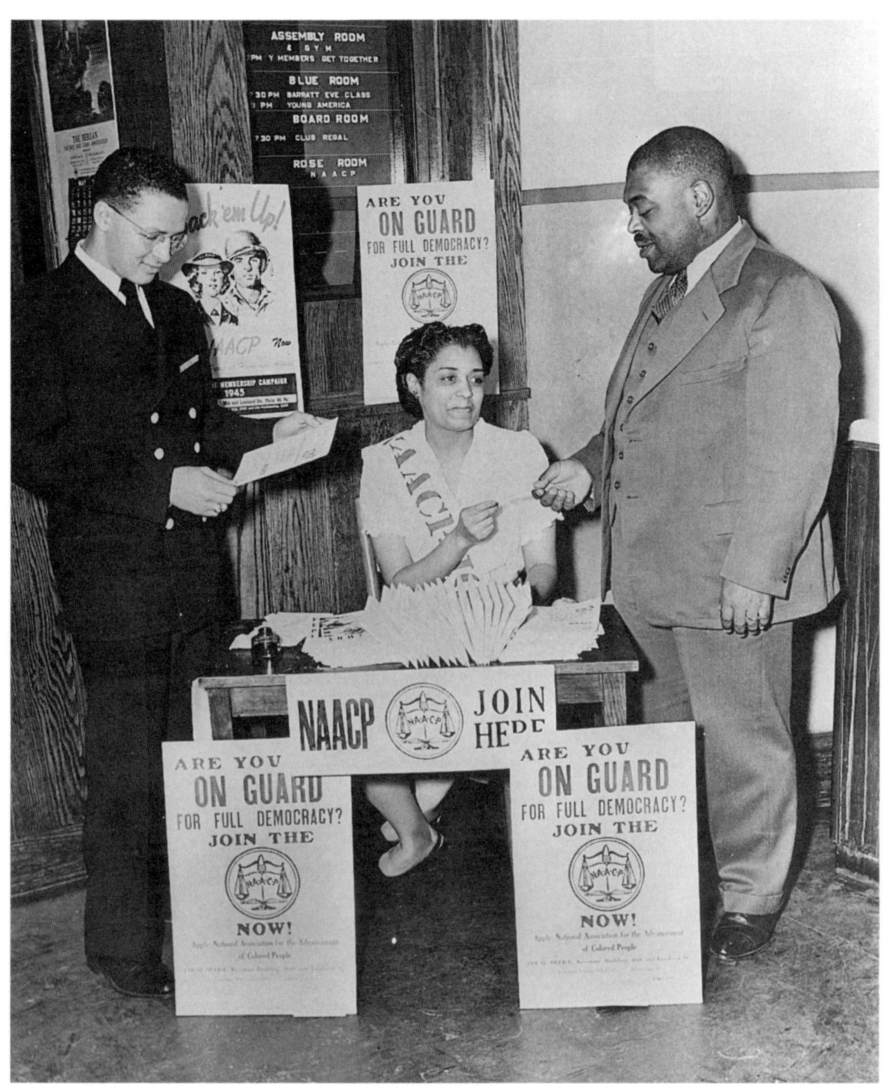

45) Dr. Robert P. Matthews makes his contributions during the NAACP Membership Drive at the Y, 1945.

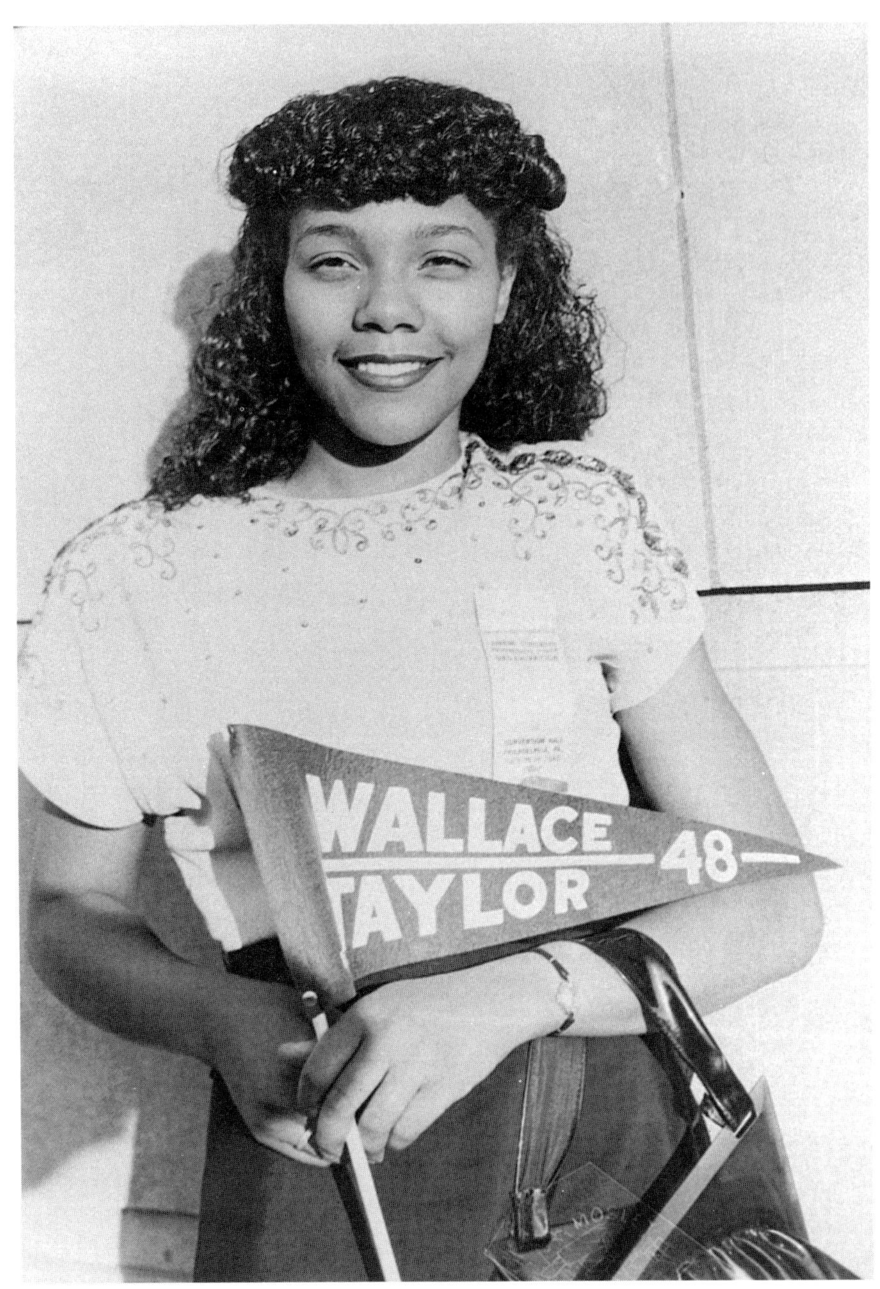

46) Delegate Coretta Scott, student at Antioch College in Yellow Spring, Ohio, attends founding convention of the Progressive Youth Organization in Philadelphia held July 25 and 26, 1948.

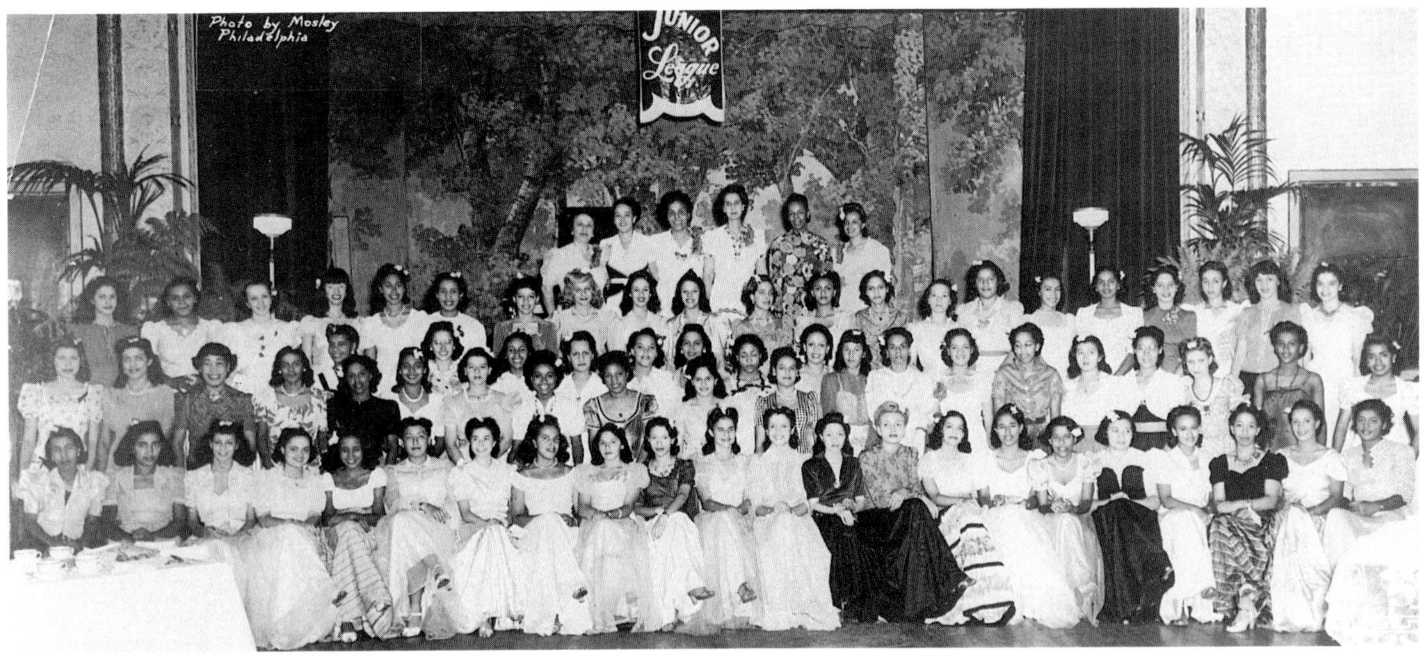

47) Women in the Junior League of Philadelphia, instrumental in assisting servicemen by organizing various activities for them during World War II, 1941.

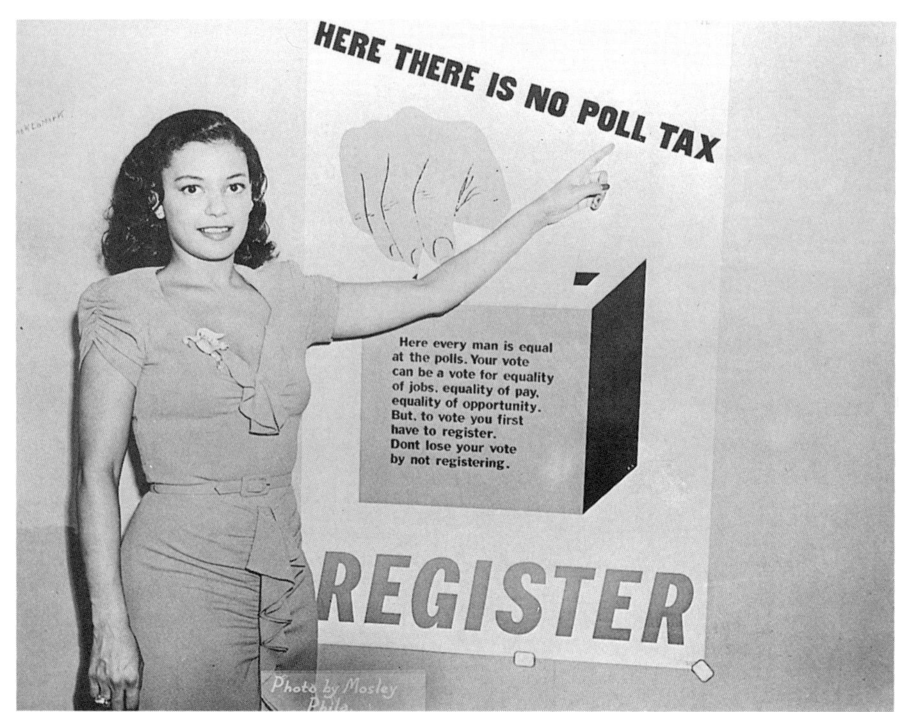

48A) Woman participates in campaign to register Philadelphia African Americans to register to vote, 1940's.

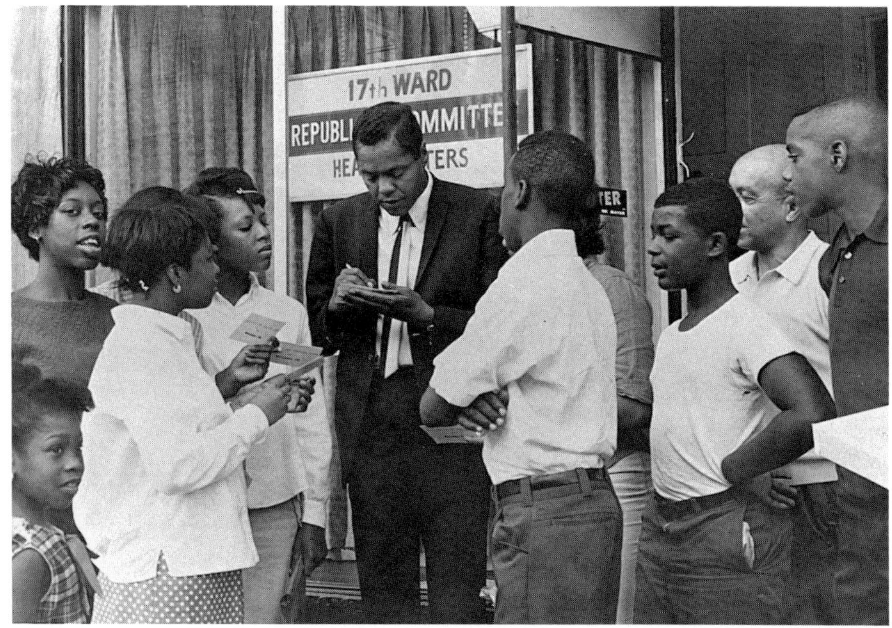

48B) Georgie Woods signs autographs for young people during Republican campaign, 1960s.

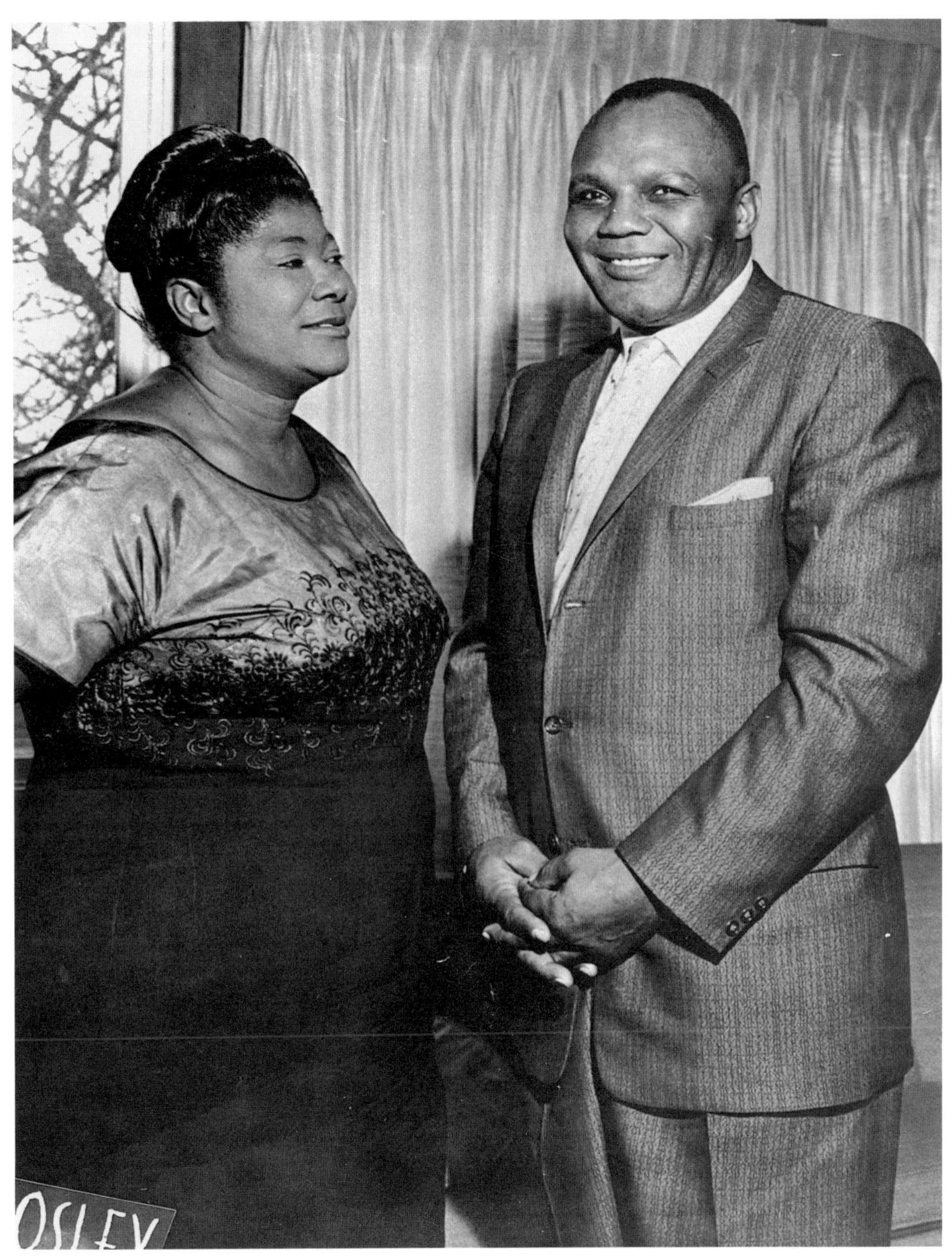

49) Mahalia Jackson (1911-1972), renowned gospel singer, with Joe "Jersey Joe" Walcott [Arnold Raymond Cream], former heavy weight boxing champion and first Black sheriff in New Jersey, 1950s.

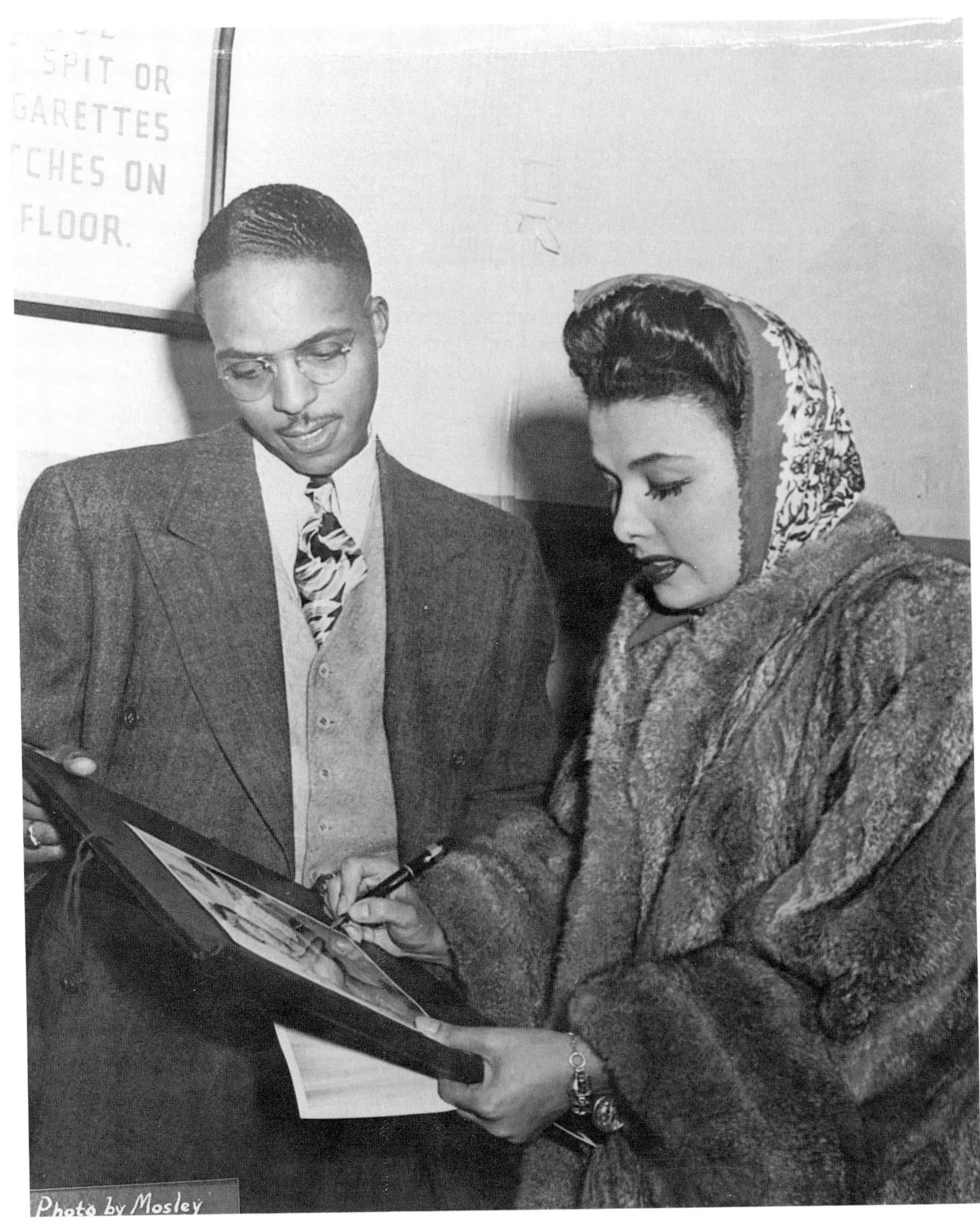

50) "Lovely Lena Horne," singer, dancer, actress and author, autographs picture for Artist Cobb, 1944.

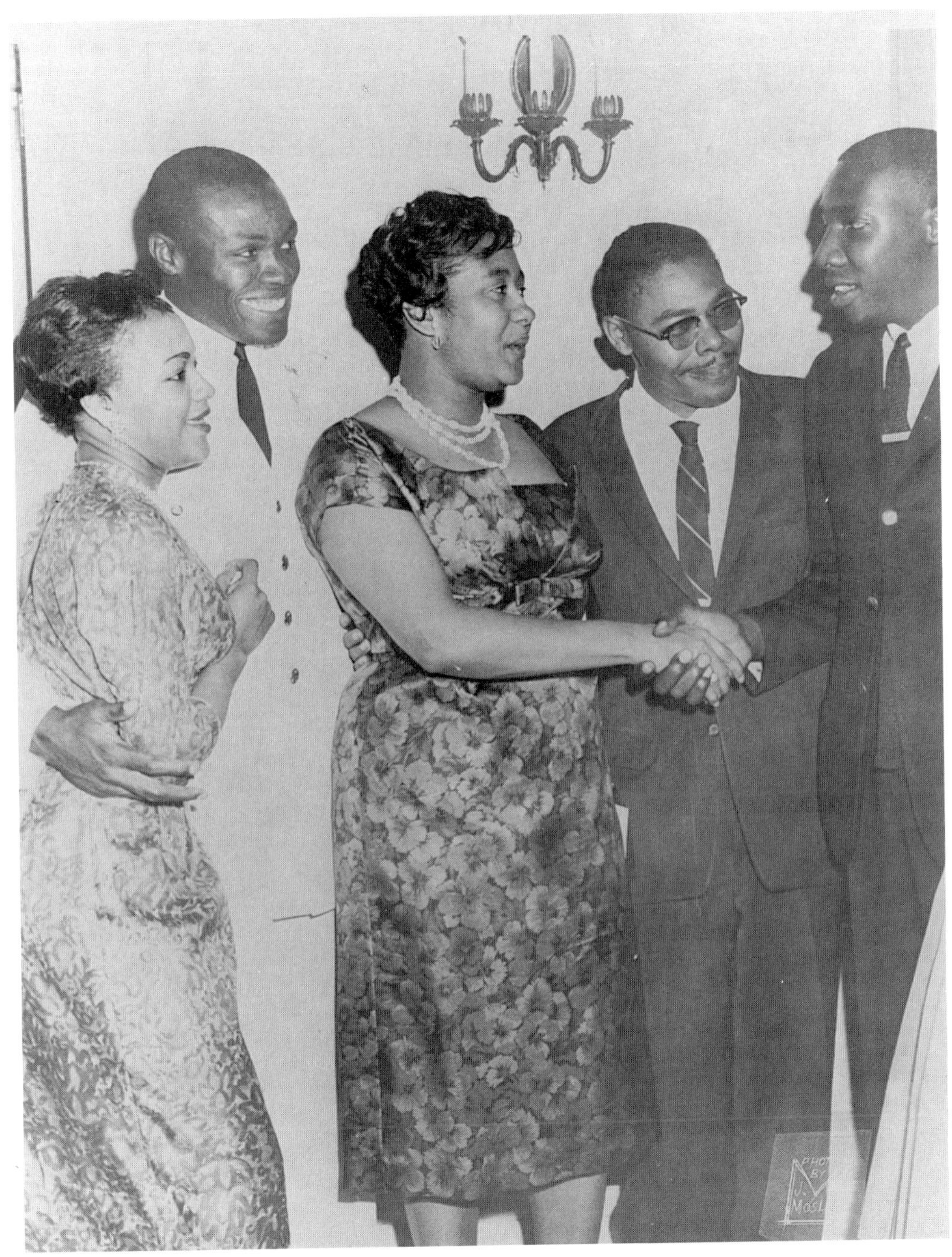

51) Dr. Constance E. Clayton (third from left), currently Philadelphia's Superintendent of schools, is introduced to another by Dr. Marcus A. Foster (fourth from left), educator, former Oakland Superintendent of Schools, slain during the Patty Hearst incident in 1973, as Irvin "Bo" Roberson (second from left), former Olympian, Dick Gregory [far right], comedian, actor and civil rights activist and woman look on, 1956.

THE COTILLION

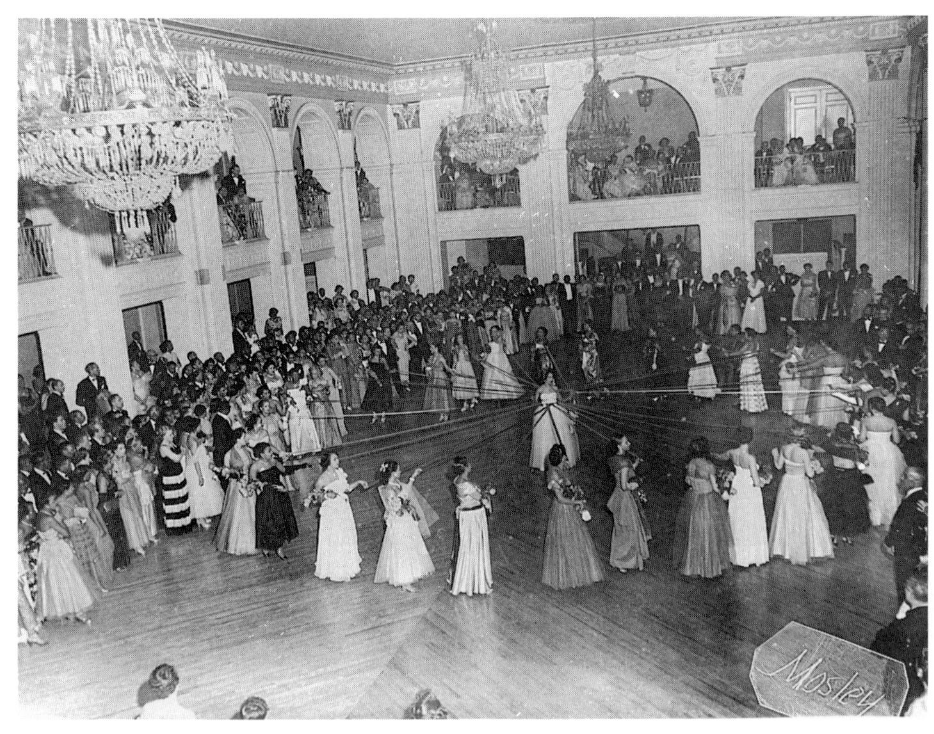

52A) The Cotillion Quadrille, 1950s.

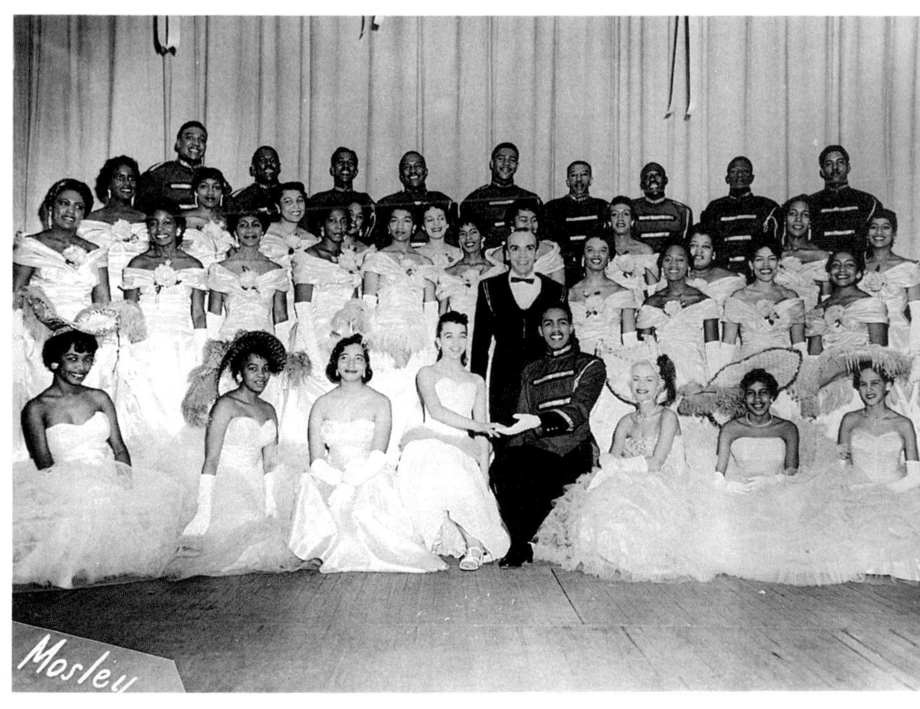

52B) Dr. Eugene Raymond Jones (center, standing), founder, with members of the Philadelphia Cotillion Society, 1950s.

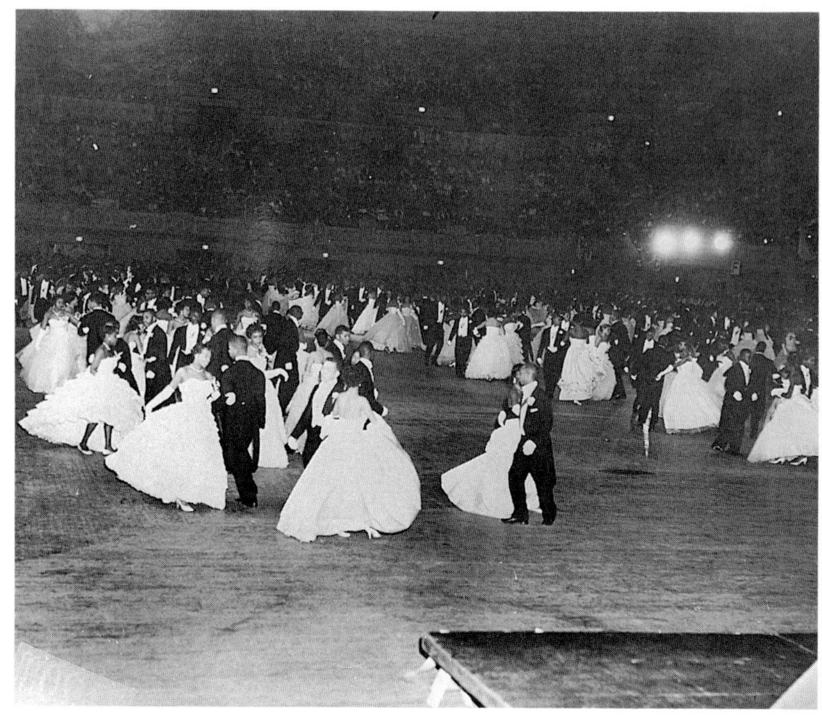

53A) Dancing with escorts, 1950s.

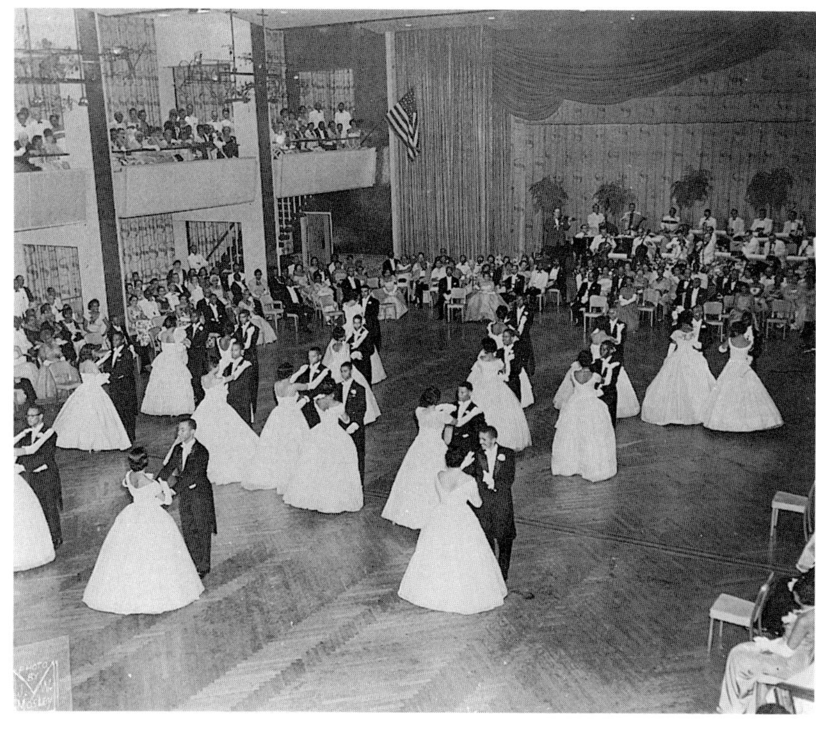

53B) Court Dancing, 1950s.

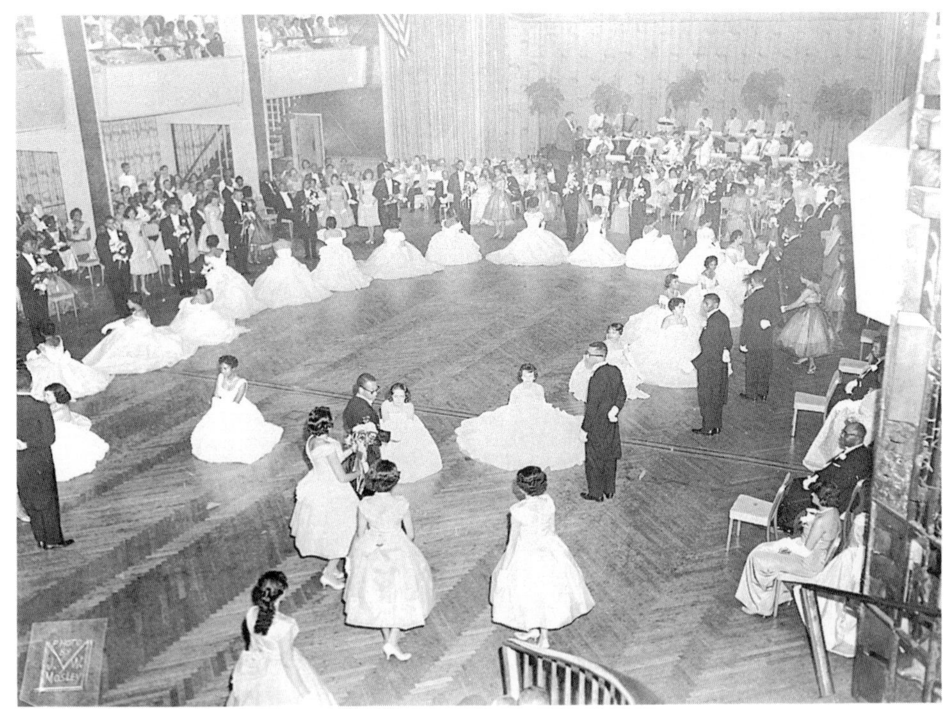

54A) Court Lines, 1950s.

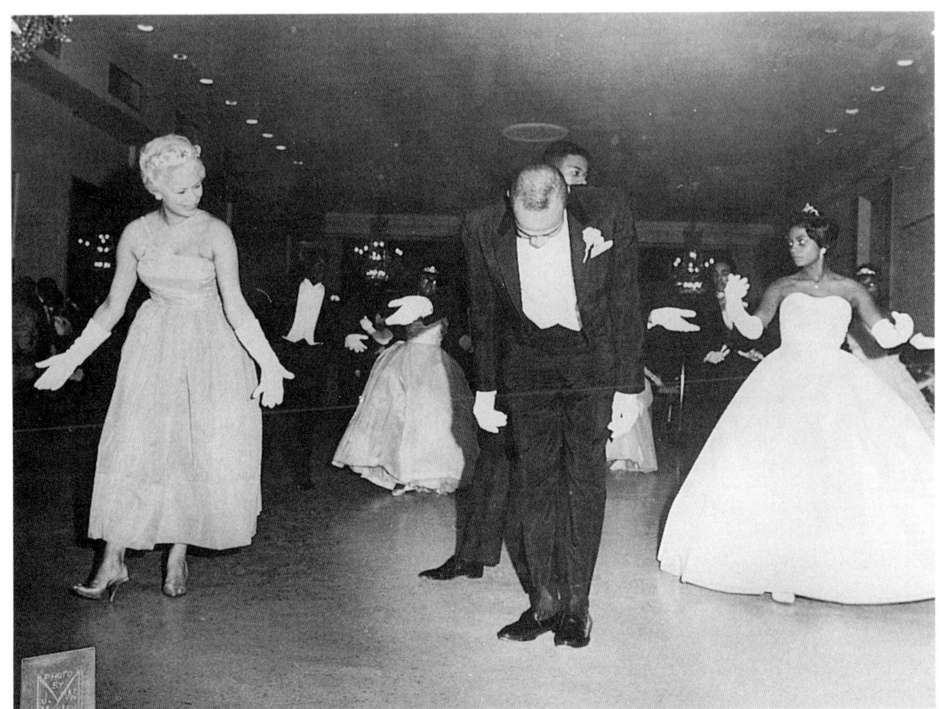

54B) Cotillion Presentation, 1950s.

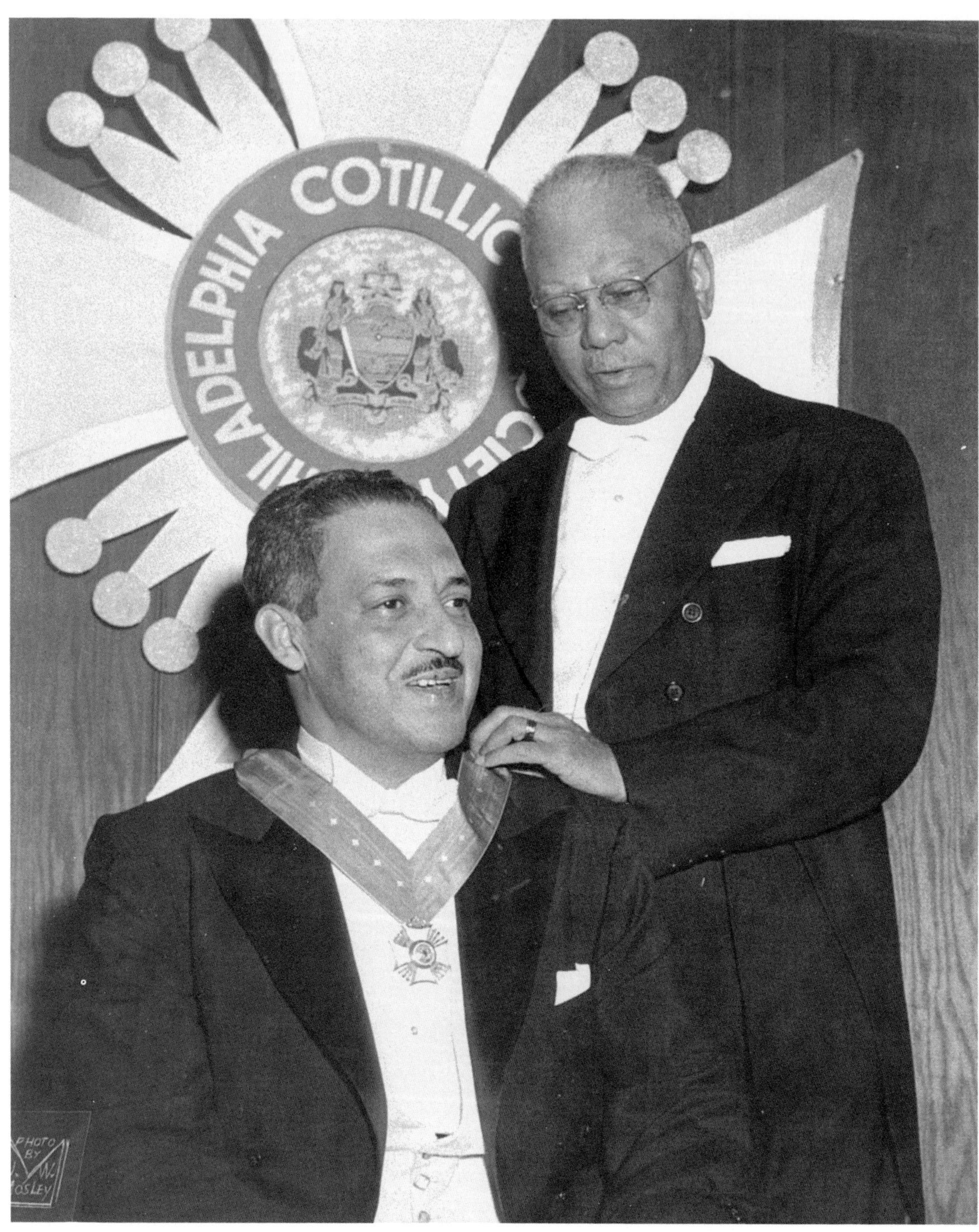

55) Judge Herbert E. Millen (standing) places The Cross of Malta, turquoise and gold, around the neck of the Philadelphia Cotillion Society honoree, Attorney Thurgood Marshall (sitting), first Black Supreme Court Justice, 1950s.

GOD BLESS THE CHILDREN

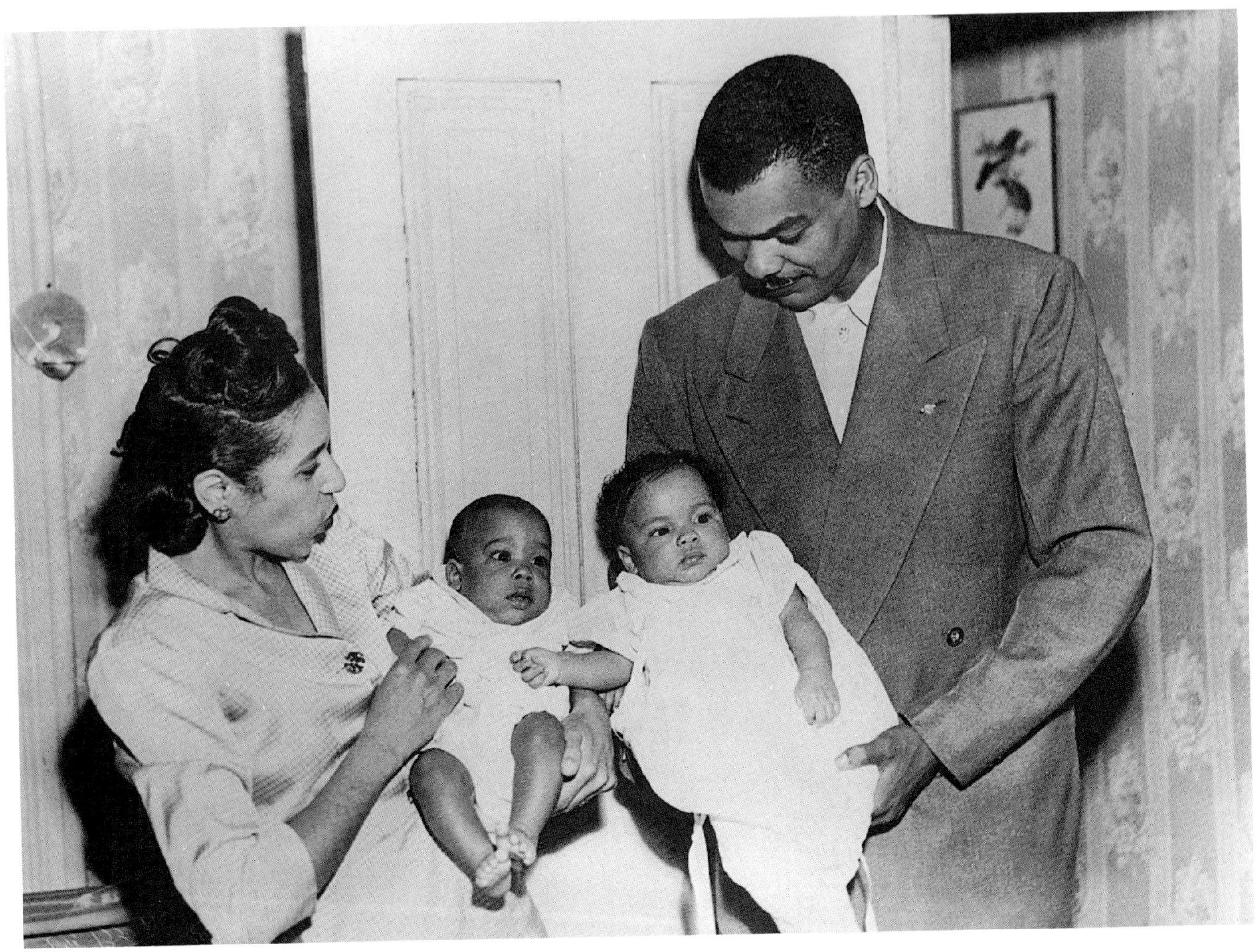

56) Future Greats, 1940s.

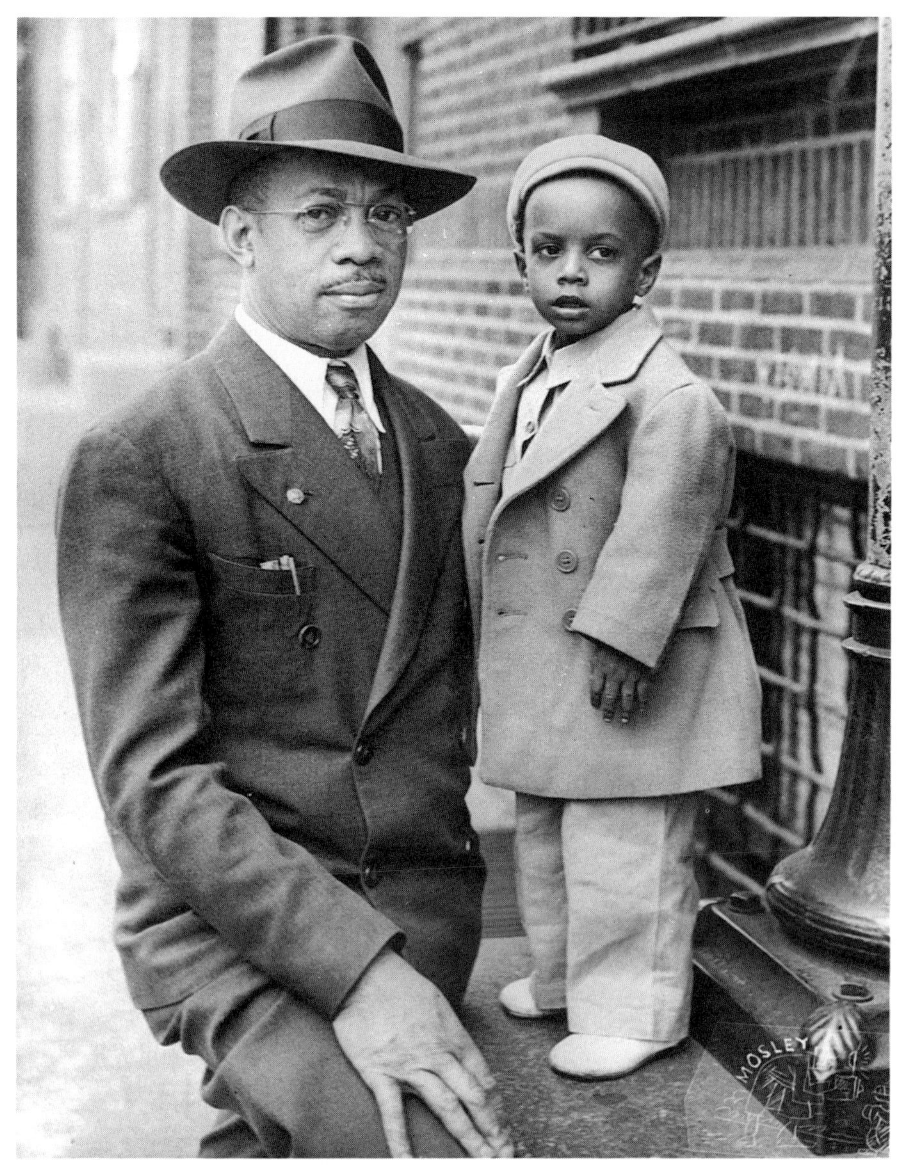

57) Mr. Cannon and grandson, May 1, 1946.

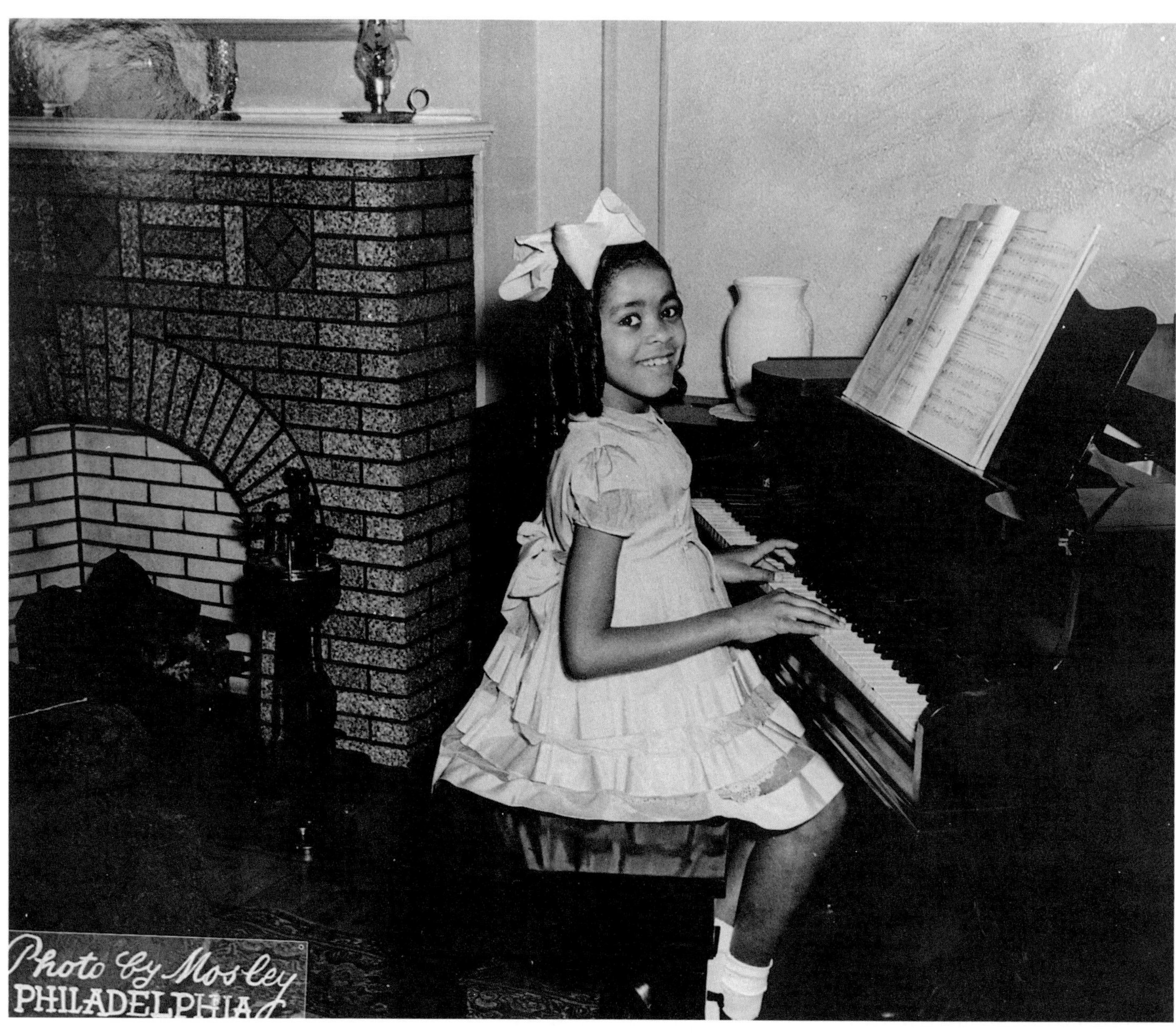

58) Practice makes perfect, 1940s.

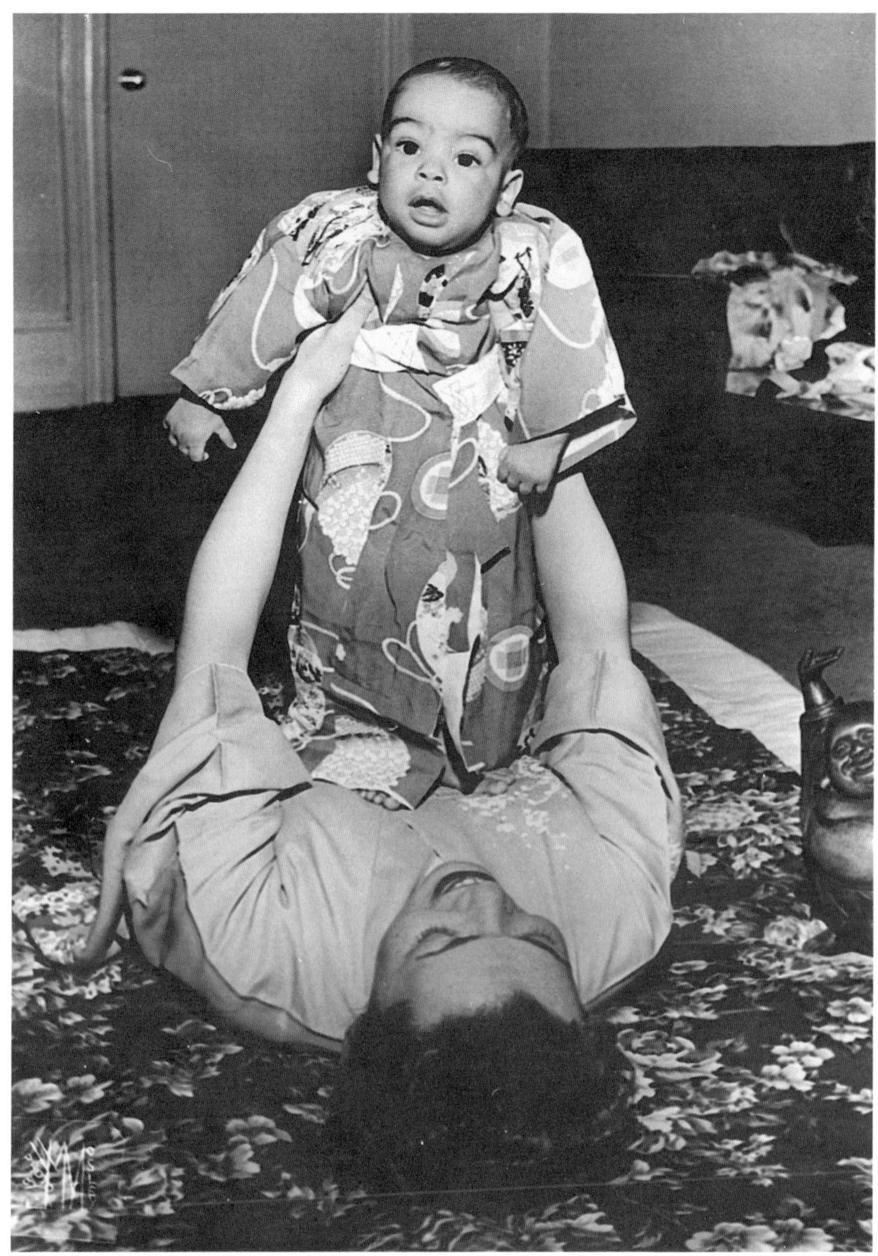

59) Mrs. Thomas L. James plays with her eight-month-old son Anthony Scott, 1940s. Her husband, Dr. James, was the first Black Philadelphian to receive a regular commission in the U.S. Navy.

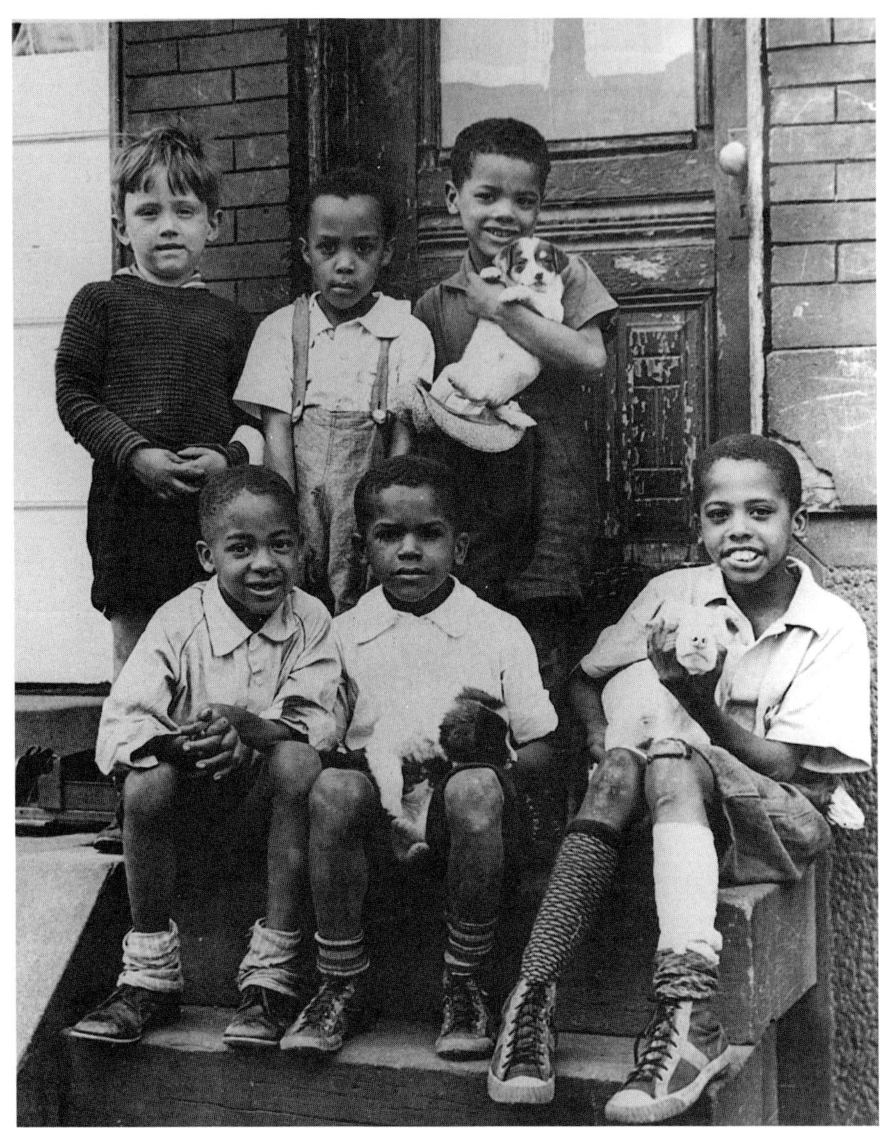

60A) Playtime, 1940s.

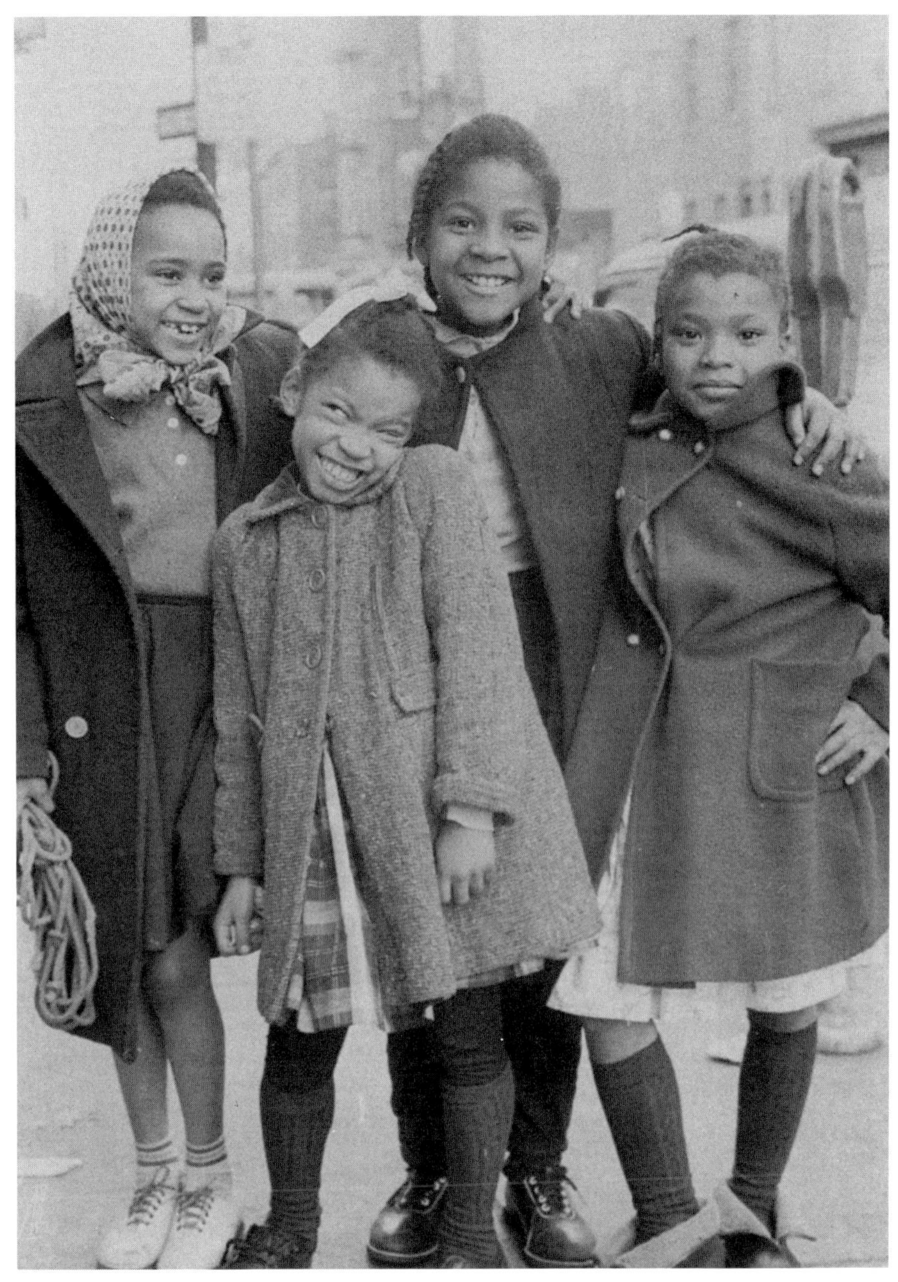

60B) Double Dutch experts, 1940s.

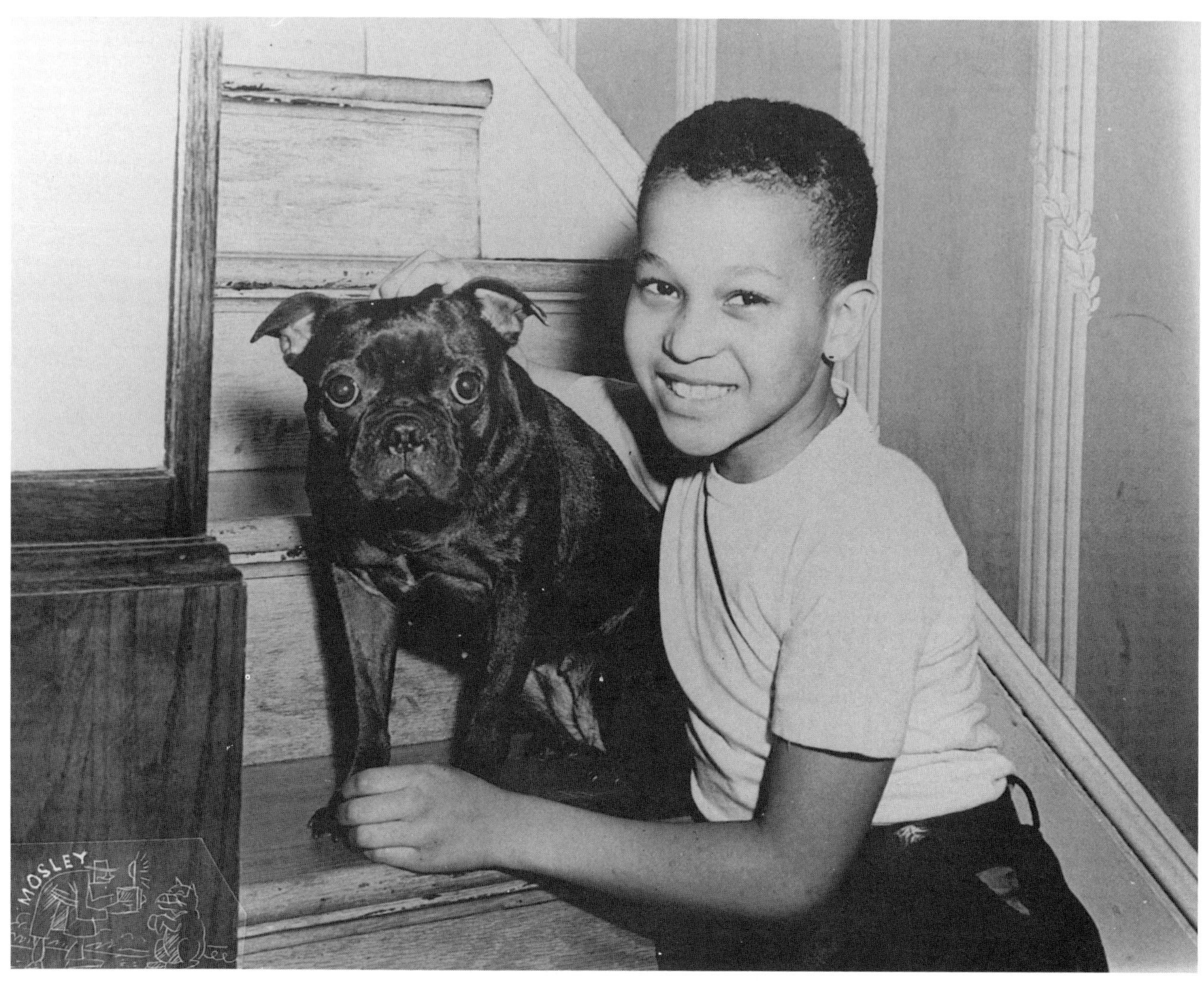

61) Little Jimmie Chew, son of Mr. and Mrs. Charles H. Chew, Jr., with his pal, Trixie, 1944.

THE LIVING IS EASY

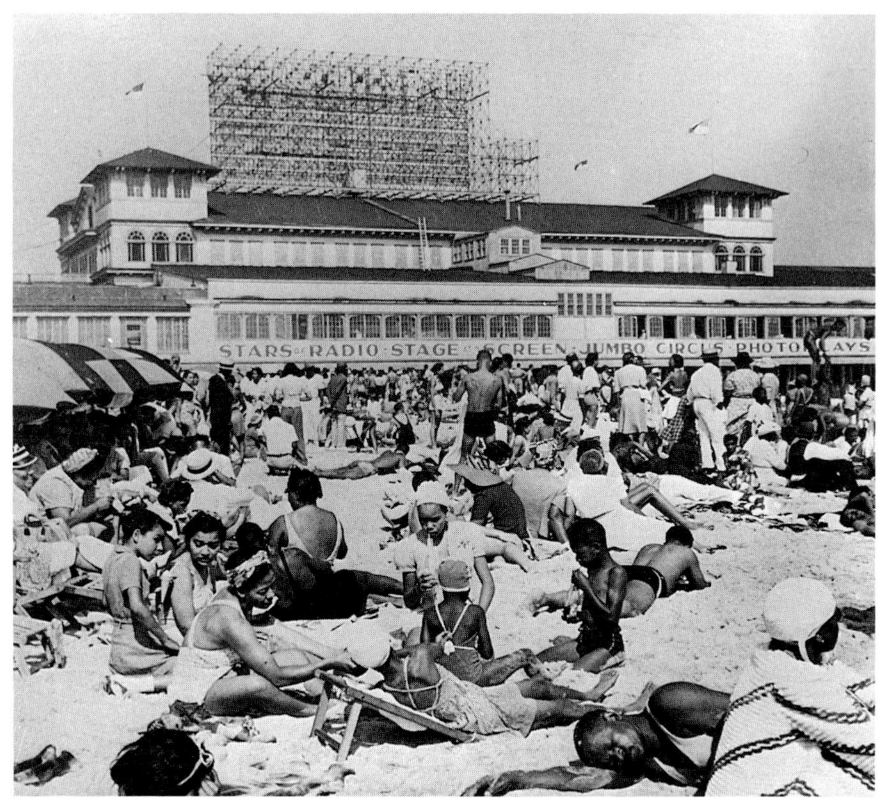

62A) Leisure time on "Chicken Bone Beach" in Atlantic City, New Jersey, late 1940s. The name of the beach was derived because of segregation.

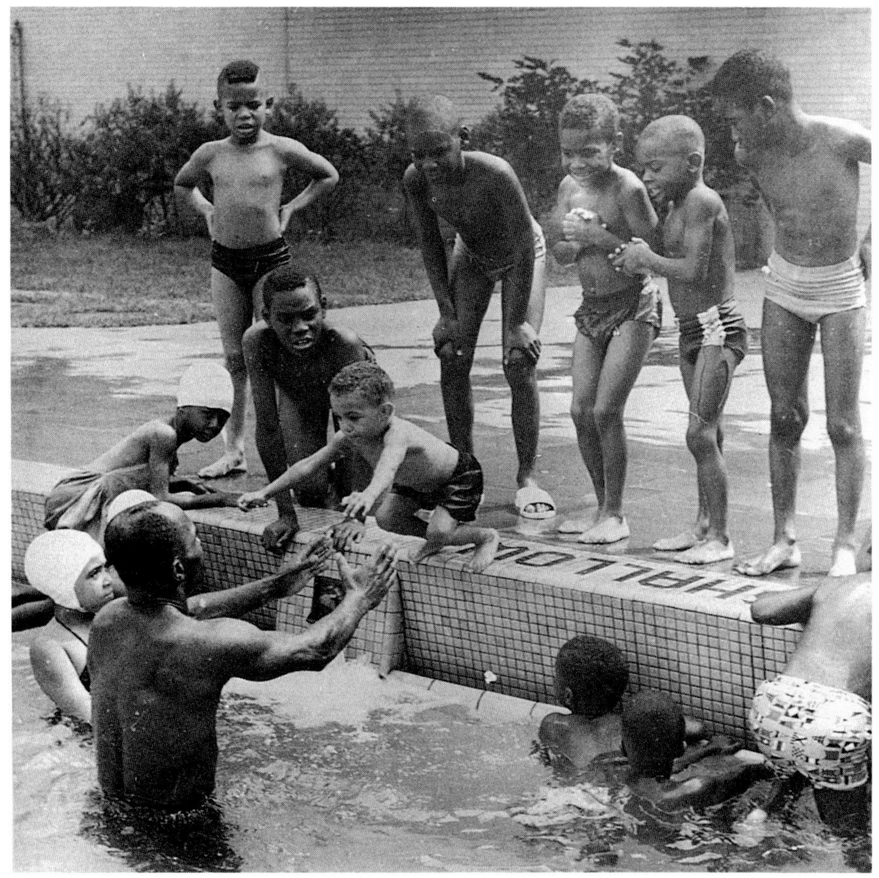

62B) Breath-taking first dive, 1950s.

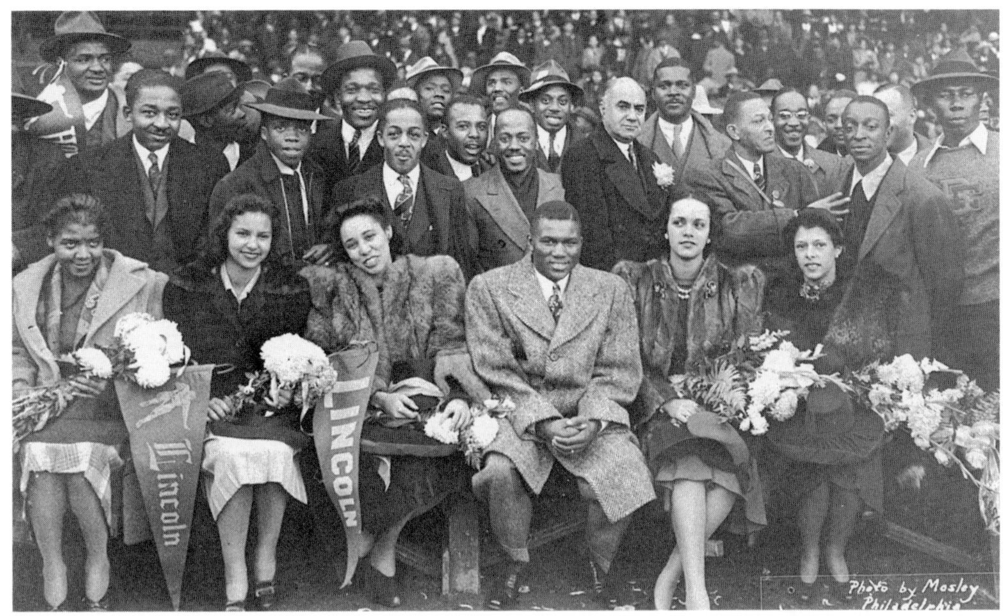

63A) Robert Montgomery (seated, fourth from left) at Lincoln-Howard football game, 1940s.

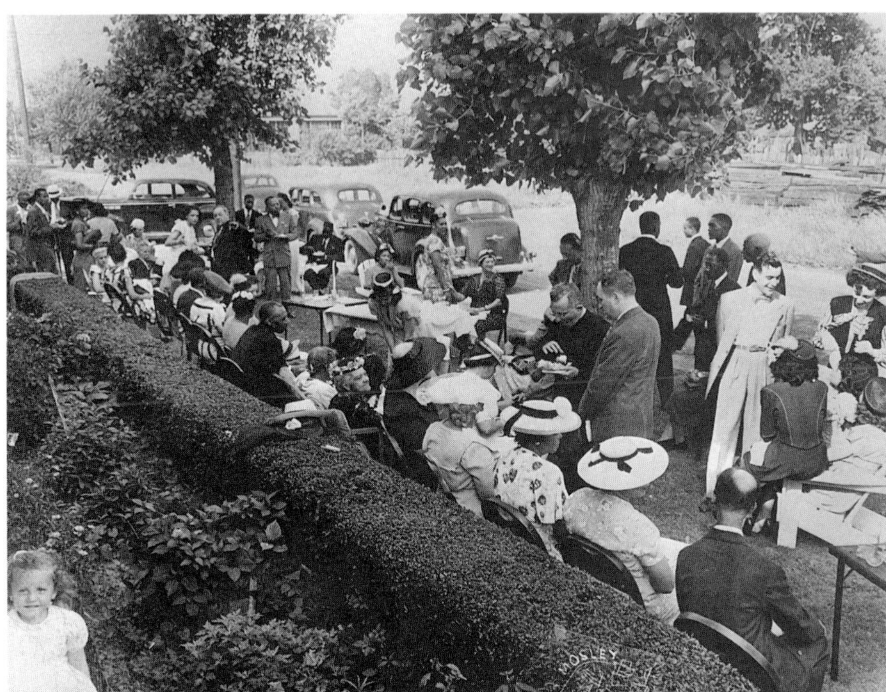

63B) Picnicking 1940s style.

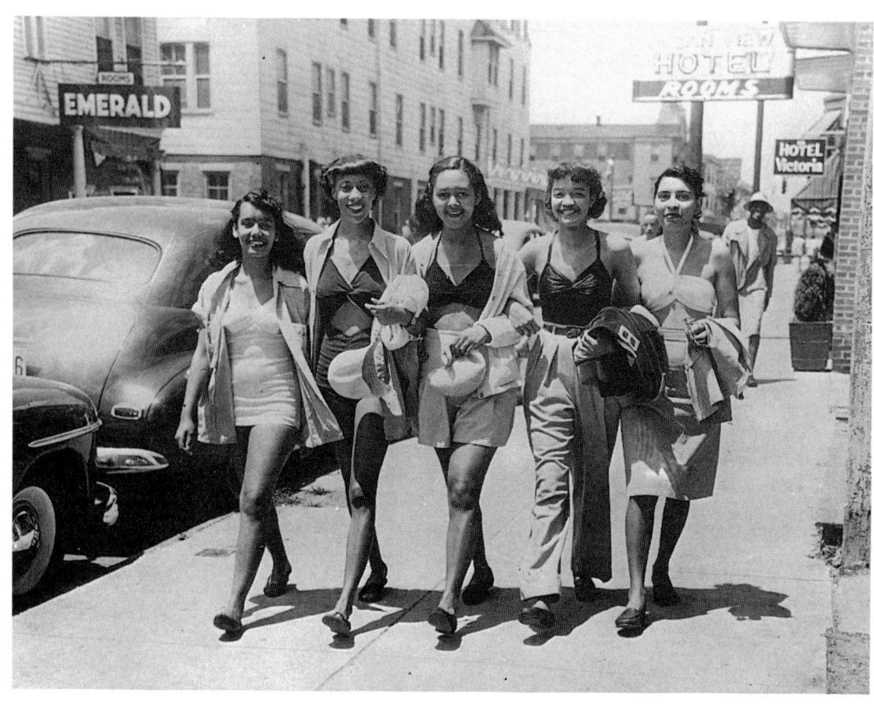

64A) Lovelies stroll down Kentucky Avenue in Atlantic City, New Jersey, 1950s.

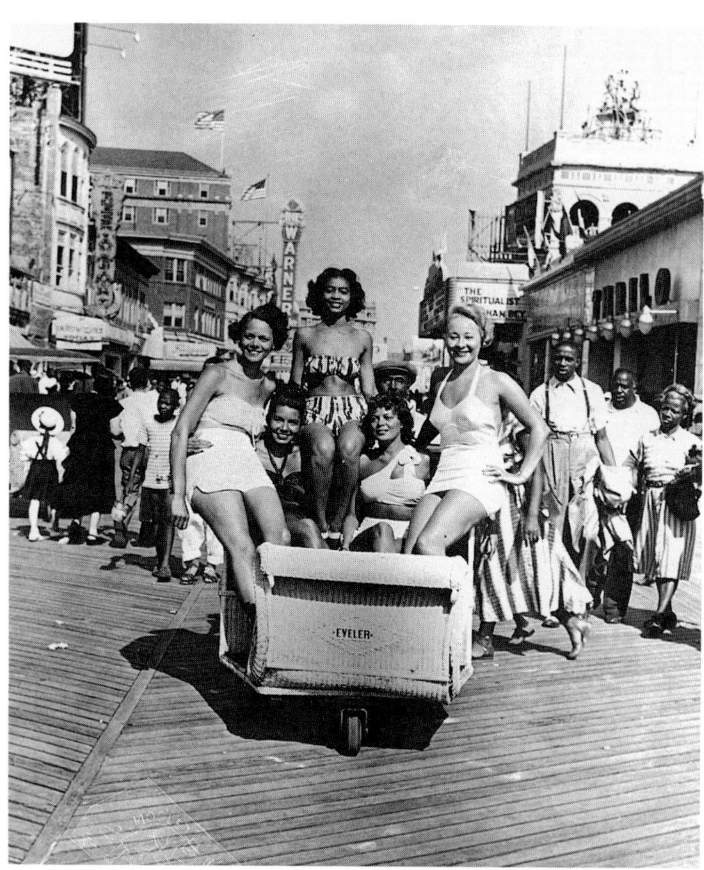

64B) Bathing beauties on the boardwalk in Atlantic City, New Jersey, late 1940s.

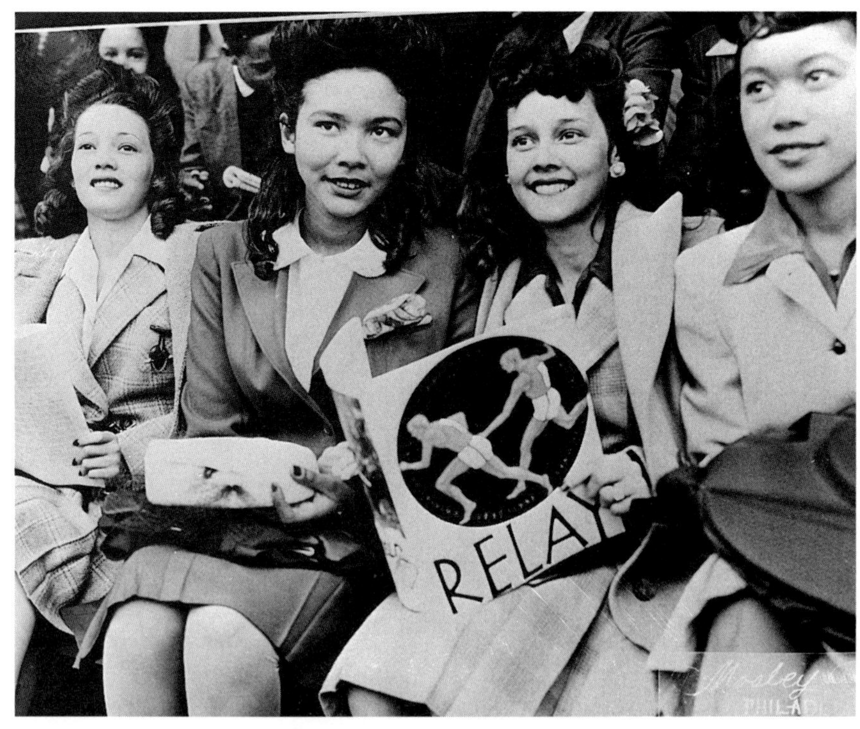

65A) Cuties at the Penn Relays, 1949.

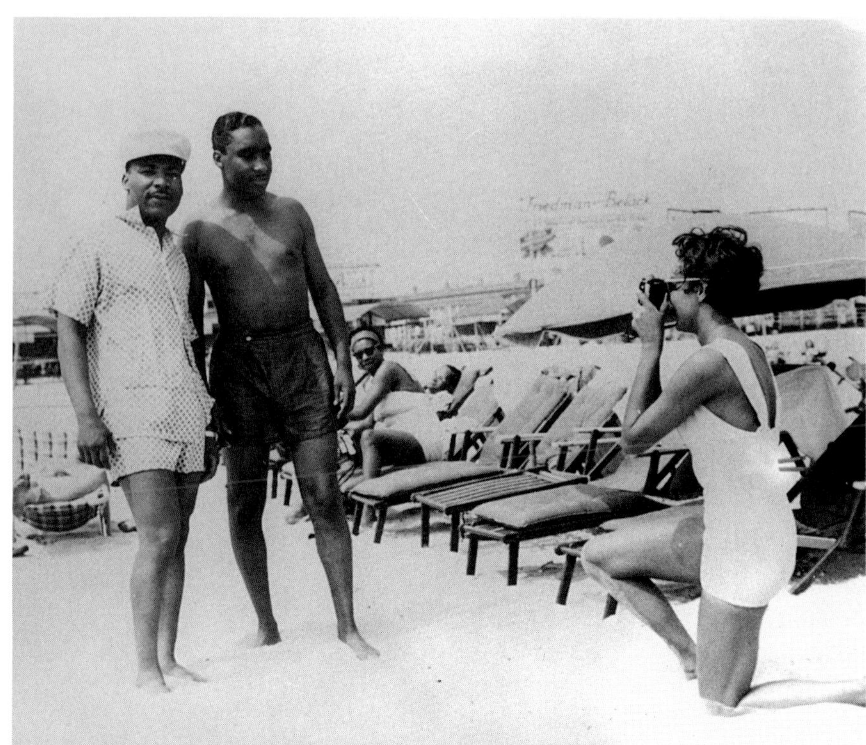

65B) The Reverend Martin Luther King, Jr. (1929-1968), civil rights leader, relaxes on Chicken Bone Beach in Atlantic City, New Jersey, 1956.

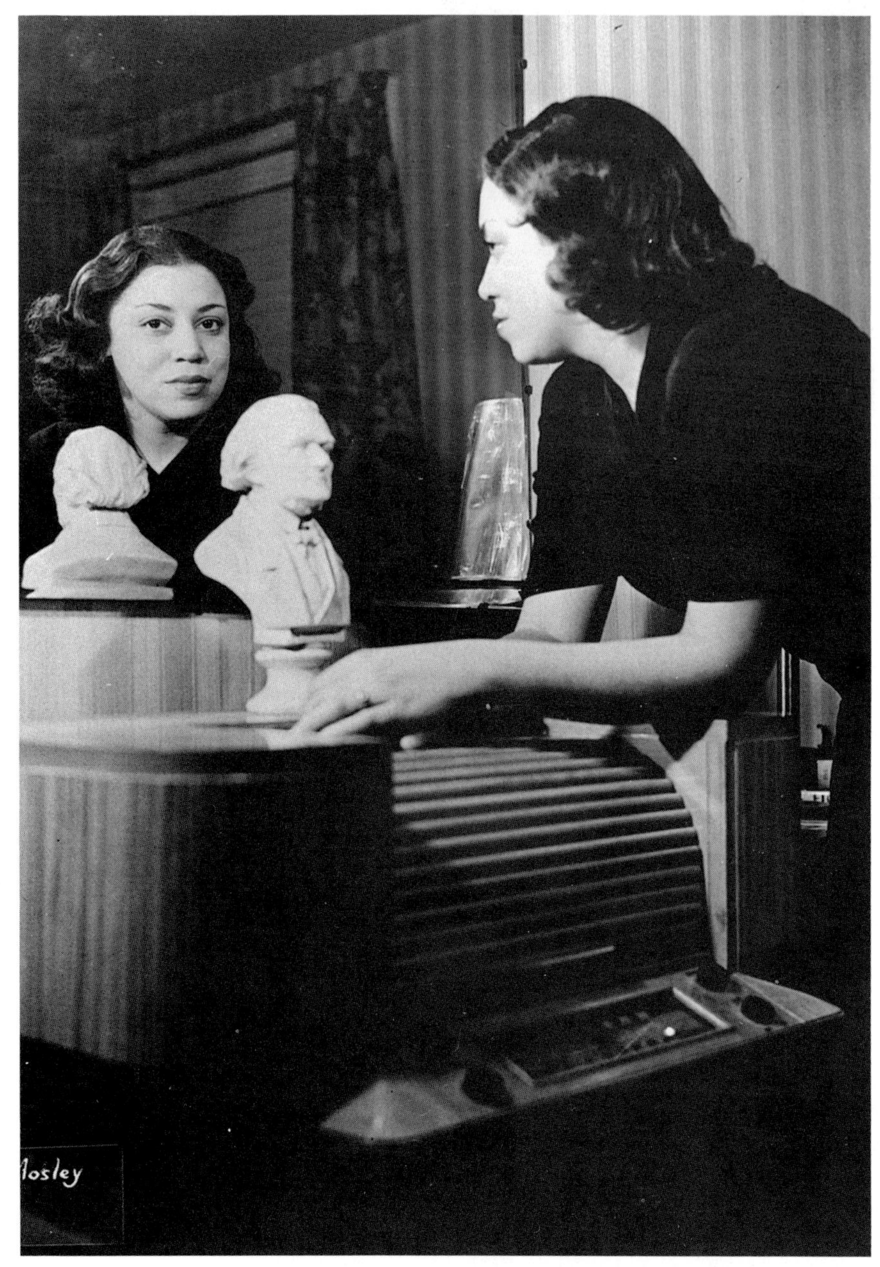

66) Reflections of beauty, 1950s.

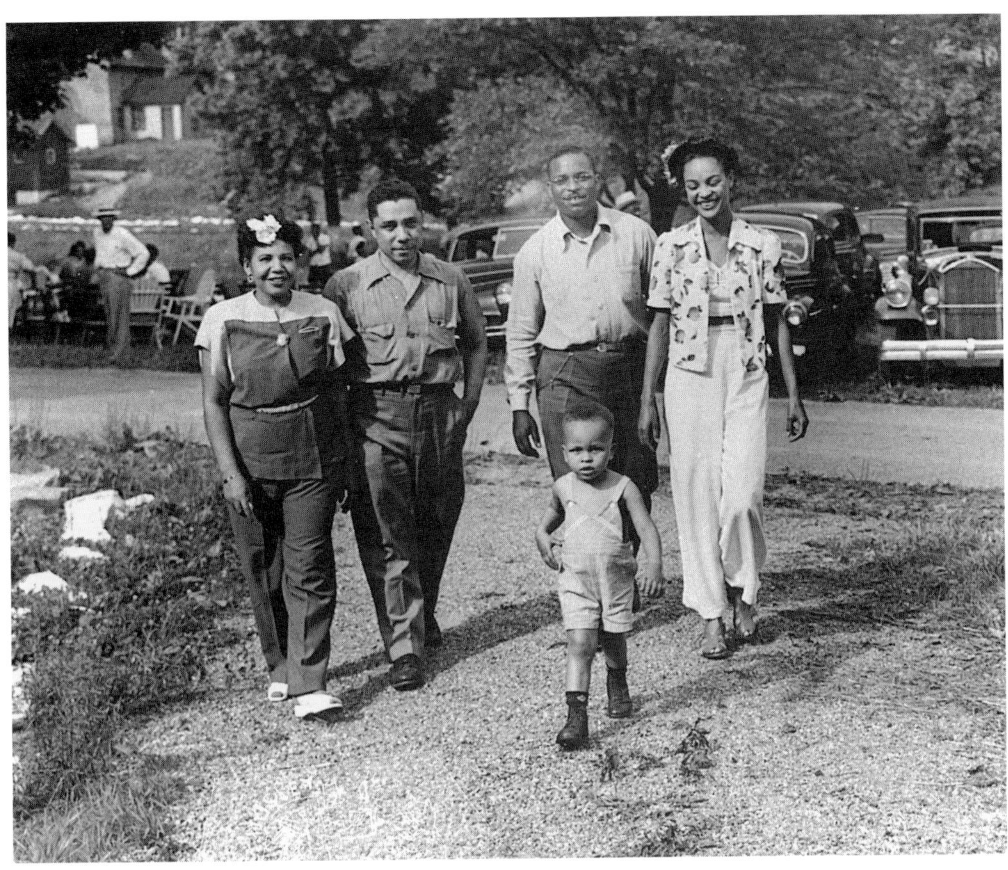

67A) Gatherers at the Pyramid Club's first annual July 4th picnic, 1944.

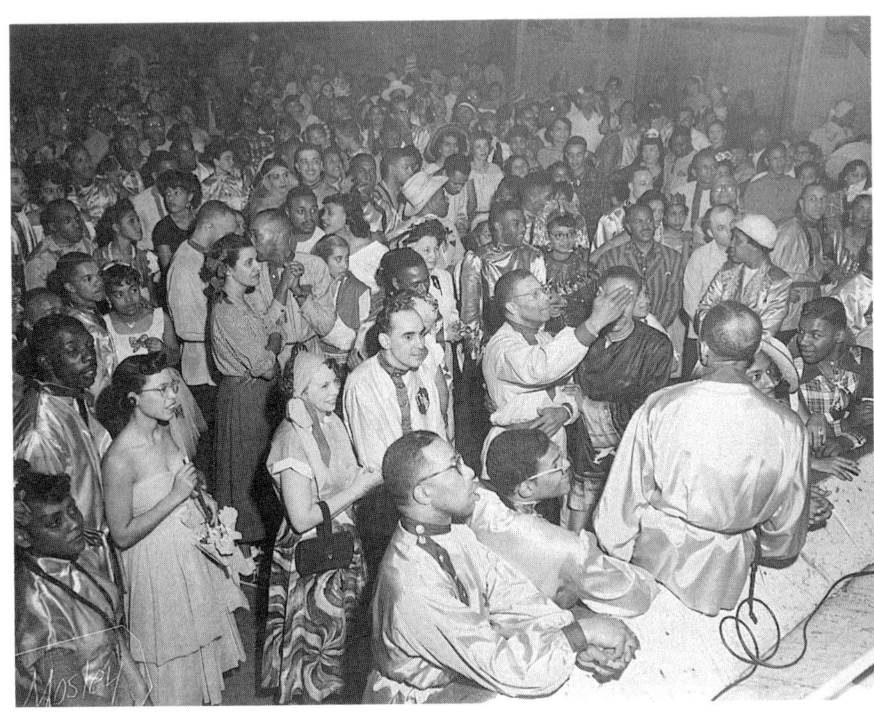

67B) Fraternal and sororal brothers and sisters attend the annual Omega Mardi Gras, 1941.

COMING ON STRONG

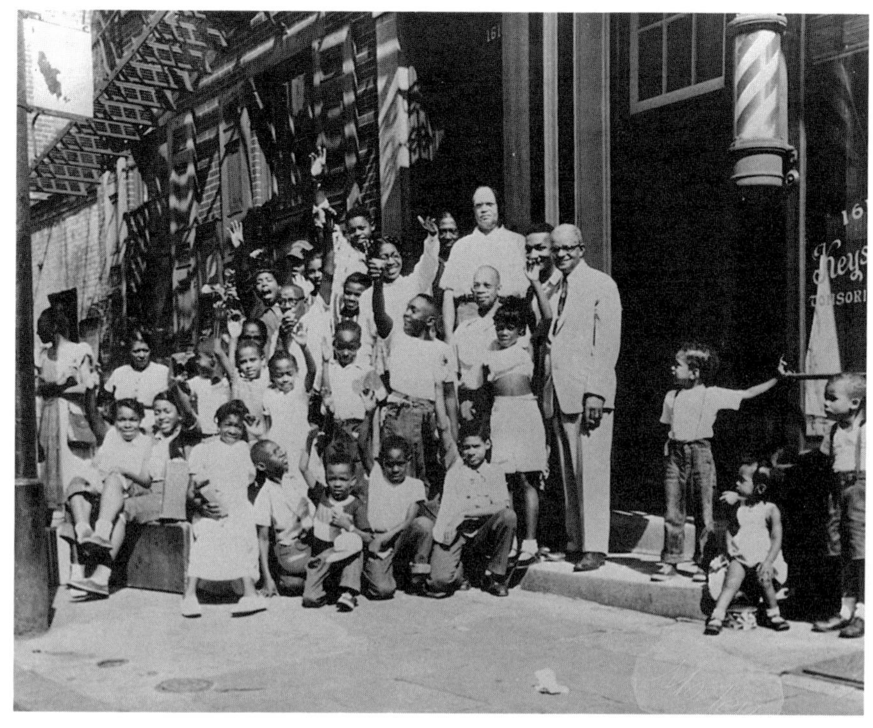

68A) New arrivals, 1940s.

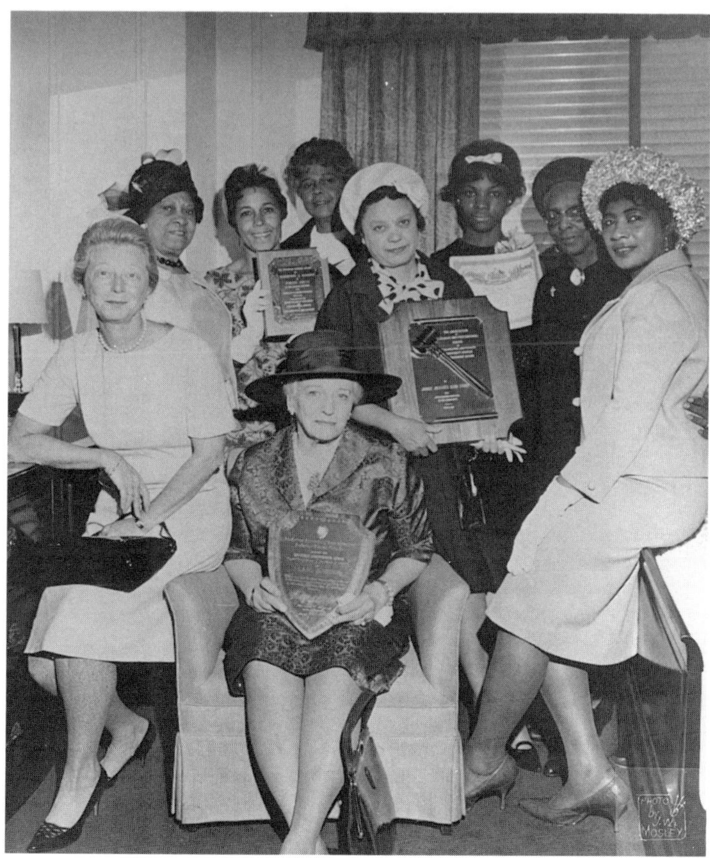

68B) Awardees Juanita Kidd Stout (forefront standing, second from left), former Judge and first Black woman to serve on the Supreme Court of Pennsylvania, and Pearl S. Buck (1892-1973) (sitting in chair), author, with other women leaders, 1950s.

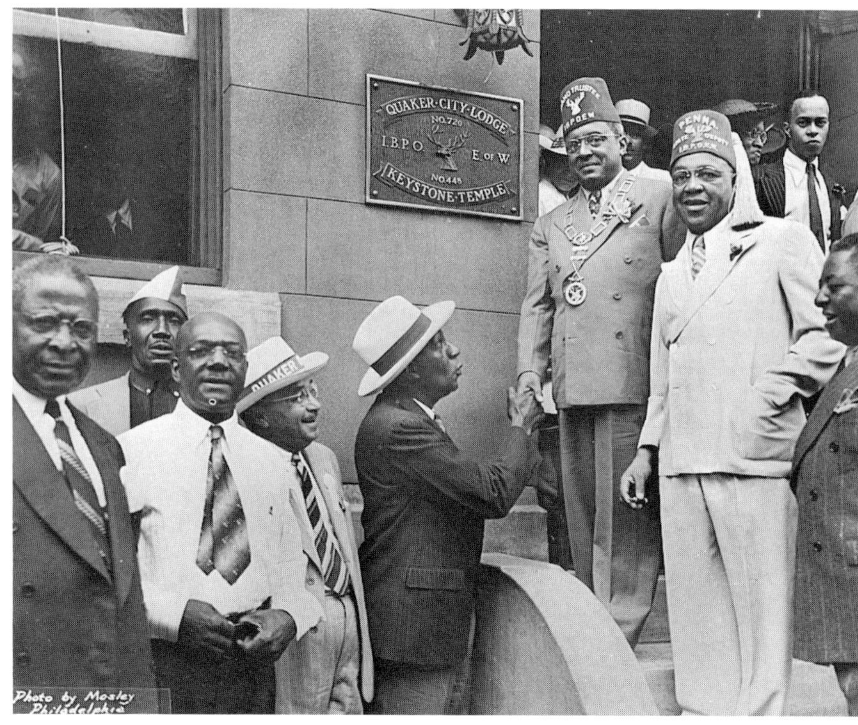

69A) Quaker City Lodge, Keystone Temple members welcome delegates at Elks' National Convention, 1943.

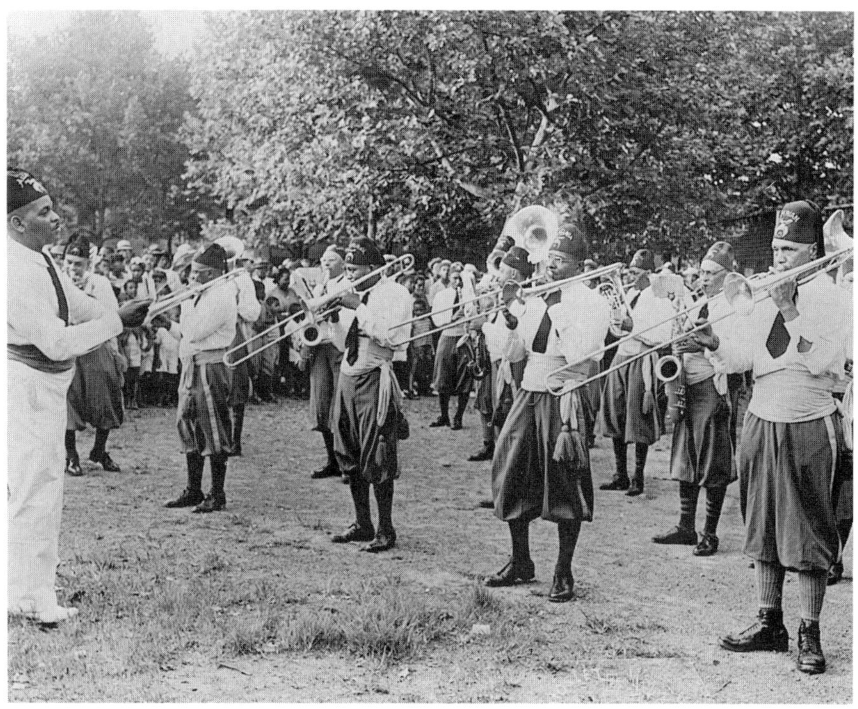

69B) Elks Band performs for spectators, early 1940s.

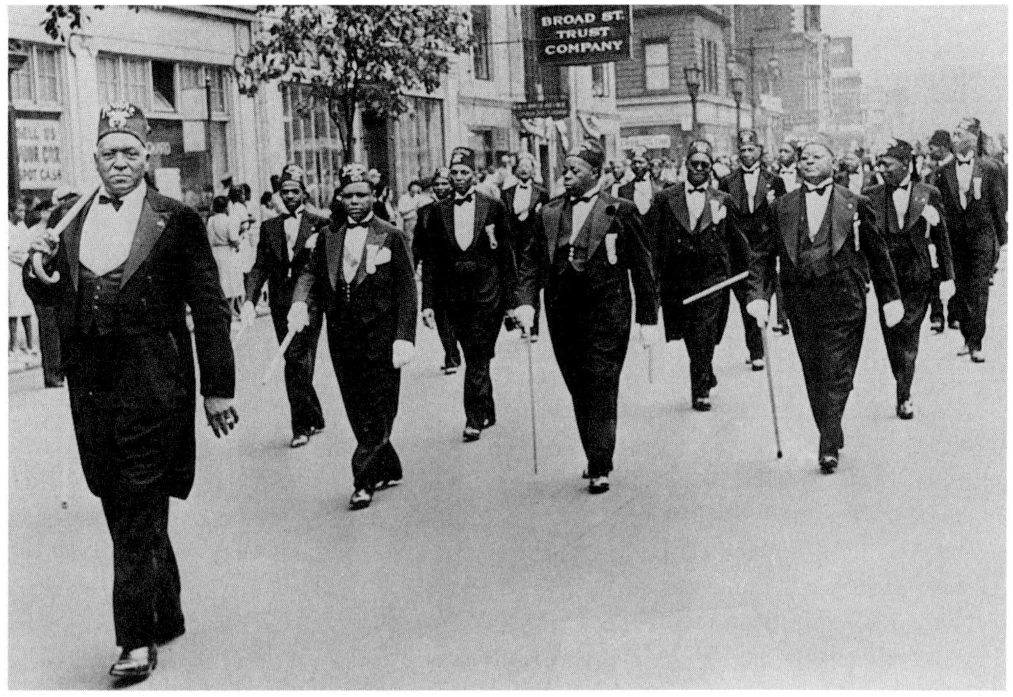

70A) In step, 1943.

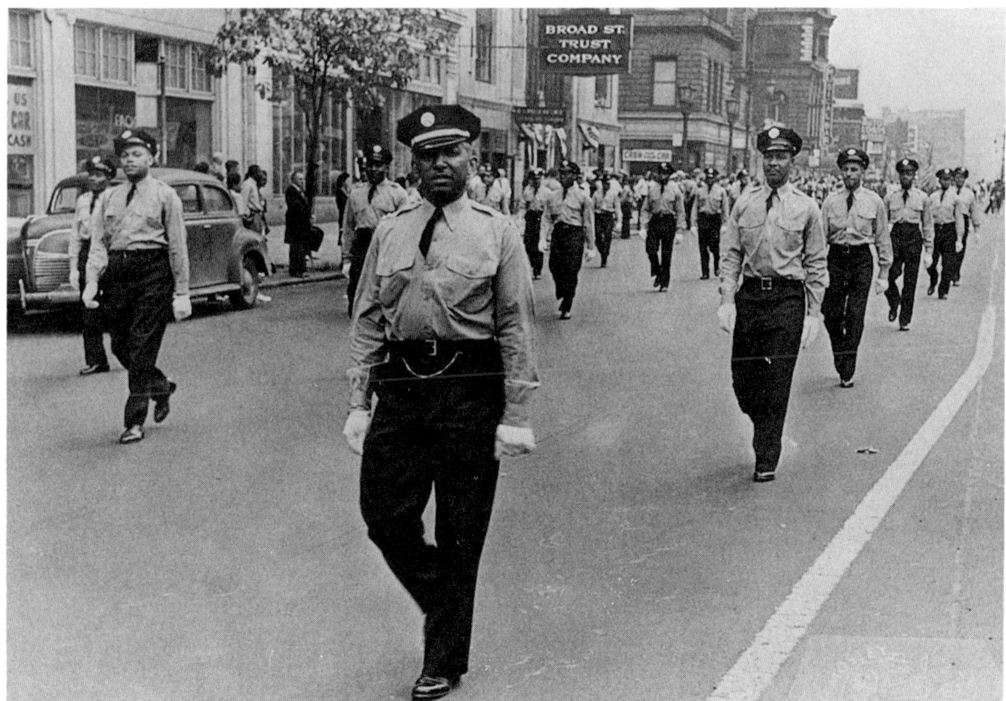

70B) The pride of their community, 1945.

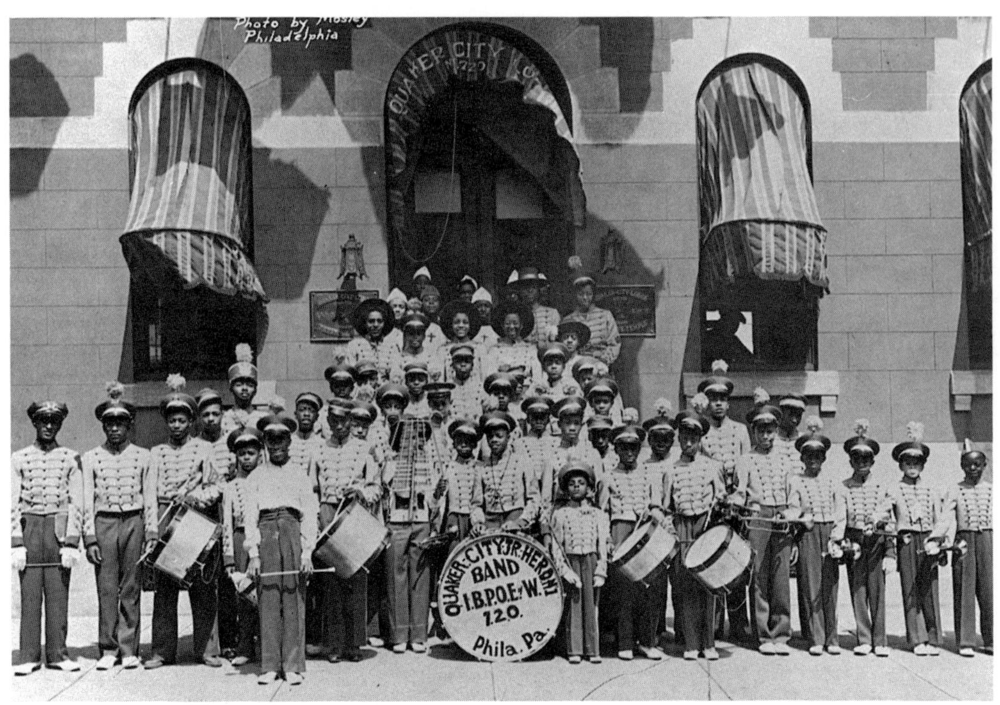

71A) Young Elks, the Quaker City Jr. Heron Band, in front of the Quaker City Elks headquarters.

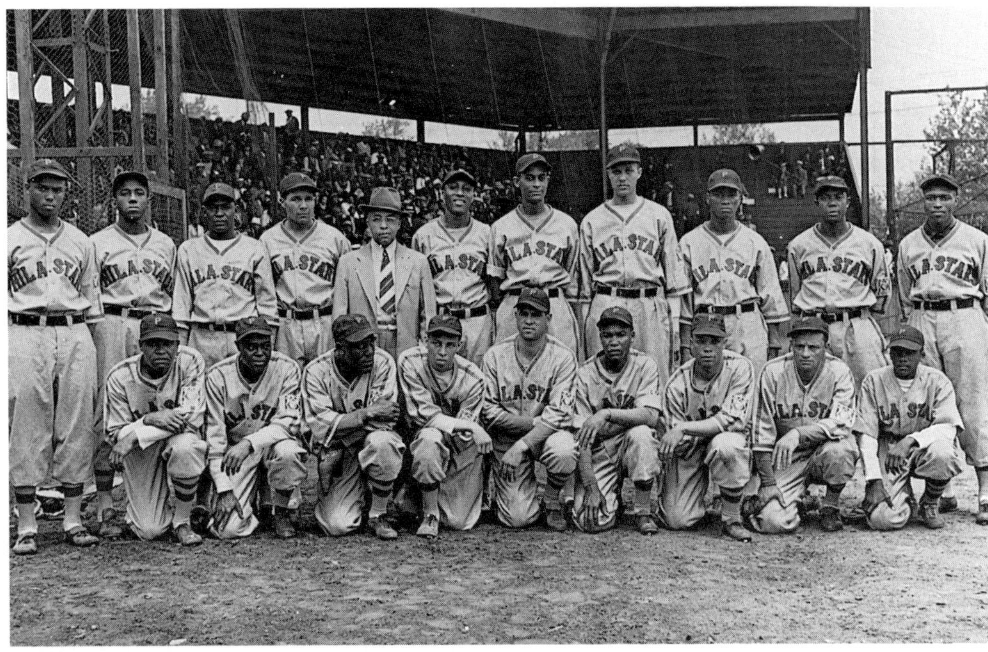

71B) Negro National League baseball team, the Philadelphia Stars, with Ed Bolden (standing, fourth from left), manager and co-owner, early 1940s. The team was organized by Bolden and his partner Eddie Gottlieb in 1939.

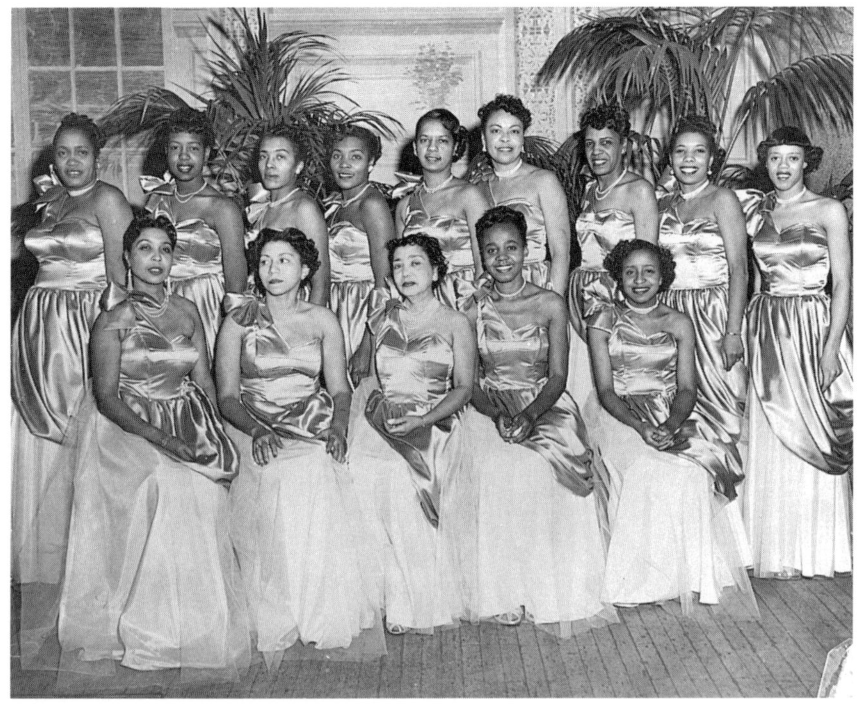

72A) The 14 ladies in Philadelphia's Piano Ensemble under the directorship of Prof. Josef Wissow. These pianists performed, in twos, on seven pianos at the Academy of Music, Convention Hall and other large music venues. Gladys Duckett (sitting, far left), Ursula Curd (sitting, third from left), and Trudy Pitts (standing, second from left), jazz pianist, composer and educator, 1947.

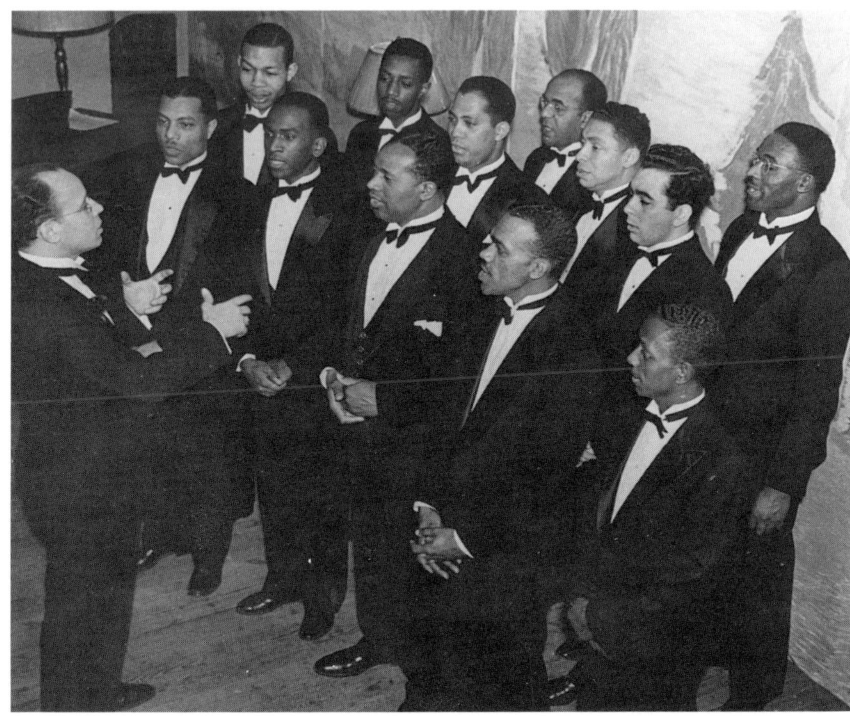

72B) Director Malcolm Poindexter, Sr., former student of Nelson Eddy, concert vocalist, concert pianist, and educator, conducts his singing group The Choristers, who performed at churches and recital halls throughout Philadelphia, 1940.

WINNERS

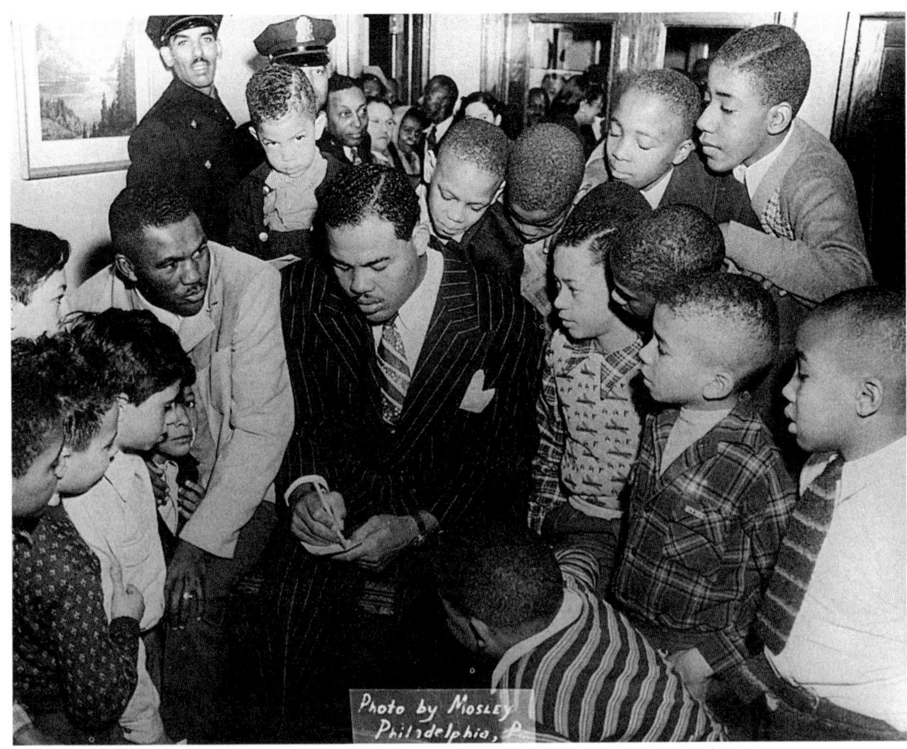

73A) Boxer Joe Louis (1914-1983) signs autographs for boys as Bob Montgomery (sitting to the left) looks on inside of the Christian Street YMCA, early 1940s

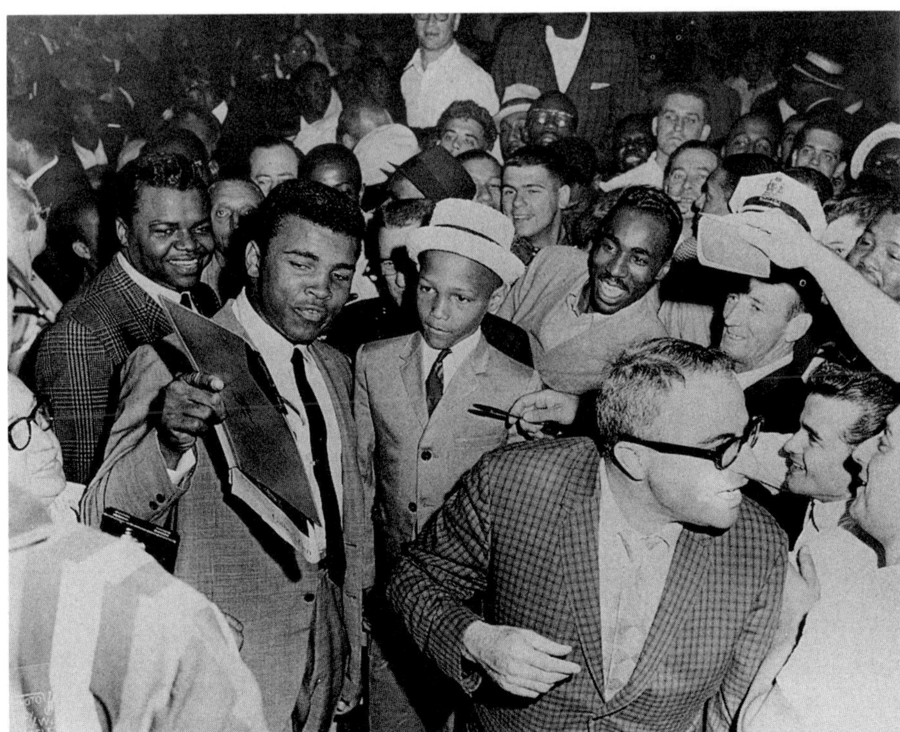

73B) Muhammad Ali, former world heavy weight champion, signs autographs for fans, 1960s.

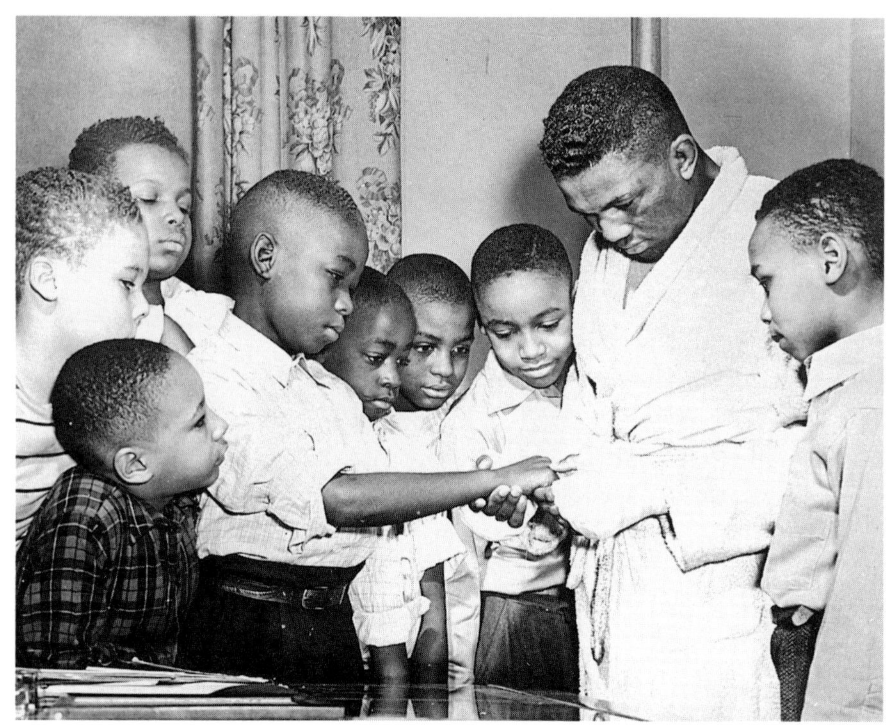

74A) Bob Montgomery teaches young males about the art of boxing at the Christian Street YMCA, 1942.

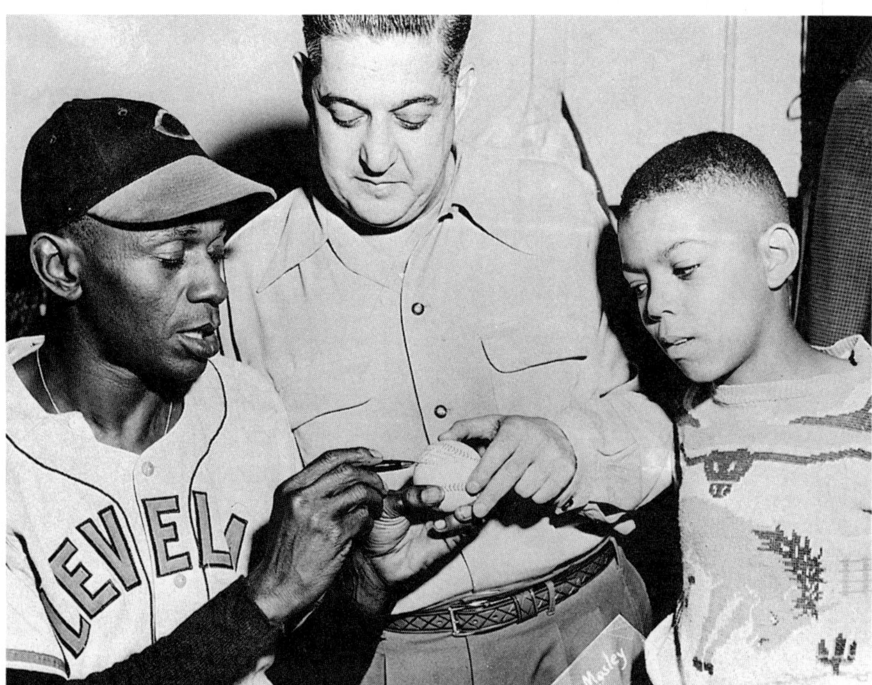

74B) Leroy Robert "Satchel" Paige (1906-1982), legendary baseball pitcher and coach, autographs baseball held by Ted Kessler for Pip Miller, one of his young fans, 1940s.

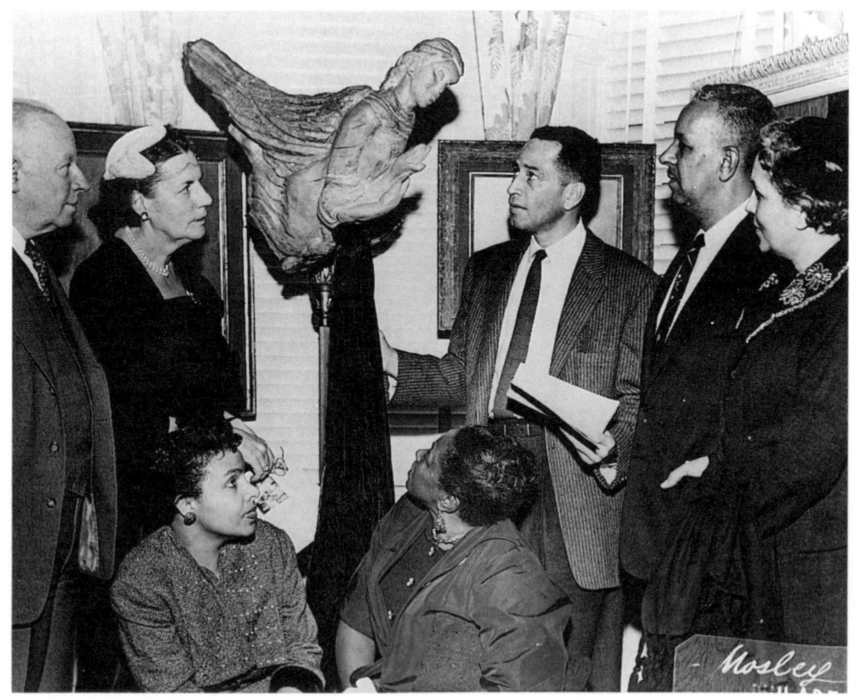

75A) Humbert Howard (standing, third from left), artist and winner in Annual Pyramid Club Art Show, views Dr. Selma Burke's (sitting, second from left) latest sculpture entitled "The Falling Angel" with Mr. and Mrs. John F. Lewis, Jr. (standing, far left), President of Pennsylvania Academy of Fine Arts, Mr. and Mrs. Hale Woodruff (standing, far right), New York University art staff, and Mrs. Bee Howard (sitting, far left), 1940s. Dr. Burke created the FDR profile for the ten cent coin.

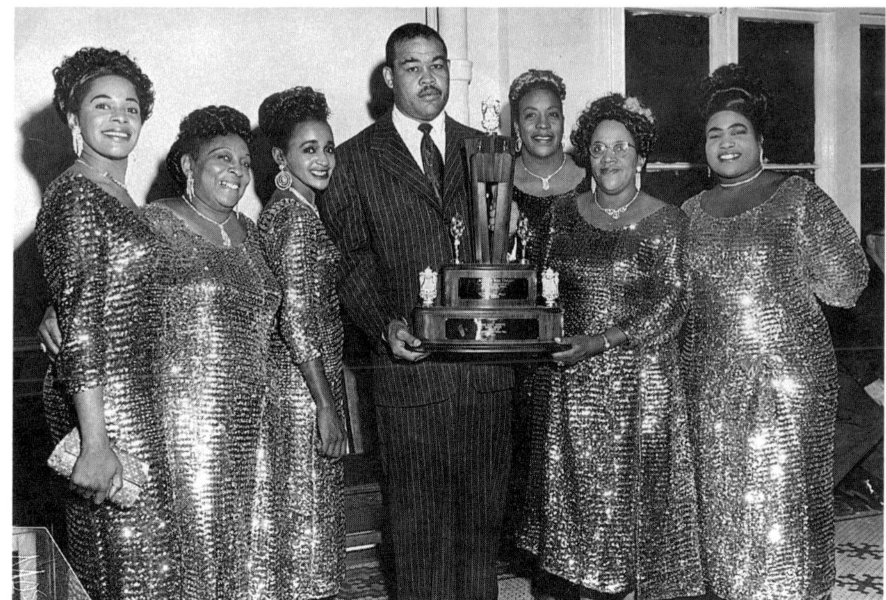

75B) Boxer Joe "Brown Bomber" Louis [Joseph Louis Barrow], former heavy weight champion, holds The Florence Mills Award given to Clara Ward (1927-1973) (third from left) and her Gospel Singers, which include her sister Willa Ward (far left), winners of the Courier Theatrical Poll, 1953.

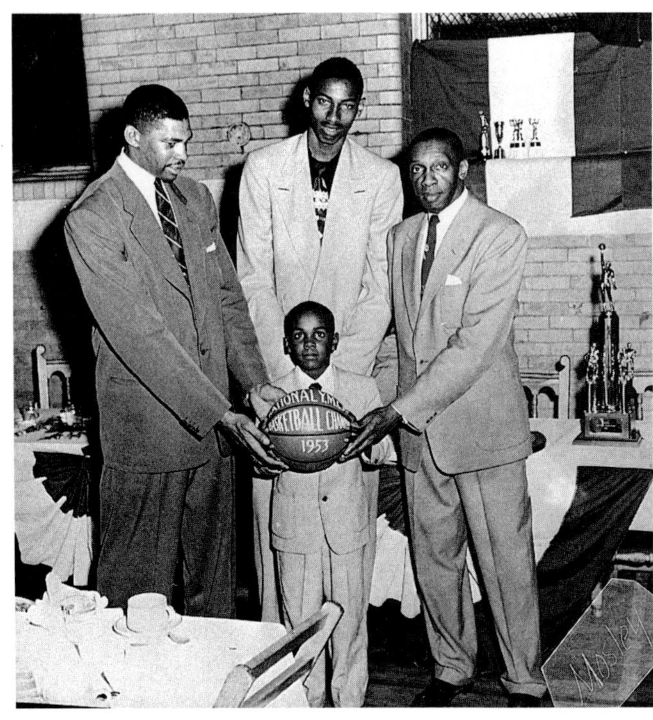

76A) Wilton Norman "Wilt the Stilt" Chamberlain, former professional basketball star, and others pose for Christian Street YMCA, the National YMCA Basketball Champions, 1953.

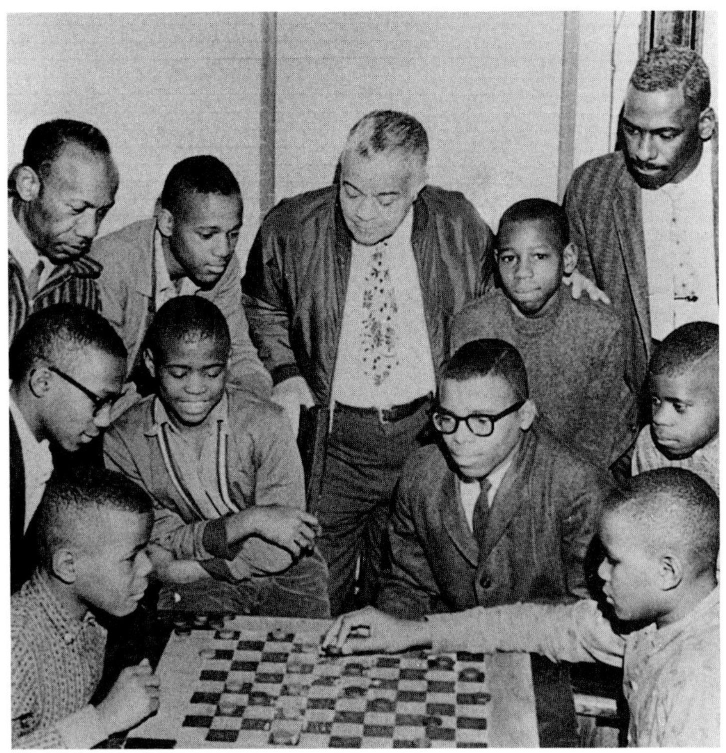

76B) A friendly game of checkers, 1950s.

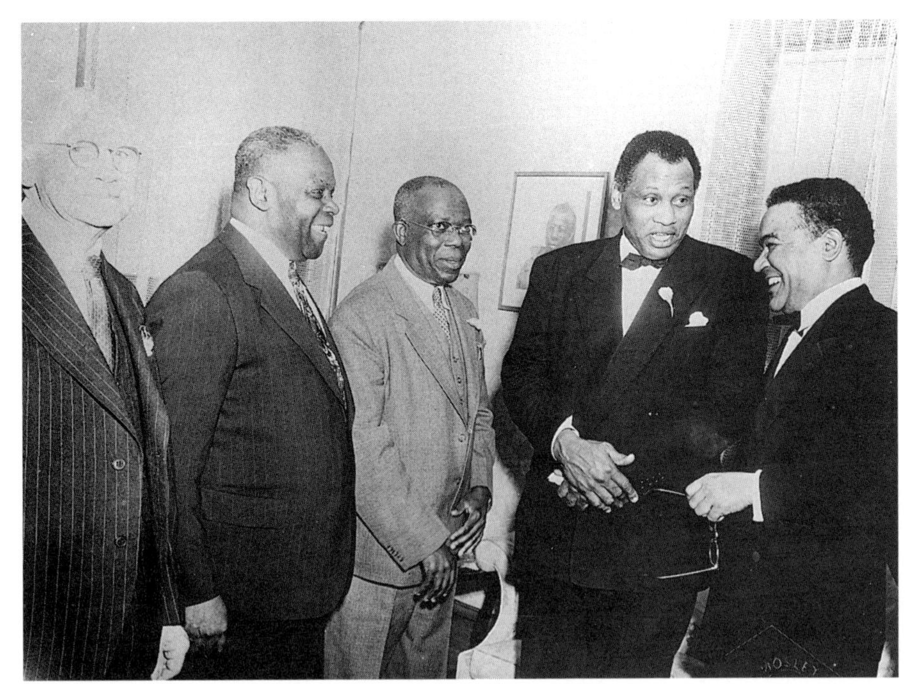

77A) Paul L. Robeson (fourth from left) chats with Dr. Horace Mann Bond (far right), first Black President of Lincoln University (1945-1957), Dr. Walter F. Jerrick (third from left), President of the Pyramid Club and others, late 1940s.

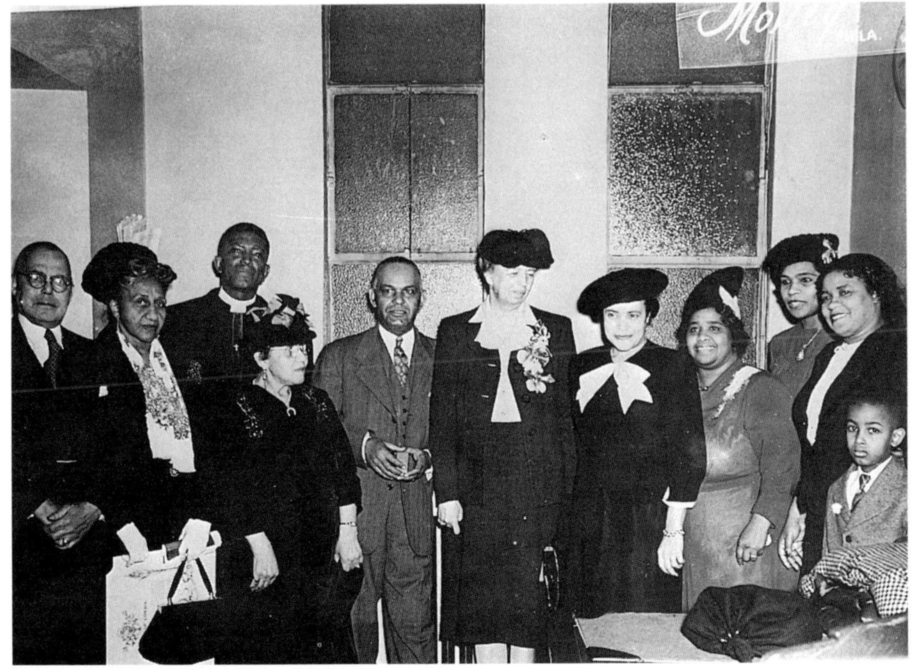

77B) Mrs. Eleanor Roosevelt (1884-1962) (sixth from left), wife of President Franklin D. Roosevelt (1882-1945), greeted by Mrs. Crystal Bird Fauset (seventh from left), Marian Anderson (ninth from left), Dr. Horace C. Scott (far left), Bishop David H. Sims (third from left) and others, 1944.

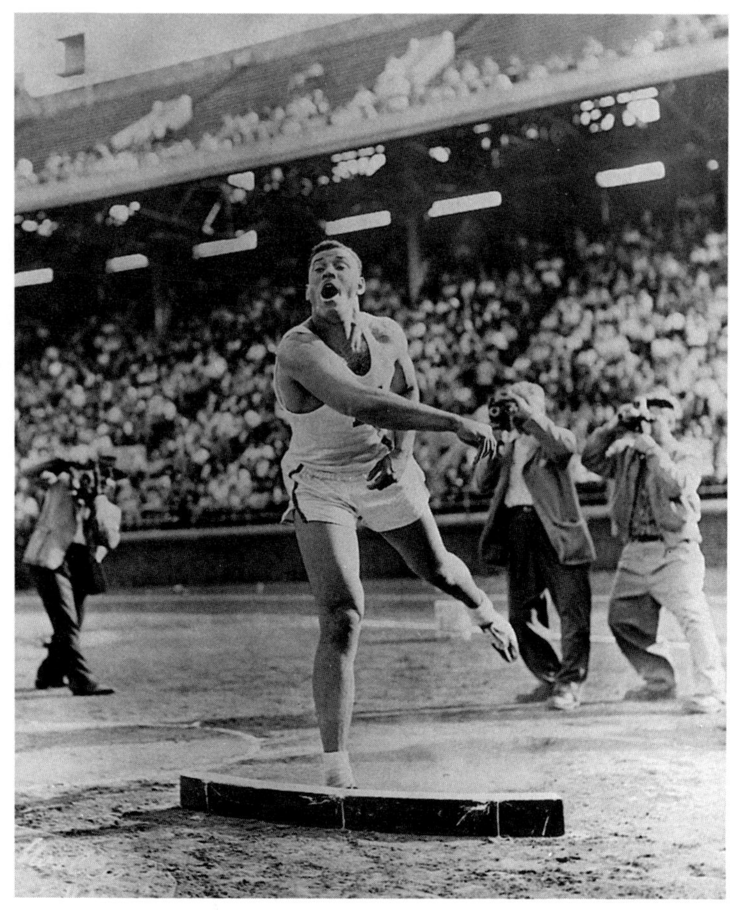

78A) Kenneth O. Bantum, Manhattan College, in the Shot Put competition at the Penn Relays, 1955.

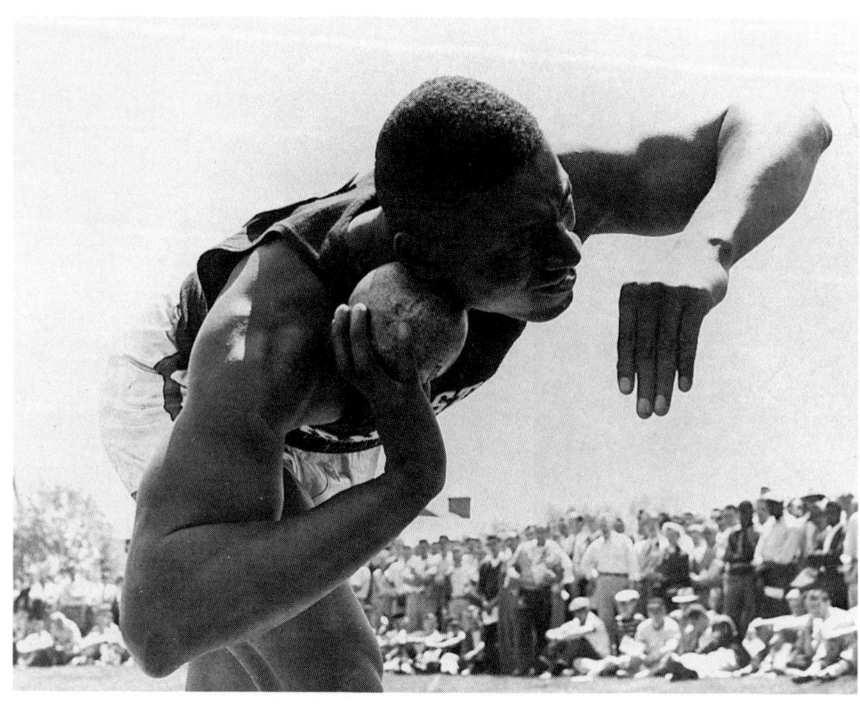

78B) Charles L. Blockson, Penn State, currently curator of the Afro-American Collection at Temple University, ready to toss the 16 lb. shot put in the competition against his rival, Bantum, 1955.

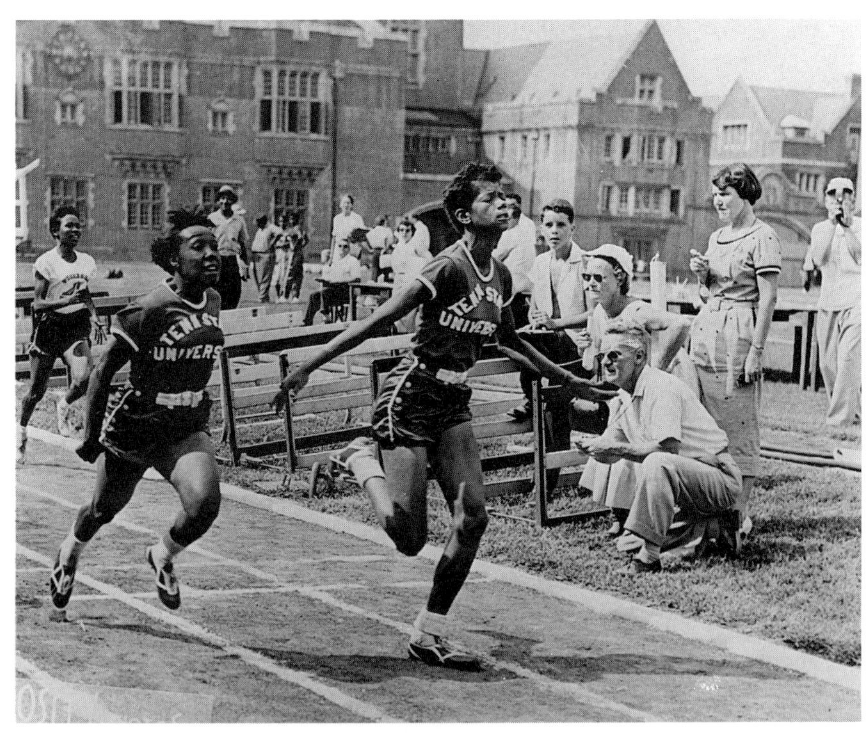

79A) Wilma Glodean Ward "Skeeter" Rudolph (first, far right), former olympic champion, competes in 100-yard dash August 17, 1959. She was known as the "World's Fastest Woman."

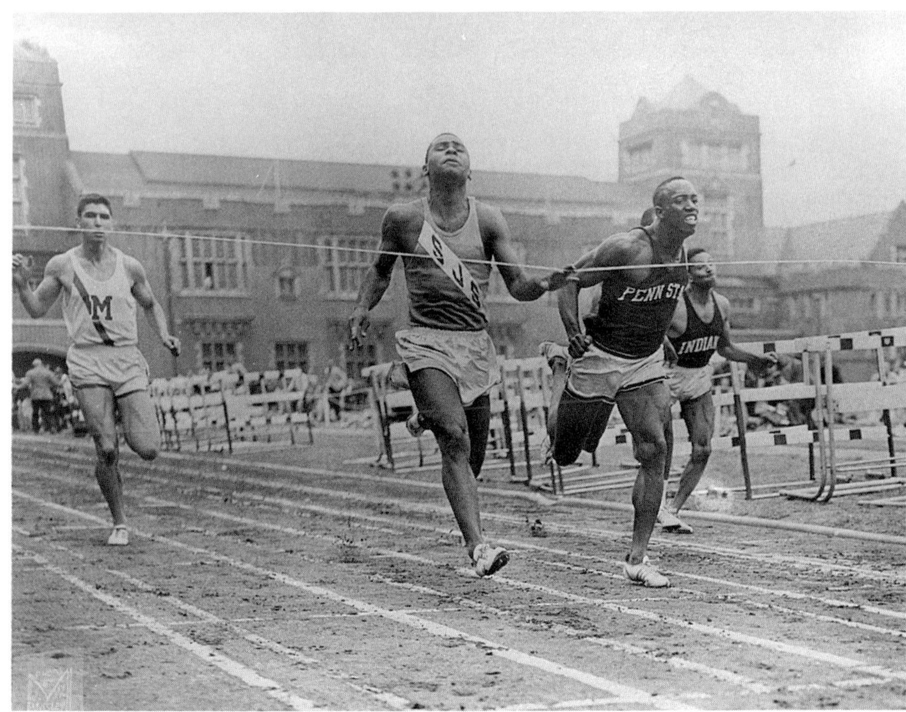

79B) Robert Brown (far right), Penn State, competes in the 100 yard dash in Penn Relays, 1960.

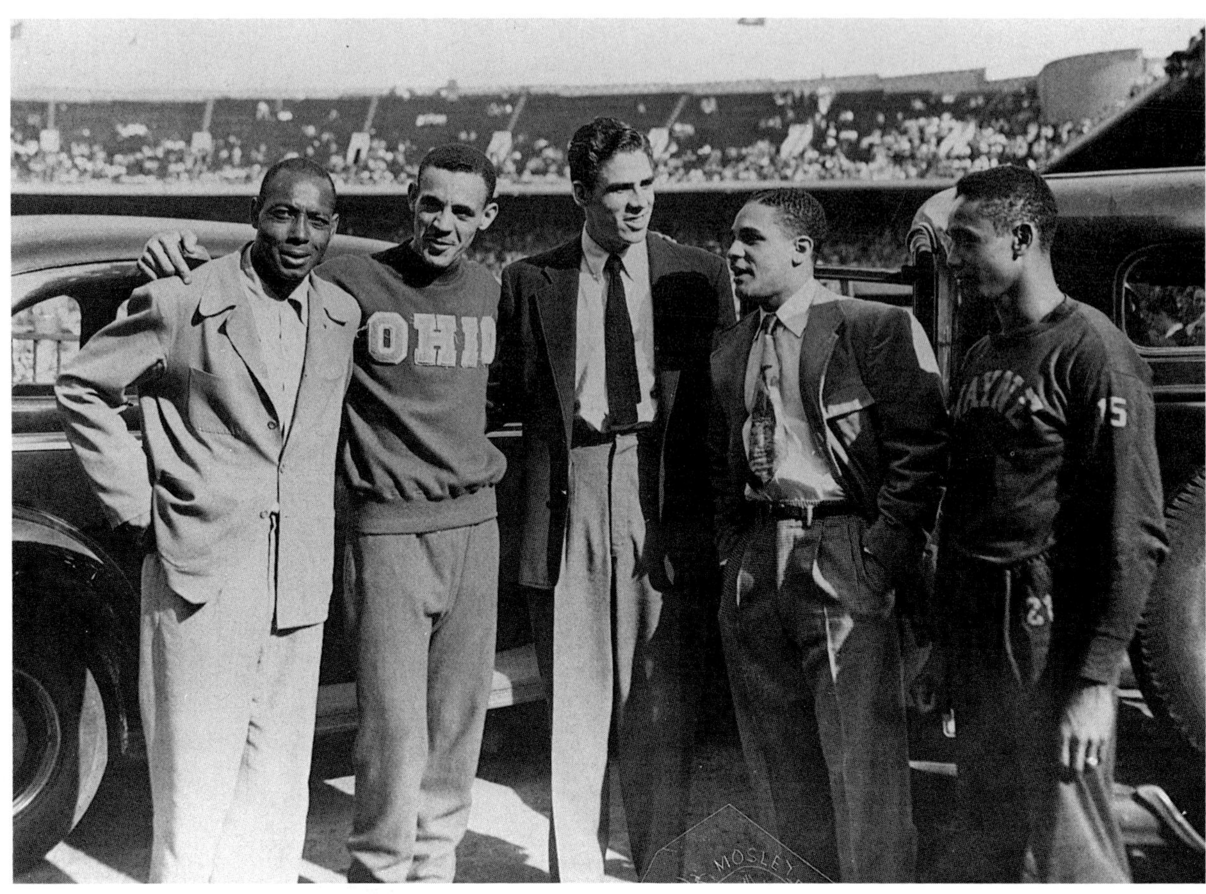

80) Olympian Track and Field Stars, (from left to right) Barney Ewell, Mel Whitfield, Ed Conwell and Lorenzo Wright at Penn Relays, early 1950s.

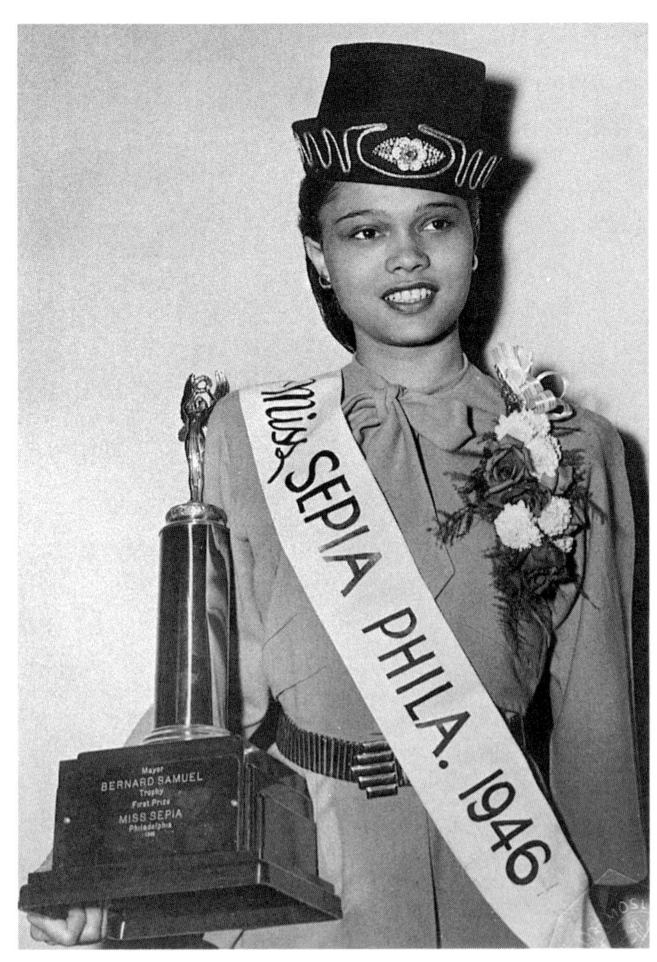

81A) Miss Sepia, the First Prize Winner, 1946.

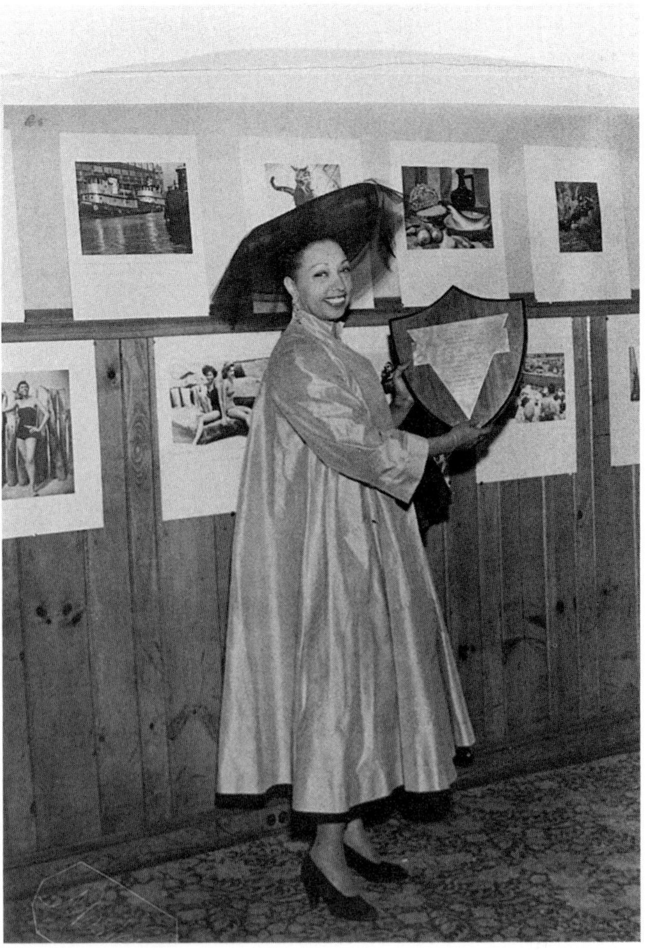

81B) Josephine Baker (1906-1975), dancer and entertainer, receives Emblem Club YMCA Award, 1950s.

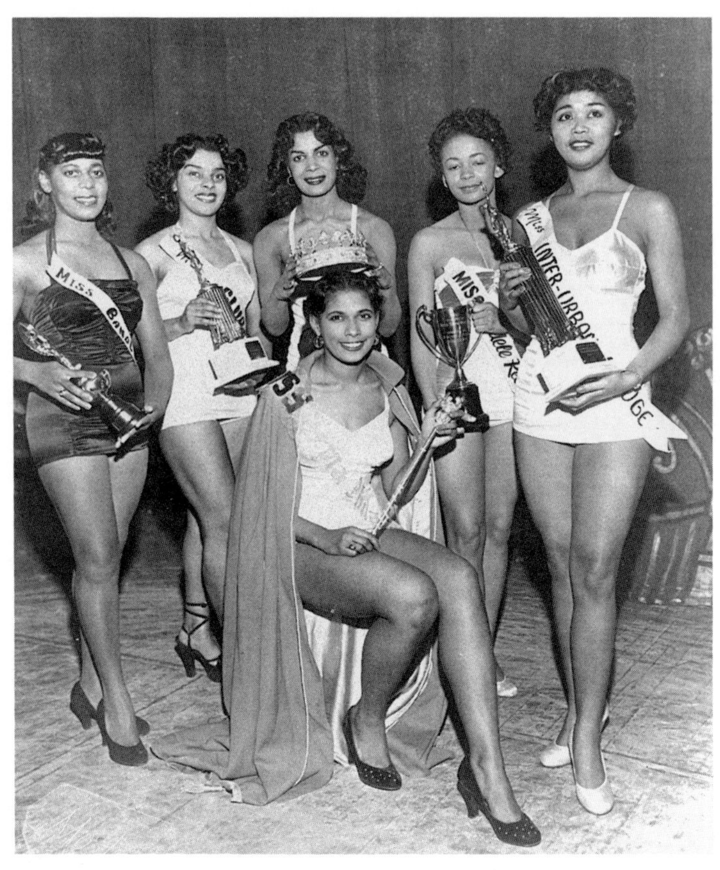

82A) Gladys Crompton (sitting), Miss Sepia 1951, crowned by Mrs. Betty Fletcher Corbin, 1951.

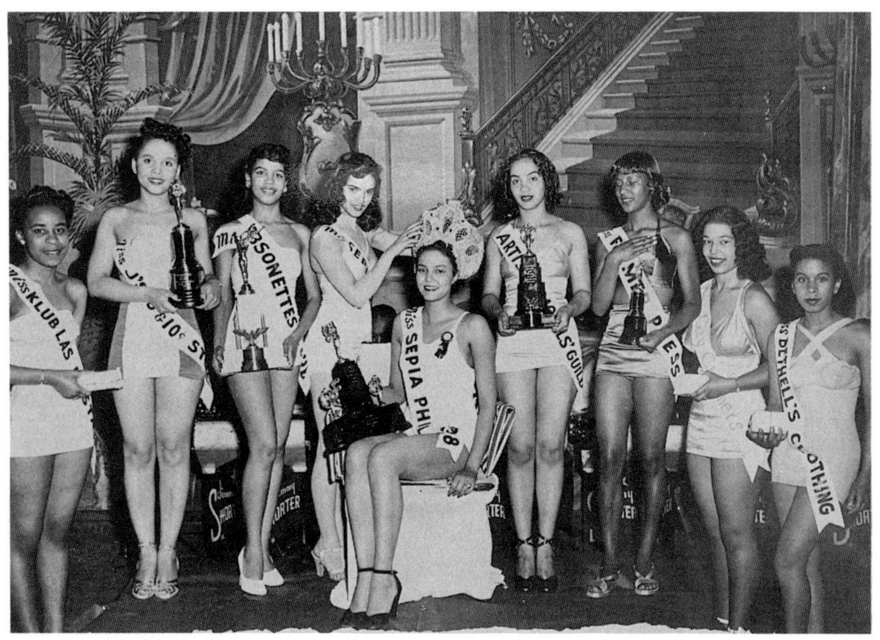

82B) Mae Madrid (center, sitting), Miss Sepia 1948, crowned by Helen Ritchie as other contestants (from left to right) Molly Mack, Grace Riggs, Barbara Carey, Barbara Frazer, Marie Caldwell, Evelyn Bell and Jackie Anderson pose for the camera, 1948.

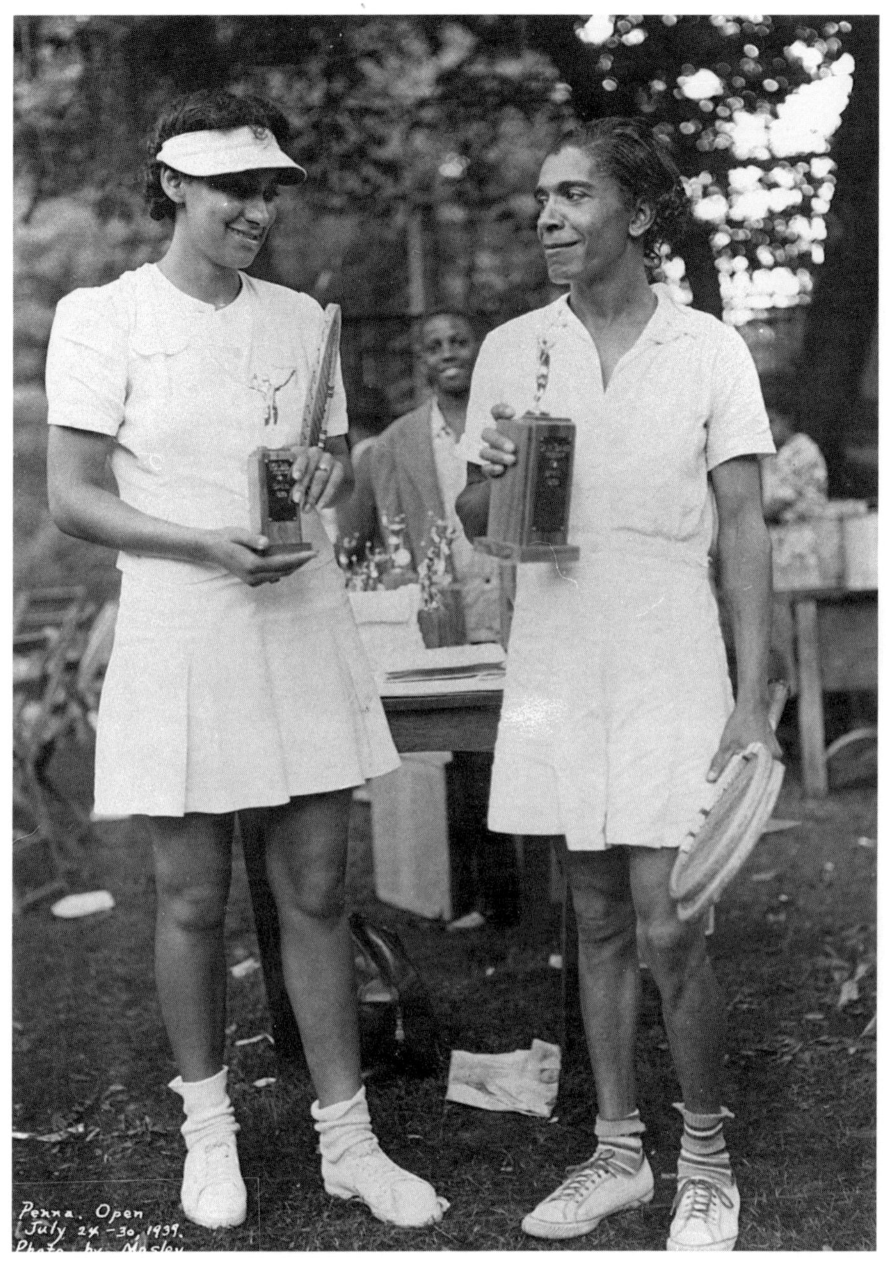

83) Ora Washington (1898-1971) (right), known as the "Queen of Tennis," holds trophy won during the Pennsylvania Opening in Philadelphia, July 24-30, 1939.

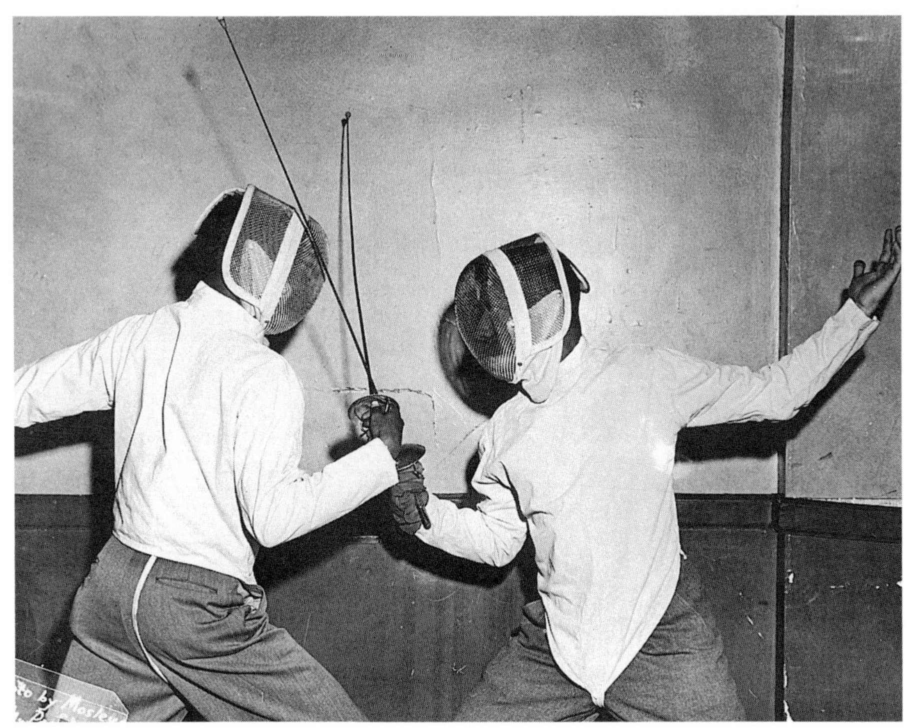

84A) Fencing - learning the art of competition, 1940s.

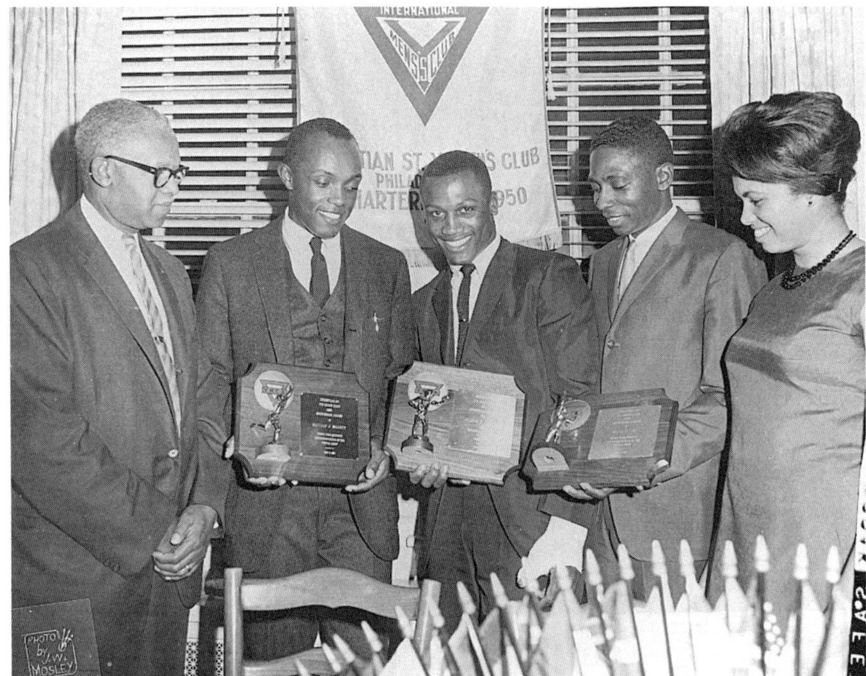

84B) Joseph "Smokin Joe" Frazier (third from left), former heavy weight boxing champion, holds award along with former Philadelphia Olympians William J. Sharpe (second from left), and Ira S. Davis(fourth from left), as Margaret Sharpe, wife of William, and others look on, 1950s.

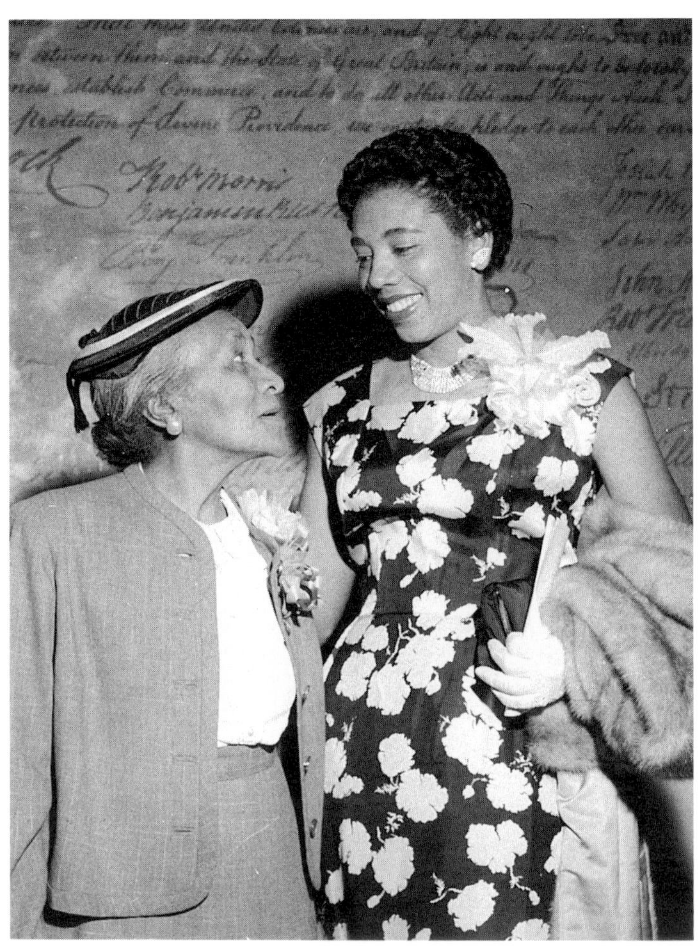

85A) Althea Gibson, tennis champion and golfer, with Mrs. Miranda Burwell at Lincoln Domes Tea, 1950's. Ms. Gibson was the first Black woman to compete in the National Tennis Championships and to win at Wimbleton.

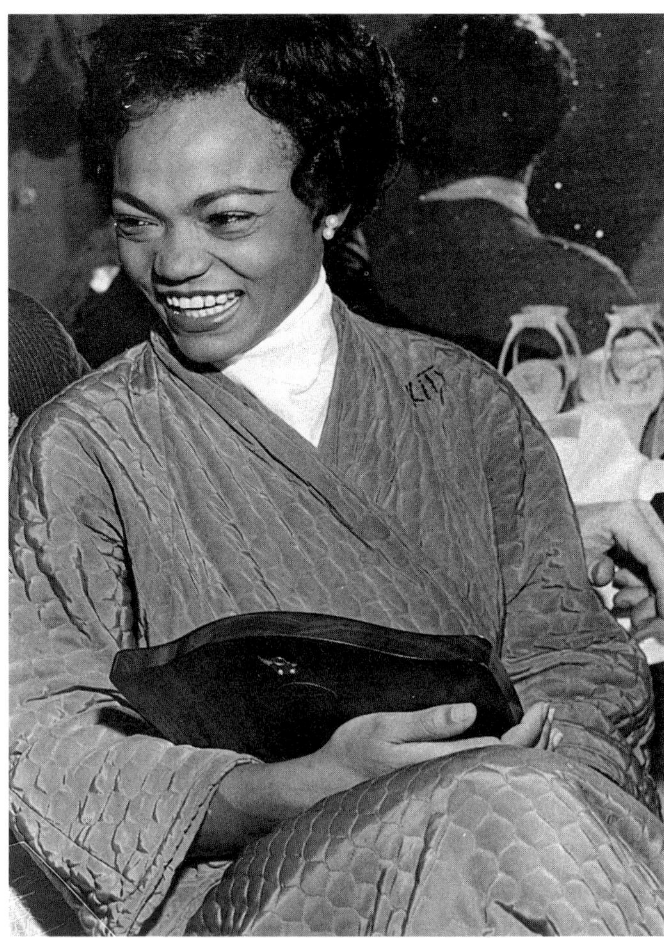

85B) Eartha Kitt, actress and singer, receives an award, late 1950s.

KEEPING THE FAITH

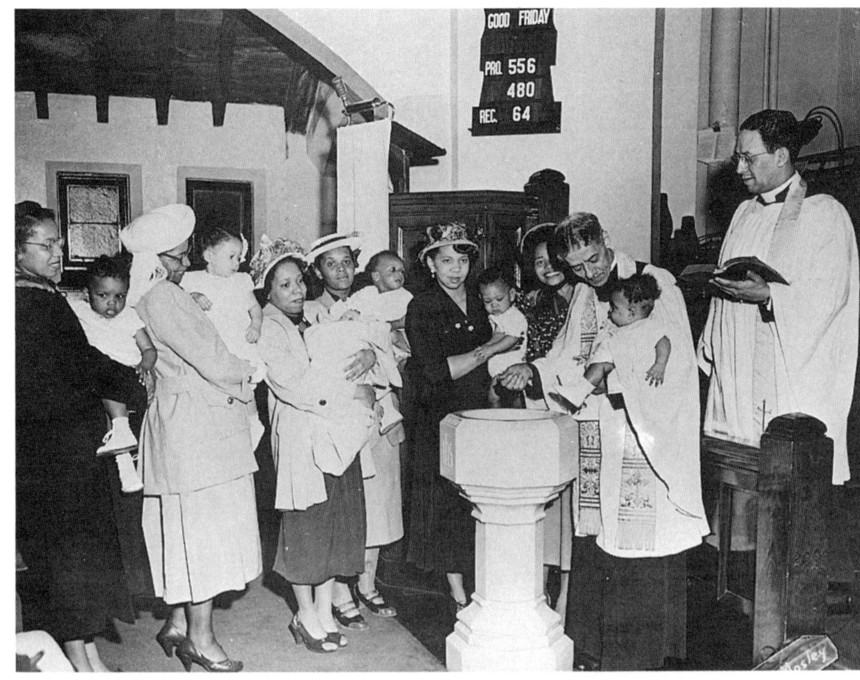

87A) Father John Richard Logan, Sr., D.D., pastor of St. Simon the Cyrenian, 22nd and Reed Streets, baptizes babies while Father John R. Logan, Jr. reads Bible passage, 1943.

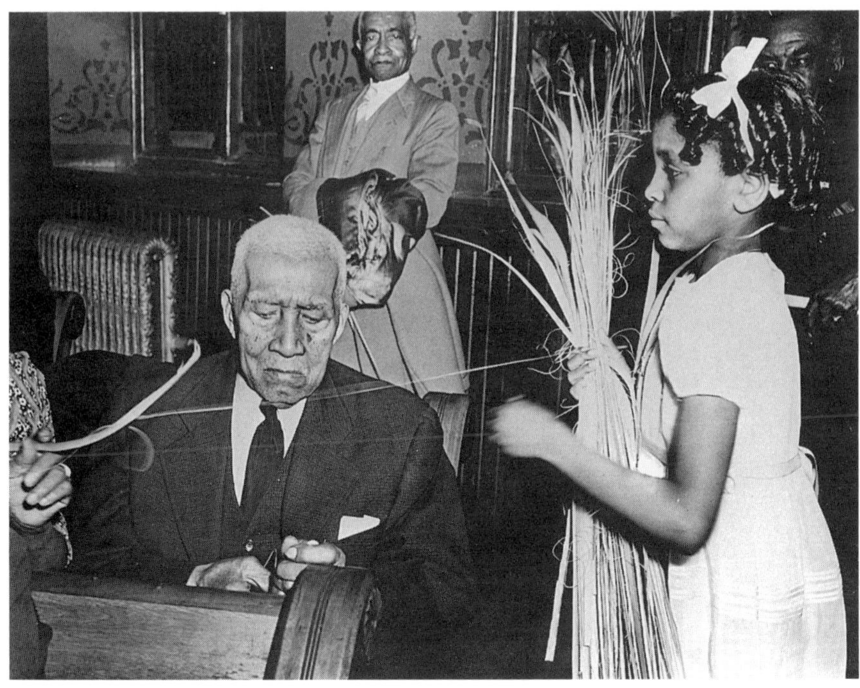

87B) Linking the past and future through the present, 1940s.

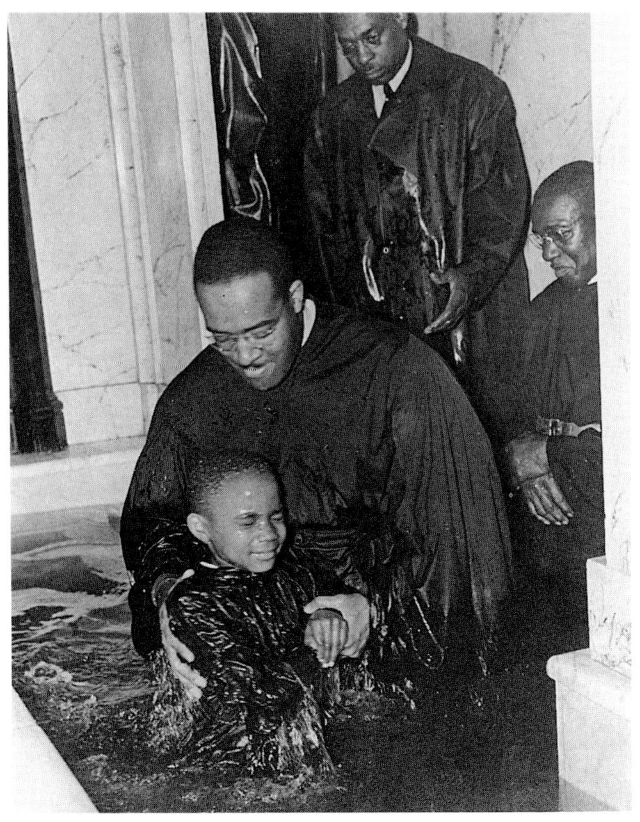

88A) The Reverend E. Luther Cunningham, Pastor of St. Paul Baptist Church, 10th and Wallace Streets, baptizes one of more than thirty followers baptized during this ceremony, January 1940.

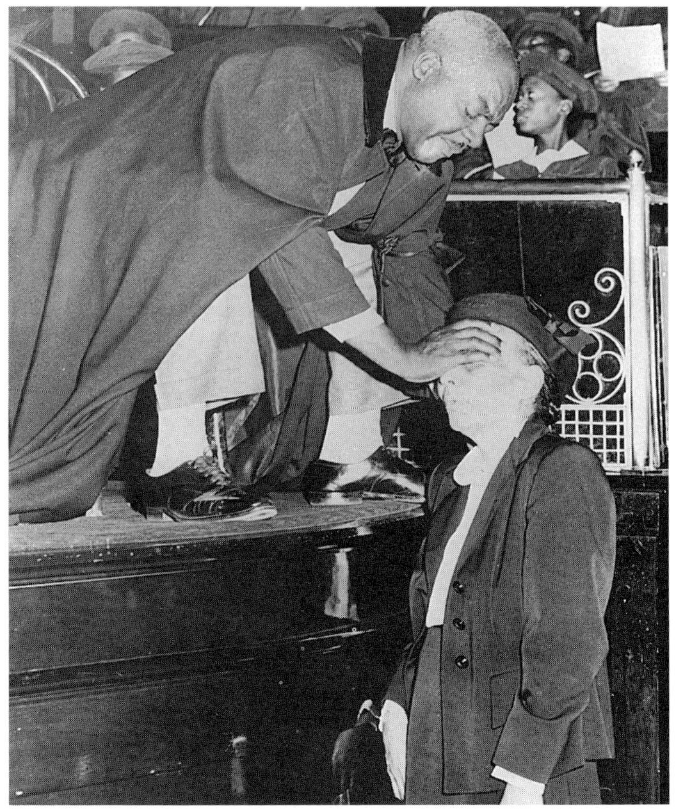

88B) Bishop S.C. Johnson, apostle and general overseer of Church of the Lord Jesus Christ, 22nd and Bainbridge Streets, spiritually heals his follower, early 1940s.

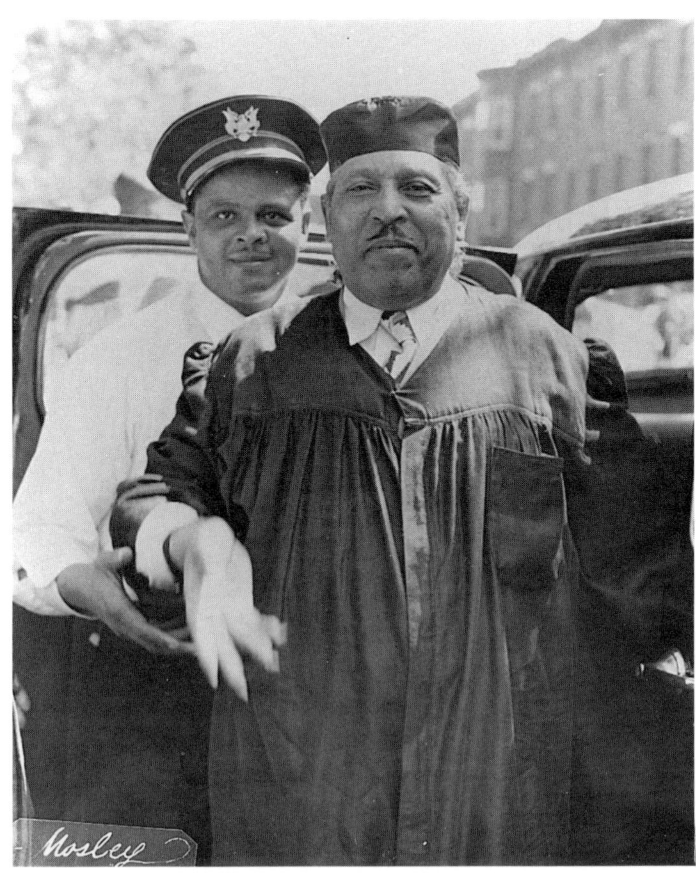

89A) Bishop Charles Manuel "Sweet Daddy" Grace (1882-1960) (right), founder of the House of Prayer for All People, visits South Philadelphia, August 18, 1946.

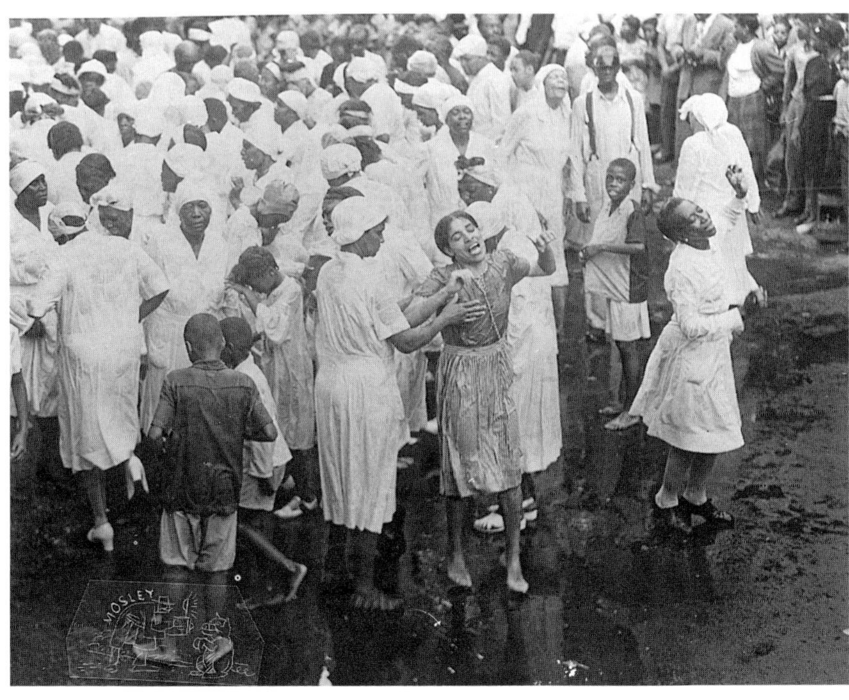

89B) Followers of Bishop Grace during mass baptism at 16th and Christian Streets in South Philadelphia, August 18, 1946.

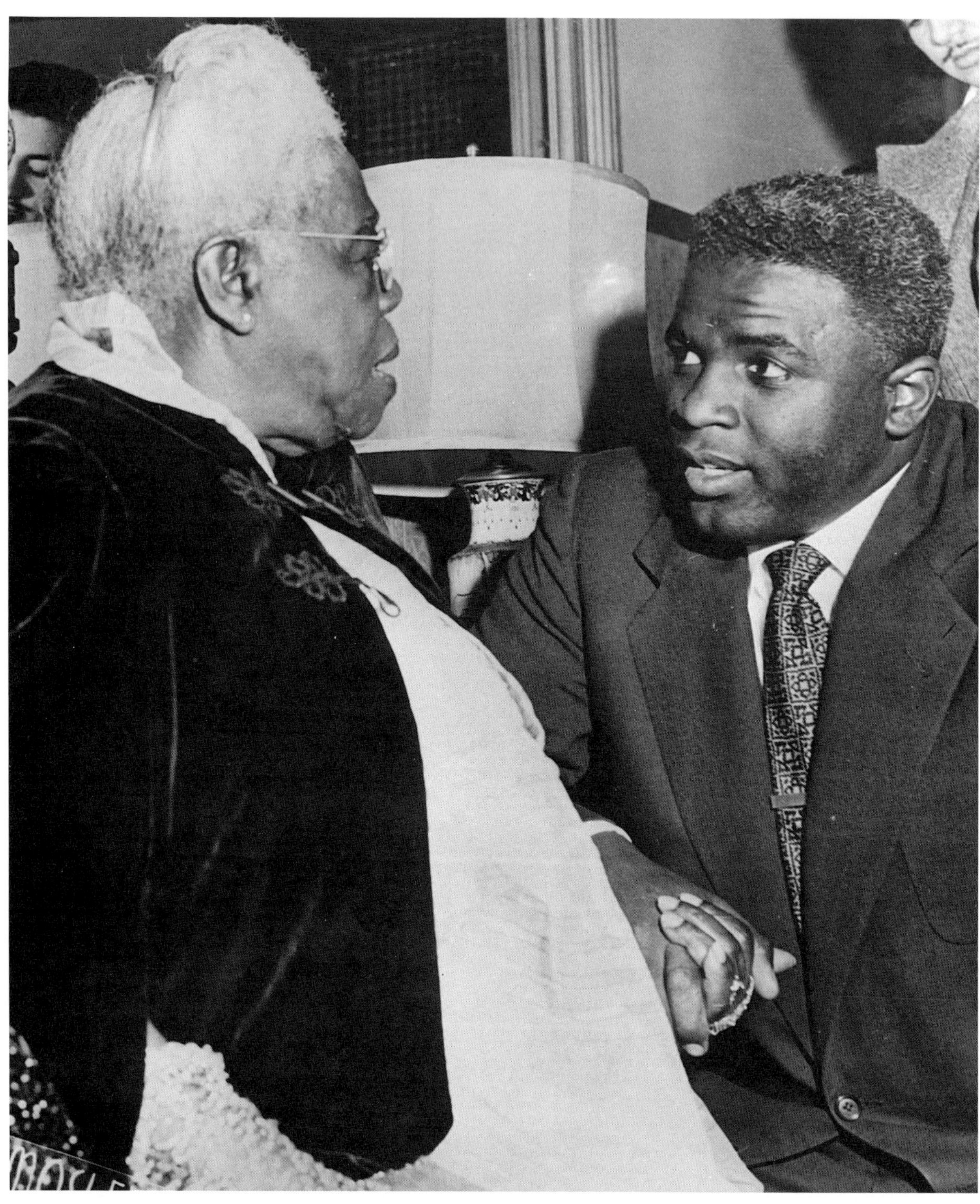

90) Dr. Mary McLeod Bethune (1875-1955)
and Jackie Robinson, 1955.

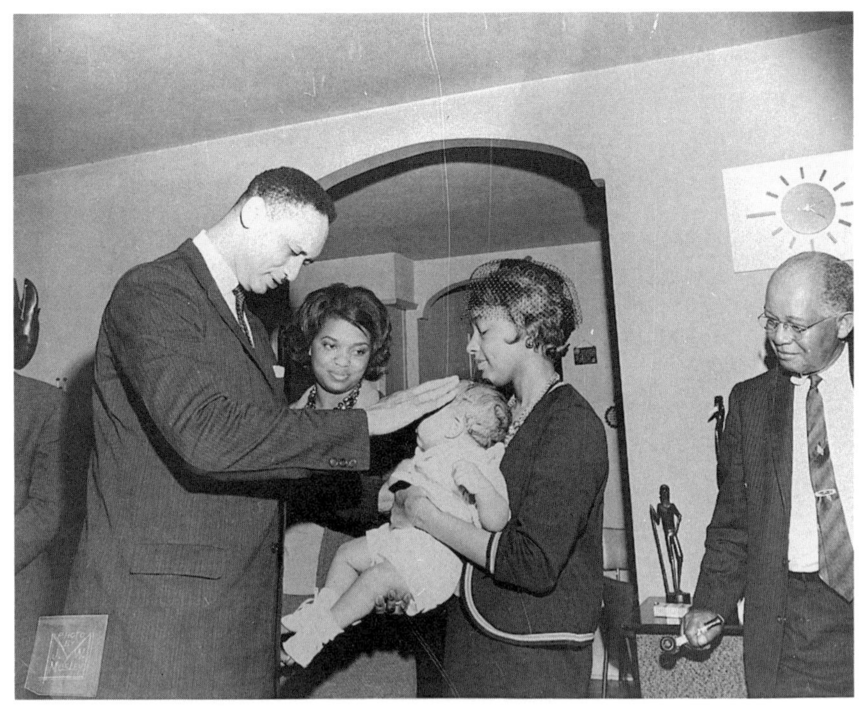

91A) The Reverend Leon H. Sullivan, pastor of Zion Baptist Church, Broad and Venango Streets, blesses a child, 1950s.

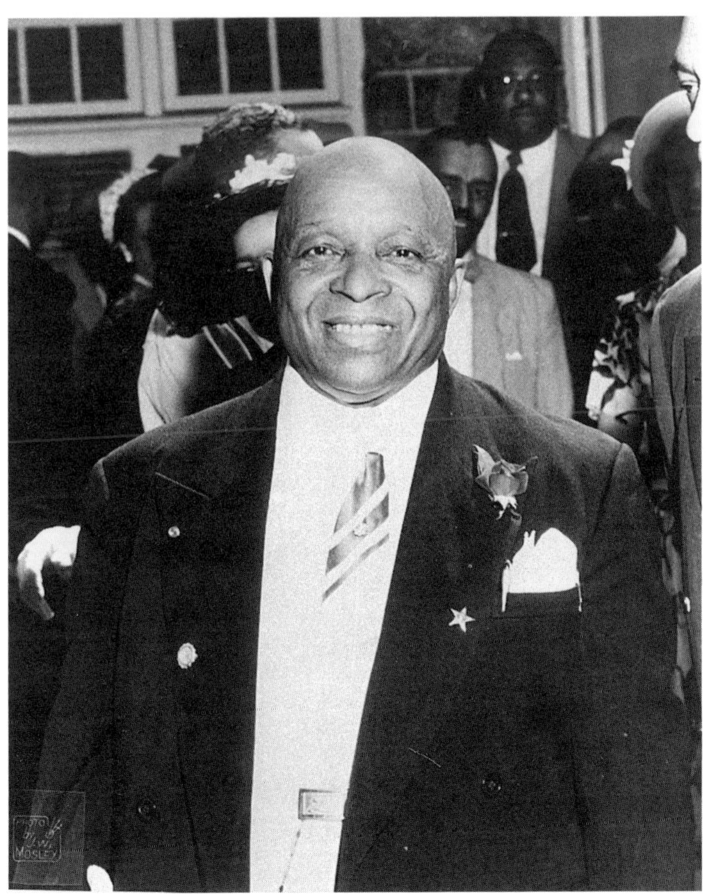

91B) Father Divine (1880-1965), leader and founder of the Peace Mission Movement, 1940s.

CLAIMING THE DREAM

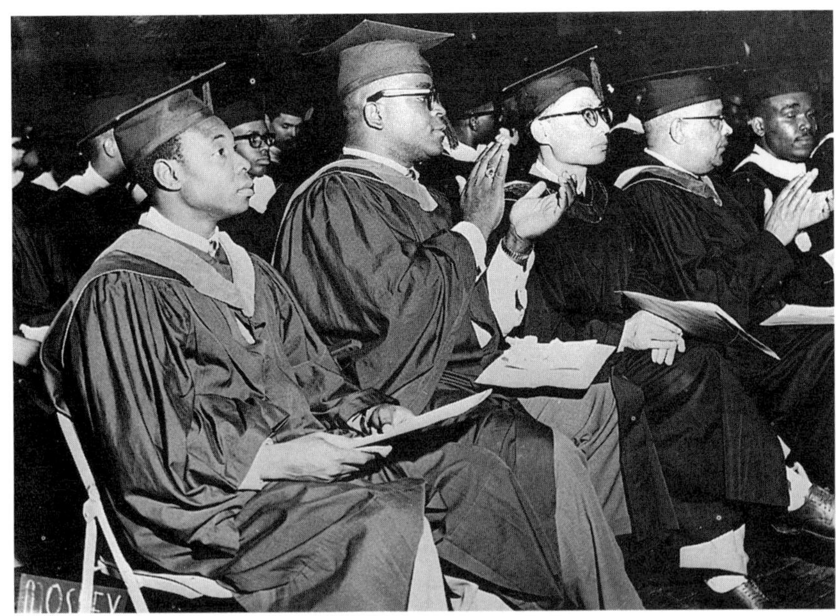

92A) The three final graduates of the Lincoln University Seminary (from left to right): Enoch Abenoyap Esian, Cameron, West Africa; Arthur Joshua Honore, Philadelphia, PA, and Hee-Bo Kim, Seoul, Korea, June 2, 1959.

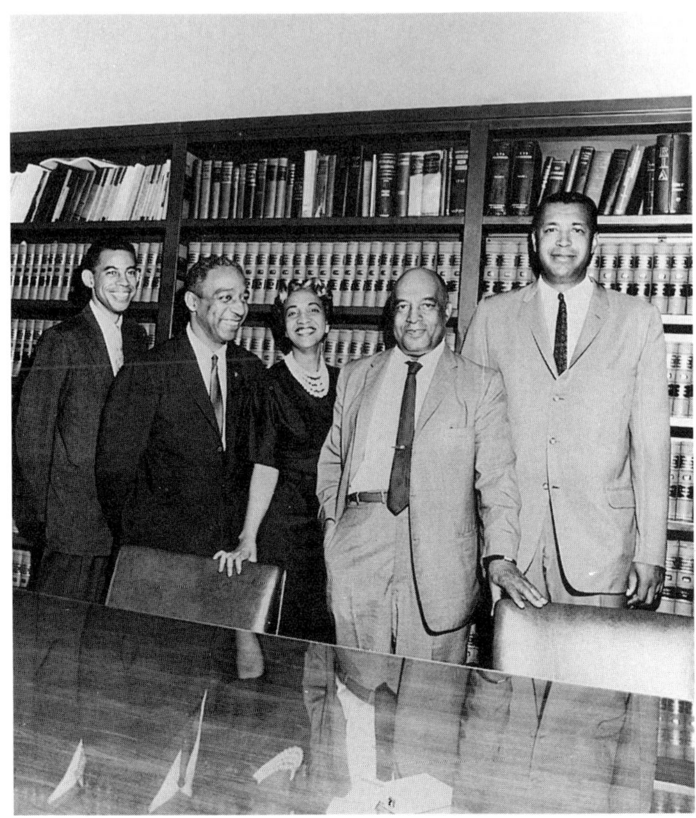

92B) William Brown, Clifford S. Greene, Doris Harris, Austin Norris (fourth from left), first Black member of the Philadelphia Board of Revision of Taxes, and Attorney A. Leon Higginbotham (far right), 1960s.

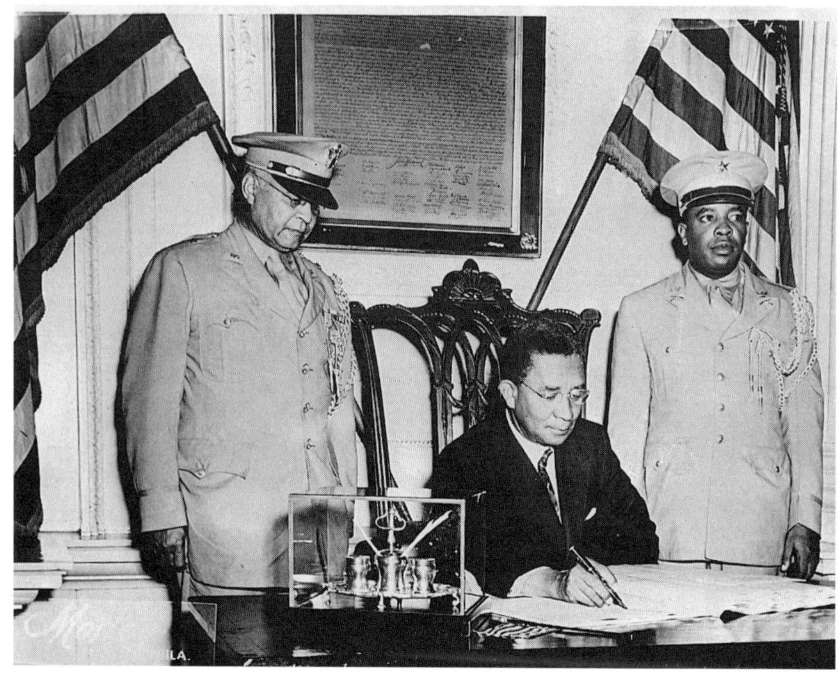

93A) Brigadier General Benjamin O. Davis, Sr. (1877-1970) (left), first Black General, U.S. Army, watches Liberian President Edwin Barclay (center) sign the visitor's register at Independence Hall as Military Aide and Captain Russ looks on, June 3, 1943.

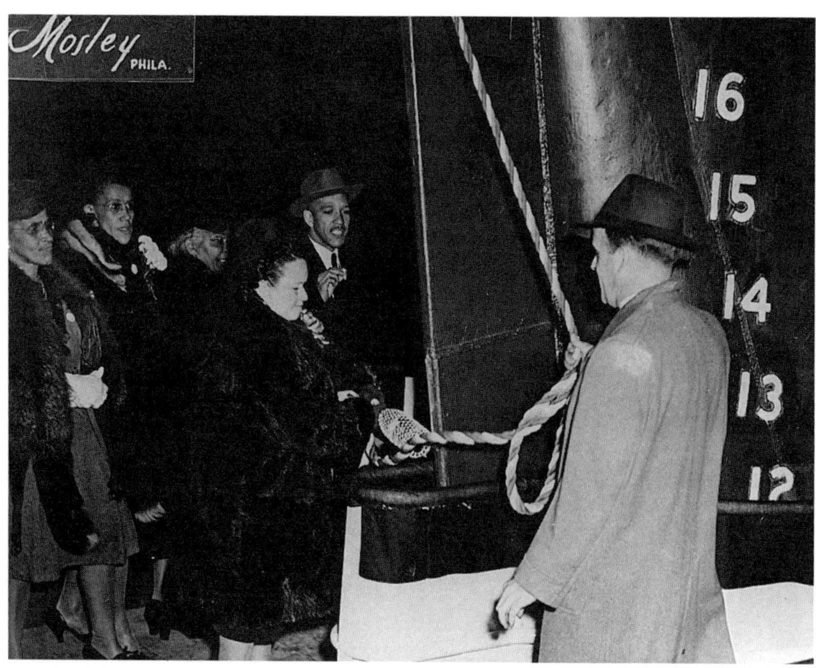

93B) The Christening of the liberty ship, Marine Eagle, the first all-Negro constructed vessel at Sun Shipbuilding Company, 1943.

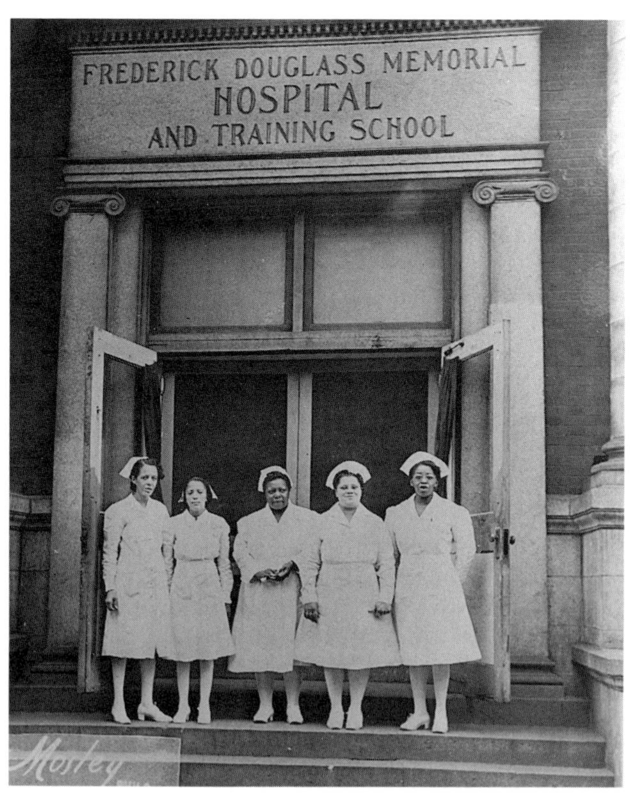

94A) Nurses stand in front of the Frederick Douglass Memorial Hospital and Training School, 1530-34 Lombard Street, organized in 1895 by Dr. Nathan F. Mossell, the first African American to graduate from the University of Pennsylvania Medical School, 1943.

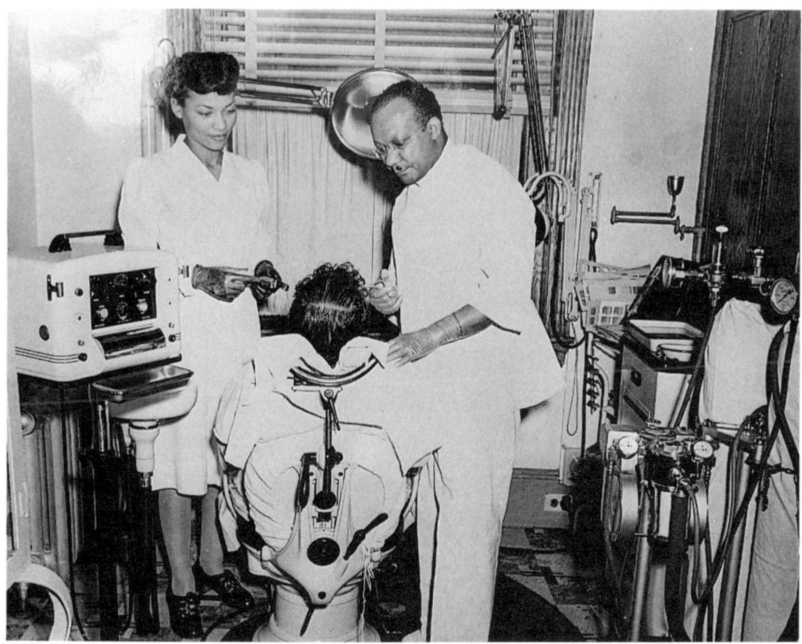

94B) Dr. John W. Sullivan examines patient as assistant watches in his oral surgery operating room at 1447 North 17th Street, 1944

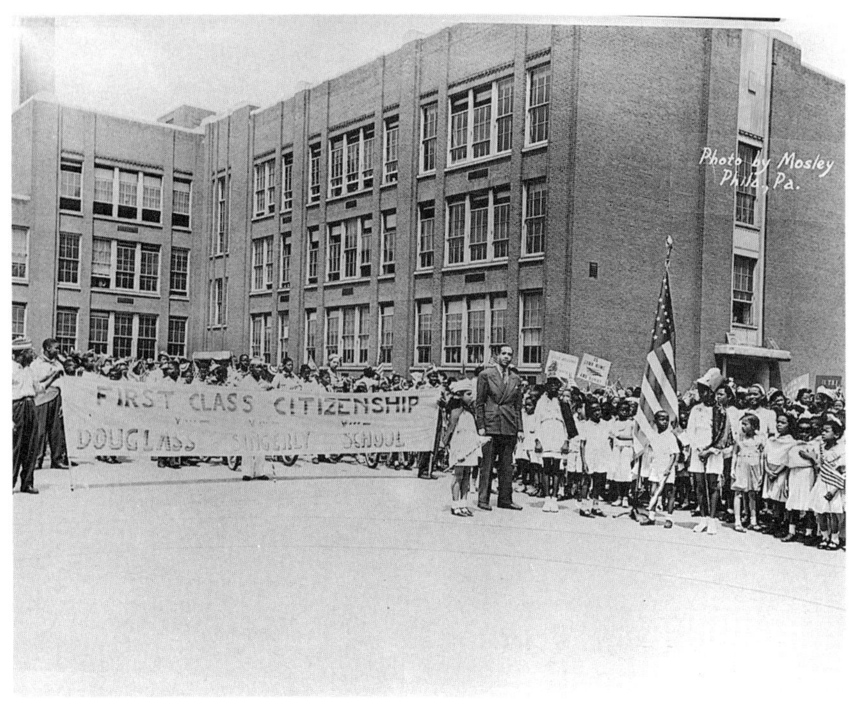

95A) Dr. Arthur Huff Fauset, author, anthropologist, civil rights activist, and former principal of Douglas Singerly School, 1904 W. Norris Street with students during May Day Celebration, 1944.

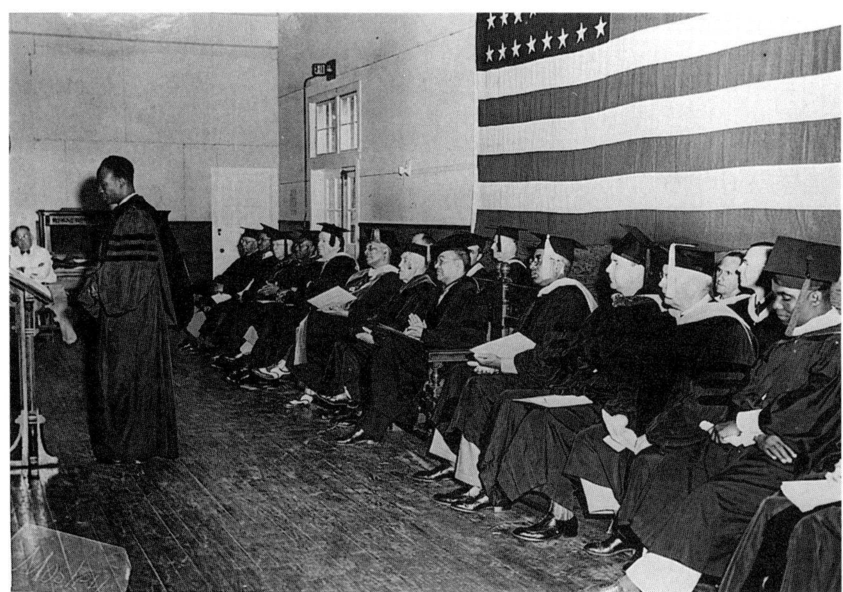

95B) Alumnus Kwame Nkrumah speaks during Lincoln University Commencement Exercise, 1940s.

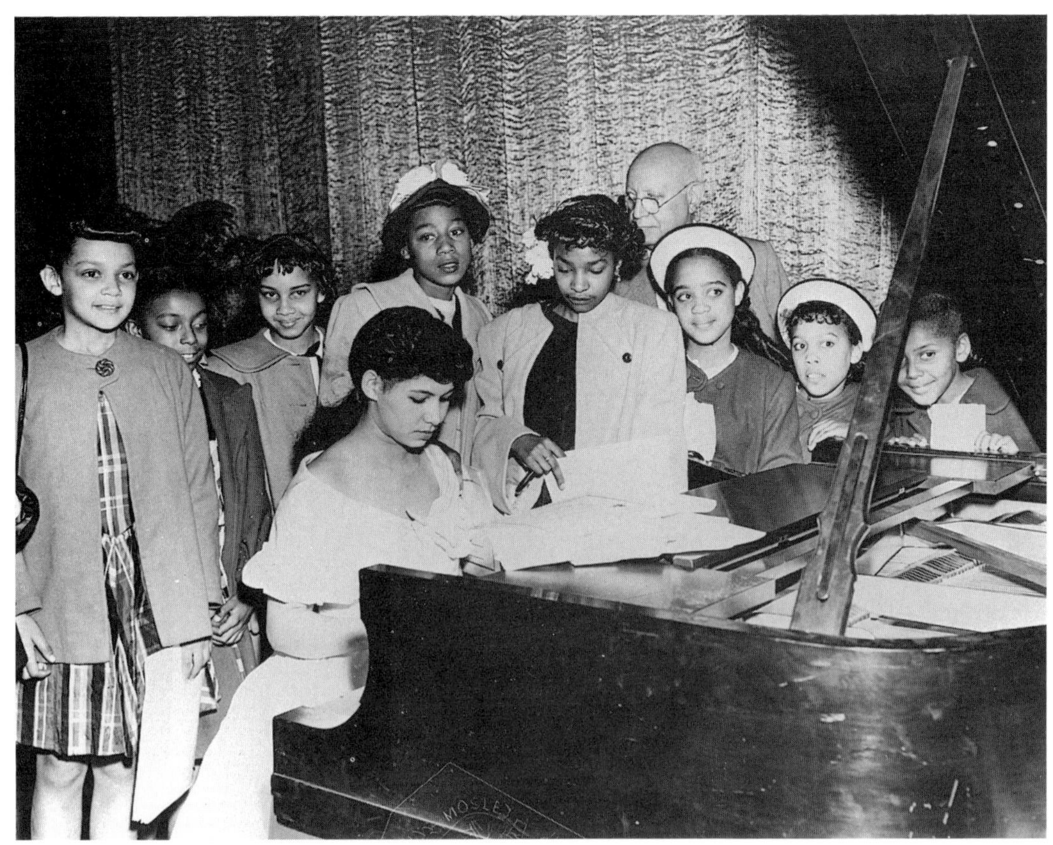

96) Philippa Duke Schuyler (1931-1967), child prodigy, composer, writer, editor, and concert pianist, the daughter of Josephine Schuyler, impresario and business manager, and George S. Schuyler (1895-1977), journalist, plays for her fans, 1950s. Ms. Schuyler died in a helicopter crash while she was a newspaper correspondent in Vietnam.

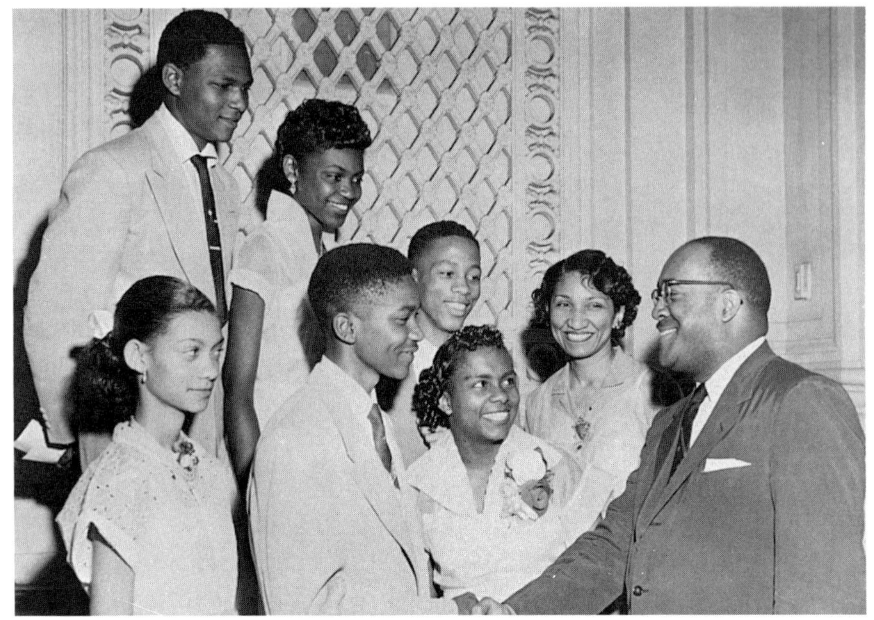

97A) McCoy Tyner (second row, far left), jazz pianist, watches Reverend E. Luther Cunningham congratulate Sam Thomas, a classmate, during Mayer Sulzberger Junior High School's Closing Exercise at School Auditorium, 48th and Fairmount Avenue, as (from left to right) (first row) Betty Burgess and Verdie Beasley; (second row) Dianna Hardy, Ronald Arnold and Dr. Marechal-Neil E. Young, Principal, look on, June 24, 1953.

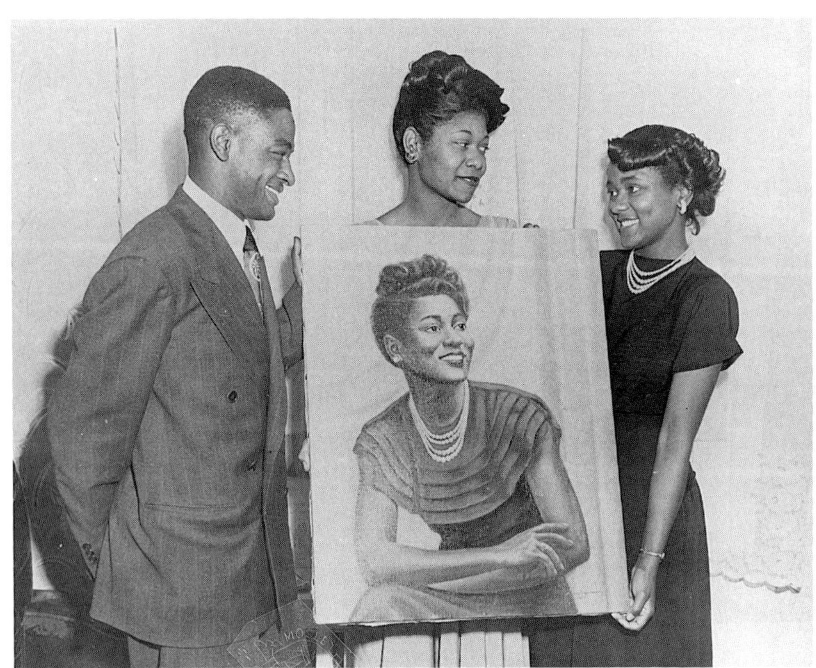

97B) Barbara Chase-Riboud (right), internationally known sculptor, writer and poet, holds portrait of her mother, Mrs. Vivian May West Chase (center) with her father, Mr. Charles Edward Chase (left), 1950s.

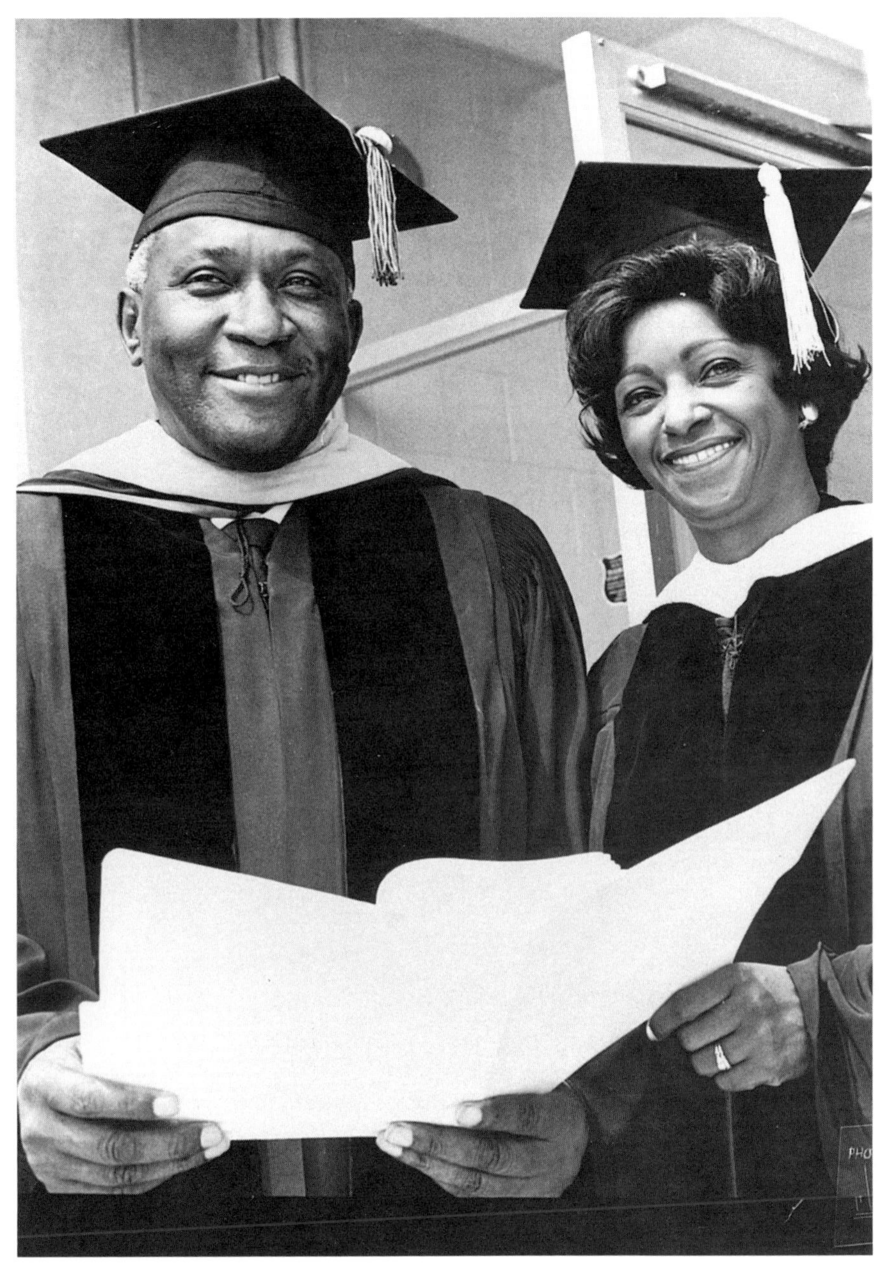

98) Dr. Wade Wilson, President of Cheyney University, during Commencement Exercises, 1960s.

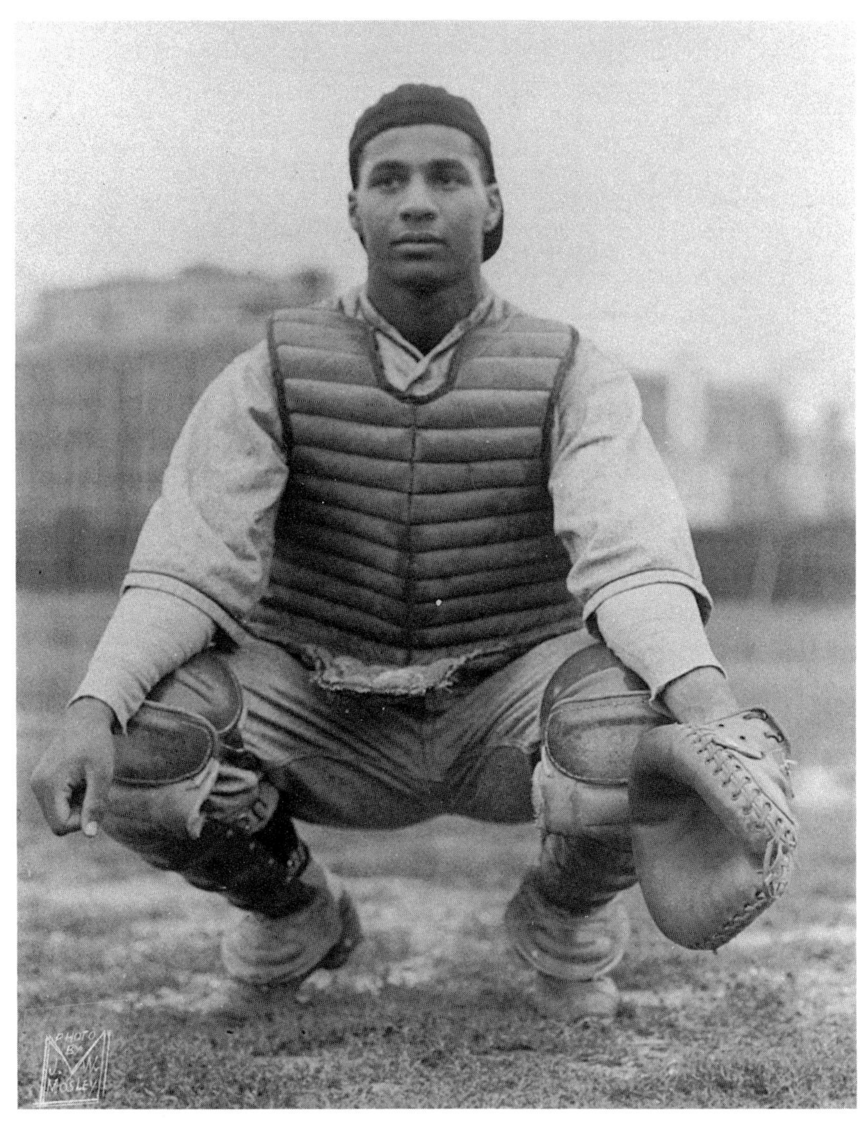

99) Roy "Campy" Campanella, former Brooklyn Dodger catcher and first Black catcher in the major leagues, late 1940s.

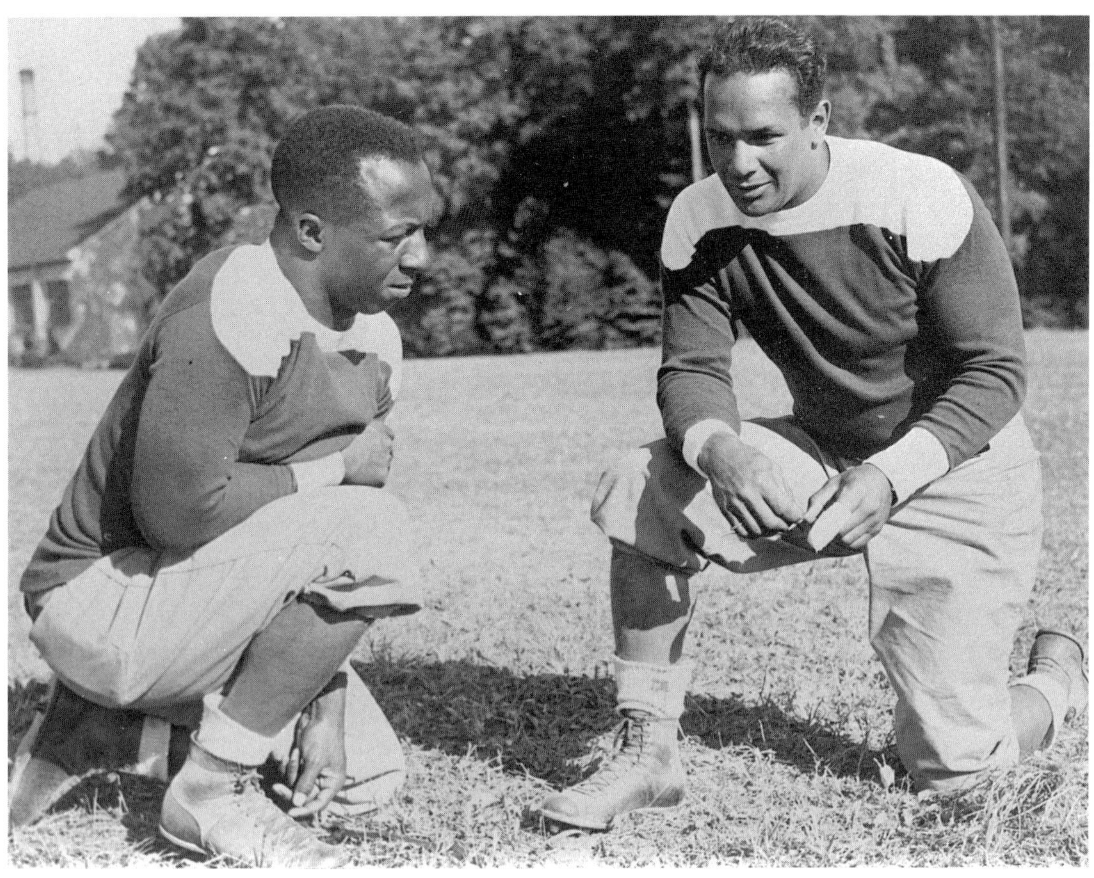

100) Dr. Jerome H. "Brud" Holland (1916-1985) (left), former Cornell All-American football player and former president of Delaware State and Hampton Universities, and Manuel "Manny" Rivero (right), Head Coach at Lincoln University, 1940.

TIME OUT FROM WAR

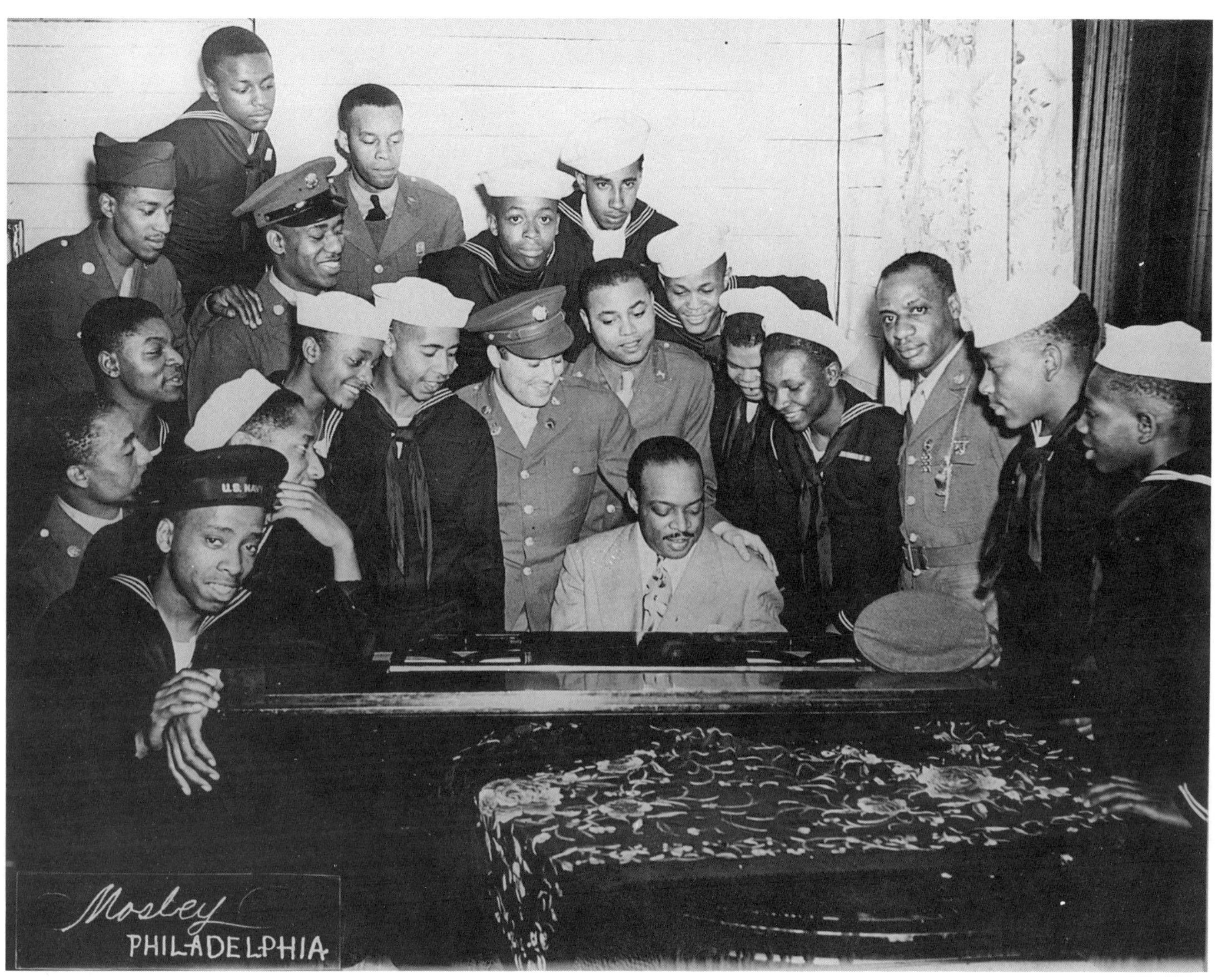

101A) William "Count Basie (1904-1984) band leader, jazz pianist and composer, performs for servicemen at the South Broad Street U.S.O., 1943.

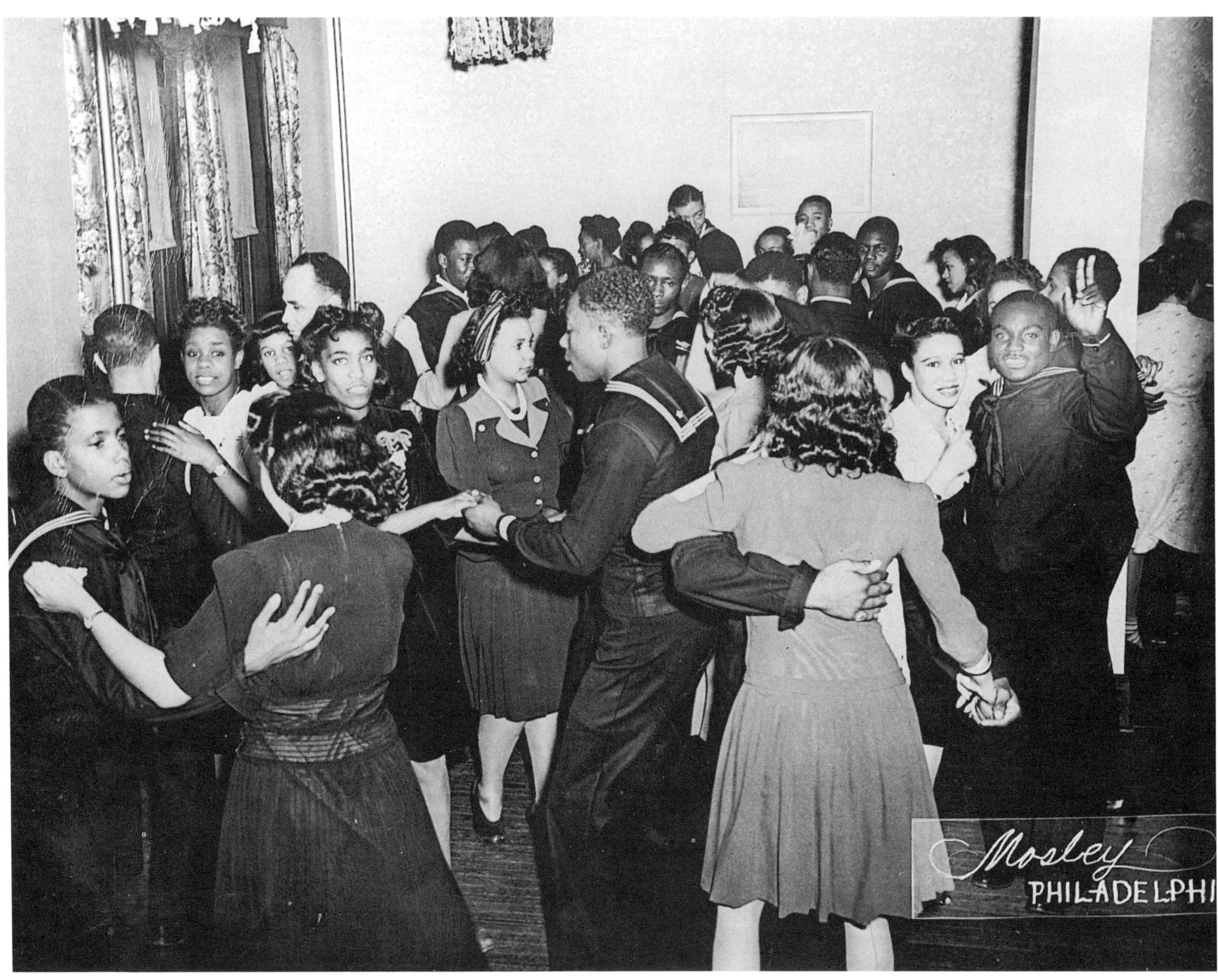

102A) Servicemen jitterbug at the Christian Street YMCA, early 1940s.

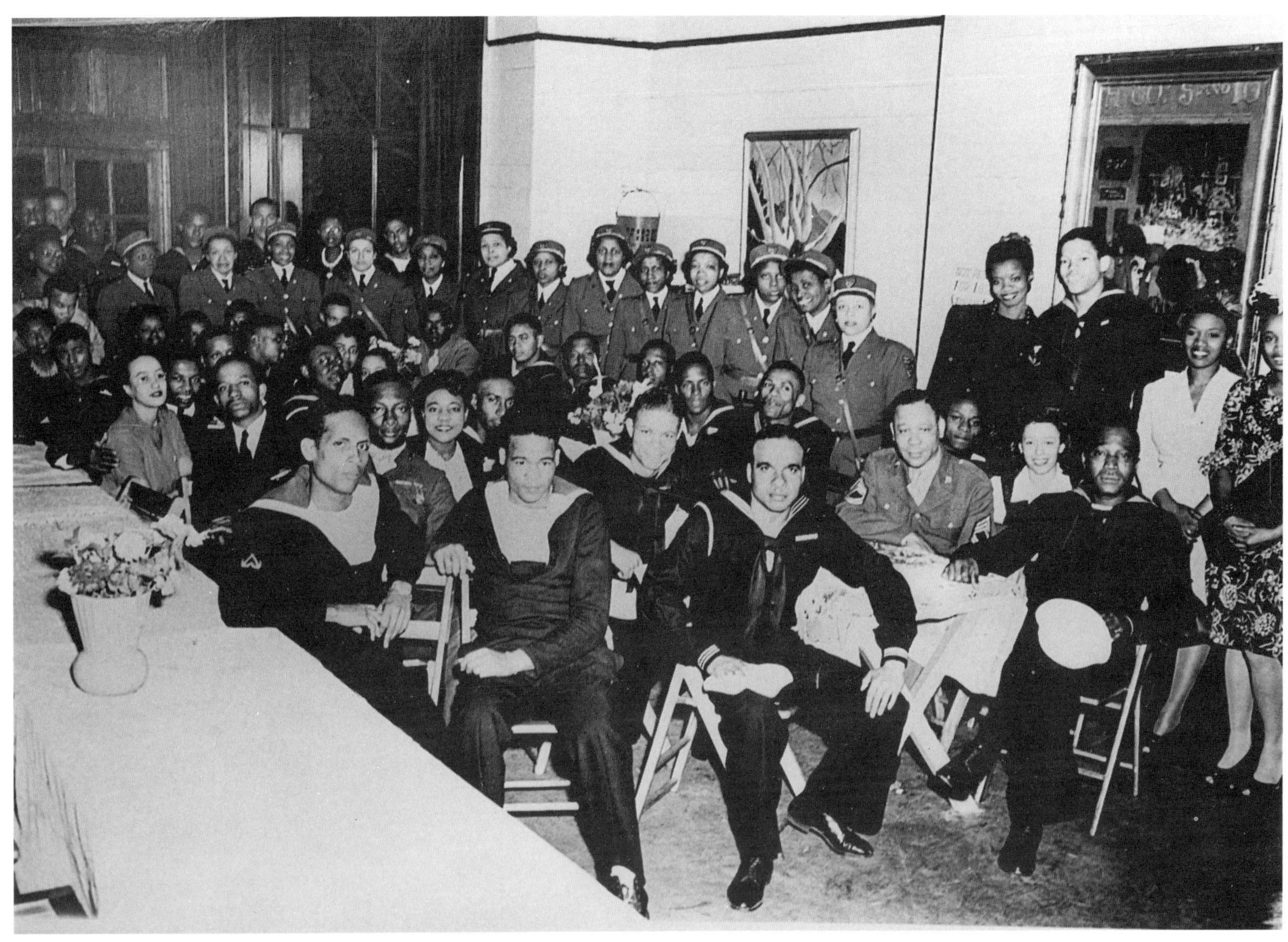

102B) Party at the South Broad Street U.S.O., early 1940s.

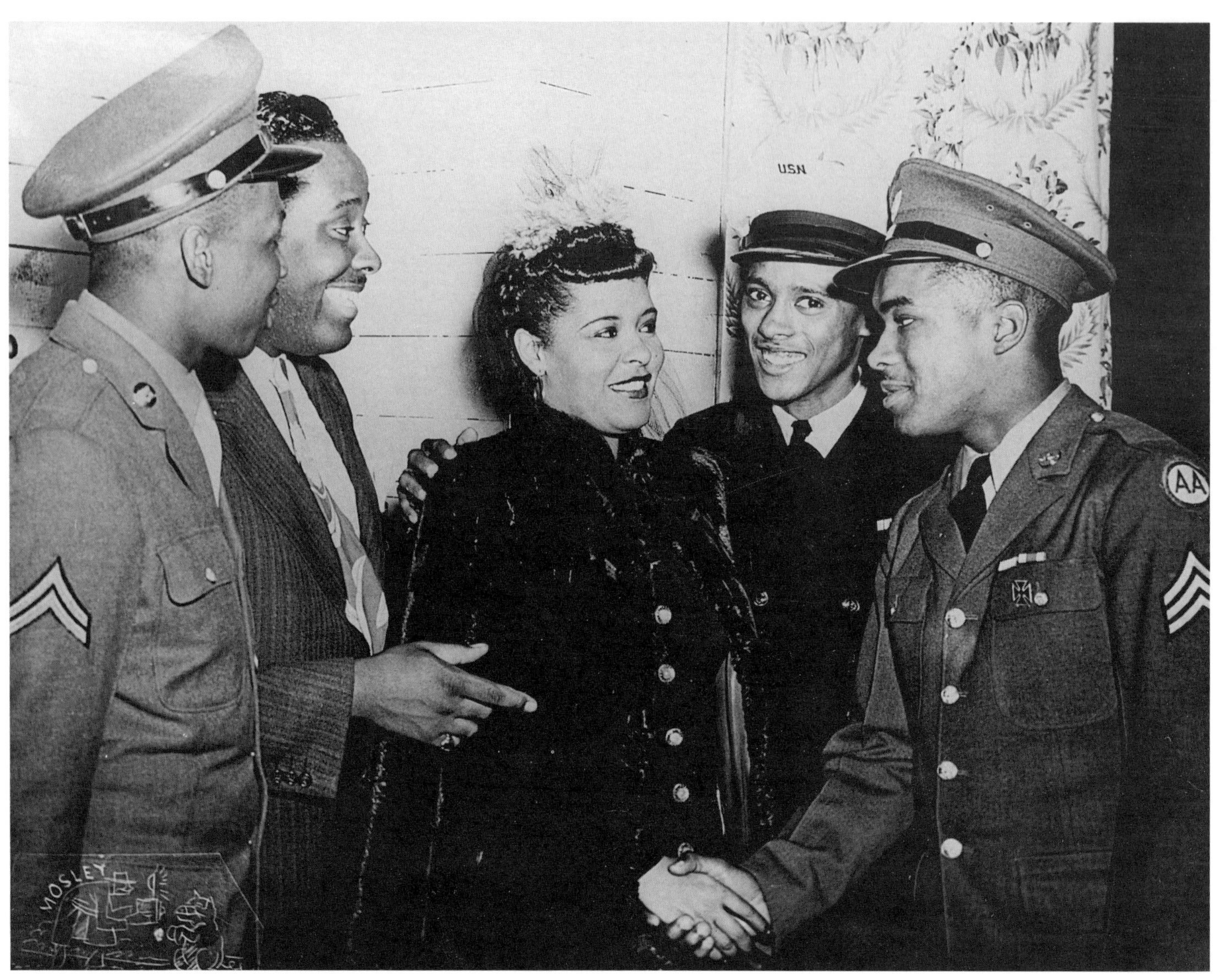

103A) Billie Holiday (1915-1959), jazz vocalist, meets a Sergeant at the South Broad Street U.S.O., 1943.

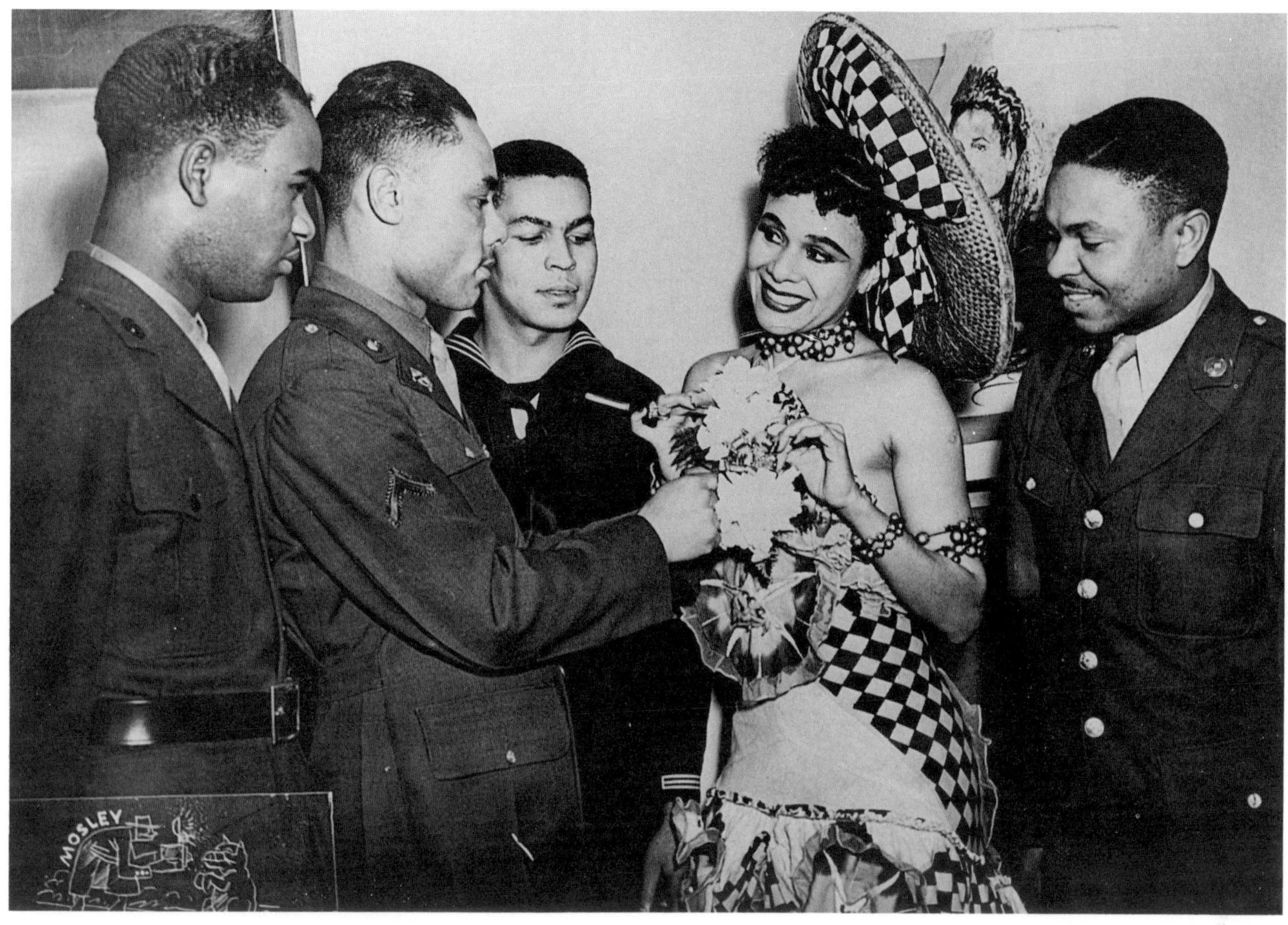

103B) Katherine Dunham accepts flowers from servicemen at the South Broad Street U.S.O., 1944.

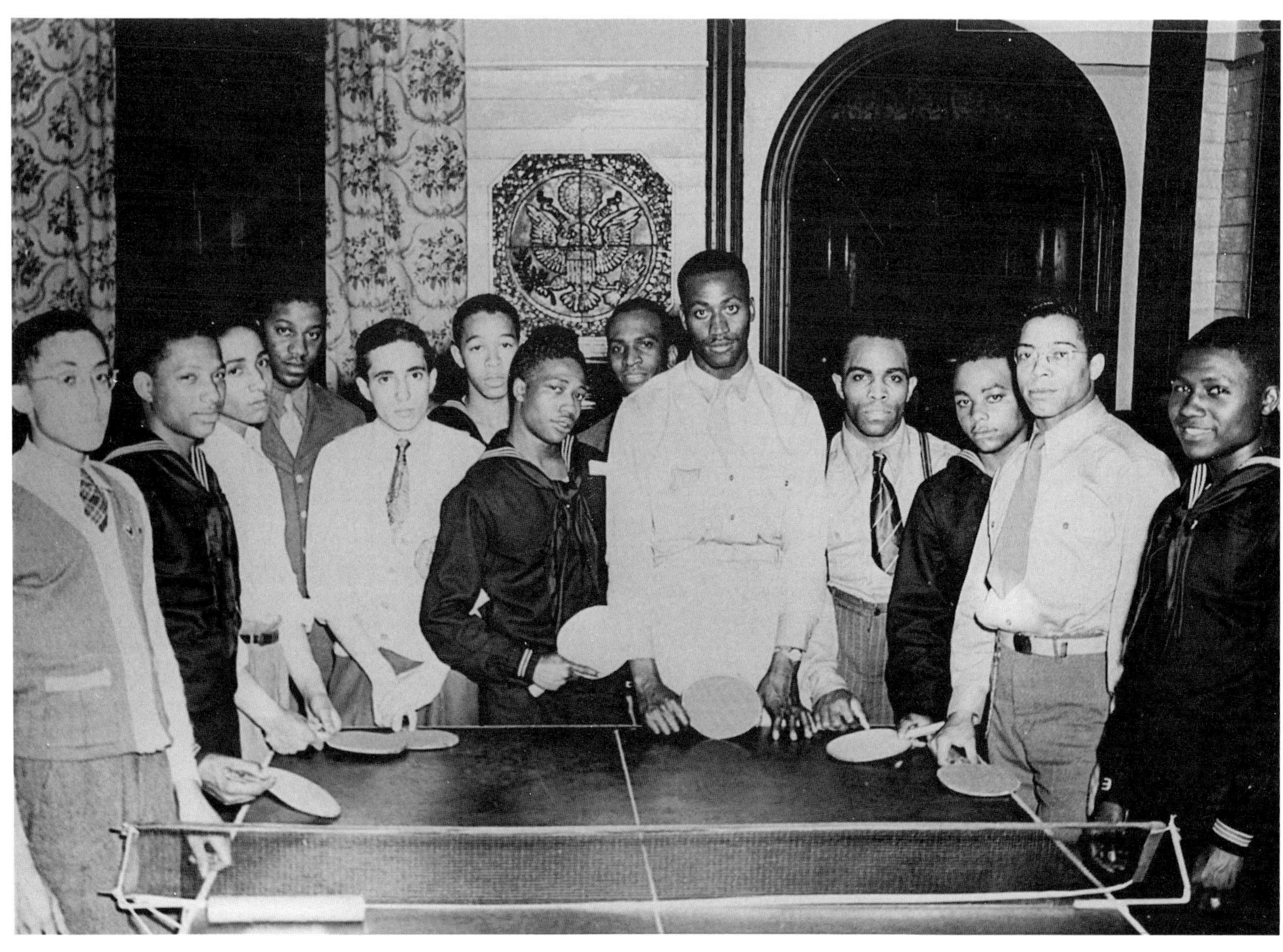

104A) Servicemen play ping pong at the South Broad Street U.S.O., early 1940's.

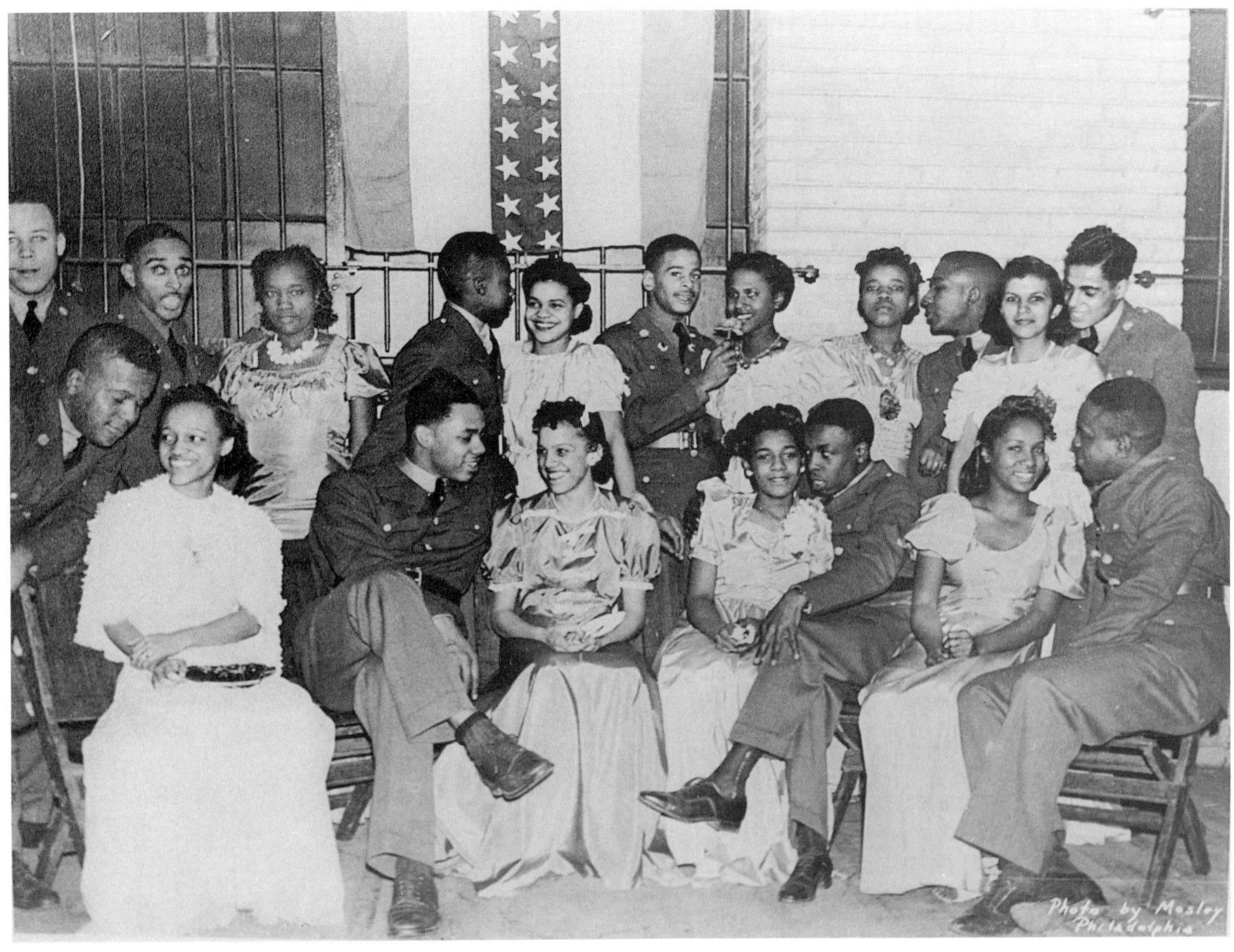

104B) Sweethearts at South Broad Street
U.S.O., early 1940s.

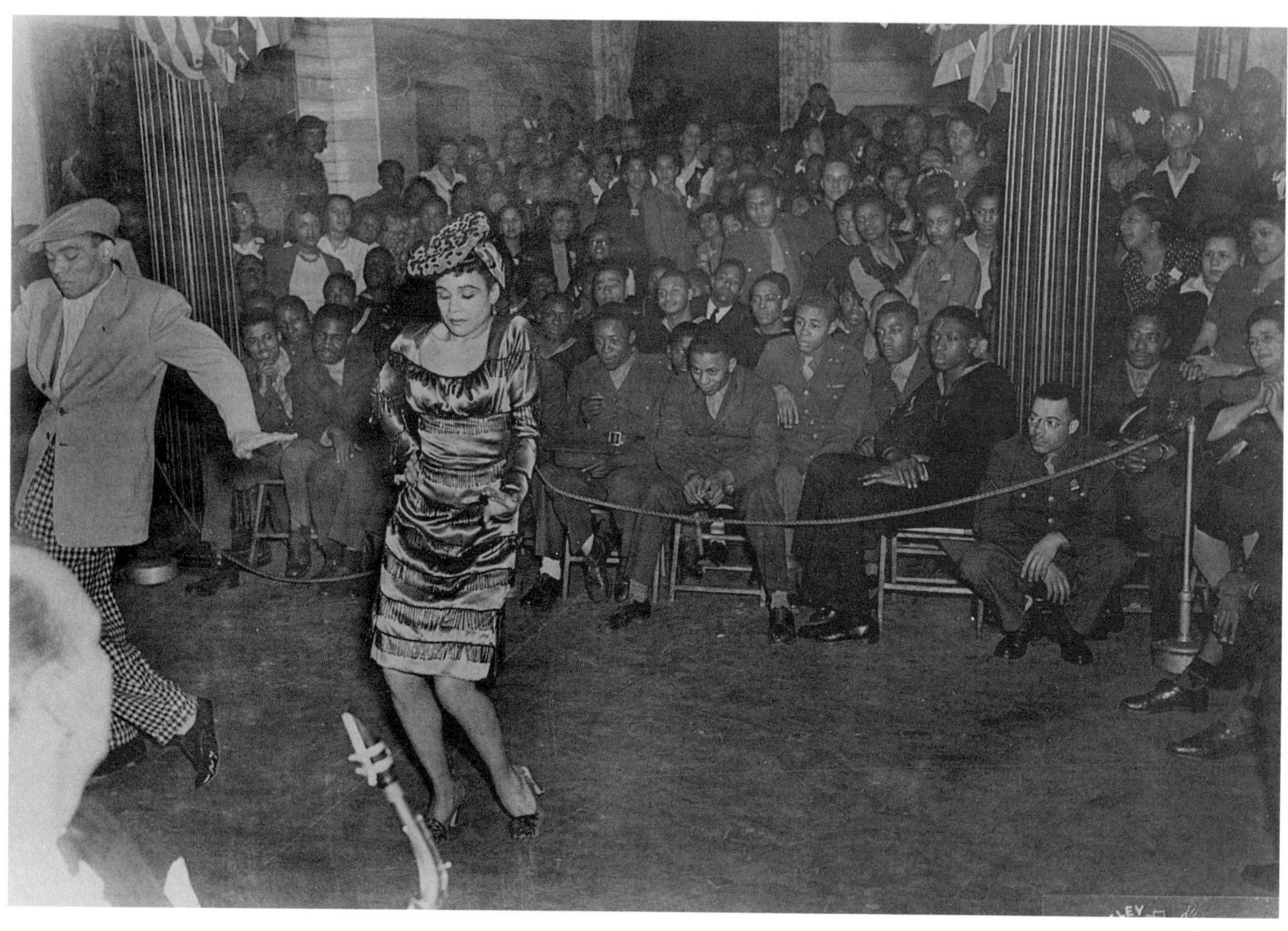

105) Katherine Dunham and Ohardiendo perform the Barrell House Boogie for servicemen at the South Broad Street U.S.O., 1944.

THE CRUSADERS

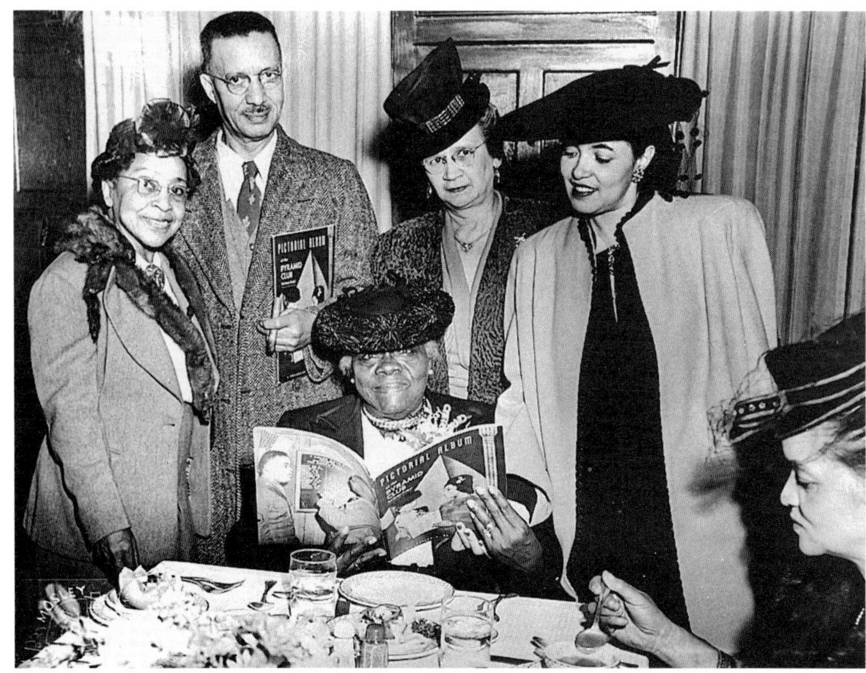

106A) Dr. Mary McLeod Bethune (1875-1955), founder and president of Cookman College, organizer and president of the National Council of Negro women, looks at Pictorial Album of The Pyramid Club, First Anniversary, as (from left to right, standing) Mrs. Walter F. Jerrick, Dr. and Mrs. Charles W. Maxwell, and Mrs. Howard E. Townes look on, 1945.

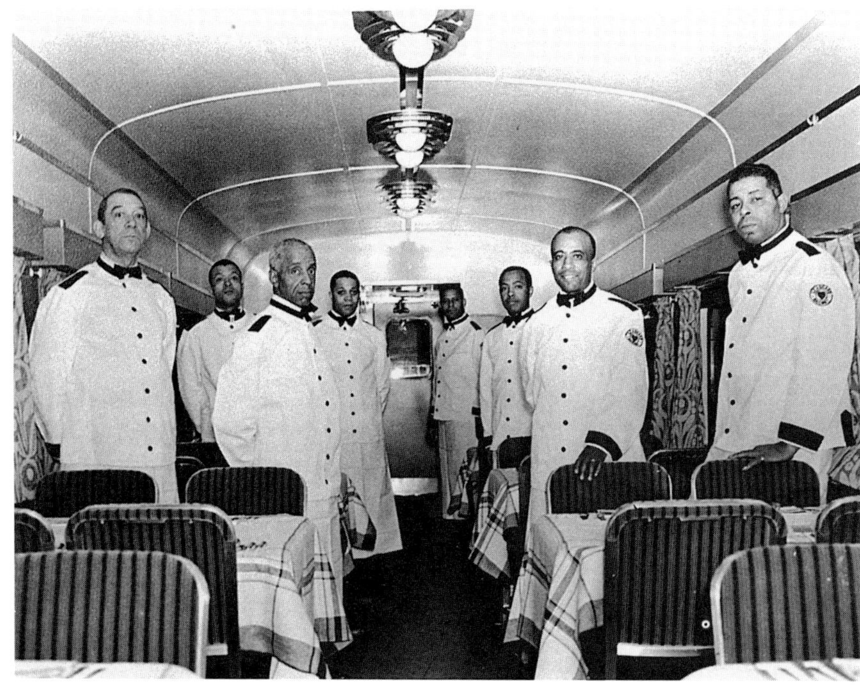

106B) Sleeping Car Porters, 1940s.

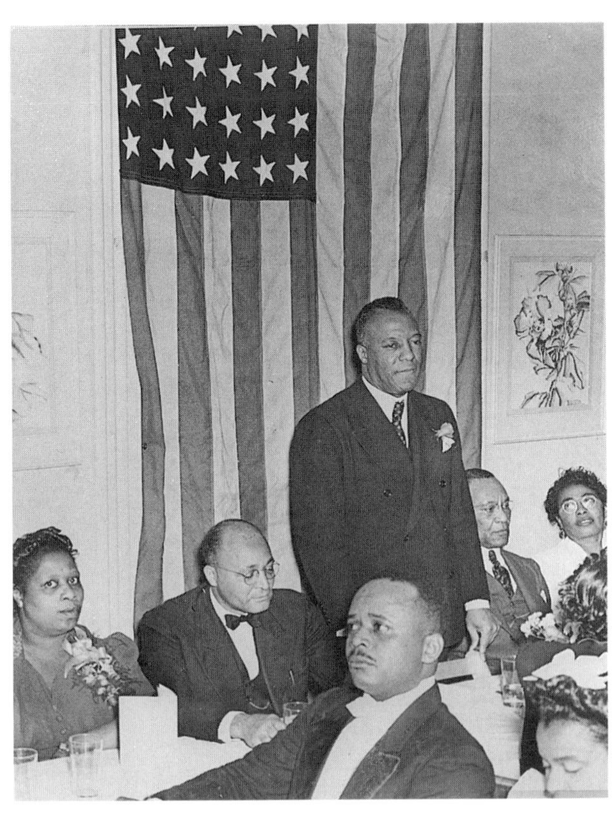

107A) Asa Philip Randolph (1889-1979), organizer and former President of the International Brotherhood of Sleeping Car Porters, pioneer labor leader, and organizer of the March on Washington, at the Pyramid Club, 1944. Known as the "Grand Old Black Liberation."

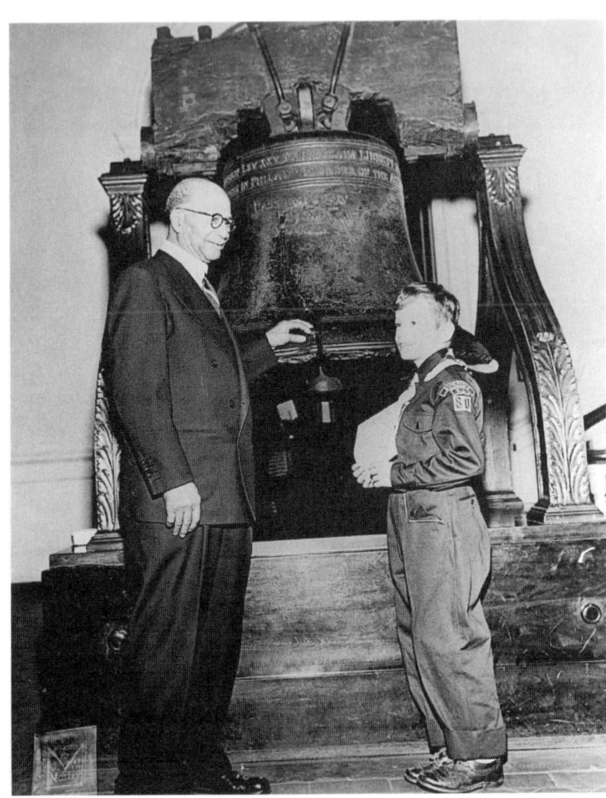

107B) Matthew A. Henson (1866-1955), co-discoverer of the North Pole, visits the Liberty Bell as a young admirer looks on, 1954.

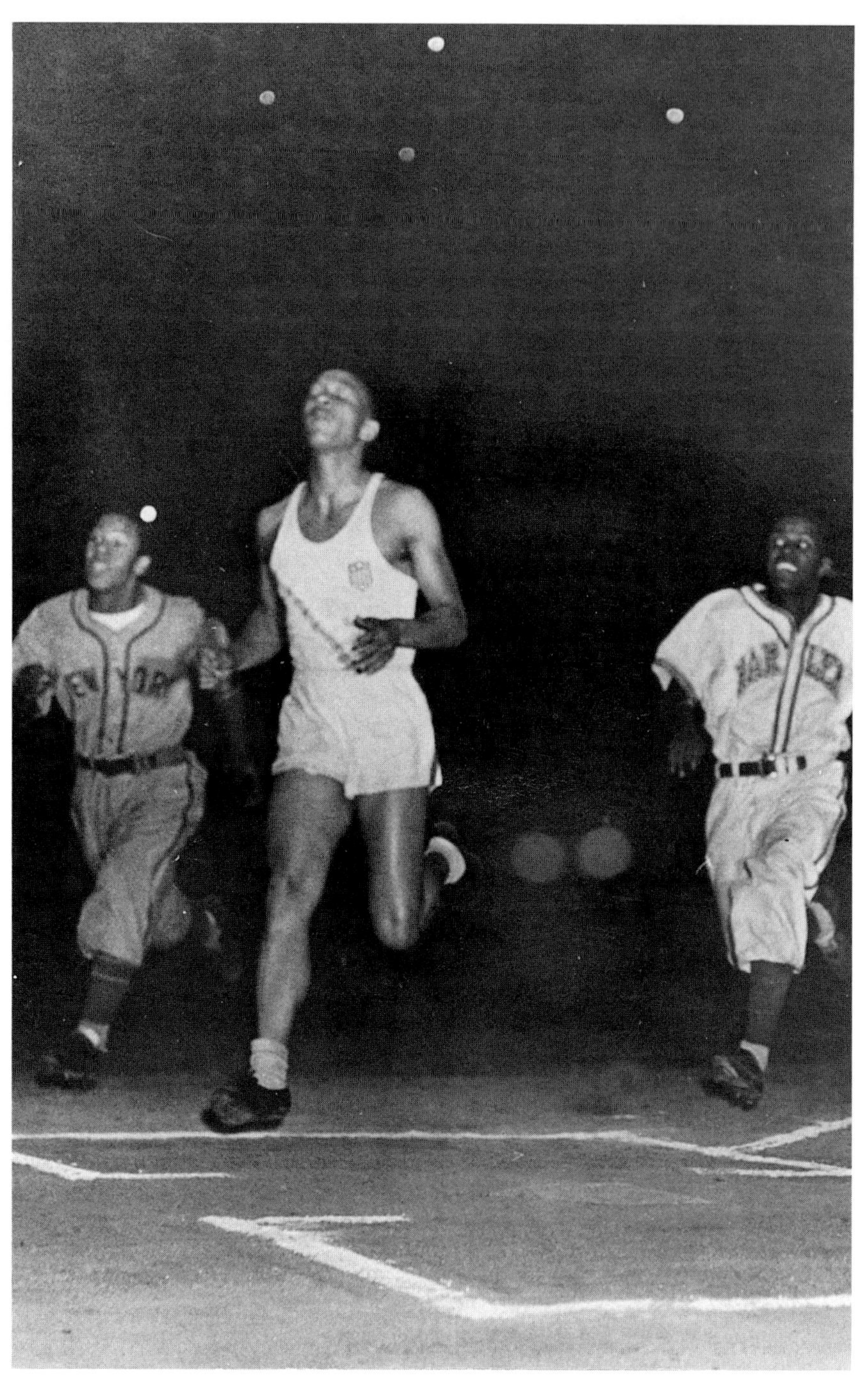

108) James Cleveland "Jesse" "J.C." Owens (1913-1980), former olympic track star, at a promotional Negro Baseball League benefit in Philadelphia, 1947. Known as "World's Fastest Human," he won four gold medals at the 1936 Berlin Olympics.

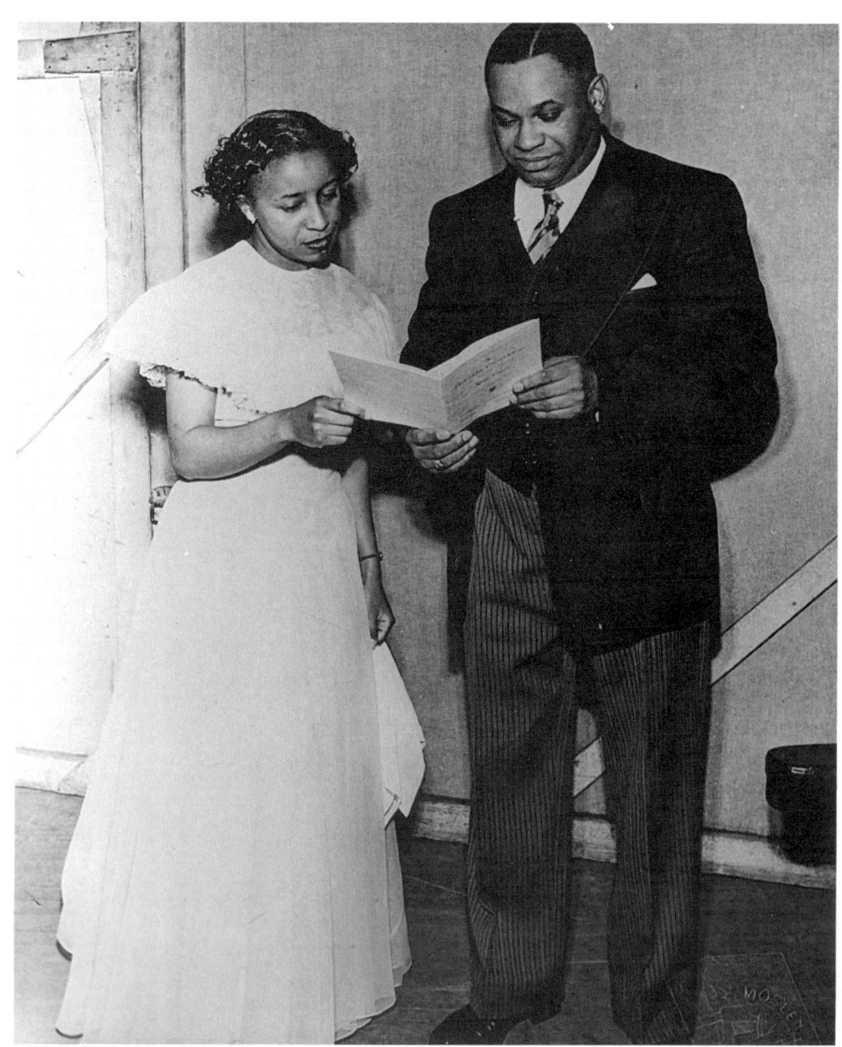

109) Raymond Lowden Smith (1896-1967), founder of the E. Gilbert Anderson Orchestra (renamed Philadelphia Concert Orchestra in 1944) presents orchestra at Town Hall, April 18, 1948. It was organized in 1930 to provide African Americans with opportunities to learn and perform European classical music at a time when the Philadelphia Orchestra practiced racial discrimination. He also organized Dra Mu, a Black opera company, in 1945.

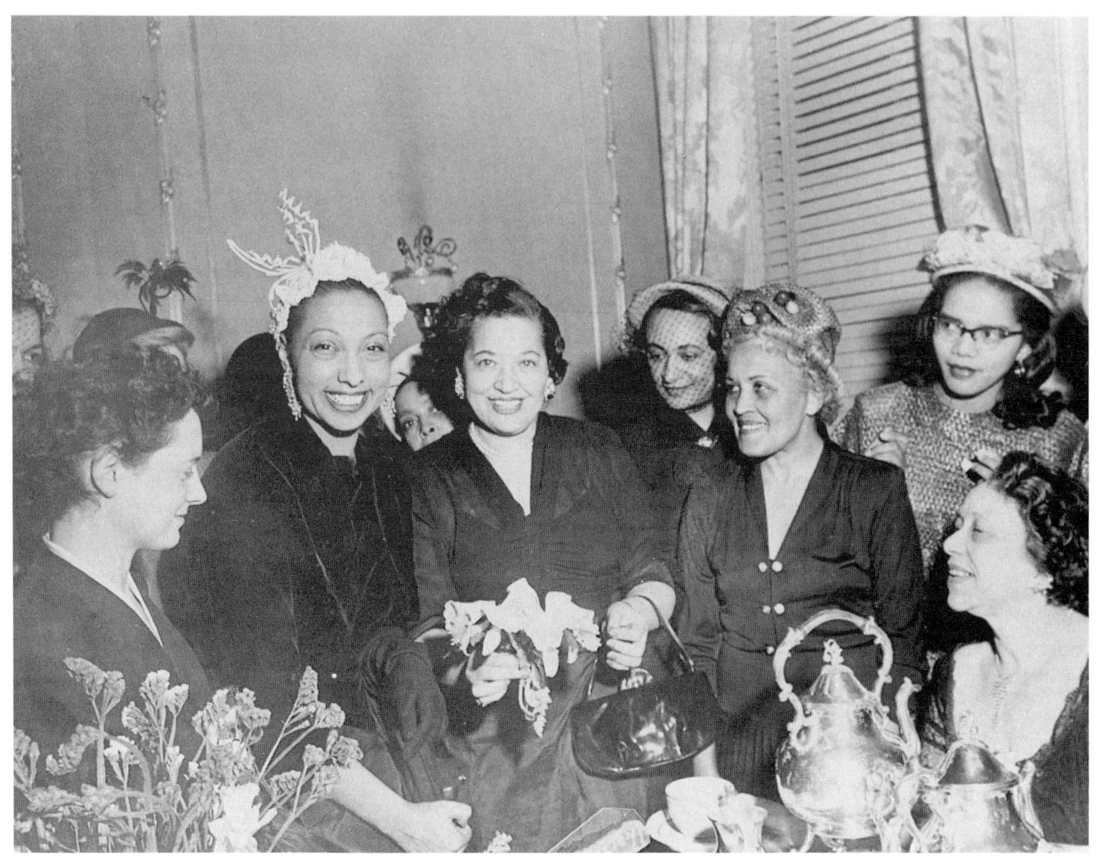

110A) Josephine Baker at the Pyramid Club, late 1940s.

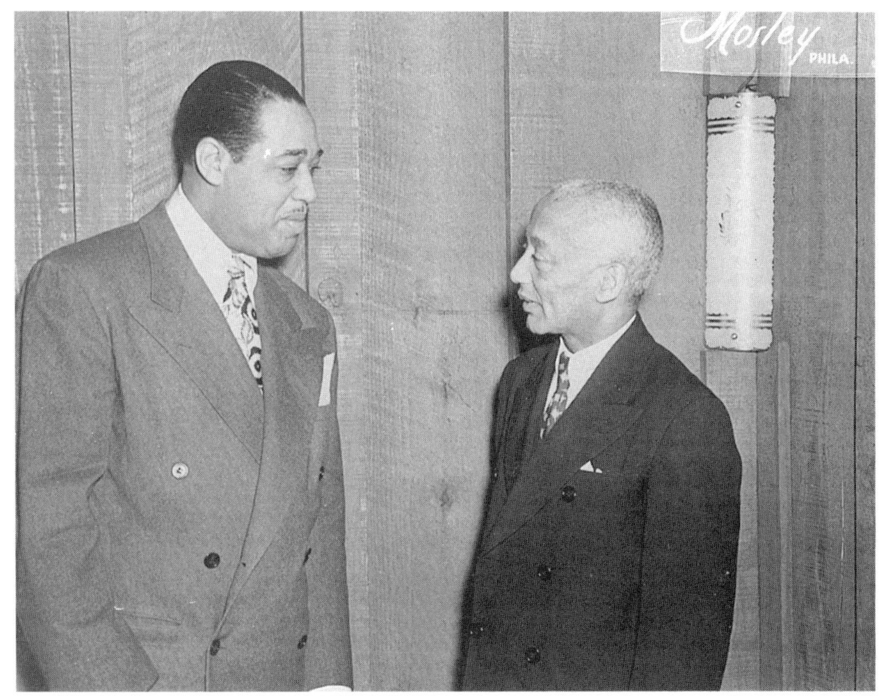

110B) Maestro Edward Kennedy "Duke" Ellington (1899-1974) (left), band leader, jazz composer and pianist, with Dr. Alain Leroy Locke of Howard University at the Pyramid Club, 1943.

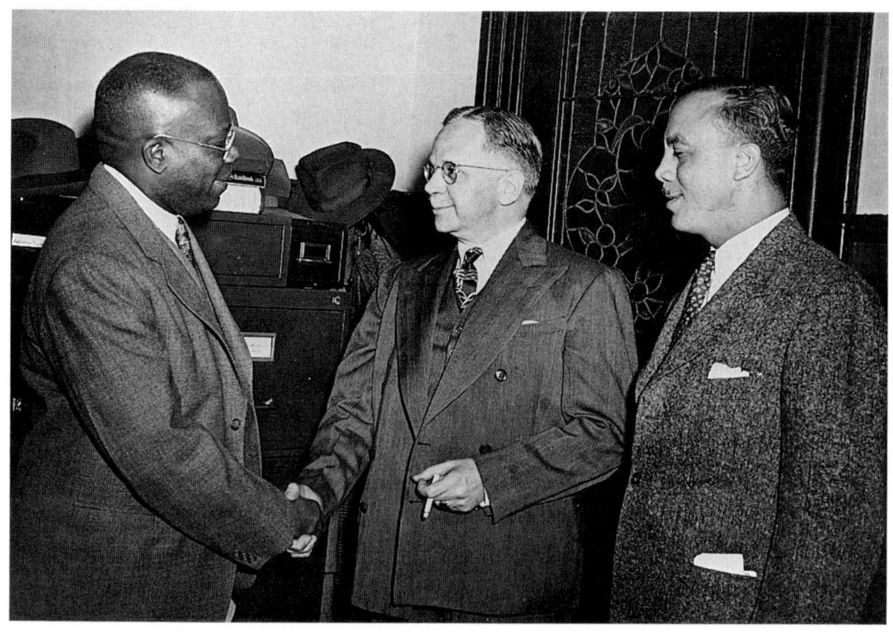

111A) Walter Francis White (1893-1955) (center), former Executive Secretary of the NAACP, civil rights leader and author, shakes hands with Dr. Walter F. Jerrick, President of the Pyramid Club, as Attorney Theodore O. Spaulding looks on inside of the Pyramid Club, prior to receiving the club's Award of Merit, 1944.

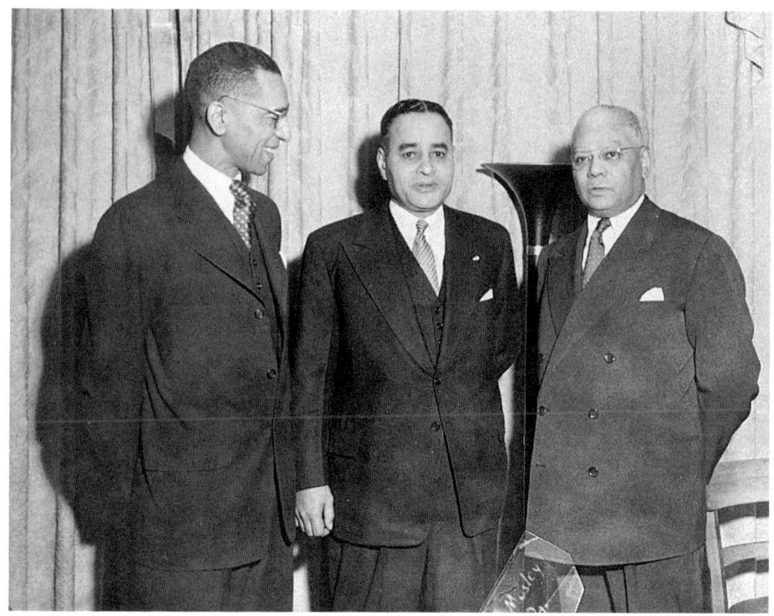

111B) Dr. Ralph Bunche (1904-1971) (center), first African American Nobel Peace Prize Winner in 1950, with Dr. Tanner G. Duckrey, Associate District Superintendent of Philadelphia Schools in 1943, and Judge Herbert E. Millen, first Philadelphia African-American Municipal Court Judge, 1950.

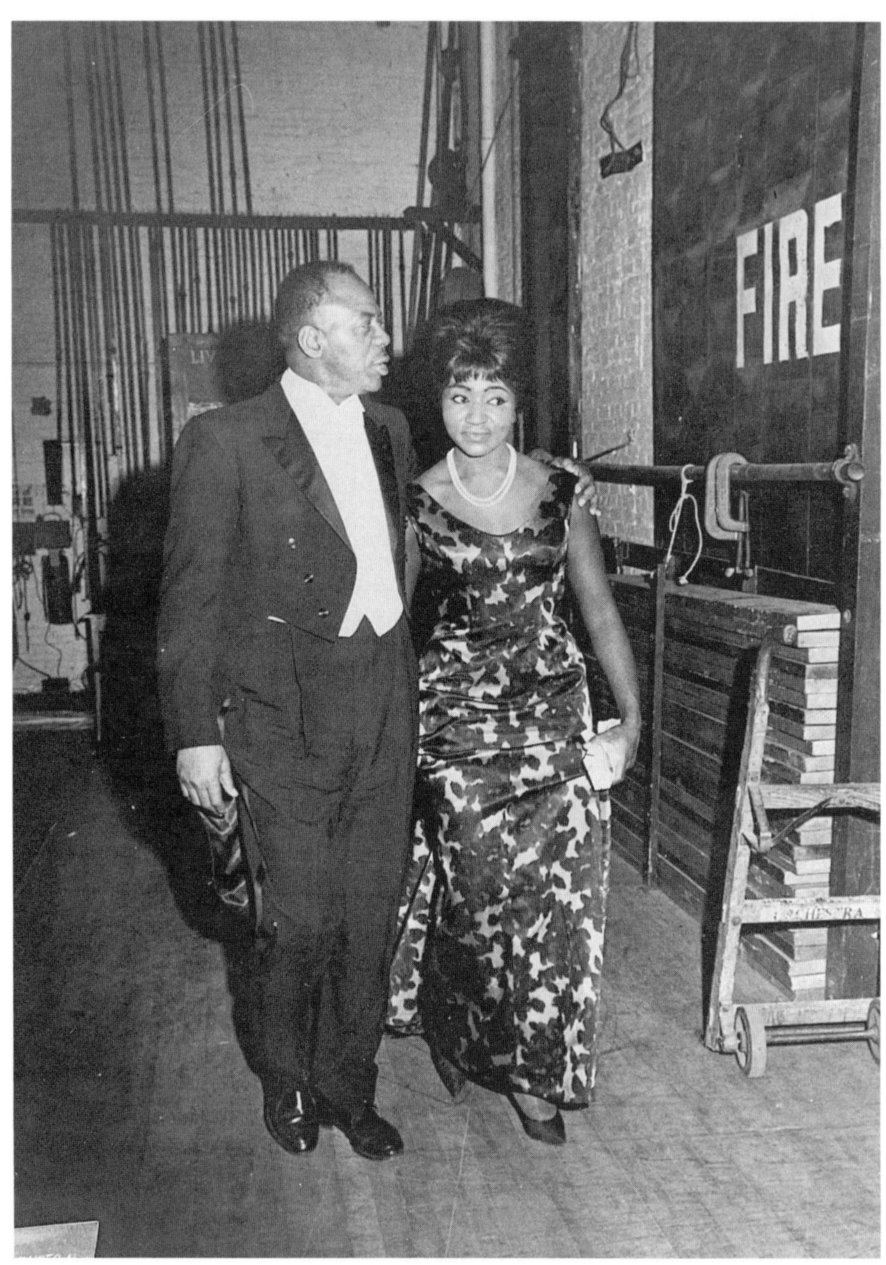

112) Samuel Evans, first Philadelphia African-American international impresario, escorts Grace Ann Bumbry, mezzo soprano opera singer, behind the stage at the Academy of Music, late 1950s.

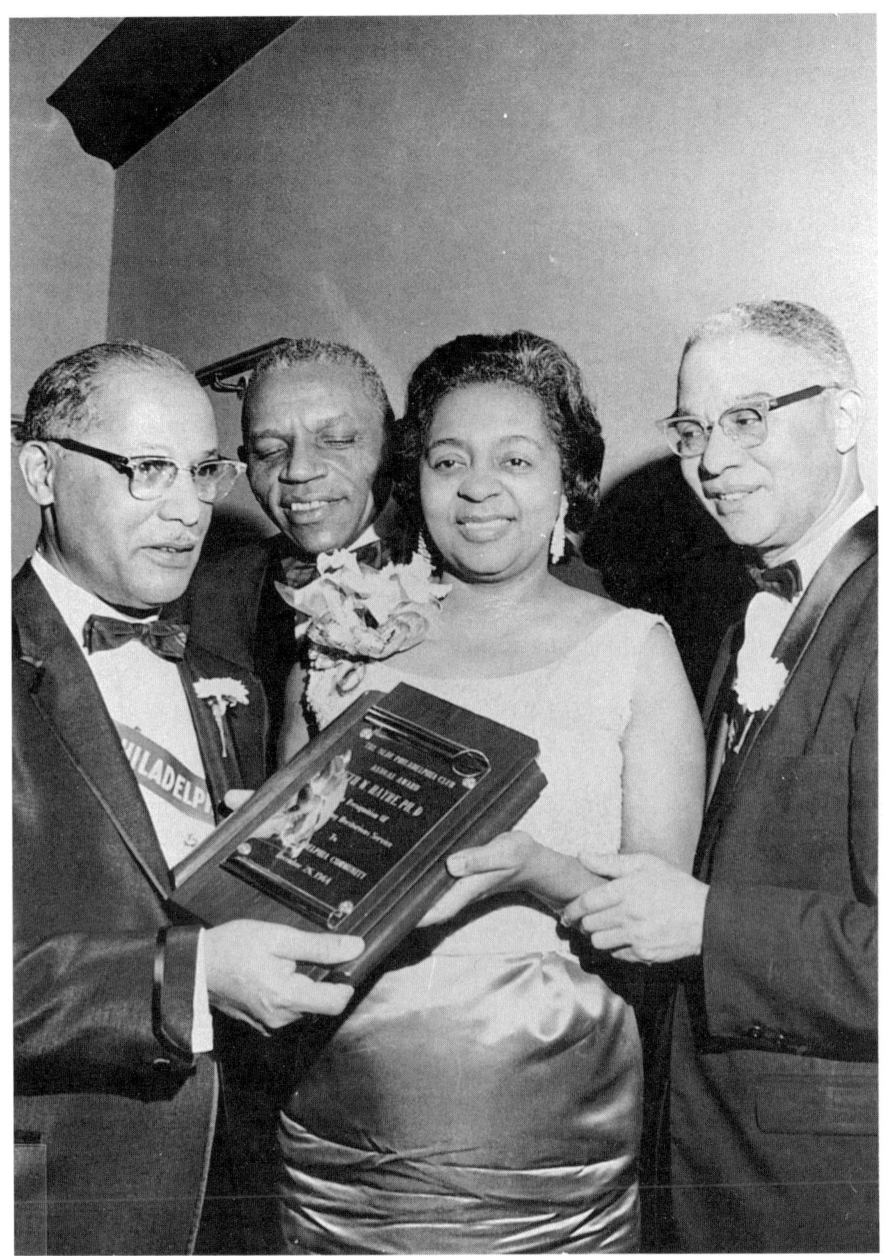

113) Dr. Ruth W. Hayre, first African-American high school principal in Philadelphia, receives The Olde Philadelphia Club Annual Award from Dr. Russell F. Minton as other club members look on, December 26, 1964.

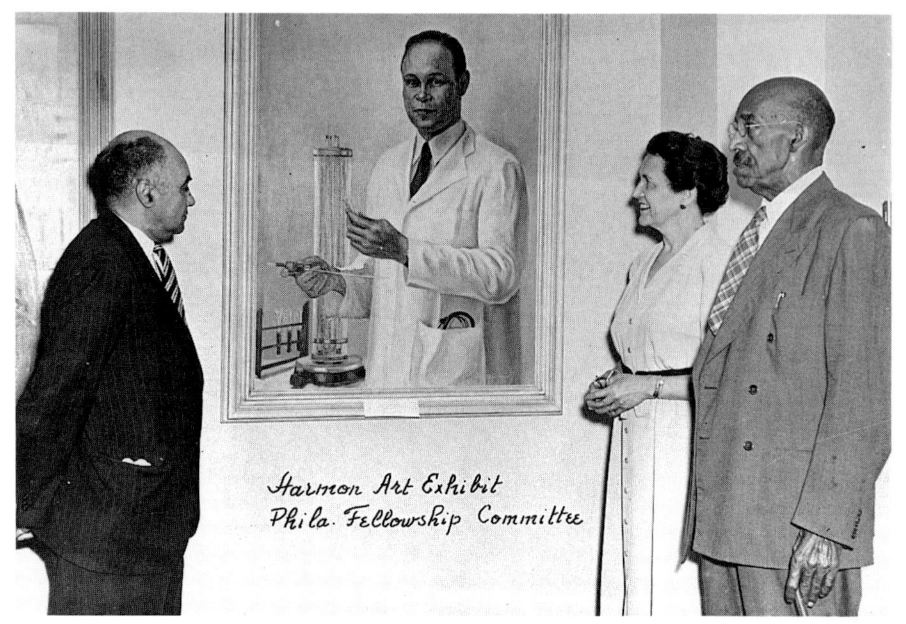

114A) Dr. Charles A. Lewis (left) and Dr. Nathan Mossell (1856- 1946) (right) view painting of Dr. Charles Drew, "Father of blood plasma and blood banks," at the Harmon Art Exhibit, early 1940s.

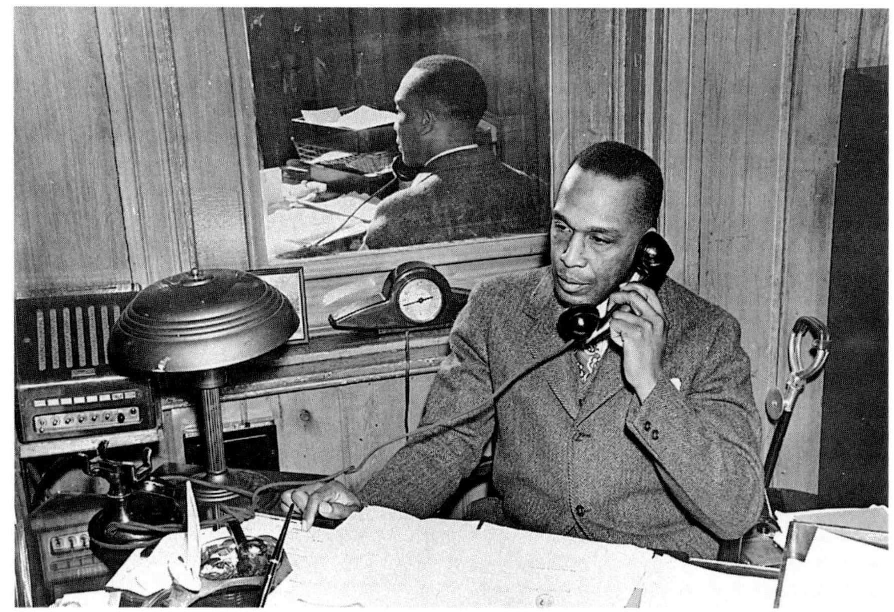

114B) Attorney Robert N.C. Nix, Sr. (1899-1987), Pennsylvania's first African -American Congressman in 1958, inside of his office, 1943.

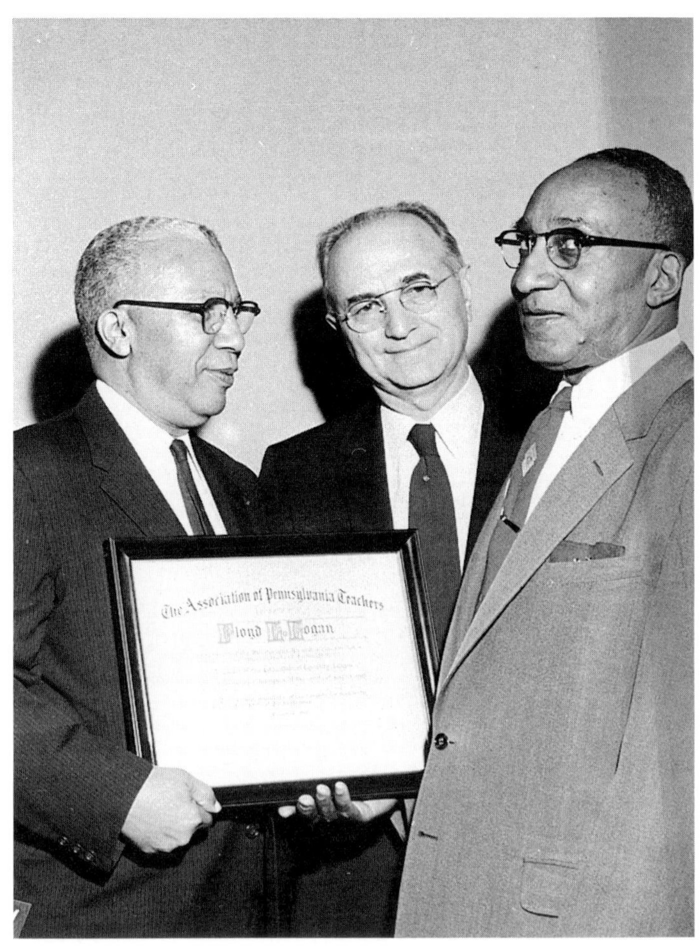

115) Floyd L. Logan (far right), organizer of the Philadelphia Educational Equality League to fight racial discrimination and segregation in the City's public schools in 1932, receives the Meritorious Award from The Association of Pennsylvania Teachers, presented to him by E. Washington Rhodes (far left), March 14, 1959.

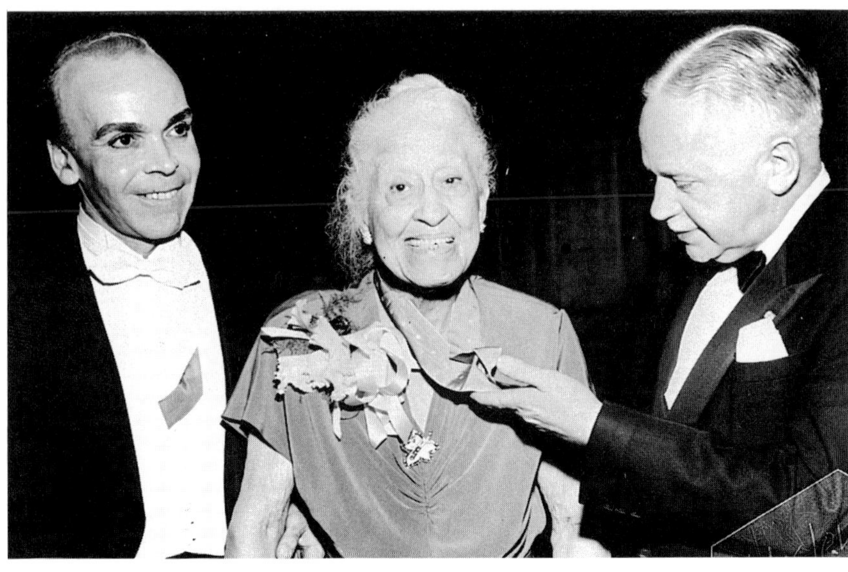

116) Mary Eliza Church "Mollie" Terrell (1863-1954) (center), civil rights pioneer, writer, educator, lecturer and first president of the National Association of Colored Women's Clubs, with Dr. Eugene Raymond Jones (left) and Walter Francis White (left), 1950.

LOVE WITH MARRIAGE

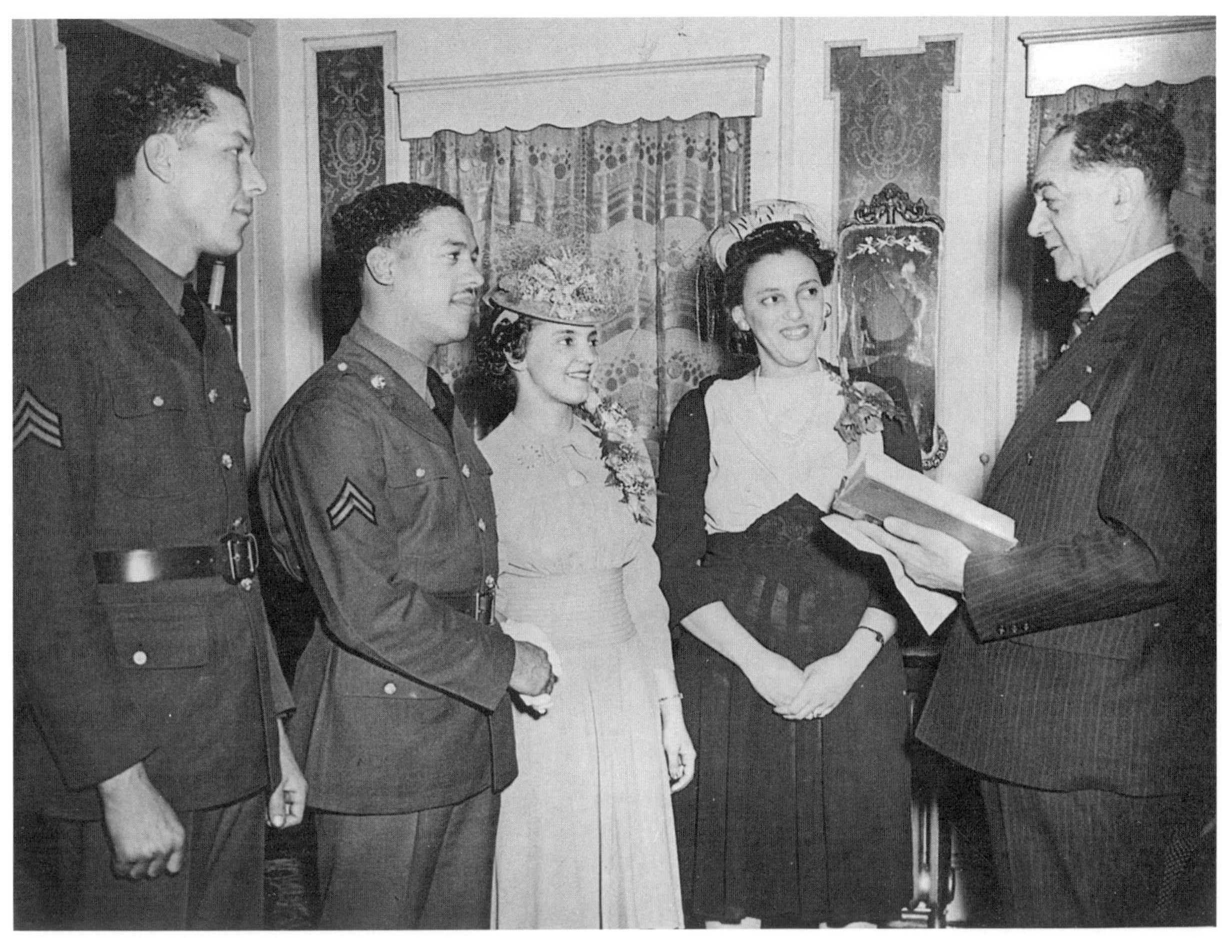

118A) Magistrate Edward W. Henry, the second African American Magistrate, reads marriage vows to serviceman and soon to be wife, early 1940s.

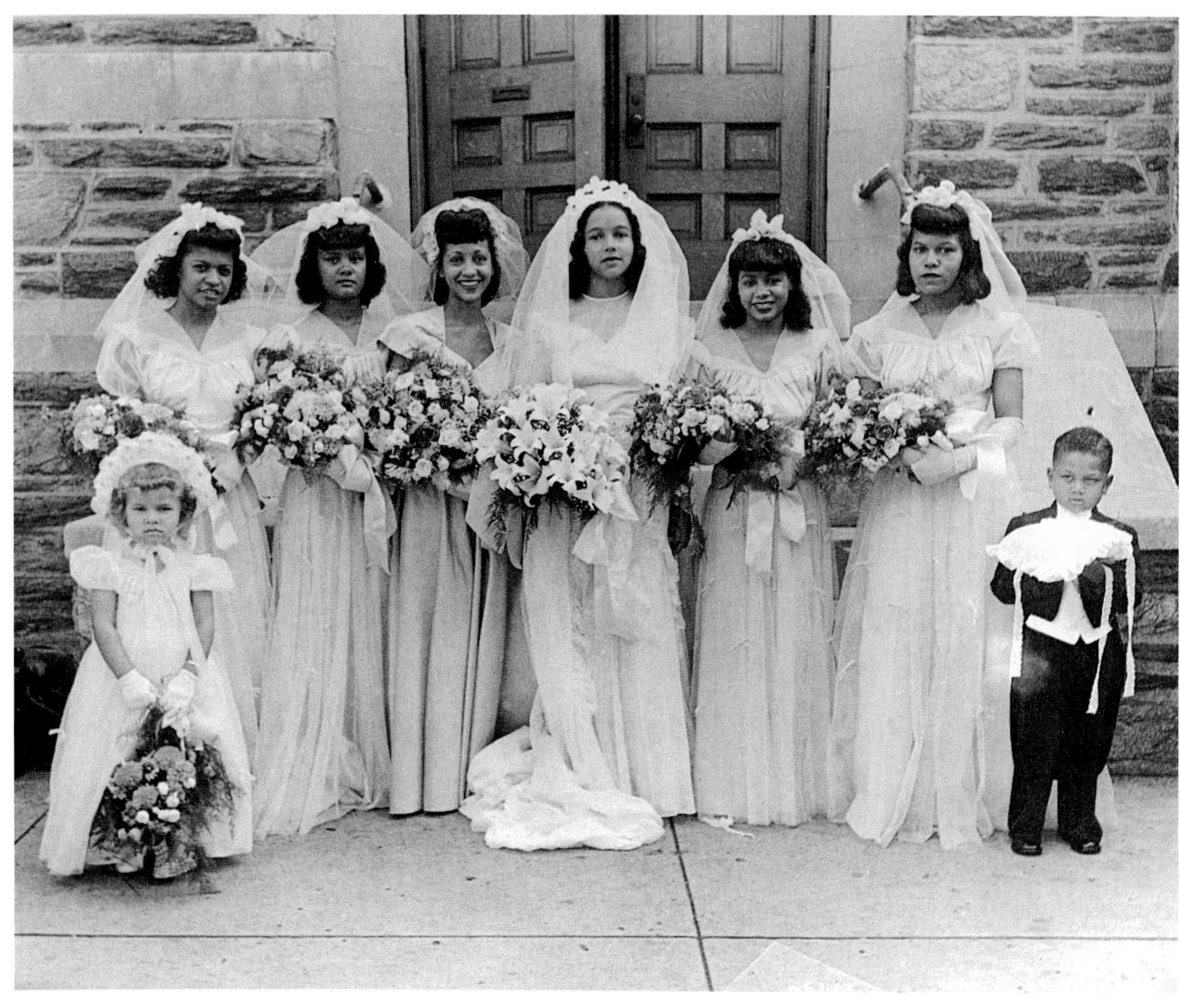

118B) "Til Death Do Us Part," early 1940s.

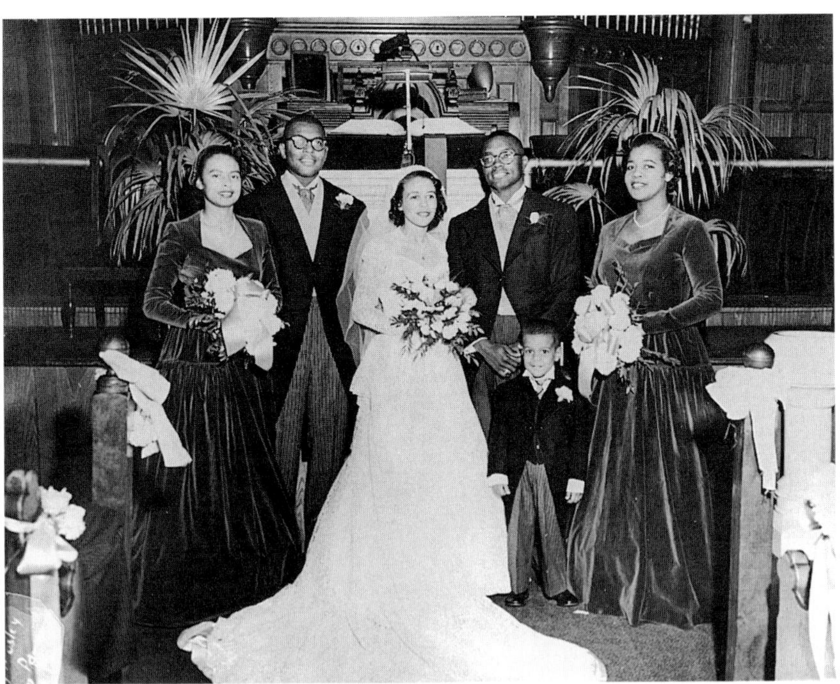

119A) Wallace Triplett, III (fourth from left), groom, one of the first Black football player to play in the Cotton Bowl, and Lenore Bevins (third from left), bride and daughter of Dr. Leon Bevins, with members of wedding party, December, 1949.

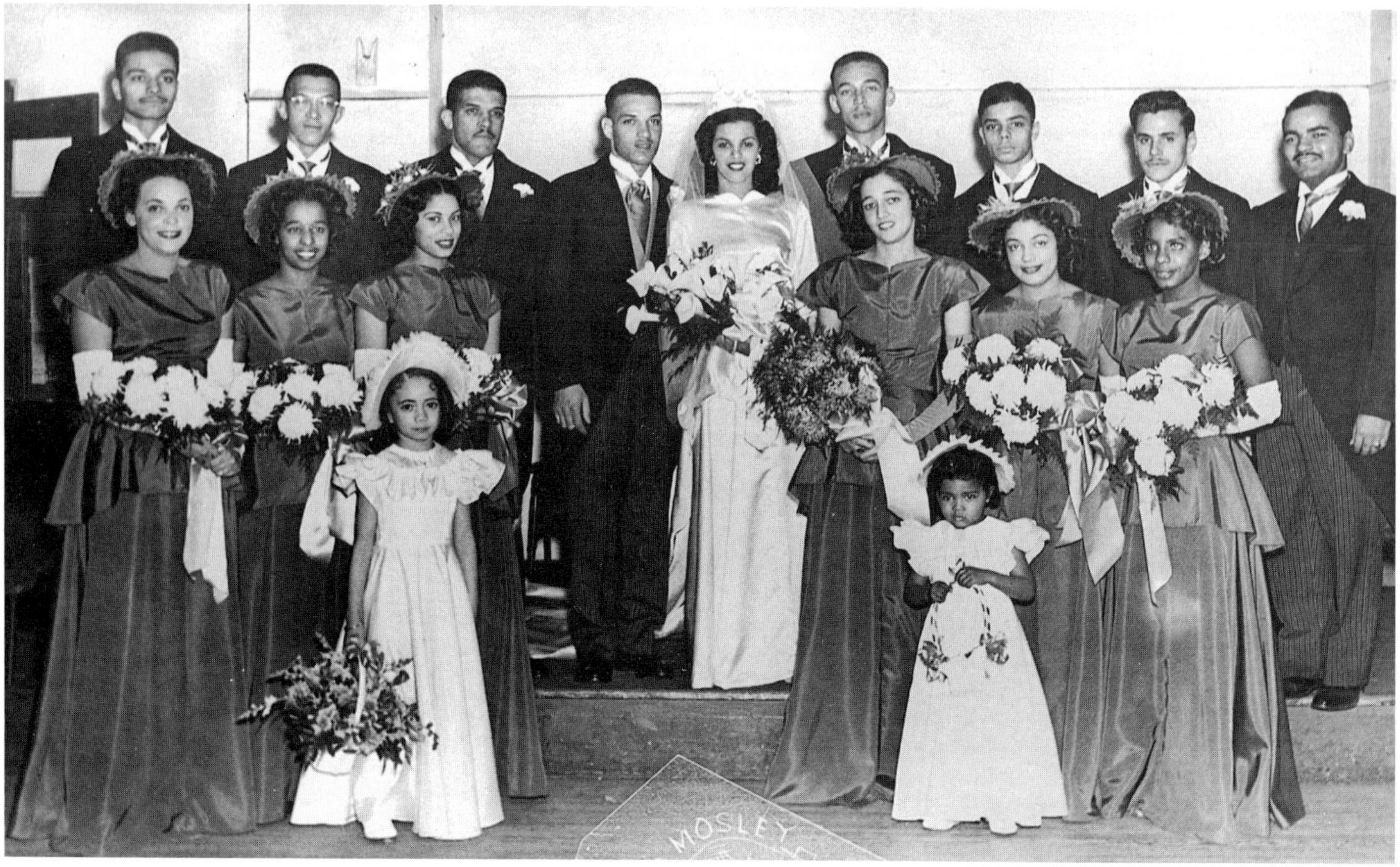

120A) Wedding party of Mr. and Mrs. Edward Chew (center couple) at St. Thomas P.E. Church, Saturday, November 22, 1947.

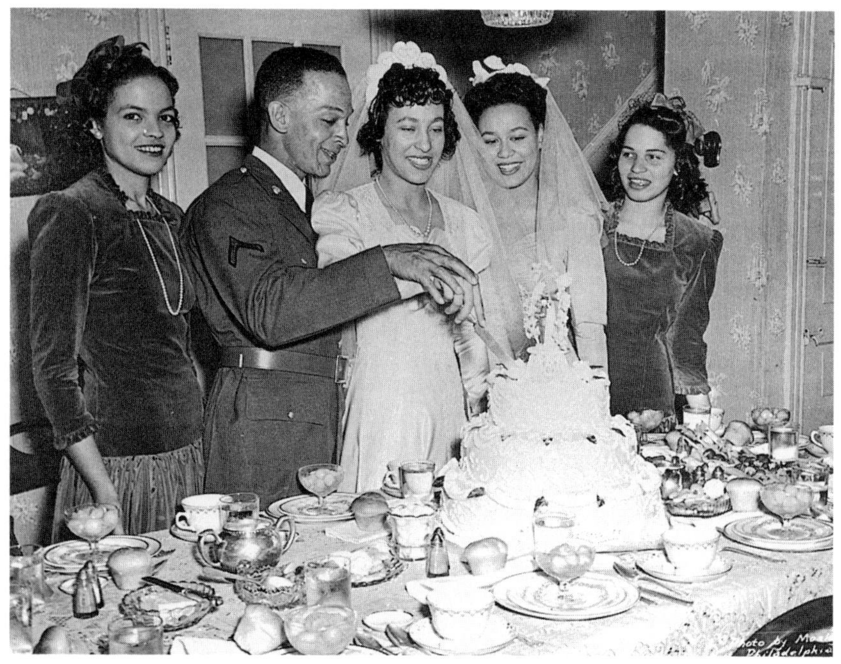

120B) Armenta Woodson's (center), wife of Lloyd Woodson, and her bridal party, late 1940s.

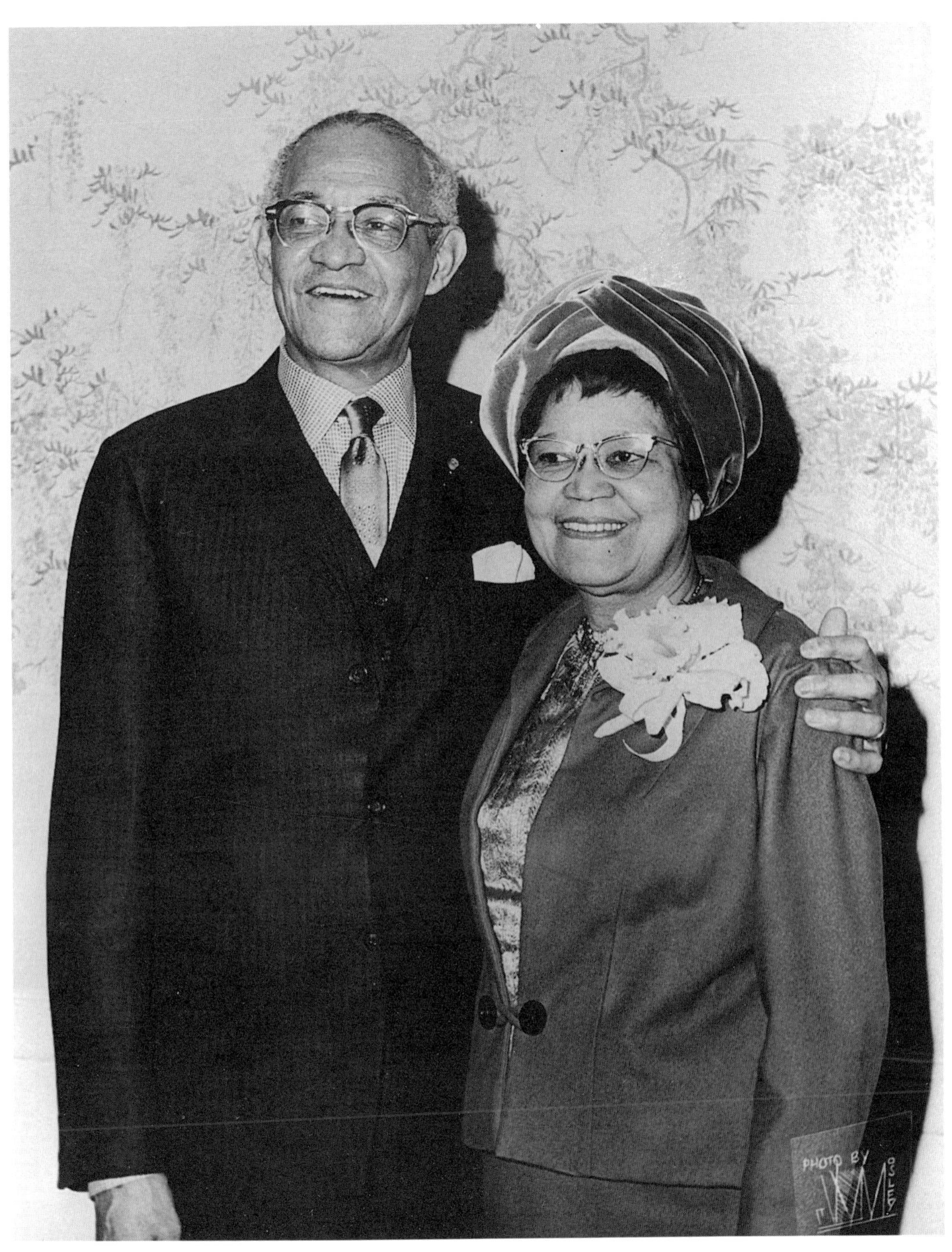

121) Judge Raymond Pace Alexander (1898-1974), first African American Common Pleas Court Judge in 1959, with his wife, Dr. Sadie Mossell Alexander (1898-1991), first African American woman to receive a Doctor of Philosophy degree at the University of Pennsylvania, 1950s.

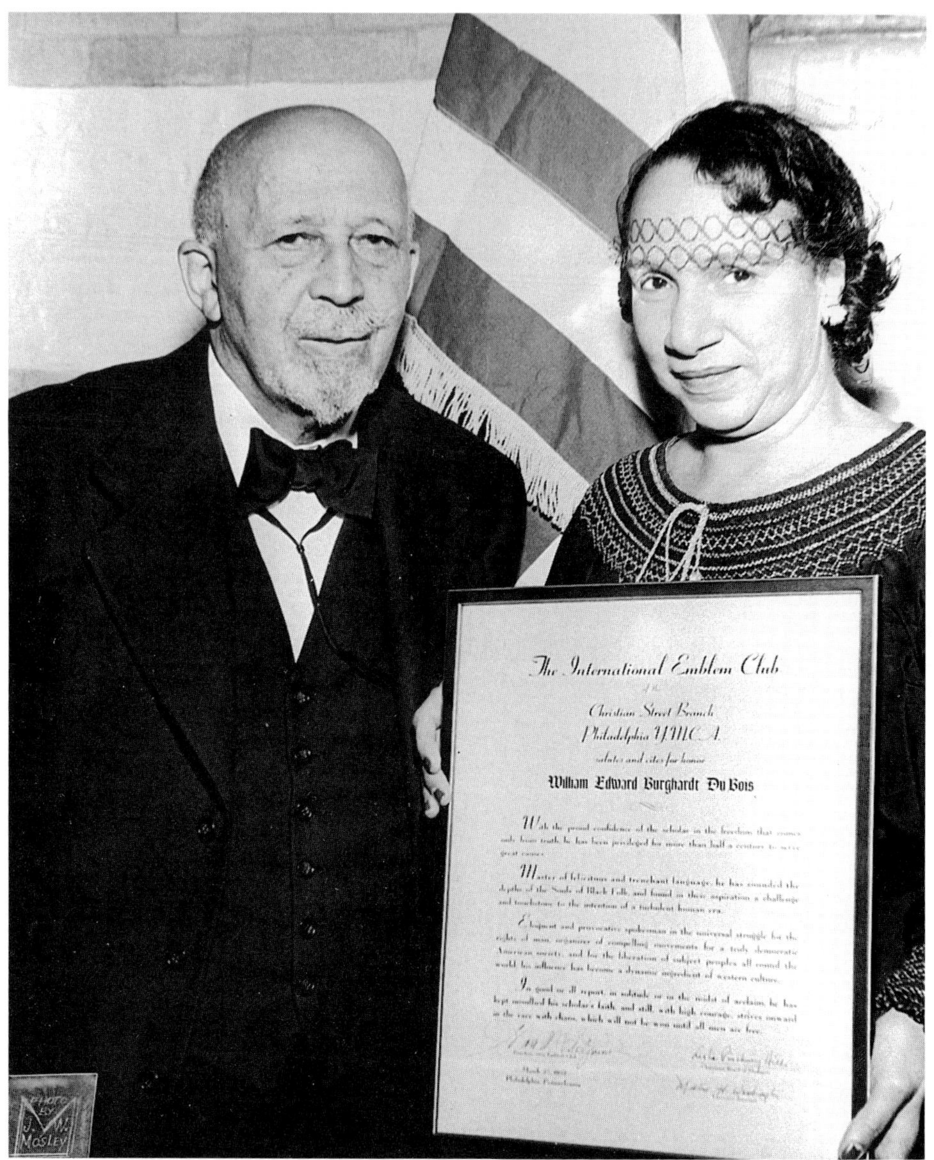

122) Dr. W.E.B. DuBois with his wife, Mrs. Shirley Graham DuBois, (1906-1977) holding his International Emblem Club Award from the Christian Street YMCA, March 27, 1953.

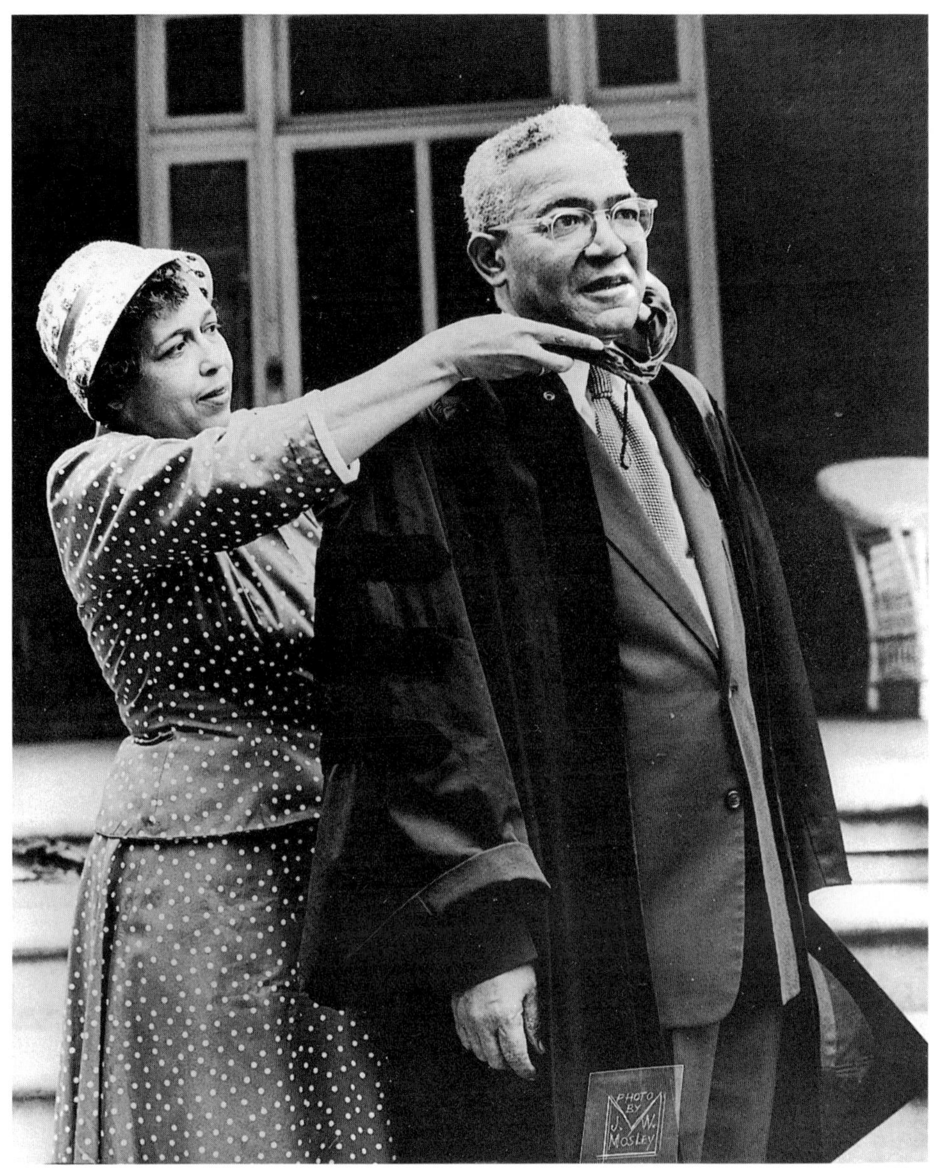

123) Dr. Horace Mann Bond and his wife,
Mrs. Julia Bond, June 1957.

IN THE GROOVE

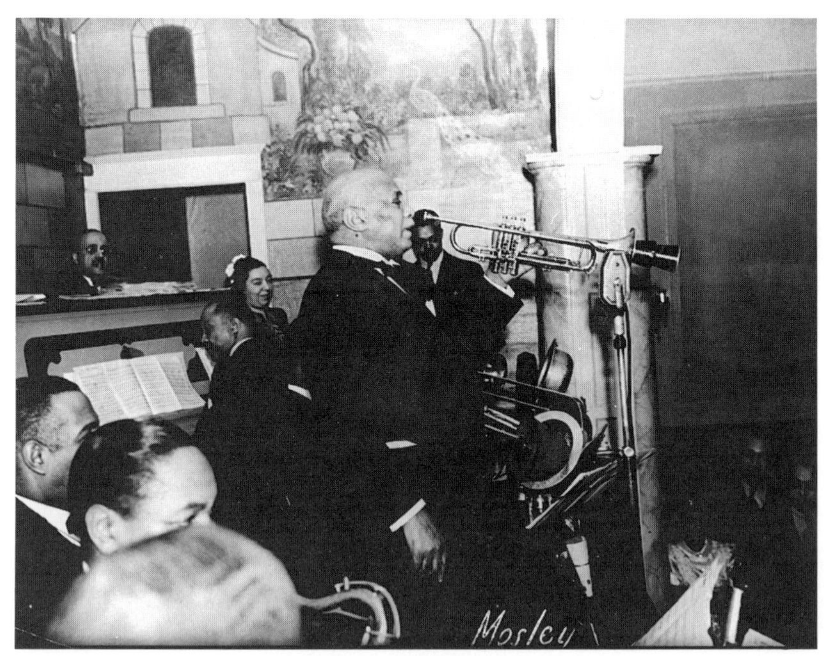

124A) William Christopher "W.C." Handy (1873-1958) (standing), performs at the Philadelphia Club Formal, 1939.

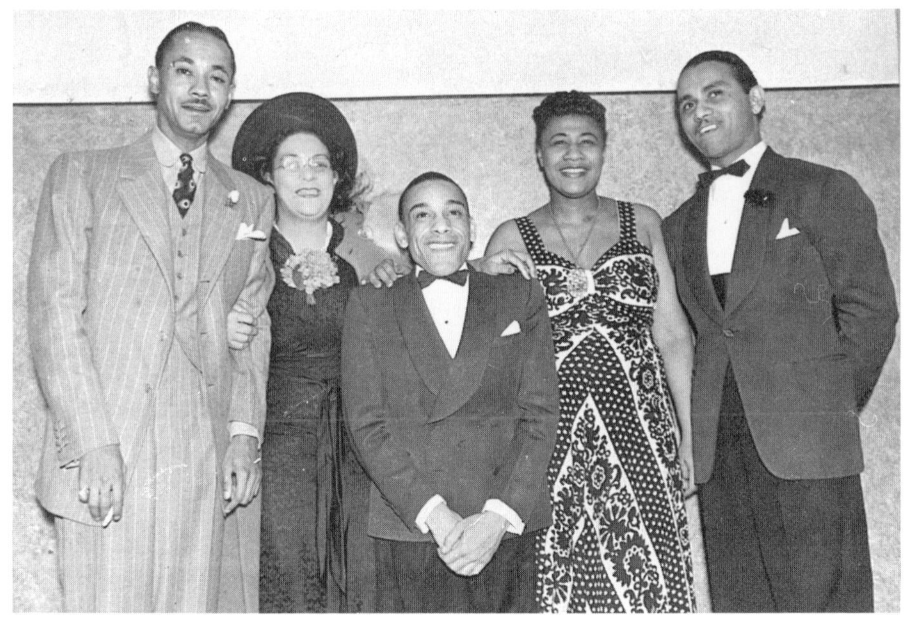

124B) William "Chick" Webb (1907-1939) (center), band leader, jazz drummer, and composer, poses with Ella Fitzgerald (fourth from left), his singing protege, before performance at Quaker City Elks Ball, June, 1938.

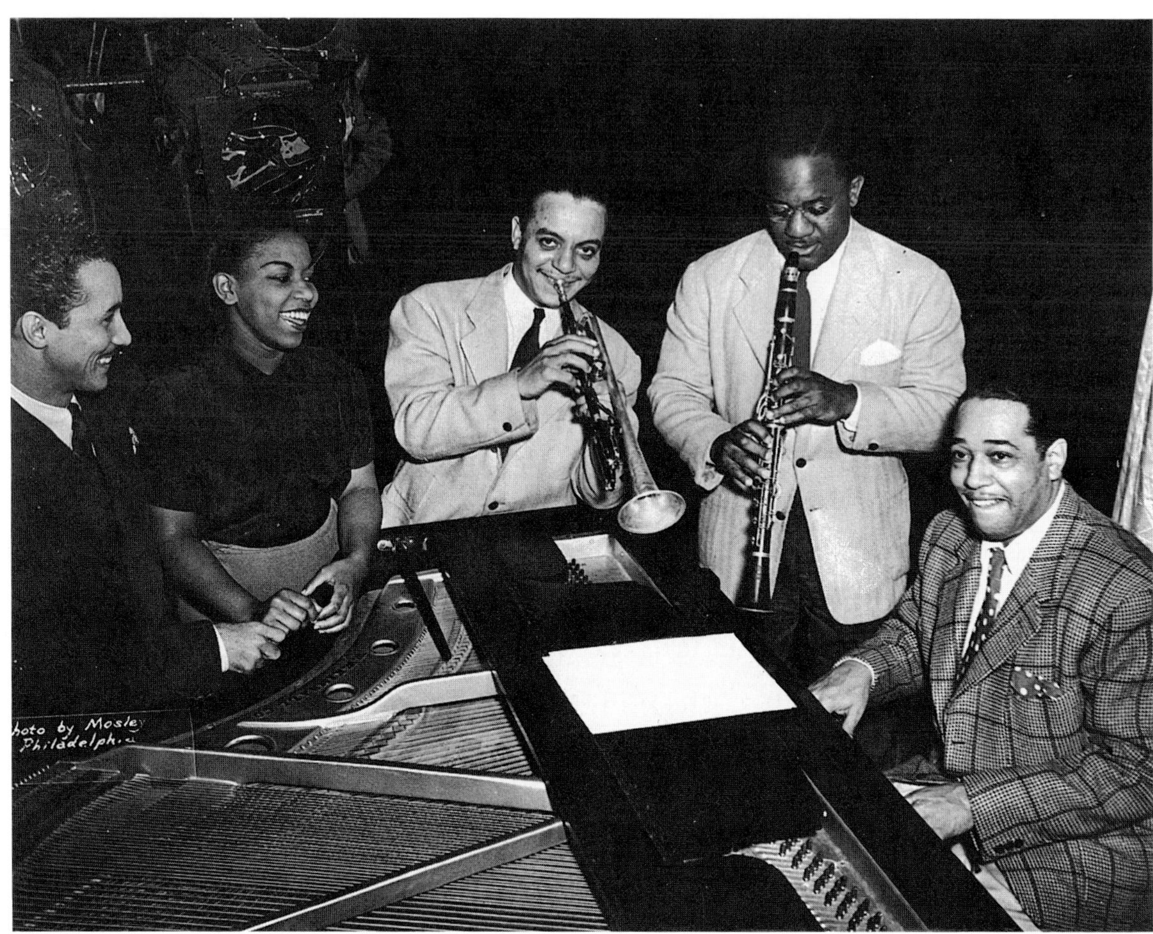

125A) Maestro Edward Kennedy "Duke" Ellington, band leader, jazz pianist and composer, jams on the piano, 1943. He brought in the swing age with his composition "It Don't Mean a Thing If It Ain't Got That Swing" during the 1930s.

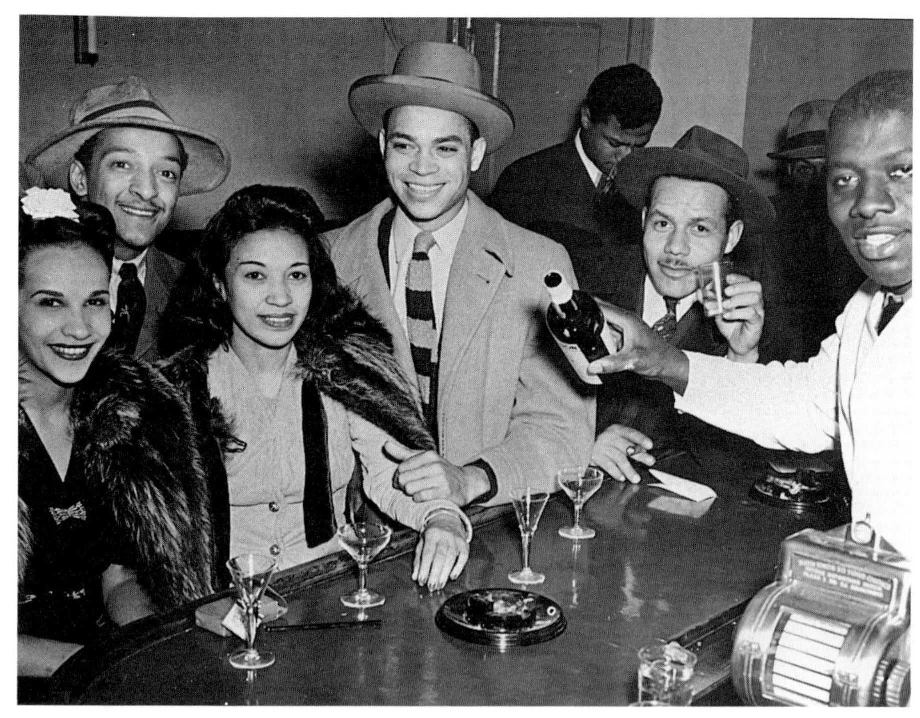

126B) Jam Session at the Show Boat Club, 1409 Lombard Street," 1943.

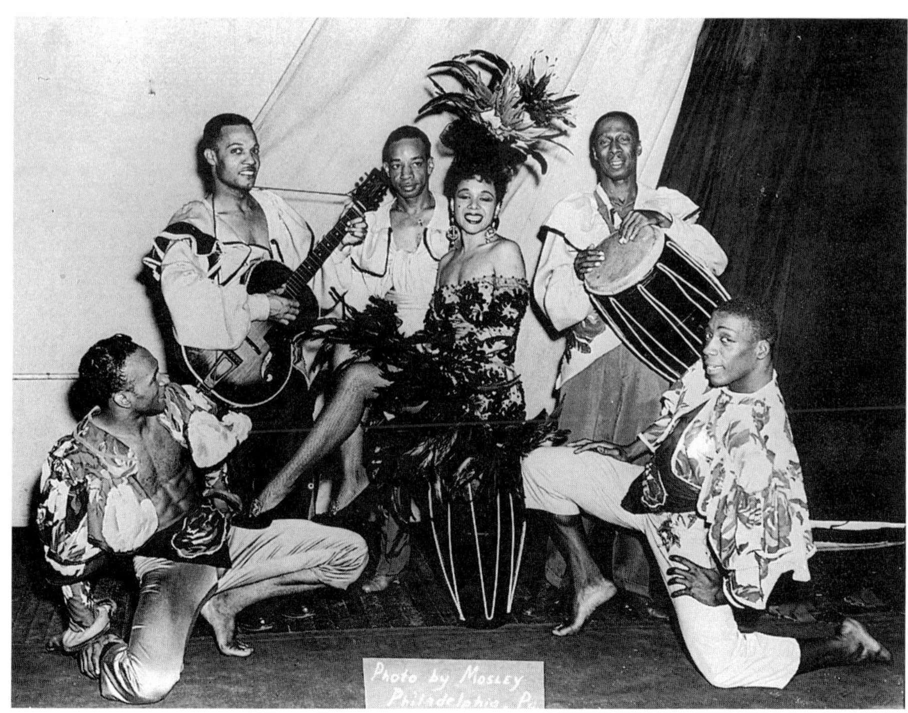

127A) Katherine Dunham performs in "Bal Negre," September 18, 1946.

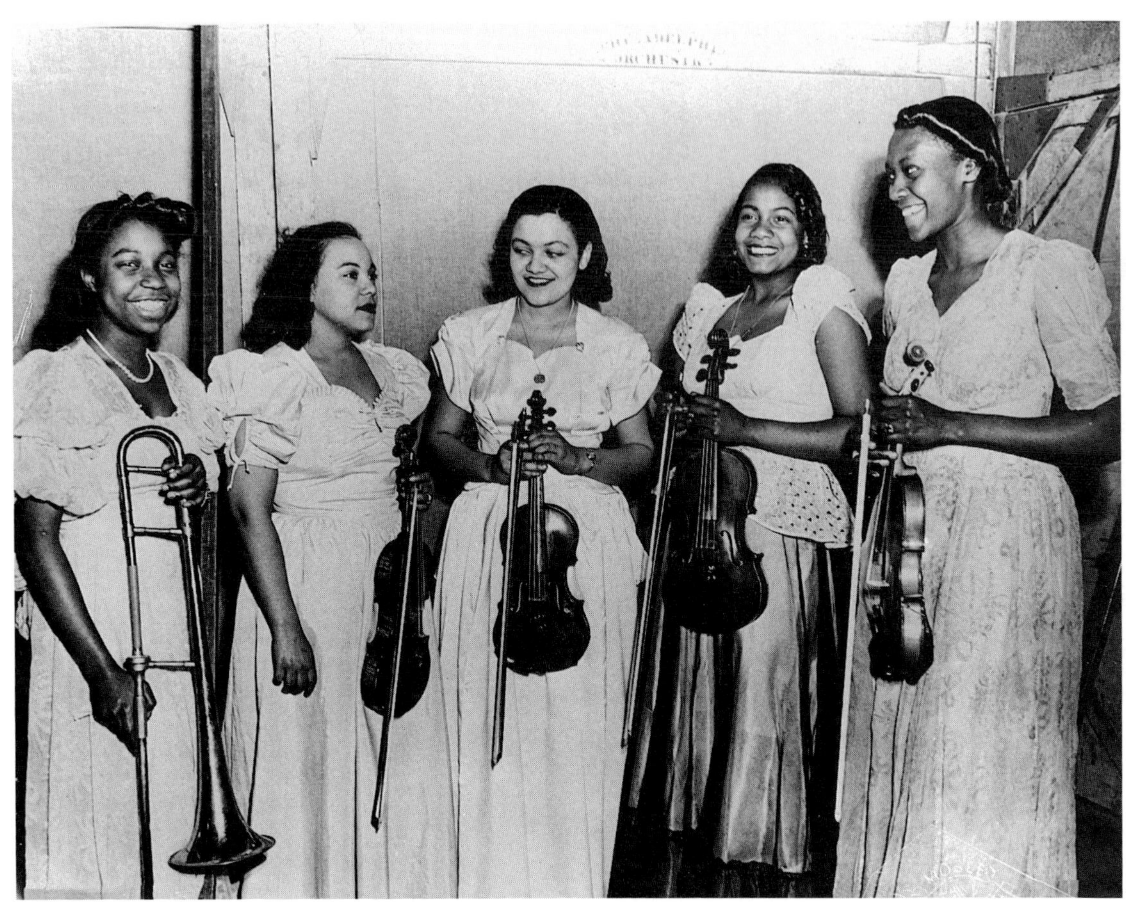

127B) Ladies of the Philadelphia Concert Orchestra performs at the Town Hall, April 18, 1948.

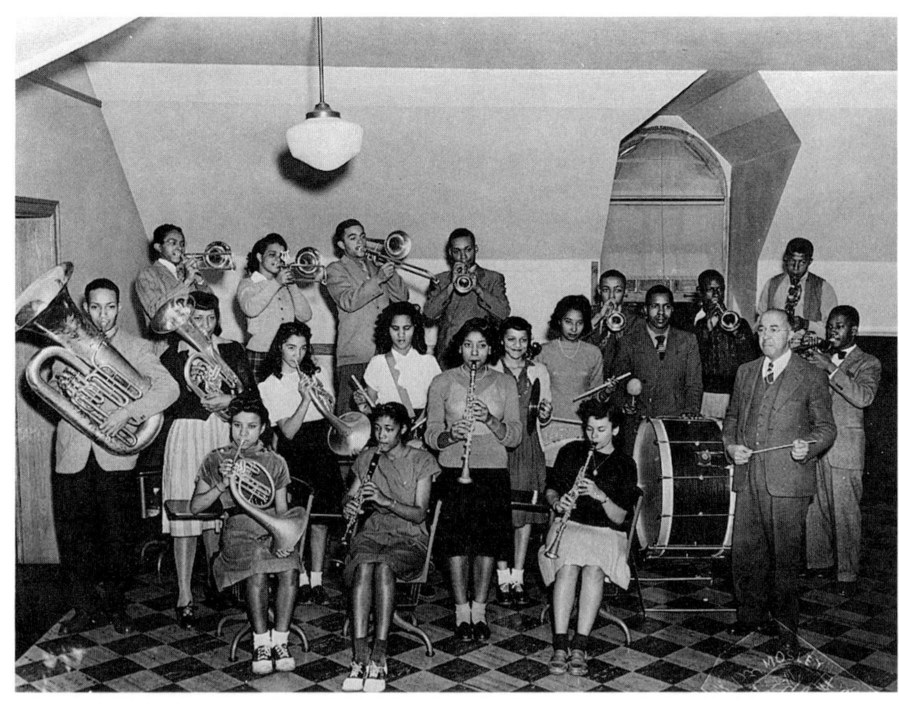

128A) School Band practices, 1940s.

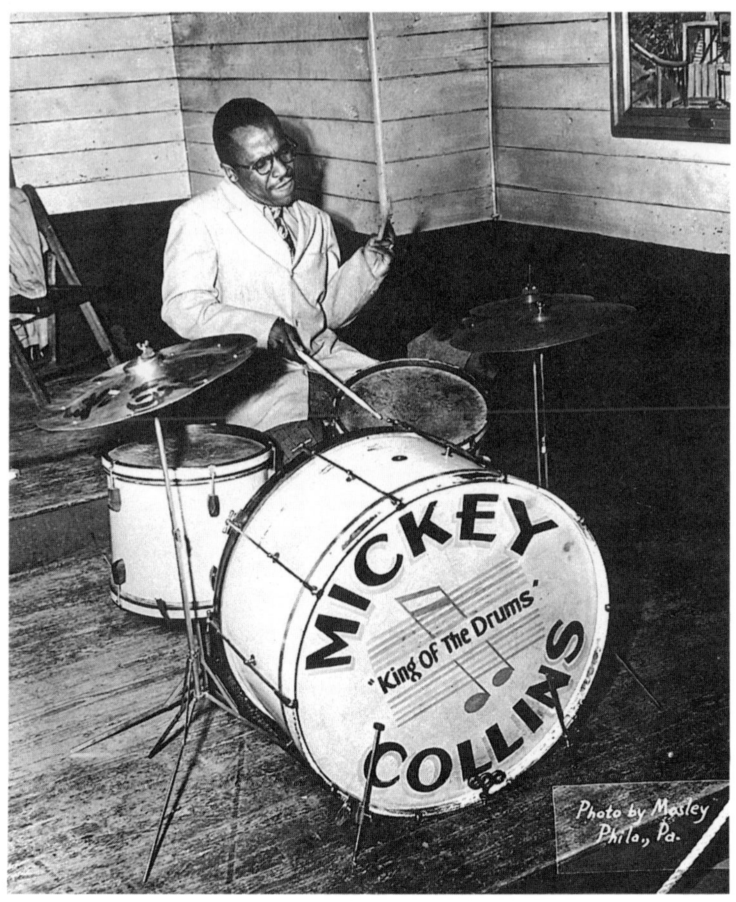

128B) Mickey Collins, "King of the Drums," performs at South Broad Street U.S.O., 1943.

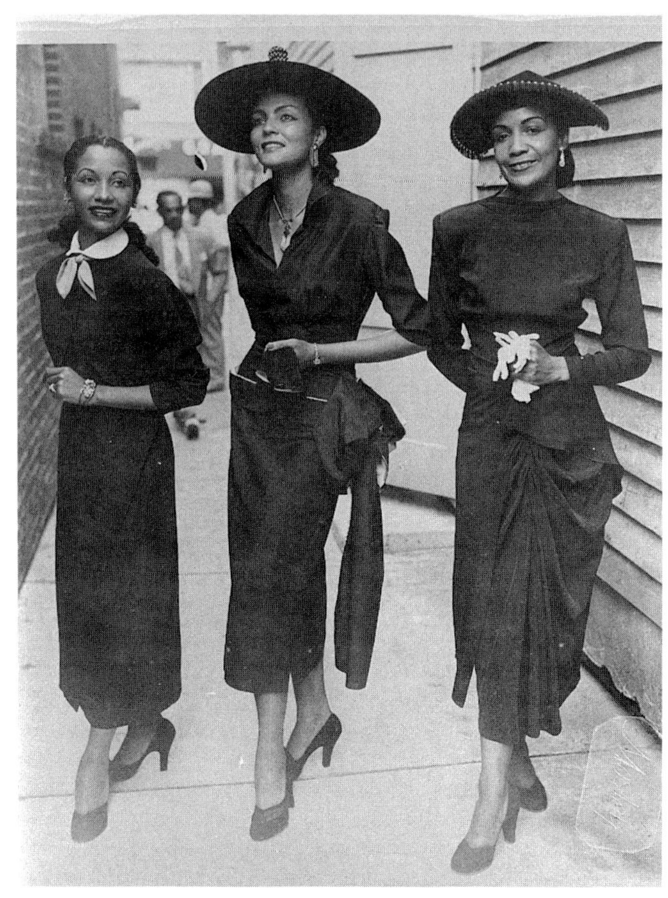

129) "A Smile to Make You Happy," 1940s.

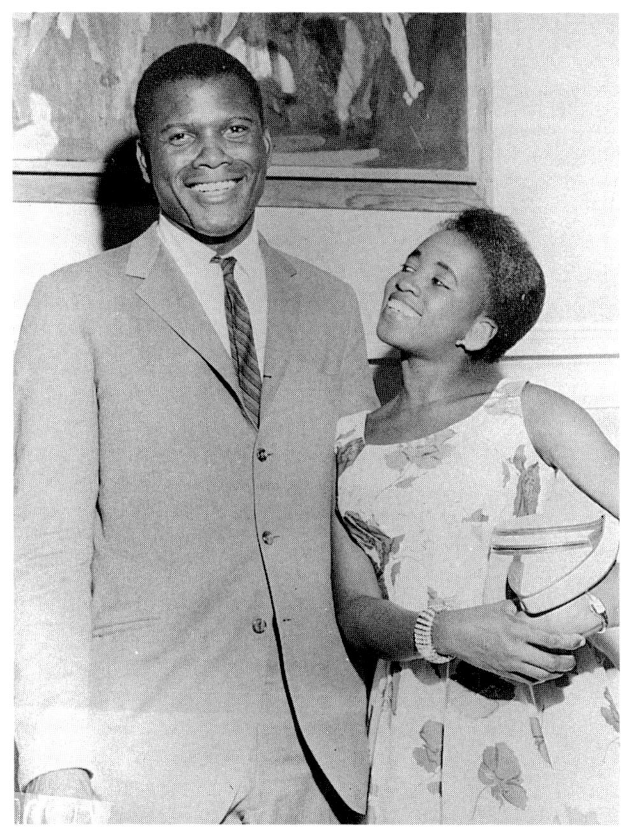

130) Sidney Poitier, actor, director, producer, activist, first Black oscar winner, and co-founder of Black Academy of Artists and Letters, with admirer, late 1950s.

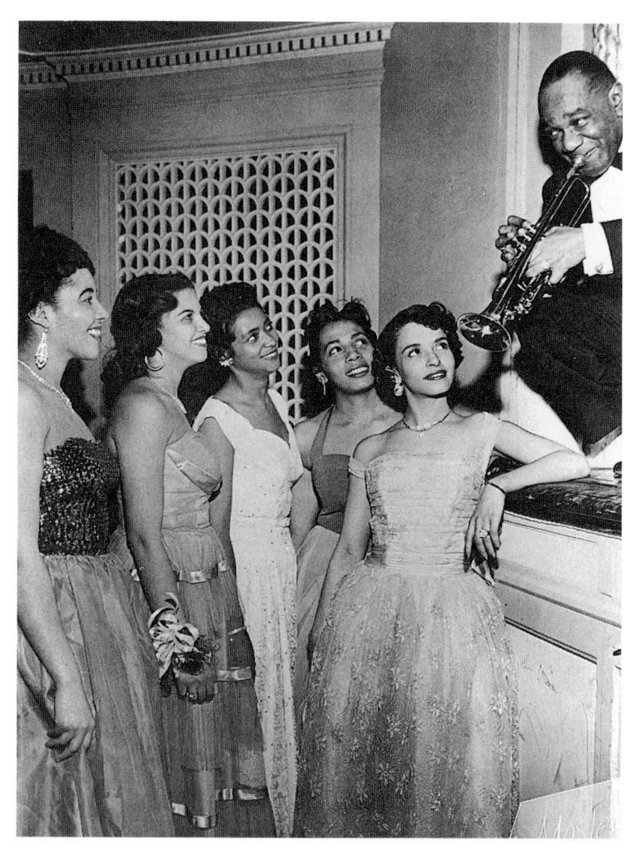

131) Charles Howard "Devil" Gaines, Sr. (1900-86), band leader, trumpeter and composer, serenades the ladies, late 1940s.

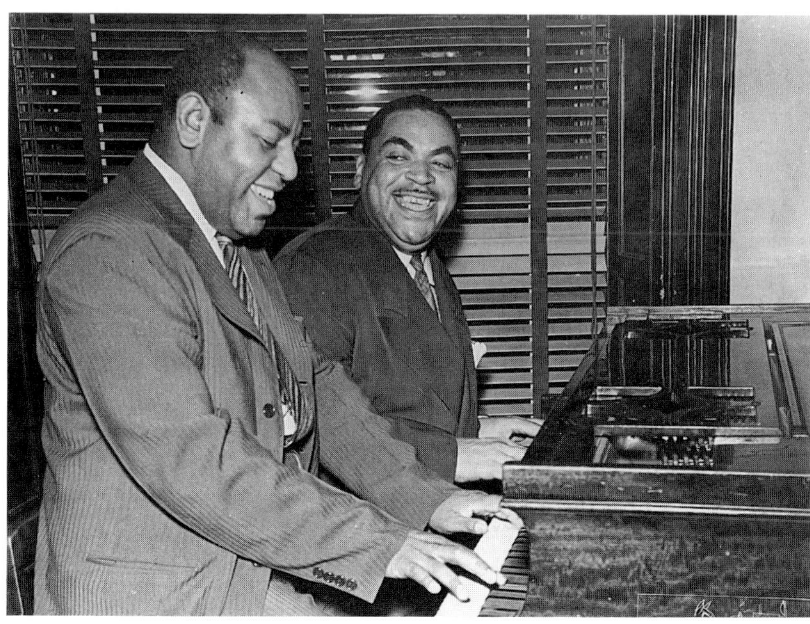

132A) Earl Kenneth " Father " Hines (1905-1983) (left), jazz pianist jams with Thomas Wright " Fats" Waller (1904 -1943) (left), jazz organist and composer, 1942.

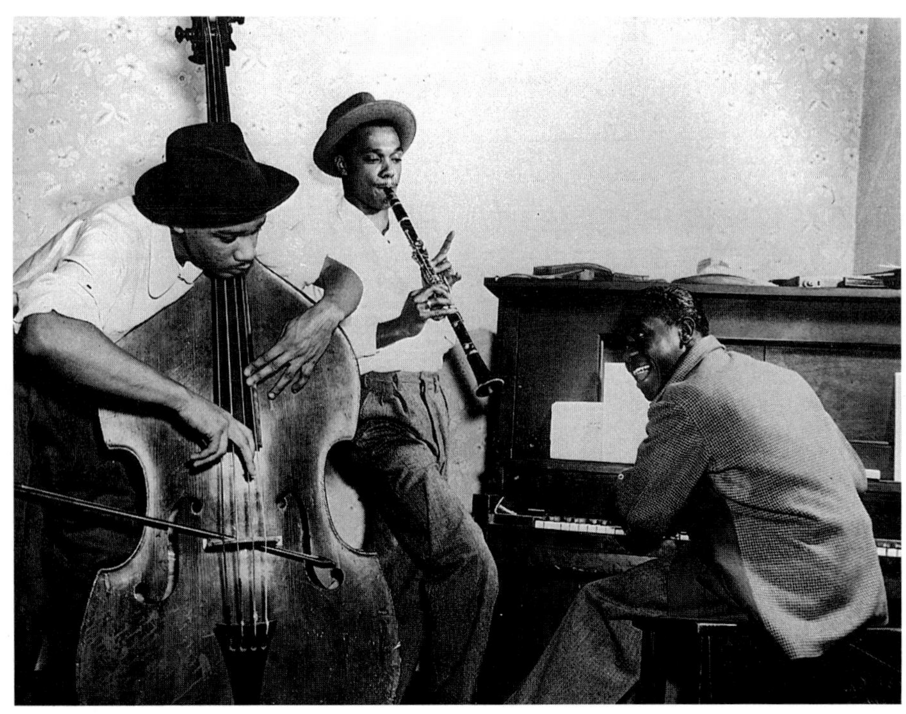

132B) Philly Jam Session, 1940s.

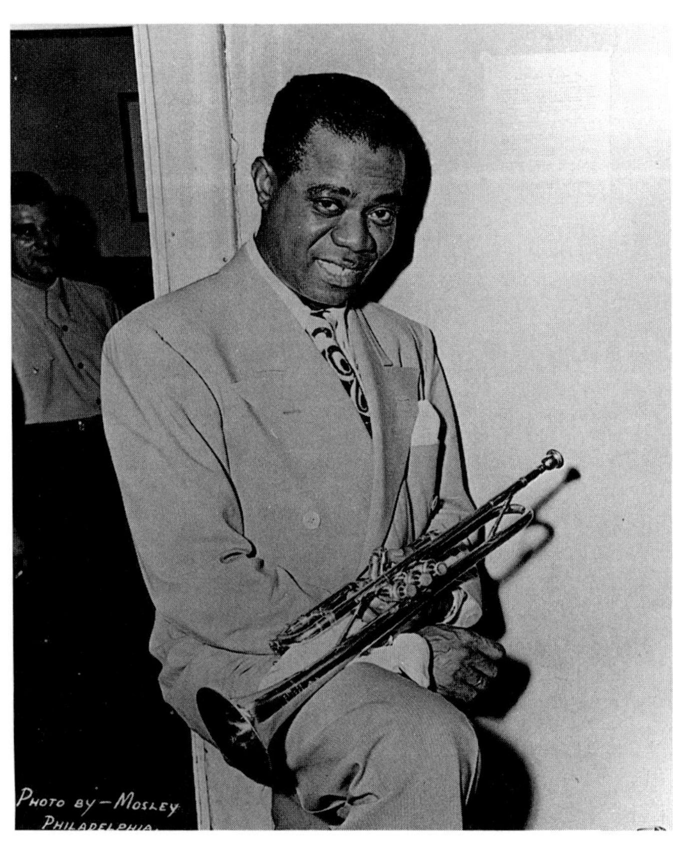

133) Daniel Louis "Satchmo" Armstrong (1900-1971), jazz trumpeter, band leader, and singer, poses, 1950s.

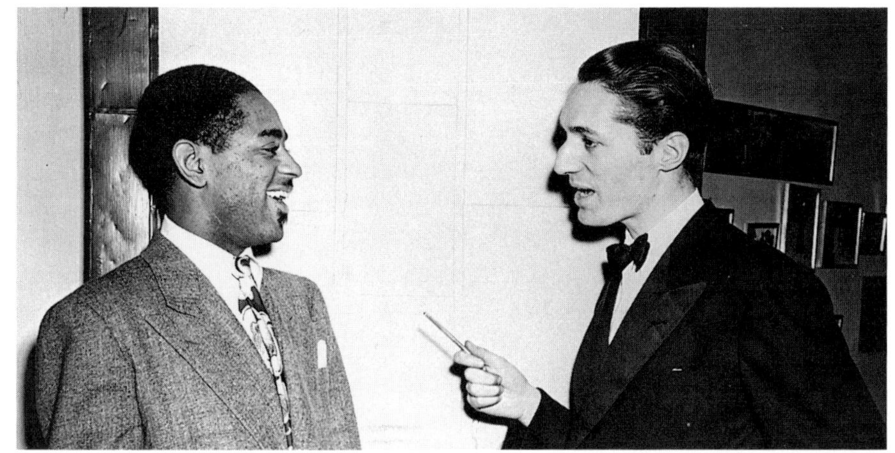

134A) John Birks "Dizzy" Gillespie, jazz trumpeter, trombone player, pianist, composer, conductor, band leader and co-founder of the "Bebop" movement exchanges with Leonard Feather, author and jazz critic, 1946.

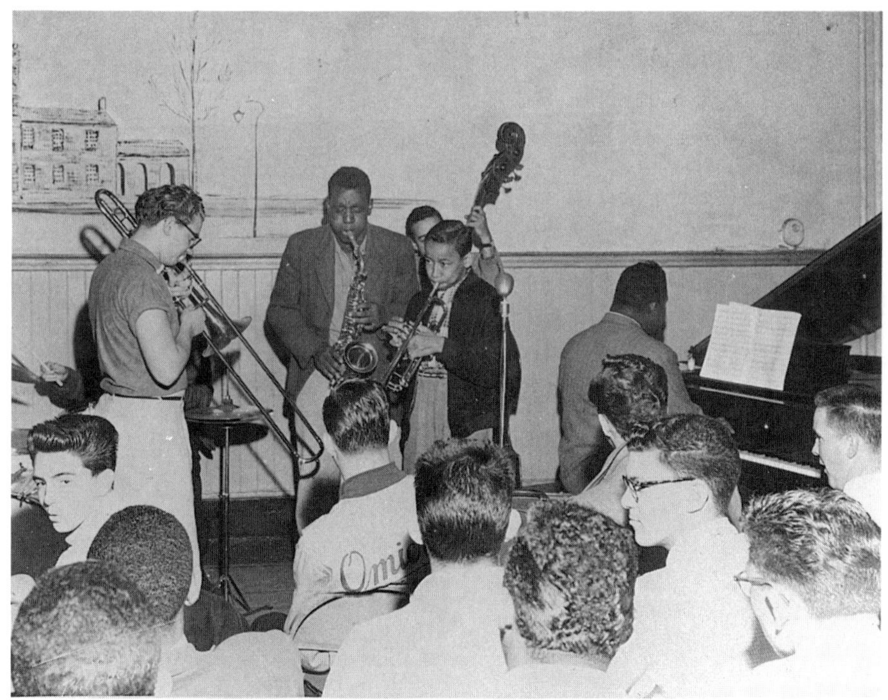

134B) Lee Morgan (1938-1972), child, prodigy, jazz trumpeter and "Hard Bop" representative, performs on his trumpet 1950s.

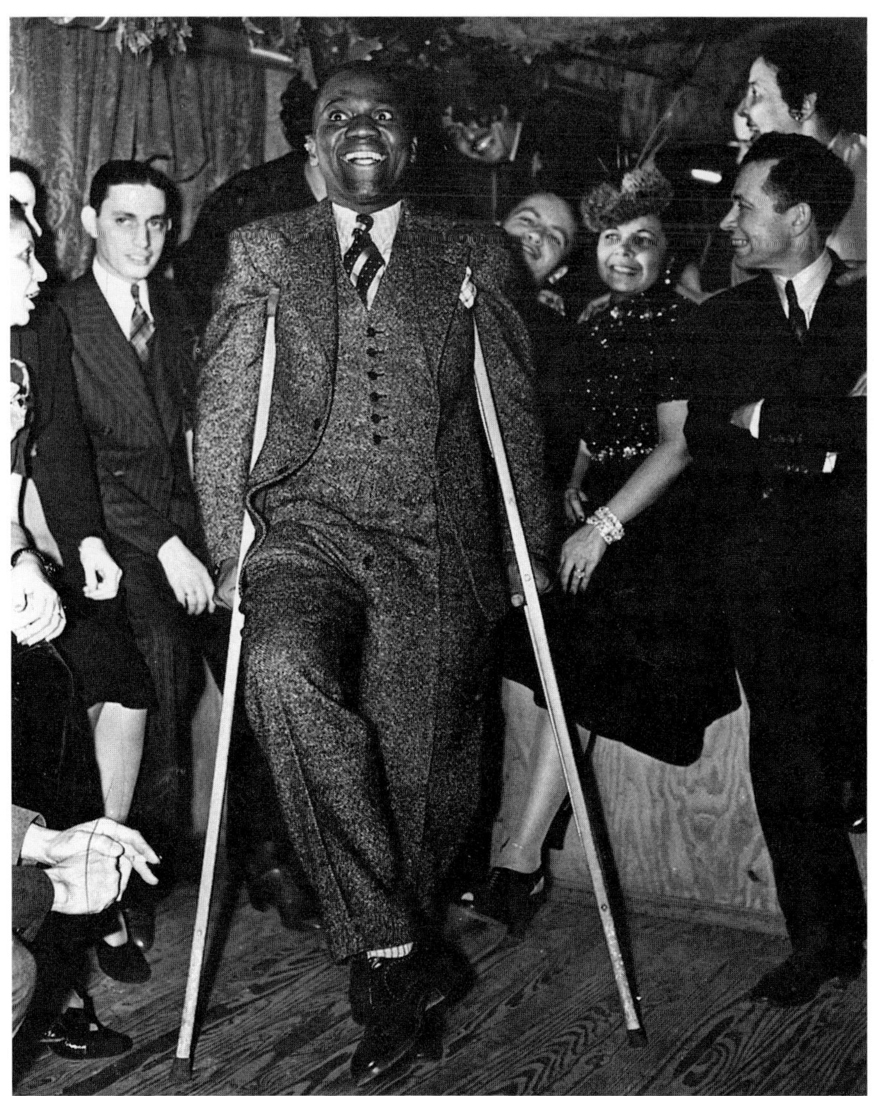

135) Bill "Bojangles" Robinson (1878-1949), actor vaudevillian, clowns around with William Stevens "Willie" H. Bryant (1908-1964) (left), jazz band leader, composer, vocalist, actor, and U.S.O. tour producer, and other friends. Mr. Robinson, known as the "Dean of Tap Dancers, coined the word "copasetic," early

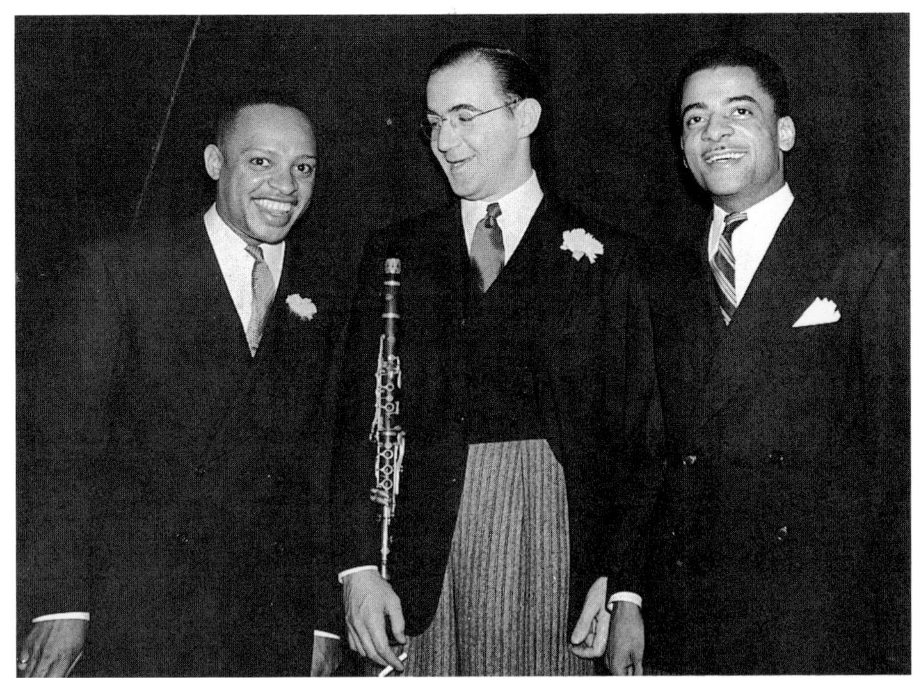

136A) Lionel Leo Hampton (left), band leader, xylophone and vibraphone player, drummer, pianist, and music professor, Benjamin David "Benny" Goodman (center), band leader and clarinetist, and Theodore Shaw "Teddy" Wilson (right), jazz pianist, first Black musician to tour with interracial jazz unit, arranger and music educator, 1939.

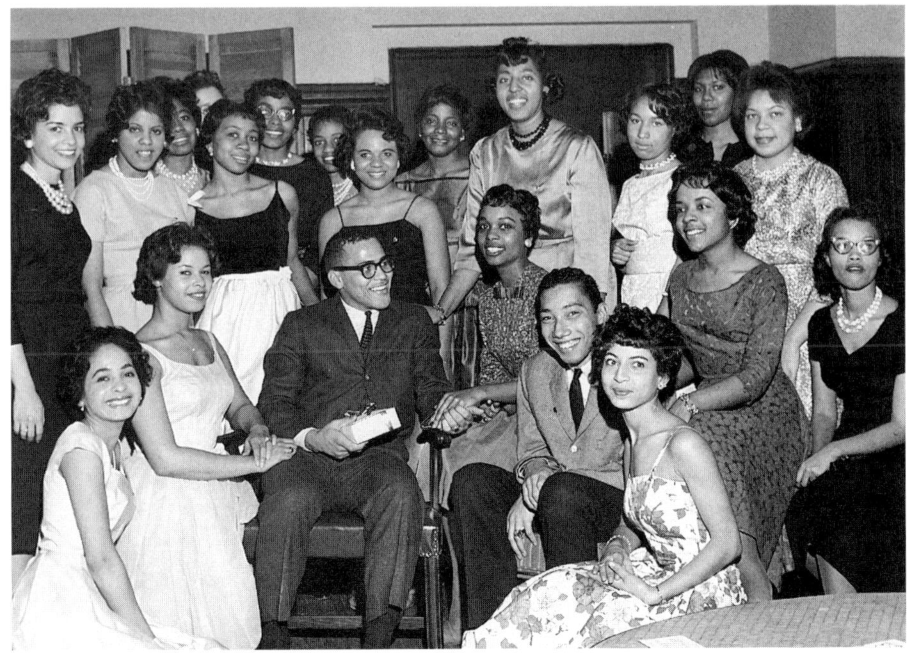

136B) Harold George, Jr. "Harry" Belafonte, folk singer, actor, director, and movie producer, and friend enjoy the hospitality of the ladies, 1950s.

LIVE AND LET LIVE

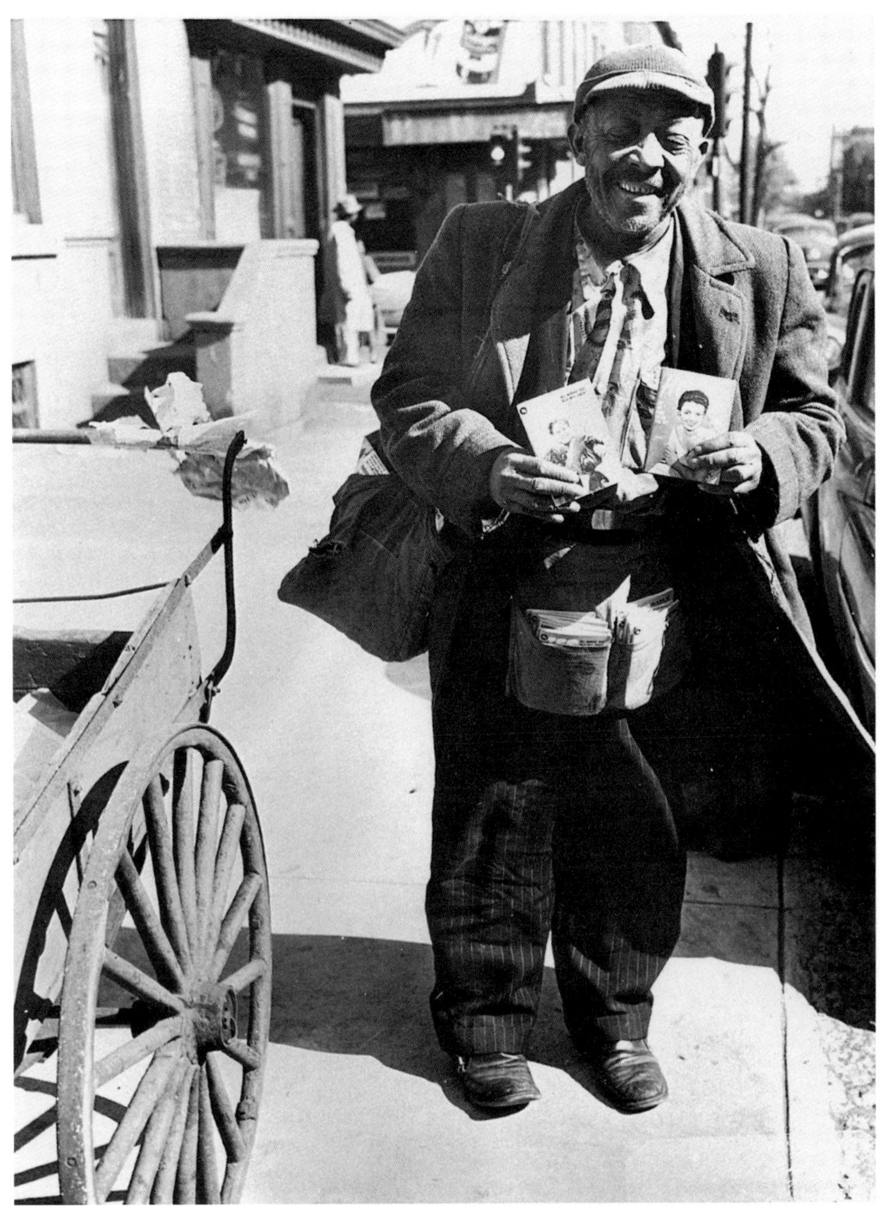

138) Newspaper cart, 1940s

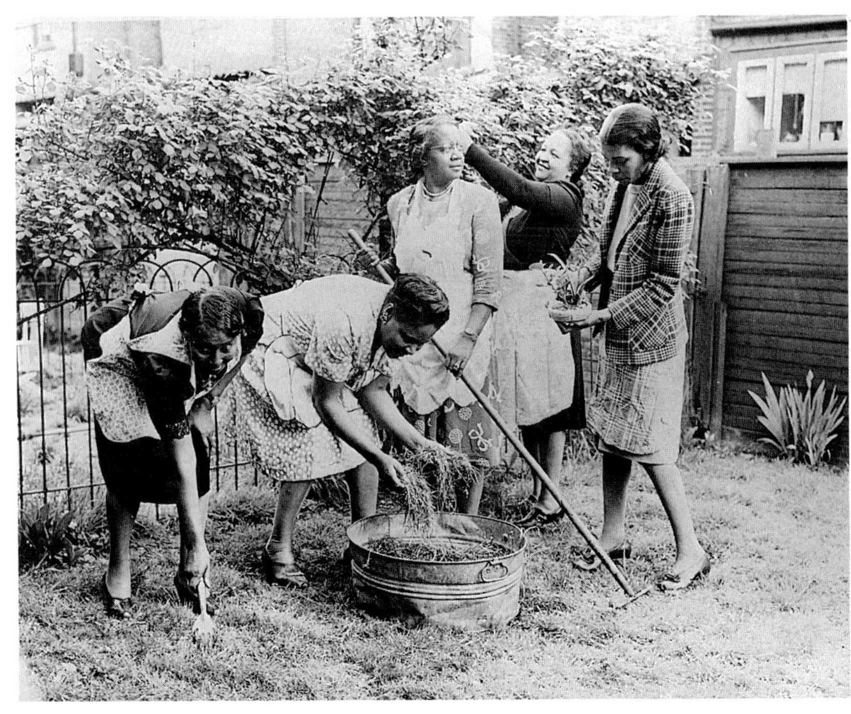

139A) Gardening, 1940s

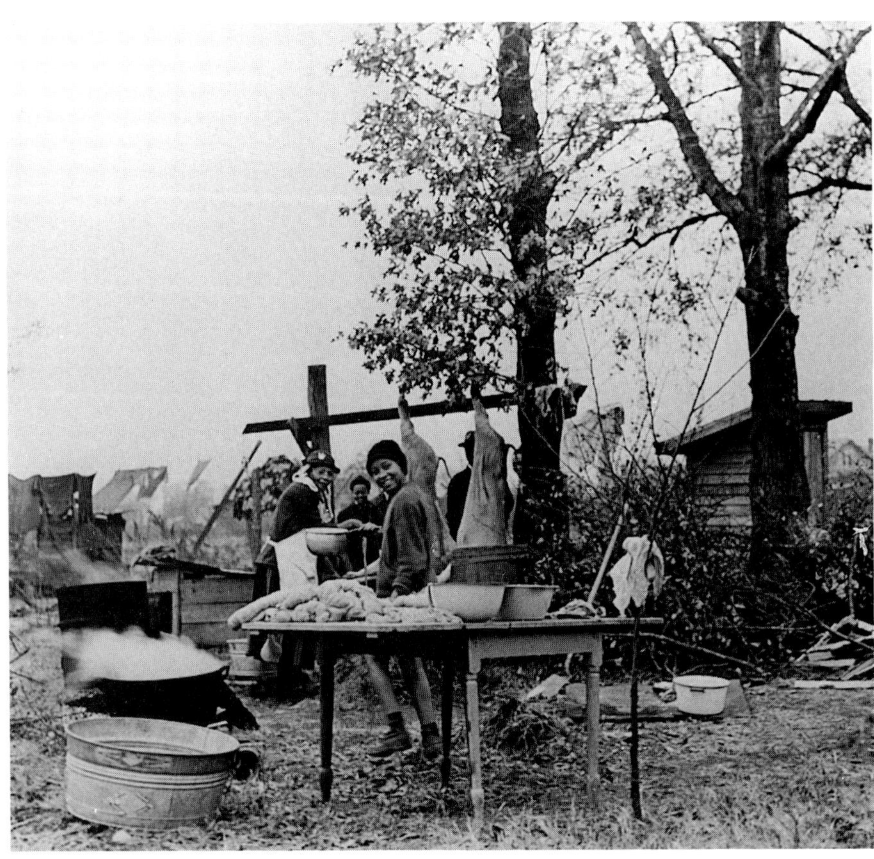

139B) Meat preparation, 1940s

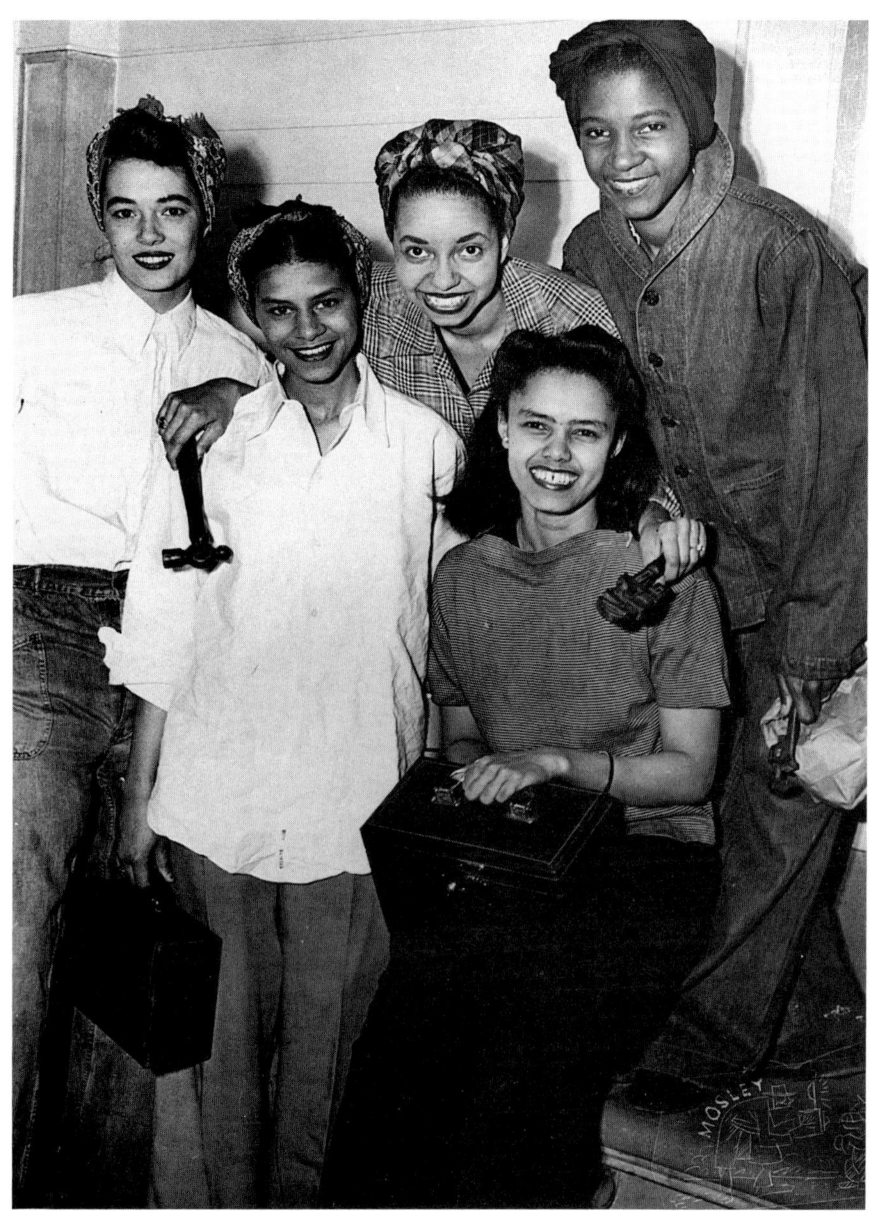

140) Second World War women workers, 1940s.

Do Lord Remember Me

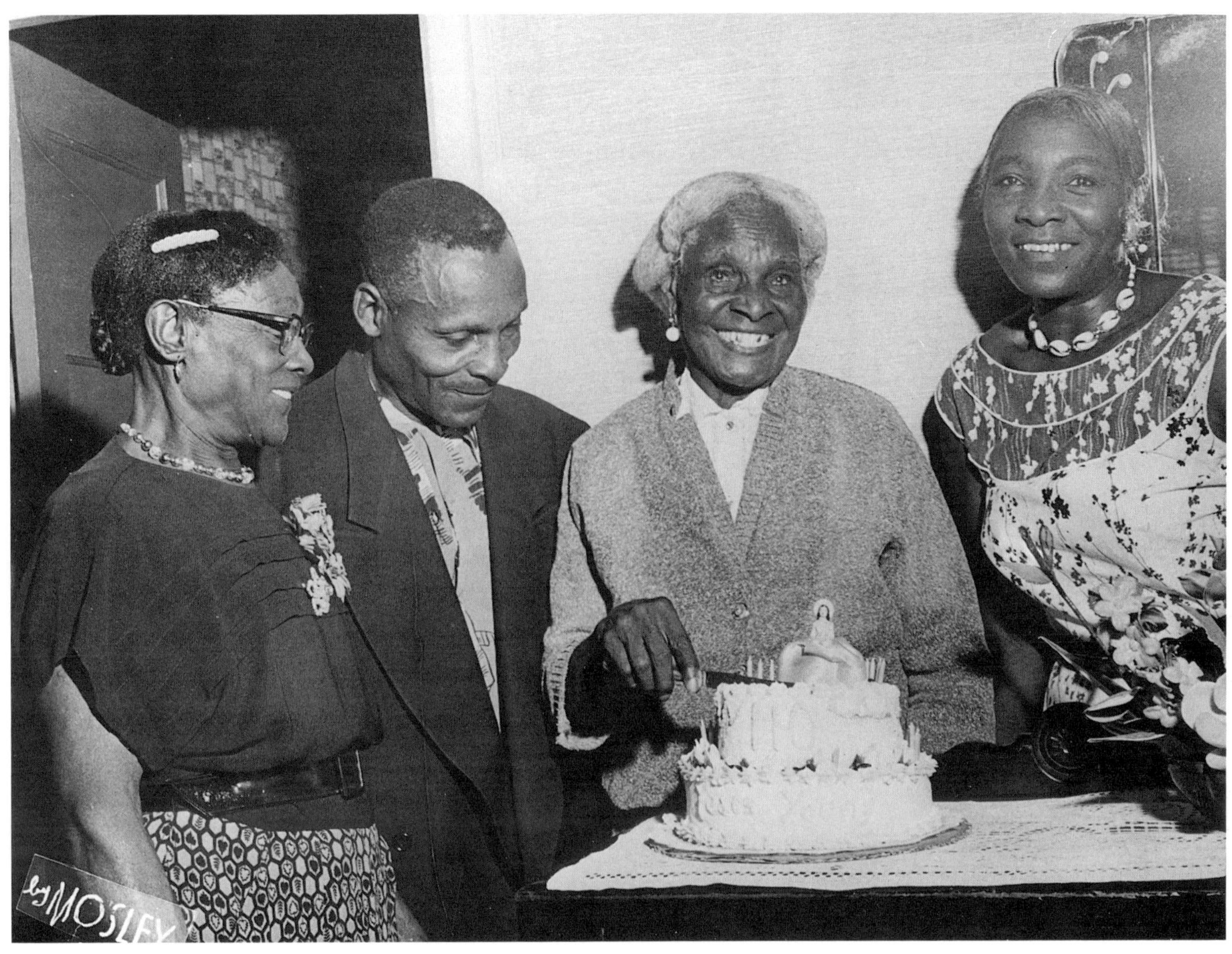

141) A lady residing at 232 S. 57th Street, celebrates her 110th Birthday, August 10, 1958.

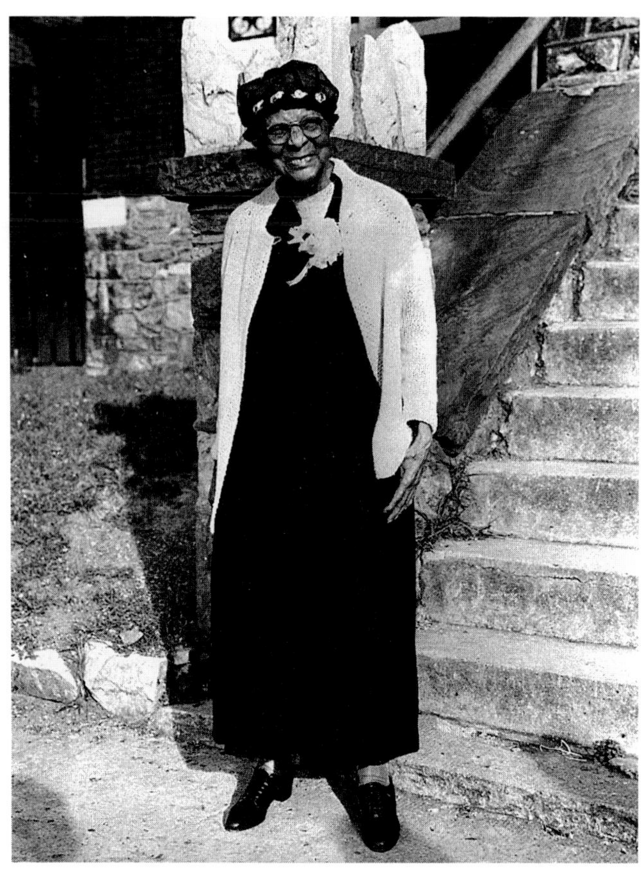

142A) Mrs Sara A. Freeman of 343 East Miner Street, West Chester, enjoys life at the age of 103 years old, 1940s.

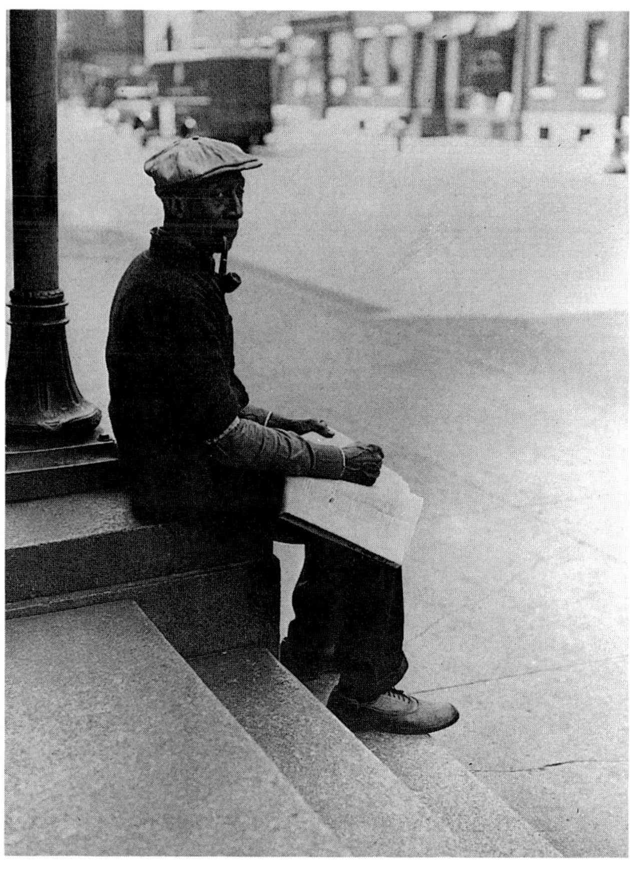

142B) Elder gentlemen indulges himself with his pipe and newspaper, 1940s.

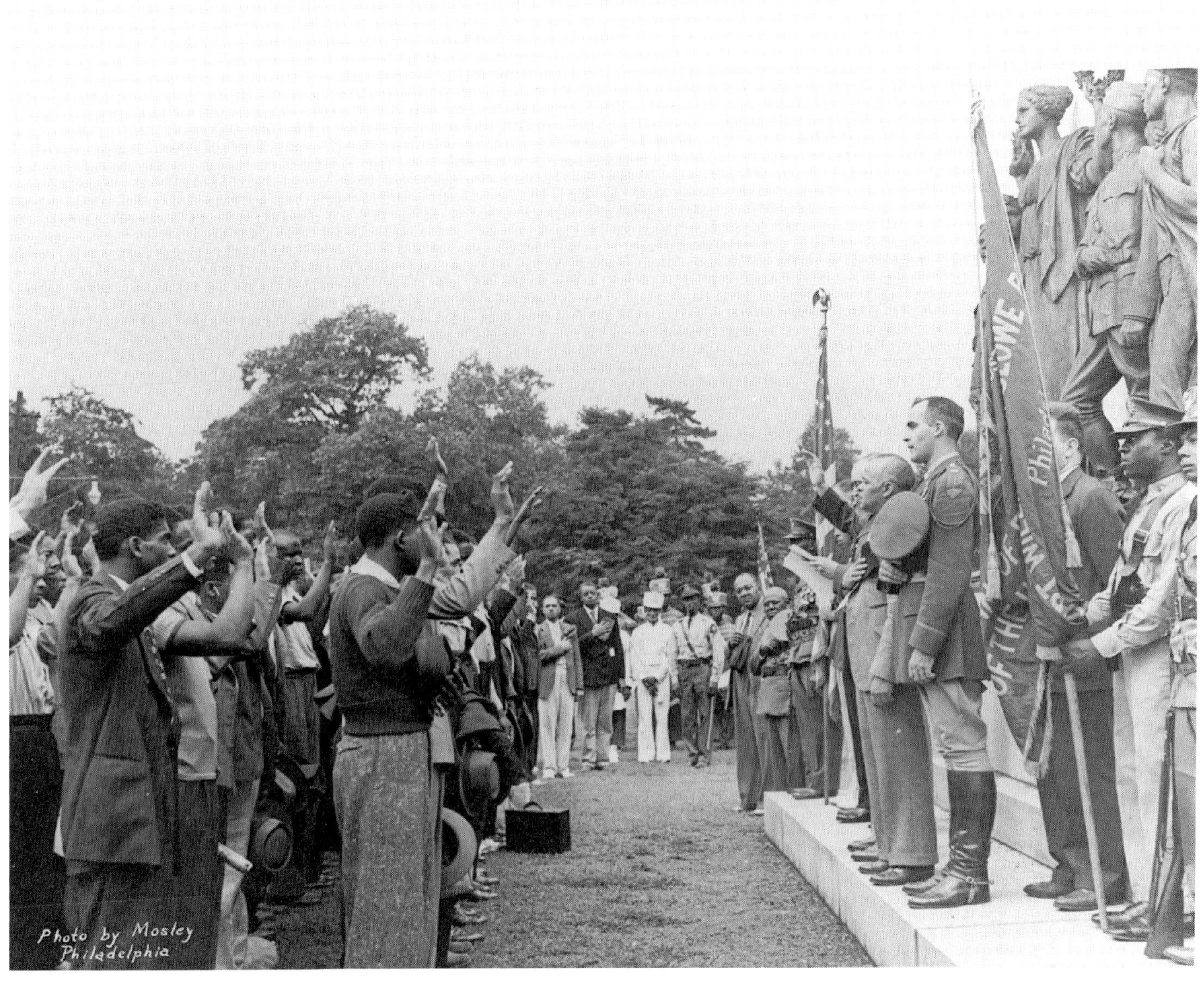

143) Volunteers in front of the Negro War Memorial, early 1940s.

BEATING AGAINST THE BARRIERS

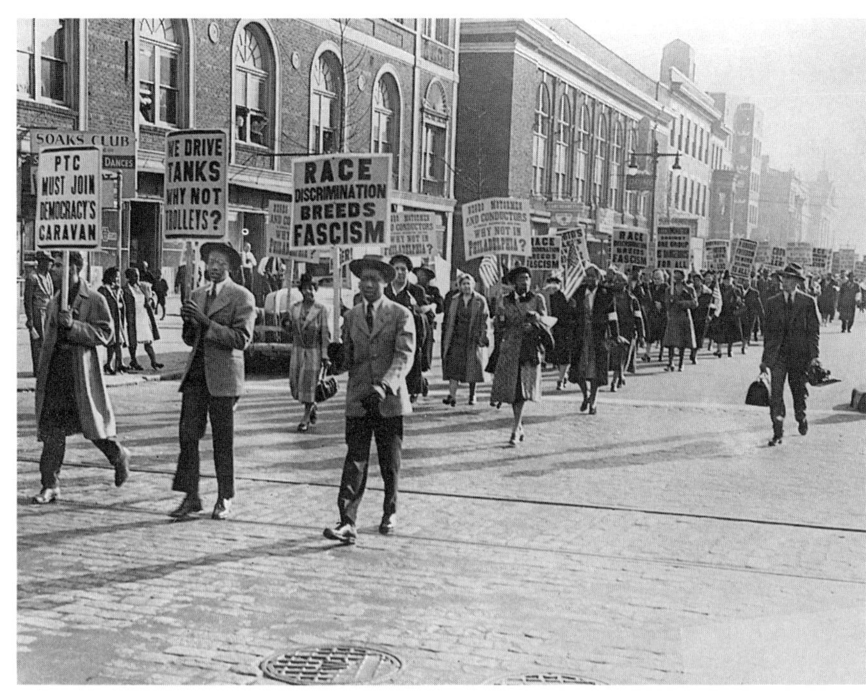

144A) Protestors march against PTC for refusal to hire African-American conductors, 1944.

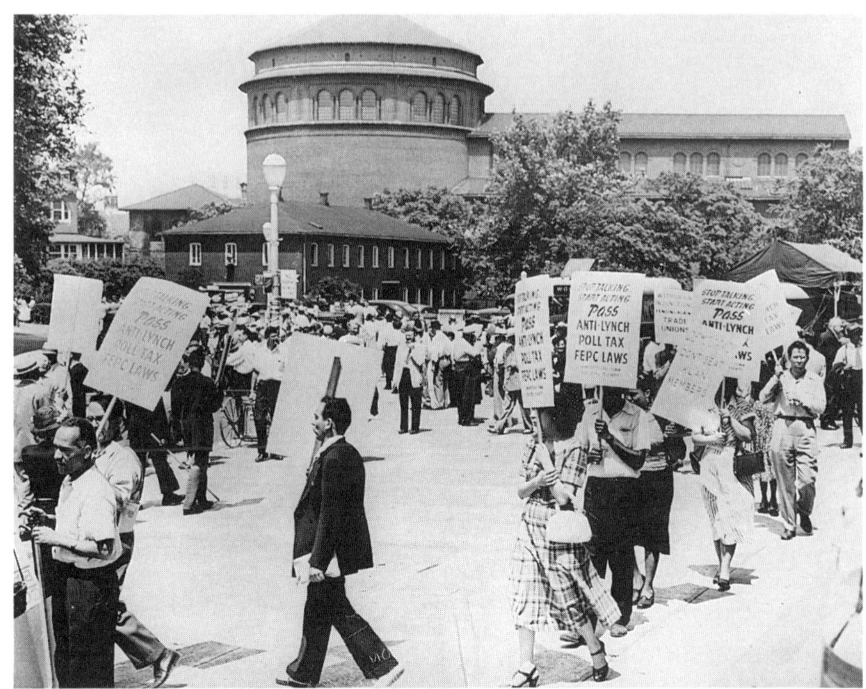

144B) Rally in support of the passage of bills to create laws for: anti-lynching, poll tax and FEPC, 1940s.

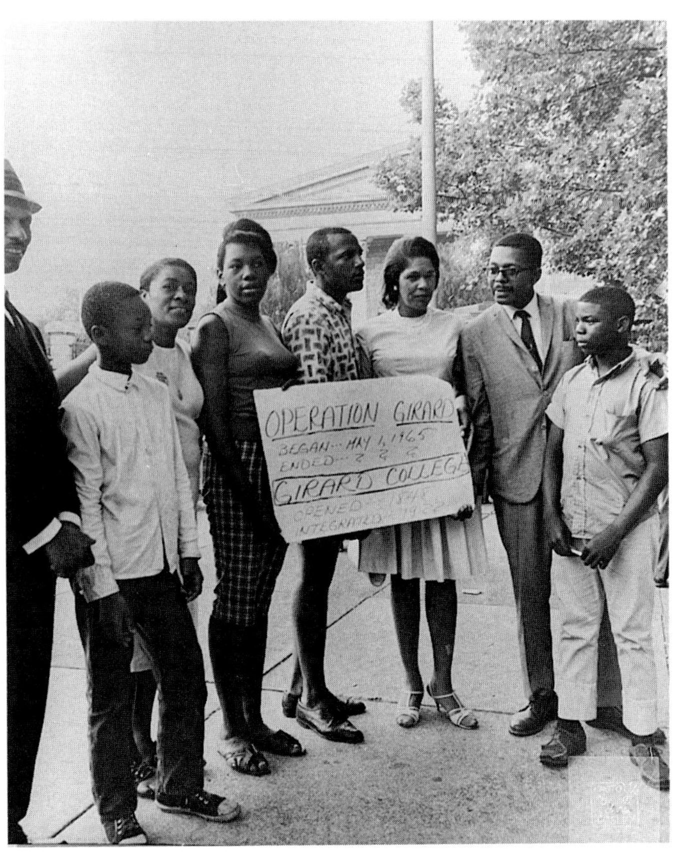

145A) "Operation Girard" to integrate Girard College, 1965.

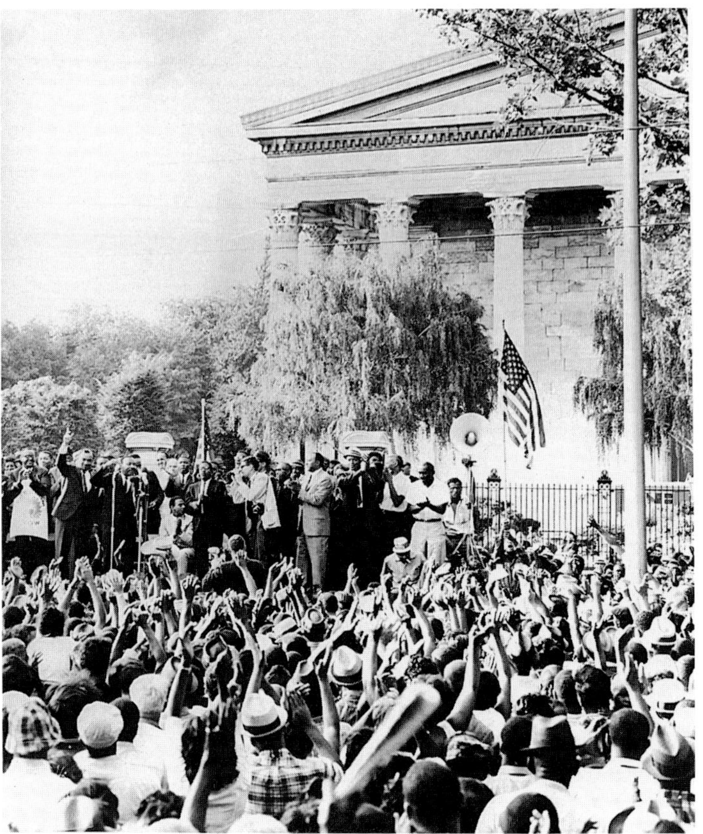

145B) Attorney Cecil B. Moore (second from left) and Rev. Martin Luther King Jr. (third from left) raise hands, as they stand on platform, in support of Girard college protesters, August, 1965.

Sitting pretty

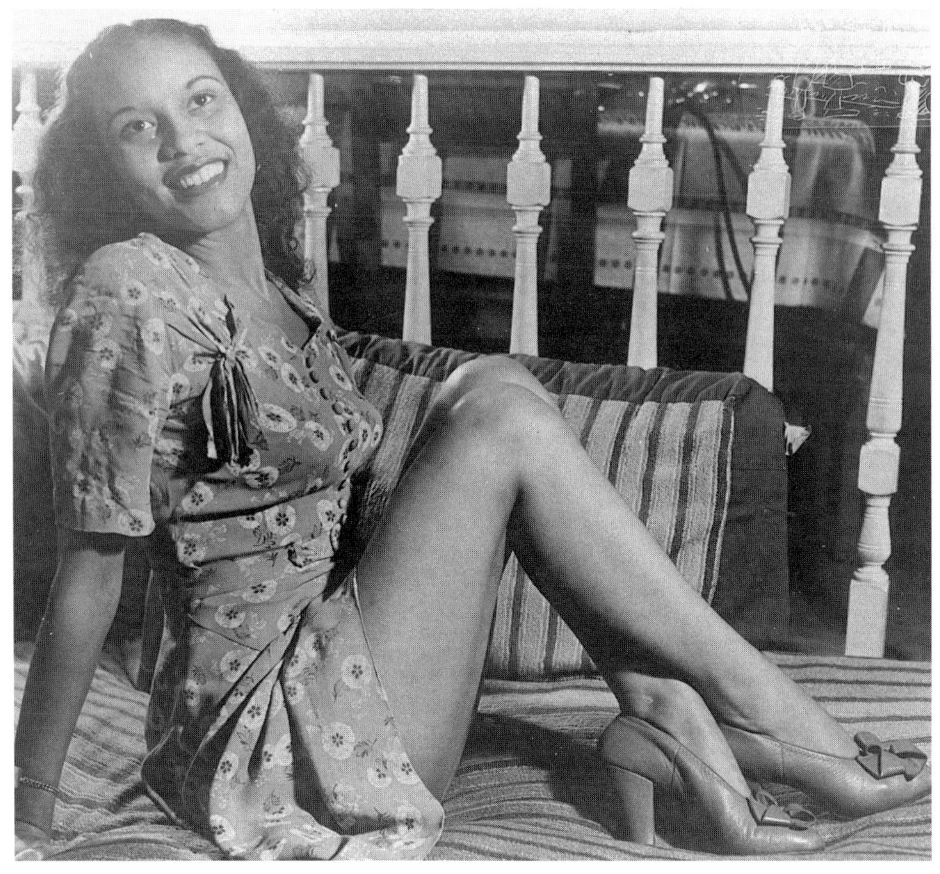

146A) Madeline Hayes of Newark, New Jersey, Miss Shore Patrol, 1944.

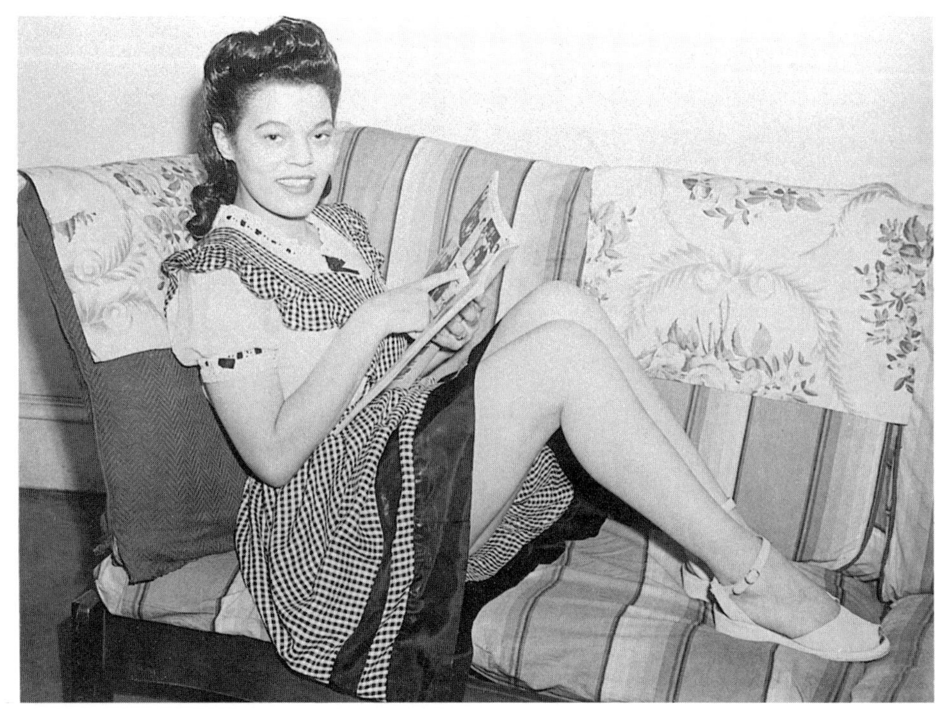

146B) "Eyes on the Book Only," 1944.

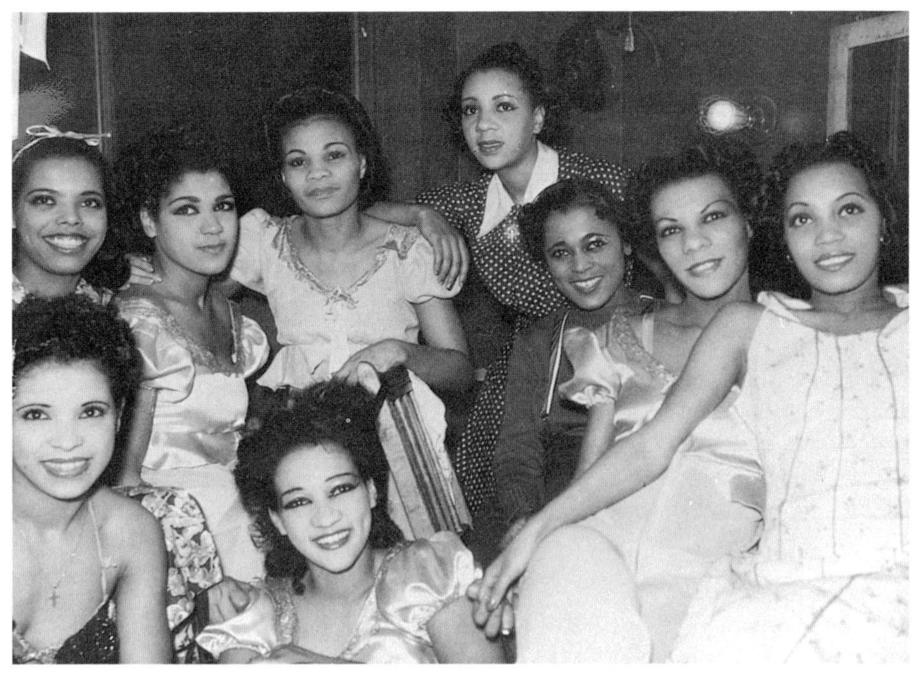

147A)"Modern Circles," 1939.

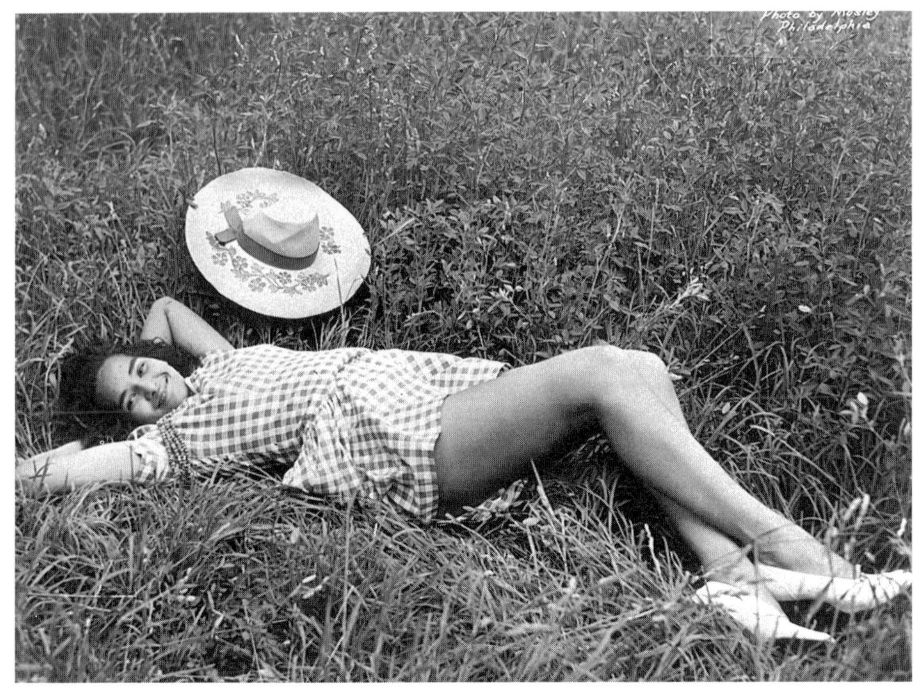

147B) Helen V. Connor, a migrant to Philadelphia from Dublin, Virginia , employed as a defense worker, posing as a "Pin-Up Lovely" early 1940s.

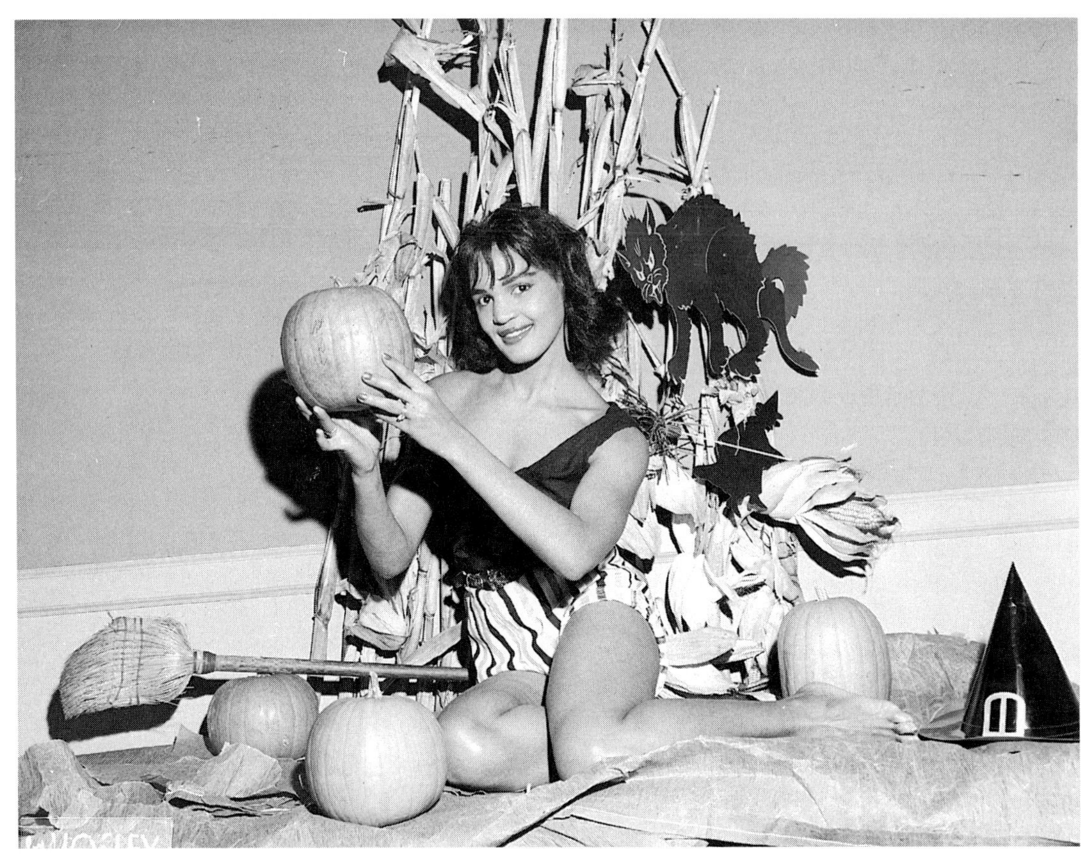

148) "Bewitching," Shirley Beasley, early 1940s.

EVERY GOODBYE AIN'T GONE

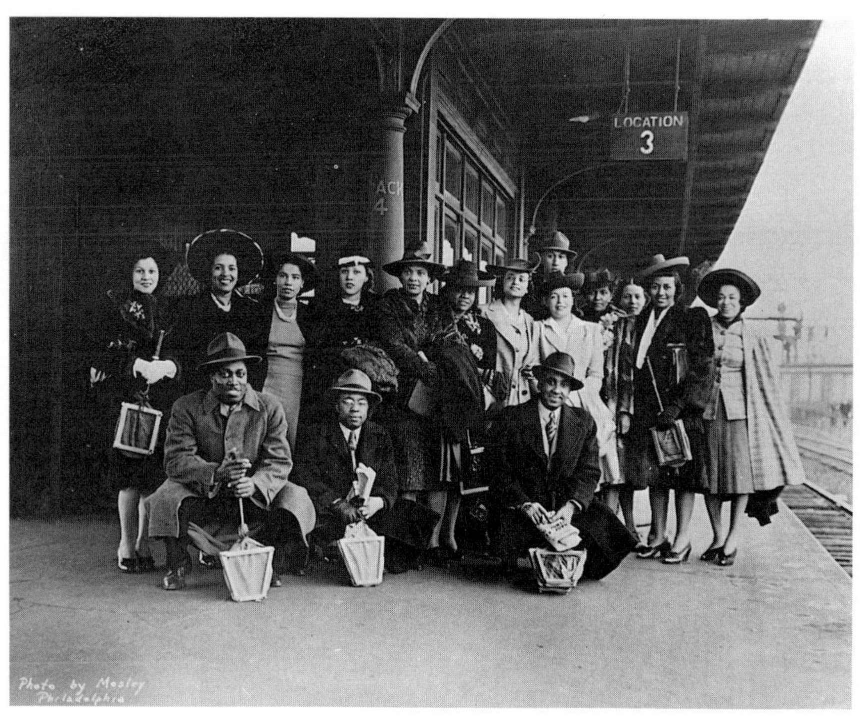

149A) Waiting for the train, early 1940s.

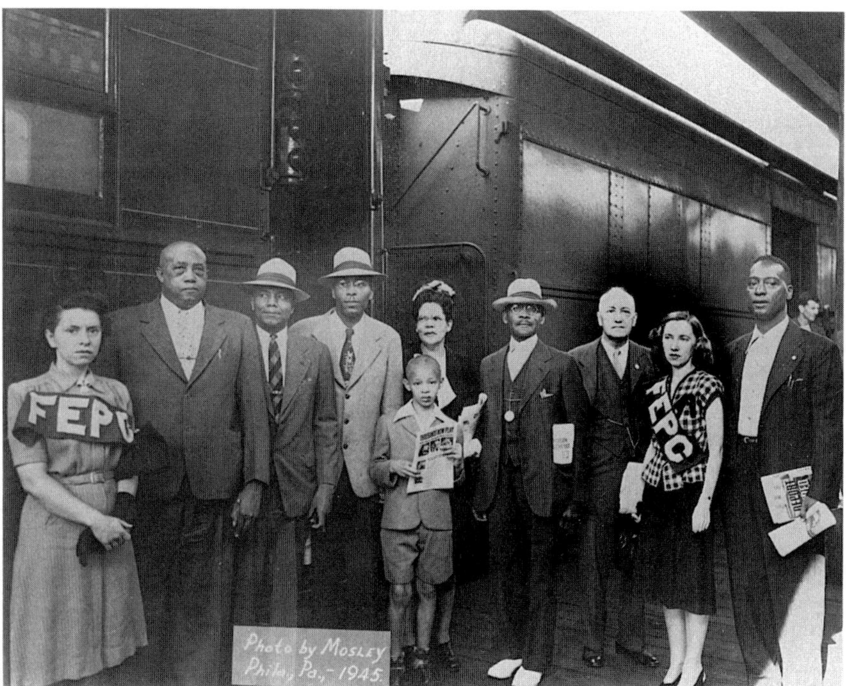

149B) Philadelphia delegation on their way to Washington DC to pursuade congressmen to support the FEPC bill, July, 1945.

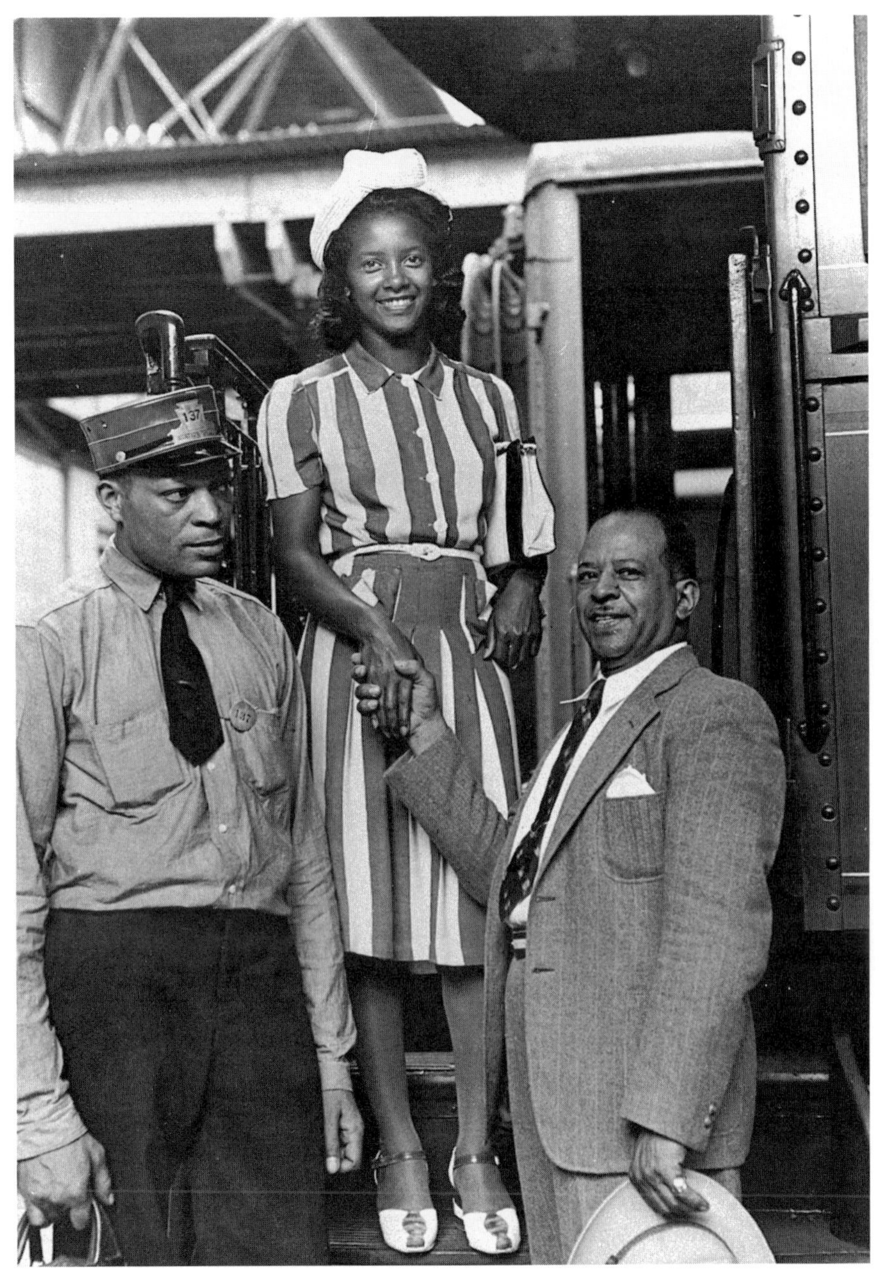

150) William L. Dawson (1886 - 1970), former U.S. Congressman of Illinois and first Vice - President of the Democratic National Committee, greets young woman, 1940s.

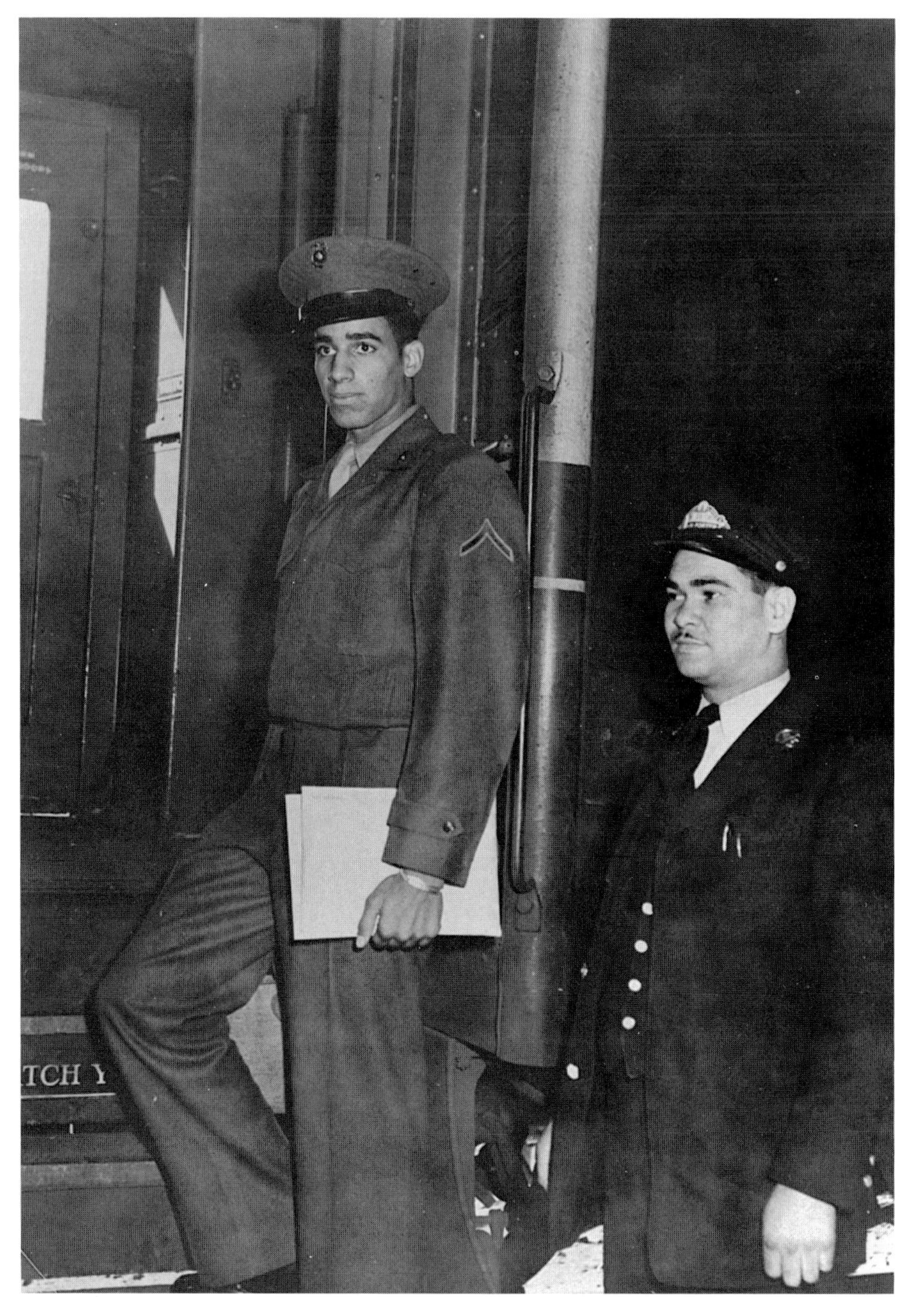

151) Going off to war, early 1940s.

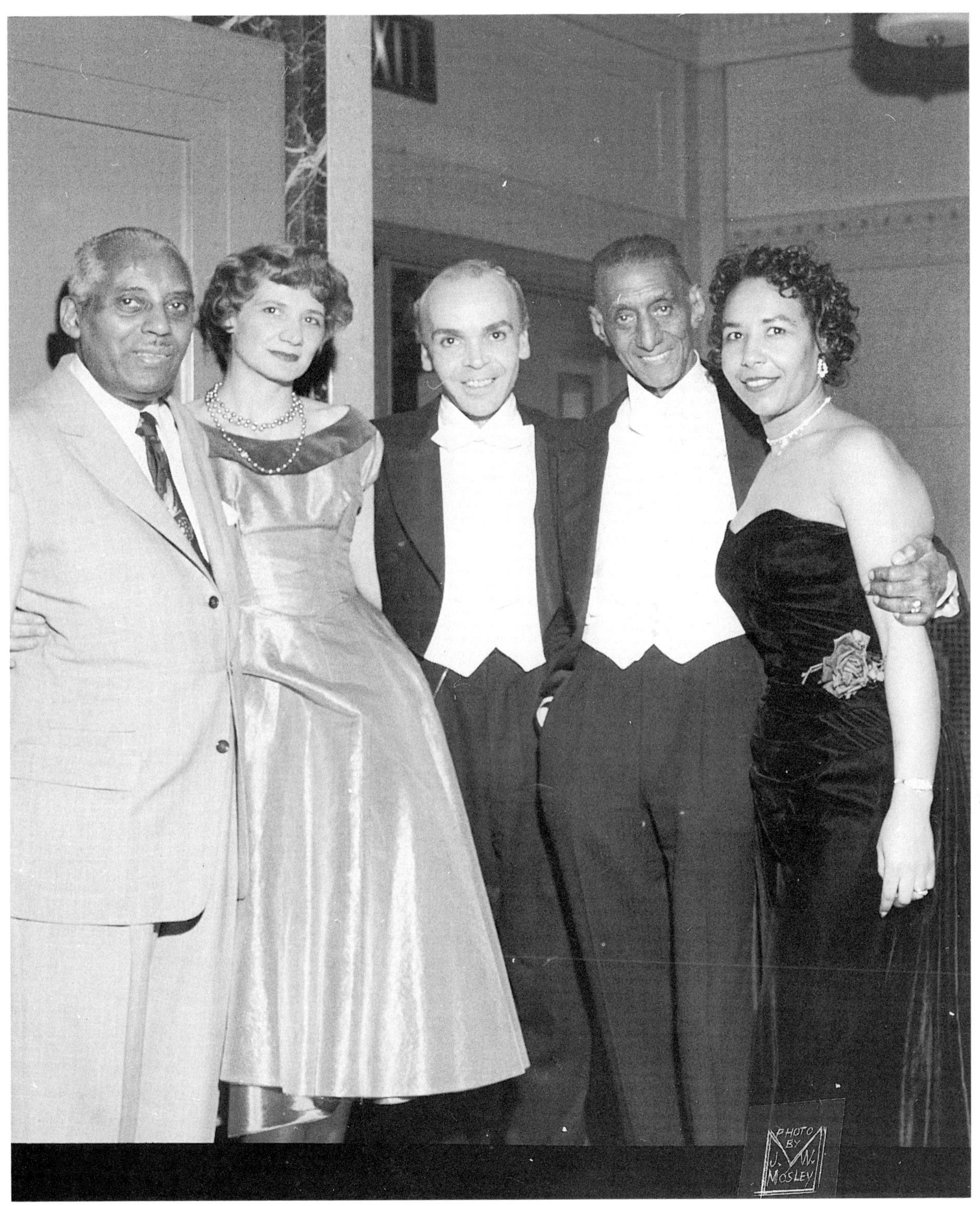

153) Mrs. Marian Cuyjet, second from left dance instructor of Judith Jamison and Dr. Eugene Raymond Jones (center), with friends.

INDEX of CAPTIONS